Word 97
SmartStart

EMILIA PLOURDE

DR. JERRY HORAZDOVSKY
Anoka-Ramsey Community College

An Imprint of Macmillan
Computer Publishing

Word 97 Smart Start

Copyright © 1998 by Que® Education and Training.

Library of Congress Catalog No.: 97-65619

ISBN: 1-57576-814-3

01 00 99 98   4 3 2

Interpretation of the printing code: the rightmost double-digit number is the year of the book's printing; the rightmost single-digit number, the number of the book's printing. For example, a printing code of 98-1 shows that the first printing of the book occurred in 1998.

Screen reproductions in this book were created using Collage Plus from Inner Media, Inc., Hollis, NH.

Publisher and President: Robert Linsky

Acquisitions Editor: Kyle Lewis

Product Marketing Manager: Susan L. Kindel

Managing Editor: Nancy E. Sixsmith

Production Editor: Geneil Breeze

Acquisitions Assistant: Ken Schmidt

Editorial Assistant: Angie Denny

Technical Editor: Ed Metzler

Cover Designer: Anne Jones

Book Designer: Gary Adair

Production Team: Aleata Howard, Daniela Raderstorf, Rowena Rappaport, and Megan Wade

Indexer: Tim Tate

Developed by David F. Noble

Composed in *Stone Serif* and *MCPDigital* by Que® Education and Training

About the Author

Dr. Jerry Horazdovsky is currently an instructor in the Business Division at Anoka-Ramsey Community College in Coon Rapids, Minnesota. His instructional experience includes teaching at the high school, community college, and university levels. He has taught business courses at all three levels and computer concept and application courses at the community college and university levels. He holds a doctorate in Vocational Education from the University of Minnesota, where he also taught educational methods courses. While serving as the Anoka-Ramsey Community College Director of Technology, he led the team that designed and implemented the college-wide computer network. He has also served as a computer consultant and trainer for numerous private businesses and state agencies.

Jerry has authored books on various versions of Microsoft Word, WordPerfect, and Windows. He also has been a reviewer/technical editor for operating system, word processing, spreadsheet, and database texts. His professional interests include microcomputer applications, instructional media, student learning styles, and teacher education. He lives in the Twin Cities with his wife Patty and their two daughters, Josie and Holly.

Acknowledgments

Que Education and Training is grateful for the assistance provided by Ed Metzler for his technical edit of the manuscript. Special thanks to David Noble, for his superb development of the manuscript.

The author would like to express his appreciation to Tina Venneman, the faculty in Suite C, and the Anoka-Ramsey Community College Technical staff for the insights and suggestions they provided during the writing of this text.

Trademark Acknowledgments

All terms mentioned in this book that are known to be trademarks or service marks have been appropriately capitalized. Que Education and Training cannot attest to the accuracy of this information. Use of a term in this book should not be regarded as affecting the validity of any trademark or service mark.

Windows and Microsoft are registered trademarks of Microsoft Corporation.

Preface

Que Education and Training is the educational publishing imprint of Macmillan Computer Publishing, the world's leading computer book publisher. Macmillan Computer Publishing books have taught more than 20 million people how to be productive with their computers.

This expertise in producing high-quality computer tutorial and reference books is evident in every Que Education and Training title we publish. The same tried-and-true authoring and product development process that makes Macmillan Computer Publishing books bestsellers is used to ensure that every Que Education and Training textbook has the most accurate and most up-to-date information. Experienced and respected college instructors write and review every manuscript to provide class-tested pedagogy. Quality-assurance editors check every keystroke and command in Que Education and Training books to ensure that instructions are clear and precise.

Above all, Macmillan Computer Publishing and, in turn, Que Education and Training have years of experience in meeting the learning demands of computer users in business and at home. This "real world" experience means that Que Education and Training textbooks help students understand how the skills they learn will be applied and why these skills are important.

A Smart Start to Learning Word 97

Word 97 SmartStart provides a hands-on approach to one of the most popular word-processing programs available. The design of the text is flexible enough to meet a wide variety of needs. The text can introduce a student to word processing, or it can supplement a student's previous learning. The abundant step-by-step, hands-on tutorials allow the student to learn either independently or within a large lab setting.

Before presenting the step-by-step tutorials, *Word 97 SmartStart* explains the purpose and practical use of each software feature. Within this context, students quickly learn how to use Word 97. The explanations and tutorials enable students to remember how to apply the particular skill and to transfer their knowledge easily to other applications. This approach ensures that students will use their skills in a practical manner.

Organization

Word 97 SmartStart uses a logical, simple-to-complex organization. Features that are easy to use and understand are presented first. The student can quickly master basic features and develop a framework for learning more complicated features. In addition, features that students can use to improve efficiency as they are learning are introduced very early in the text.

Each chapter begins with an introduction explaining why the features in that chapter are used. Learning objectives are listed after the introduction and then repeated at the appropriate points within the chapter.

Each chapter contains an abundance of hands-on tutorials, tables, and screen illustrations to facilitate learning. Each chapter ends with a summary to help the student absorb and remember the chapter skills. The end-of-chapter exercises include objective questions and hands-on projects to help students check and apply their skills.

Distinctive Features

Following are some of the distinctive features of the book:

- Each chapter begins with a set of objectives.

- Key terms are defined in the margin next to where they are first used in the text.

- Frequent illustrations will aid your learning.

- *Tips* and *Notes* provide helpful hints and additional information to enhance learning.

- *If You Have Problems* sections act as a teaching assistant in the lab by anticipating where common student errors occur and offering practical assistance.

- Many hands-on exercises are interspersed throughout the chapters at the points where doing the exercise can best clarify the immediately preceding discussion.

- The early chapters are designed to build quickly the "critical mass" of material necessary for you to start creating more complex documents on your own.

- Questions at the end of the chapter point out important concepts in the chapter and enable you to verify your understanding of the material.

- The numerous end-of-chapter exercises focus on developing and applying critical thinking skills—not on rote memorization.

- Continuing projects are provided throughout the text. The continuing projects help learners "pull the pieces together."

- An appendix, "Working with Windows 95," helps students get up to speed quickly in Windows 95 basics.

- An alphabetical index helps users quickly locate information.

To the Student

Although this *SmartStart* provides a step-by-step approach, it is much more than a button-pushing book. In response to your requests, we have included a short explanation of the purpose for each feature. Our focus is on teaching you to use Word 97 effectively rather than on simply listing its features. We want to make sure that you remember how to apply your knowledge of Word 97 long after you have taken this course.

You will not spend a great deal of time simply typing documents. We have provided you with data files containing example information for many of the hands-on projects. You can then spend your time completing interesting projects with real-life scenarios.

To the Instructor

The *Instructor's Manual* includes a Curriculum Guide to help you plan class sessions and assignments. Each chapter in the *Instructor's Manual* contains a list of objectives, a variety of tips to facilitate teaching and learning, answers to Checking Your Skills questions, answers to Applying Your Skills exercises, PowerPoint slides, additional hands-on projects, and test questions and answers.

The disk that is packaged with the *Instructor's Manual* includes the electronic files of the *Instructor's Manual* text, the student data files needed for completing the tutorials, solutions for the Instructor, and a PowerPoint presentation.

The *Instructor's Manual* is available to the adopters of *Word 97 SmartStart*, upon written request. Please submit your request on school letterhead to your local representative or to Que E&T Sales Support, Macmillan Computer Publishing, 201 W. 103rd Street, Indianapolis, IN 46290-1097; Fax: 317-581-3084.

Look for the following additional *SmartStarts* in versions for Windows 3.1 and Windows 95, as well as Microsoft Office 97:

Access 2

dBASE 5.0

Excel

Lotus 1-2-3

Novell NetWare

Paradox

PowerPoint

Quattro Pro

Windows

Word

WordPerfect

For more information call:

1-800-428-5331

Contents at a Glance

Table of Contents

9 Merging Files   291

10 Increasing Your Productivity   325

Introduction

Microsoft Word 97 is the best-selling word processing program that meets the needs of people in a variety of industries and professions. Word easily supports basic word processing features, such as formatting characters and paragraphs and checking the spelling and grammar in the document. Word also supports far more sophisticated features that are used in creating, editing, and publishing documents—features such as automating work by using styles and macros, inserting commonly used text or graphics with the AutoText feature, building tables, adding borders and shading, and displaying columns and graphics. Word now includes many features that you expect to find only in high-end desktop-publishing applications.

The following list includes some of the Word features that you can use to save time and increase productivity:

- The WYSIWYG (*what-you-see-is-what-you-get*) feature enables you to see on-screen all text in the font and size that you have chosen.

- You can use many fonts and font sizes, as well as add emphasis by choosing boldface or italic type. You also can define paragraph styles and apply them throughout a document.

- You can easily move text by dragging it with the mouse.

- You can automate repetitive work by using *macros* and *templates*.

- You can import pictures from Word's library of clip art or other sources.

- You can easily create headers and footers.

- You can save frequently used text or graphics, and then quickly insert them into your document by typing only a few characters.

- You can create newspaper-style columns that start anywhere on a page. You can have different numbers of columns within a document and even on a single page.

- You can change the shape of text and then rotate the text in your document.

- You can print some pages of a document in portrait orientation (vertically) and others in landscape orientation (horizontally).

- You can enhance pages with borders and shading.

- You can choose to display one or more toolbars, each of which provides instant access to commands and provides shortcut methods of performing various tasks. From a toolbar, for example, you can number lists or create bulleted entries, cut and paste text, open or save existing documents, and start new documents. You can customize toolbars to suit your needs.

- You can create polished, professional documents by using Word's spelling and grammar checkers and the thesaurus.

- You can use a screen-preview feature to check the contents of a document before you open it. This feature makes file management easier.

In the pages that follow, you will find systematic instructions for using all these features and more.

What's New in Word 97?

Microsoft has modified some existing features and added a number of new ones to Word 97. You receive instruction on many of these features in this text, including:

- *Revised toolbars.* Some of the buttons may have changed on your favorite toolbars. There are also a few new toolbars in the latest release of Word. To make the Word window easier to read, inactive toolbar buttons are no longer displayed in the raised position—inactive buttons are now flat against the toolbar.

- *The Office Assistant.* An interactive screen character that provides quick access to the topics included in the Word Help program.

- *AutoComplete.* A feature where, at various times, Word "guesses" that you are typing a date, day of the week, month, your name, or an item in the AutoText list and provides you with the opportunity to let Word complete the entry for you.

- *A combined spelling and grammar checker.* The spelling and grammar checkers are now combined in the same dialog box to speed the proofing of your documents.

- *Document Map.* A new feature that utilizes the styles applied to various document headings to create a "map" of your document and enable you to move quickly to any portion of your document.

- *Online Page Layout view.* A new "view" of your document that displays your document in a similar manner to what it would look like if it were published online. This view also displays the Document Map.

- *Draw Table feature.* This feature literally enables you to use a pointing device to draw the rows and columns of your table into your document. Using this feature makes it very easy to create cells of unequal dimensions in the same column or row.

- *New wizards.* As with other releases of Word, Microsoft has created some new wizards for the latest release of Word. You can use the wizards when you need to quickly create a standard type of document that requires a number of formatting features.

- *AutoShapes.* Word now makes it easy for you to add a variety of shapes (such as ribbons and star bursts) to your document by choosing AutoShape designs displayed in palettes or menus.

Who Should Use This Book?

This text is designed to be used by students who are enrolled in a semester-length microcomputer word processing course. These courses typically cover beginning to intermediate level word processing features and are often taught in business departments, CIS departments, and in continuing education.

The text can also be used in corporate training, where trainees often complete half-, one-, or two-day classes. The book can also be used by those who want to learn Word on their own.

What Does This Book Contain?

Microsoft Word 97 SmartStart shows you how to use many of the most commonly used Word features to help you create polished and effective documents. The book is organized into the following chapters:

Chapter 1, "Getting Started," introduces the Word environment, the procedures for completing basic word processing tasks, and how to use the Word Help and Office Assistant features.

Chapter 2, "Editing Documents," shows you how to open and change the content of existing documents by inserting and deleting text; moving and copying selected text is also discussed.

Chapter 3, "Proofing Your Work," covers the use of the Find, Replace, and Go To features; the spelling and grammar checkers; the thesaurus; and the AutoCorrect features.

Chapter 4, "Formatting Characters," shows you how to improve the appearance of a document by changing the character formatting and inserting special characters into your documents.

Chapter 5, "Formatting Lines and Paragraphs," illustrates paragraph-formatting options, such as aligning text, indenting text, double-spacing text, setting up tables in a document by using tabs, controlling line breaks, and inserting bulleted and numbered lists.

Chapter 6, "Formatting Pages," shows you how to format pages; set margins, paper size, and orientation; use page numbering; insert page breaks; divide a document into sections; create headers and footers; and create footnotes and endnotes.

Chapter 7, "Managing and Printing Files," presents methods for managing files, such as viewing file information, creating folders in storage locations, moving and copying files, finding files within your computer system, placing one file inside another, and experimenting with various printing options.

Chapter 8, "Using Tables," shows you how to create tables within your documents and how to edit and format tables. Use of the new Draw Table feature that enables one to actually draw a table into a document is discussed. Finally, the chapter shows you how to change tabbed lines of text into tables and how to change tables into tabbed lines of text.

Chapter 9, "Merging Files," introduces the powerful and time-saving Mail Merge Helper, which guides you through the process of merging information from a type of database file into a standard (form) document file.

Chapter 10, "Increasing Your Productivity," introduces you to the use of features for automating the repetitive aspects of your work: styles and templates, Wizards, the AutoFormat and AutoText features, and macros.

Chapter 11, "Introduction to Desktop Publishing," shows you how to display your information in newspaper-style columns, add special shapes (such as ribbons and stars) to your document to bend and shape the appearance of selected characters, apply borders and shading to paragraphs and pages, insert Drop Caps, and insert and manipulate pictures.

Appendix A, "Working with Windows 95," is a step-by-step tutorial on Windows 95.

Conventions Used in This Book

The conventions used in this book have been established to help you learn to use Word quickly and easily. As much as possible, the conventions correspond with those used in the Word program and documentation.

The keys that you press and the text that you type appear in **boldface**. Key combinations are joined by either a plus sign or a comma. The key combination ⬆Shift+F5 indicates that you are to press and hold down ⬆Shift, press F5, and then release both keys. The key combination ⬆Shift, F5 indicates that you are to press and release ⬆Shift and then press and release F5.

CHAPTER 1

Getting Started

Word processing is the most common task completed by micro-computer users. This text helps you learn to use Microsoft Word 97 (Word), one of the most popular and powerful microcomputer word processing software packages available today.

Document
A file that contains the work created by a program.

In this chapter, you learn the fundamental procedures for creating, printing, and saving a *document* when using Word. After you learn how to start the program, you examine the elements found in the Word window. After you are comfortable using the Word window elements (menus, toolbars, scroll bars, and so on) you'll find that you can quickly create attractive documents for both personal and business use.

After you create your first document on-screen, you'll learn how to save, print, and safely close the document. This chapter also introduces the Word Help feature, a tool that you may find quite valuable as you continue to work in Word. Finally, you'll learn the proper way to exit Word so that your documents do not become lost or damaged. These basic techniques provide the necessary foundation for you to work effectively and efficiently in any Word document.

Objectives

By the time you finish this chapter, you will have learned to

1. Start Word

2. Work with the Word Window Elements

3. Create a New Document

4. Save a Document

5. Preview and Print a Document

6. Close a Document

7. Access Help

8. Exit Word

Objective 1: Start Word

If you have used other software programs written for Windows 95 (or later versions of Windows) or Windows NT, you'll see that Word uses the same standard Windows features as many other Windows-based applications. In this section, you learn how to start Word from the Windows desktop. If you are unfamiliar with using the mouse or Windows 95, see Appendix A, "Working with Windows 95," at the end of this text for help in working with the basic Windows procedures.

Starting Word

The Windows operating system must be running before you can start Word. After Windows is running, you can start Word by following these steps:

❶ Click the Windows taskbar Start button to display the Start menu (see Figure 1.1).

If your copy of Windows has been left in its default configuration, the Start button is in the lower-left corner of the desktop, at the left end of the taskbar. If the taskbar is not visible, try resting the mouse pointer along the bottom (or one of the other borders) of the Windows desktop; this action usually displays a "hidden" taskbar. (Your Windows desktop may be configured to hide the taskbar when it is not in use, thereby allowing more screen space for your programs. In the next few pages, you'll learn more about the taskbar.) If you can't find the taskbar, ask your instructor or computer support department for help.

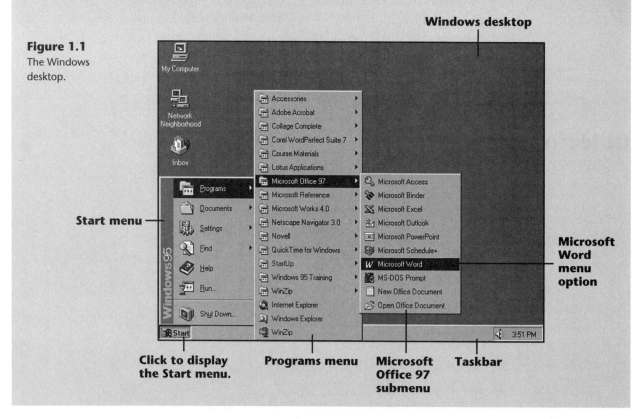

Figure 1.1
The Windows desktop.

2 Rest your pointer on the **P**rograms option on the Start menu; a menu of available programs is displayed.

The next step is to locate the Microsoft Word menu item. You may see the Microsoft Word menu item on the **P**rograms menu; if you do, move to step 3. If you don't see the Word item on the **P**rograms menu, look for an option that says something similar to MS Office, MS Office 97, or Word Processing, and click that item to display a submenu of program choices. Many computer users install the entire Microsoft Office 97 Suite (Word, Excel, PowerPoint, Access, and Outlook) on their computers. These users may choose to display a general Microsoft Office 97 entry, or something similar, on the **P**rograms menu to conserve space. Usually, choosing the broader option causes another menu to be displayed that includes the Microsoft Word menu choice.

If you have problems... If you cannot find the Microsoft Word menu option, check with your instructor or computer support department for help.

3 Choose the Microsoft Word menu option.

The opening Word logo is displayed for a moment, and then the opening Word screen is displayed (see Figure 1.2).

Figure 1.2
The Word window.

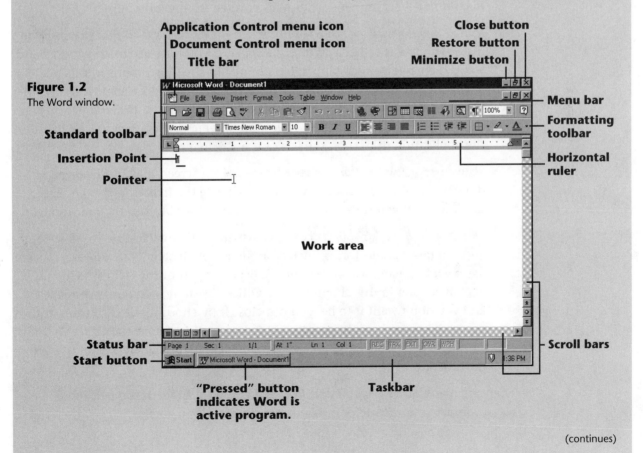

(continues)

④ At this point, the Word window should be displayed on your screen. Leave the Word window open for the next exercise.

Note

This chapter is designed to take you through the essential concepts for creating a simple document in Word. If you need to stop your Word computing session before finishing the chapter, refer to objectives 6 and 8 before you turn off your computer. These objectives show you how to safely close documents and exit Word.

Word uses a numbering pattern for temporarily identifying unnamed documents until you name and save them. At the beginning of a Word session, the initial blank document is named *Document1*. If a second blank document is opened anytime during the session, it is named *Document2*. This numbering pattern continues throughout the Word session.

Don't worry if your Word window appears slightly different from the figures in the text. Depending on how the software and your computer system were set up, your Word window may

- *Appear smaller than the one in the text.* The application window may not be maximized—maximizing windows is covered in Appendix A.

- *Include another window displayed in the work area of the application window.* The inside window is called a *document window*. If you have an inside window and want to change your display to look more like the illustrations in this text, locate the three small buttons on the right side of the document window title bar; then click the middle button (Maximize). Clicking this Maximize button enlarges the work area in the window and merges the document title bar into the application title bar at the top of the screen.

- *Show more or fewer buttons on your toolbars.* Your screen may be displayed at a different resolution from the one used to create the figures in this book, so don't worry if you see either more buttons or fewer buttons on your toolbars.

- *Display the Office Assistant.* The Office Assistant is a new feature to Word 97 and can take various forms, such as an image of Einstein, Shakespeare, a paper clip, or a bouncing ball. The Office Assistant is part of the Help system and is explained later in this chapter. If the Office Assistant is currently displayed and you don't want it to be, you can close it by choosing the X button in the upper-right corner of the graphics box. You can also move the Office Assistant by dragging its title bar to an appropriate location anywhere within the Windows desktop.

There are many other ways to start Word. If you want to learn some of these ways, contact your instructor or computer support department.

Objective 2: Work with the Word Window Elements

At this point, it is important to learn a little about the Word window. If you have used other Windows applications, you already may be familiar with many of the window elements. However, if you are just starting to use Windows applications, the window elements may, at first, be a little confusing. This section provides an overview of the major components of the Word window.

Default
The original settings for a program when it is first installed on a computer system. Most default settings can be changed to reflect your preferences.

Table 1.1 lists the *default* Word application window elements and gives a brief description of each element. As you read through the table, refer to your screen (or to Figure 1.2) to locate each of the elements within the window.

Table 1.1   Word Screen Elements

	Element	Description
W	Application Control menu icon	Click the Control menu icon on the application window title bar to display the application's Control menu. Double-click the application window Control menu icon to exit (or close) the application.
	Document Control menu icon	Click the Control menu icon on the menu bar (or the document window title bar) once to display the document's Control menu. Double-click the document window Control menu icon to close the document.
	Title bar	The top line of an application or document window. When the document window is maximized, the application window title bar displays the name of the application and the current document's name.
	Minimize button	Click the title bar Minimize button to minimize the application window. Click the Minimize button in the menu bar (or document window title bar) to minimize the document window.
	Restore button	In Figure 1.2, the Restore buttons are displayed because the application and document windows are maximized. Click either Restore button to restore the window to a smaller or previous size, and the button changes to a Maximize button.
	Maximize button	Only appears in a window that is not already maximized. Click the Maximize button in the application window title bar, and the application window fills the desktop. Click the Maximize button in the document window title bar, and the document window fills the application window's work area. When a window is maximized, the Restore button is displayed in place of the Maximize button.
X	Close button	Click the Close button in the application window title bar to close the application window. Click the Close button in the menu bar (or document window title bar) to close the current document window.

(continues)

Table 1.1   Word Screen Elements (continued)

Element	Description
Menu bar	The second line of the application window that lists the menu options that can be used to customize Word documents. Menu options can be accessed by using either the mouse or the keyboard.
Standard toolbar	A strip of buttons that you choose with the mouse to access frequently used features. Each button contains a picture that represents the feature. The Standard toolbar includes shortcuts for opening, saving, and printing documents.
Formatting toolbar	A strip of buttons that provide quick access to commonly used text editing and text layout features.
Ruler	A reference to view how your document is displayed across the page. It provides convenient ways to change margins, adjust indents, set tabs, and change the width of table columns.
Work area	The blank area where you type, edit, and format your document.
Insertion point	The vertical blinking line that indicates your location on-screen and where the next text or graphic entry will be placed in the window work area.
Pointer	The marker that moves around the screen as the mouse is moved. When in text, the pointer looks like the end view of an I-beam. The marker changes shape depending upon its location in the window and the procedure being completed.
Scroll bars	Accessible only with a mouse, the vertical scroll bar is used to move up and down in a document; the horizontal scroll bar is used to move from left to right in a document.
Scroll box	A box inside a scroll bar. The location of the scroll box indicates the position of the currently displayed information in relationship to the entire document.
Status bar	Displays the current page, section, position of the insertion point, and indicates if an operation is in progress.

Note

When you first start Word, the Word window is usually maximized to fill the desktop. The document window is usually maximized inside the Word window. This is typically the preferred setting because it shows as much of the document as possible.

If your Windows taskbar is visible, it's usually displayed at the bottom of the screen, below the Word status bar. If you want to hide the taskbar (thereby

Right-click
To click the right mouse button.

Shortcut menu
A context-sensitive menu that appears when you right-click.

creating a slightly larger application window) and make it come into view only when you need it, point to a blank area of the taskbar and click the right button on your mouse (this technique is called *right-clicking*). A *shortcut menu* is displayed. From this menu, choose **P**roperties, choose the **Au**to hide option in the dialog box, and click OK. This hides the taskbar from view. When you need to access the taskbar, simply move the pointer to the edge of the screen where the taskbar is "hiding." The taskbar will be displayed while the pointer is positioned in it; moving the pointer out of the taskbar will again cause it to be hidden. The illustrations in this chapter display the Windows taskbar so that you can become familiar with it. The illustrations in the remaining chapters do not display the taskbar. Hiding the taskbar enables the Word window to fill the entire screen and display as much of your document as possible.

Using Menus

The menu bar lists the names for the Word menus. When you click one of the names on the menu bar, a group of related commands "drops down" from the menu name. You then choose a command by clicking it or by pressing the (Alt) key at the same time you press the underlined letter in the command name. If a command is dimmed (usually displayed in a gray shade), it is not available for the current procedure.

To choose menus and commands, follow these steps:

1 In the open Word window, place the tip of the pointer on the word **F**ile in the menu bar and click the left mouse button.

This opens the **F**ile menu, which "drops down" into the document window, as shown in Figure 1.3. This menu contains a number of file-management commands.

Figure 1.3
You may access many of the file management commands from the File menu.

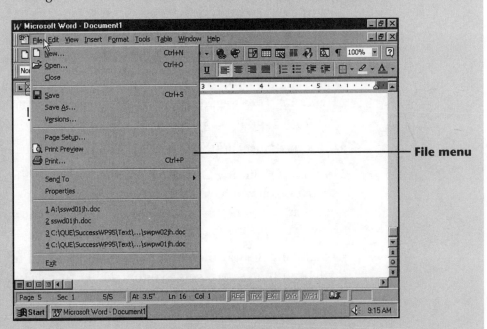

File menu

(continues)

Tip

If you open a menu by mistake, you can quickly close the menu by clicking in an area outside the menu, such as in the title bar or work area. Do not click a toolbar button to close a menu; clicking a button may activate a Word function.

Alternatively, you can close a menu by pressing the ⎋Esc key twice. The first key press closes the menu; however, the menu bar still remains active. The second key press deactivates the menu bar and returns you to the work area of your window.

---

❷ Move the mouse pointer up and down the menu (without clicking) to highlight the various options.

Each command name automatically highlights when you touch it with the pointer. The highlighting (by default) appears as a blue bar that covers the command name; highlighted commands (usually) appear in white.

Some menu commands, such as **S**ave, are followed by a "shortcut" key combination (Ctrl+S) to indicate that you can activate the command by pressing those keys instead of opening the command's menu and choosing the command. In this case, you would hold down the Ctrl key, press S, and then release both keys to activate the Save command. Shortcut keys will not work when the menu bar is displaying an open menu.

Some menu commands, such as the **O**pen command, are followed by an ellipsis (...). (The **O**pen command also includes a shortcut key combination.) When you choose a command followed by an ellipsis, a dialog box opens. Word uses dialog boxes to enable you to make one or more choices about the current procedure you are completing.

❸ Point to the **O**pen command in the **F**ile menu to move the highlight bar to that command; then click to choose the **O**pen command.

Choosing the **O**pen command displays the Open dialog box, as shown in Figure 1.4. The Open dialog box lets you open files stored on a floppy disk or on your computer's hard drive.

❹ Click the Cancel button in the upper-right side of the dialog box.

In this case, clicking Cancel clears the dialog box without making any changes. You will have many opportunities to make selections in dialog boxes as you work through this book. For now, concentrate on learning how to use the menus.

To simplify the way menu commands are shown throughout this book, you will be instructed to access a command like this: "Choose **F**ile, **O**pen." This command tells you to open the **F**ile menu, and then click the **O**pen command (as you did previously in steps 1 and 3). The bold letters represent the letters in the command that appear underlined on your screen in case you want to use the keyboard rather than the mouse to open menus.

Figure 1.4
Use the Open dialog box to open the file you want to work with.

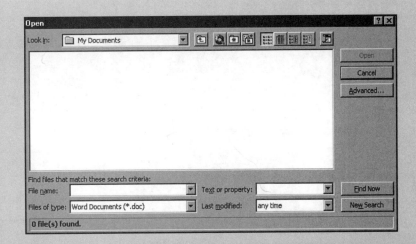

Note

When you see a command such as "Press Alt+F" in this book, you should press and hold down the Alt key while you press the F key; then release both keys. When you see a command such as "Press Alt, F," you should press and release the Alt key and then press and release the F key.

❺ Press Alt+F to open the **F**ile menu.

To select a command from an opened menu, simply press the command's underlined letter.

❻ Press O.

Pressing the letter O chooses the **O**pen command, which displays the Open dialog box. Now use the keyboard to cancel the dialog box.

❼ Press Esc to remove the Open dialog box from the screen.

Pressing Esc provides the same results as clicking the Cancel button in the Open dialog box.

❽ Choose **V**iew to open the **V**iew menu.

Some menu commands are followed by a right-pointing arrowhead. This symbol indicates that when you rest the pointer on the command or click the command, a submenu of related commands will appear next to the original menu.

❾ Choose **T**oolbars to display the Toolbars submenu (see Figure 1.5).

If a menu command has a check mark next to it, that command is currently selected, or "active." Choosing the menu command turns off the feature; choosing the command again turns it back on. These types of commands are sometimes called *toggle switches* because the same command turns the feature on and off.

(continues)

Using Menus (continued)

Figure 1.5
The View menu
and Toolbars
submenu.

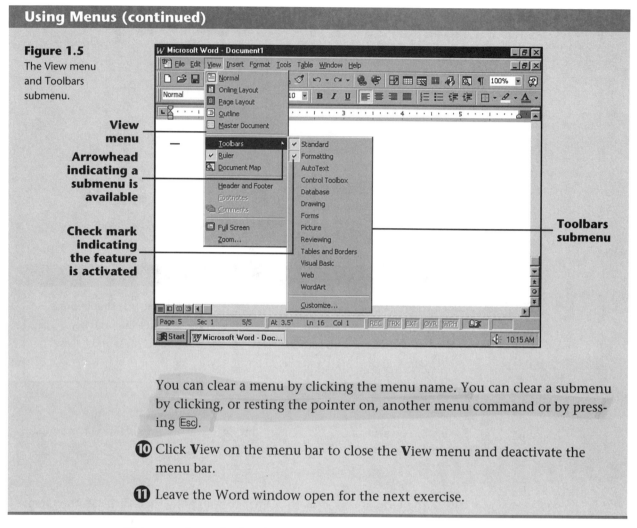

View menu

Arrowhead indicating a submenu is available

Check mark indicating the feature is activated

Toolbars submenu

You can clear a menu by clicking the menu name. You can clear a submenu by clicking, or resting the pointer on, another menu command or by pressing Esc.

🔟 Click **View** on the menu bar to close the **View** menu and deactivate the menu bar.

⑪ Leave the Word window open for the next exercise.

This completes the brief exercise on using Word's menus. You may have noticed that some of the menu commands display a picture in front of the command name. A picture in front of a command represents the button on one of the Word toolbars (or the horizontal scroll bar) that can be chosen to produce the same result as choosing the menu command. In the next exercise, you learn to work with the buttons on the toolbars.

Using Toolbars

When you first start Word, the screen displays the Standard and Formatting toolbars (see Figure 1.6). To use Word efficiently, you should become familiar with the functions that you can access from these toolbars. They save keystrokes or extra mouse movements so that you don't have to use the drop-down menus.

In addition to the Standard and Formatting toolbars, Word has toolbars that you can display to help you with specific tasks. The following information applies to all the toolbars in Word.

Most users find that the Word toolbars make working in Word easy and efficient. To display the Open dialog box, for example, you can click the **F**ile menu and then click the **O**pen command, or you can simply click the Open button on the Standard toolbar. (The Standard toolbar is located just below the menu bar.)

Note

If a ScreenTip is not displayed when you rest the pointer on a toolbar button, the ScreenTip option may be turned off. To turn on this option, choose **T**ools, **O**ptions; click the View tab; check the ScreenTips check box; then choose OK.

1

Using the Standard Toolbar

To display the Open dialog box using the Open toolbar button, follow these steps:

1 Position the mouse pointer (but don't click) on the Standard toolbar's Open button. The picture on the Open button is an open yellow file folder.

By default a yellow rectangle—known as a *ScreenTip*—is displayed by the button. A button's ScreenTip identifies or briefly describes the function of the button (see Figure 1.6).

Open button

Figure 1.6
Place the mouse pointer on a toolbar button to display a corresponding ScreenTip.

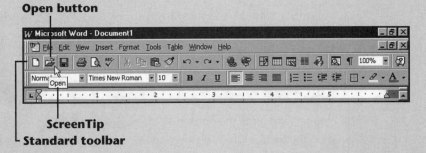

ScreenTip
Standard toolbar

2 Click the Open button.

The Open dialog box is displayed.

You are not quite ready to work with opening files yet, so at this point, just close the dialog box.

3 Click the Close button in the upper-right corner of the dialog box to close the dialog box.

Note

In most cases, you can close a dialog box, without initiating any changes to the current document or Word settings, by choosing the Close button, choosing the Cancel button, or pressing Esc.

So far, the illustrations in this text have shown the Standard and Formatting toolbars in their normal position and shape (their *default* settings). For most of your work in Word, it is highly recommended that you leave these two toolbars in their default positions.

(continues)

Using the Standard Toolbar (continued)

When people need to share a computer, however, they sometimes find that a previous user has moved a toolbar or, even worse, totally removed a toolbar from the screen! The next steps show you how to position and shape a toolbar, and how to add and remove a toolbar from the window. As you complete this exercise, you return the toolbars to their default settings.

❹ On the Standard toolbar, place the pointer on the thin gray line between the sixth and seventh buttons: the Spelling and Grammar button and the Cut button; then double-click the mouse.

Note

Remember, *double-click* means to keep the mouse steady and quickly tap the left mouse button twice. Refer to Appendix A if you need a refresher on basic Windows concepts and procedures.

The toolbar immediately changes shape and moves into the work area. Notice that the toolbar now is displayed in its own window that includes a title bar.

Note

You can also place the pointer on the gray line separating toolbar buttons and drag the toolbar into the window work area.

Your window should now look similar to Figure 1.7.

Figure 1.7
The Standard toolbar is "floating" in the window work area. The Formatting toolbar is "docked" above the window work area.

Standard toolbar

Window work area

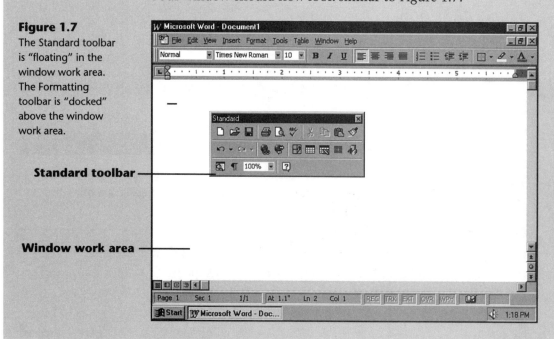

The Standard toolbar is now in a "floating" position, meaning that it can be moved anywhere on the screen. (The Formatting toolbar is still in the "docked" position.) You can move the window displaying the Standard toolbar by dragging the title bar to the desired location. This window can be sized (to a few predetermined sizes) by dragging a window border.

To return the Standard toolbar to its default position, complete the next step.

5 Double-click the title bar of the Standard Toolbar window.

Note

If you should find the Formatting toolbar positioned above the Standard toolbar, it is easy to switch the toolbar locations back to their default positions. Place the pointer on a gray line separating two buttons on the Standard toolbar; then drag the pointer toward the top of the window until you see the dotted line representing the top border of the Standard toolbar positioned in the menu bar. Release the mouse button. The Standard toolbar should now be positioned immediately below the menu bar.

Word uses a variety of toolbars to help you accomplish specific tasks. In the next steps, you learn to quickly add and remove toolbars.

6 Choose **V**iew, **T**oolbars, Drawing to display the Drawing toolbar.

The default location for many of the Word toolbars (such as the Drawing toolbar) is along the bottom of the Word window. Other toolbars are usually found along a side of the Word window. Word displays toolbars in their default location unless the previous user moved the toolbar to a different location and then removed the toolbar before exiting Word. In these cases, Word will usually display the toolbar in its last location within the Word window.

A list of toolbars is displayed when you choose **V**iew, **T**oolbars, or when you right-click on any part of a toolbar. (Right-clicking a toolbar displays a shortcut menu listing the available Word toolbars.) A check mark in front of a toolbar name means that the toolbar is currently displayed in the Word window. To remove a toolbar from the window, choose the toolbar name to deselect it (this also removes the check mark in front of the toolbar name).

7 Right-click in the blank area on the right side of the Drawing toolbar.

The toolbar shortcut menu should be displayed (see Figure 1.8).

8 Remove the Drawing toolbar by clicking the Drawing option in the shortcut menu. (You can use either the right or left mouse buttons when clicking in a shortcut menu.)

9 Leave the Word window open for the next exercise.

(continues)

Using the Standard Toolbar (continued)

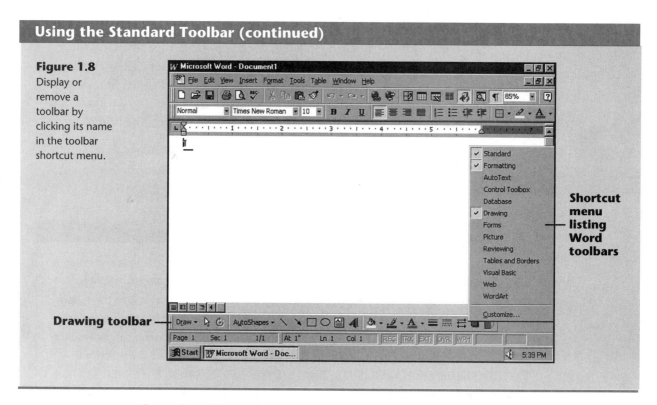

Figure 1.8
Display or remove a toolbar by clicking its name in the toolbar shortcut menu.

Shortcut menu listing Word toolbars

Drawing toolbar

Changing Views

Word can display several views of the same document. You can use these views to focus on various aspects of your document and to simplify editing. However, sometimes when you are sharing a computer with others, you may finish your Word session in one view and exit the program. Later, when you return to your document, another person may have used the computer and left Word in a different view. This section briefly explains the different views in which Word can display your document and shows you how to quickly change among the Word views.

You can display a document in many different views, including:

- **N**ormal
- Onlin**e** Layout
- **P**age Layout
- **O**utline
- **M**aster Document
- F**u**ll Screen

Normal view is the default view and generally the most useful one. You probably will do most of your work in this view. Most of the illustrations in the text will display the documents in Normal view.

In Normal view, you can see character and paragraph formatting; alignment; tab positions; and line, section, and page breaks. In this view, you do not see headers, footers, or side-by-side columns; neither do you see how the document will actually look on a printed page.

2   Page Layout is another commonly used view. It shows all the formatting in the document—including headers, footers, footnotes, columns, and graphics—and shows all elements in their correct positions. A vertical ruler is added at the left side of the screen. You can edit and format text in this view; you also can move graphics by dragging them with the mouse. The screen response, however, is usually a little slower than in Normal view.

3   Online Layout view displays a screen view that is optimized for reading online documents. Text appears larger and wraps to fit in the window. In this view, Word turns on the document map, which makes it easy to move from one location in your document to another.

4   Outline view enables you to work with a document in outline form, providing that you have applied suitable heading styles to titles and subtitles in the document. In Outline view, the various levels of headings are indented automatically to show the structure of a document. You can collapse a document so that only headings are displayed.

Master Document view is useful when you are preparing long documents and need a quick way to keep the document organized.

For those preferring to display just their document on the screen, choose Full Screen view to remove all other window components from the display.

All the views just discussed can be accessed from the **View** menu. In addition, choosing a button from the group of buttons attached to the left side of the horizontal scroll bar can access one of the first four views listed.

In addition to enabling you to change to a predefined view, the **View** menu also lets you access the Word Zoom feature. When you choose **View, Zoom,** the Zoom dialog box is displayed. You use this dialog box to choose the percentage you want your document displayed at on your screen. The default percentage is 100%, but you can display the document from 10% to 500%. The lower the magnification, the more you will see of your document on your screen. You may choose to use a higher magnification when you want to work on a specific portion of your document, such as when editing a graphic.

Alternatively, you can activate the Zoom feature by choosing the drop-down arrow of the Zoom button on the Standard toolbar to display a list of Zoom settings similar to those displayed in the Zoom dialog box. In addition to specific numerical settings, the Zoom options also include choices such as Page Width.

Print Preview is useful for seeing how your document will print *before* you actually send it to the printer. While in this view, you can make edits to your document and then print it. You use this view later in this chapter, just before you print your first document.

The following exercise gives you a chance to type some text and then display your document in a few different views. Most of the exercises in this text have you working in Normal view. If your Word screen is initially displayed in a different view, completing this exercise will help you learn to quickly change views.

Insertion point
The flashing vertical bar in the work area of the document.

Before you begin the following exercise, you need to understand the role of the insertion point. The *insertion point* is the flashing vertical bar in the work area of the document. It marks the place where text you type is inserted into a document. In a new document, the insertion point appears in the upper-left corner of the work area. As you type, text appears immediately to the left of the insertion point, and the insertion point moves to the right. You can move the insertion point—using the keyboard or the mouse—to the right of the last character or space, but you cannot move the insertion point beyond that location.

The short horizontal line in the work area marks the last line in a document. In a new document, this line occurs immediately below the first line because the document contains no text.

Displaying a Document in Three Different Views

❶ In the blank Word window, type your first and last name; then press `⏎Enter`.

Don't worry if you press an incorrect key while you are typing; at this point, we'll disregard any typos in your document. If you want to correct a mistake, however, you can press the `⬅Backspace` key to remove the character to the left of the insertion point. Pressing the `Del` key removes the character to the right of the insertion point.

For now, use the arrow keys to move the insertion point. These keys are located to the left of the number pad and are in an inverted "T" formation near the bottom edge of the keyboard. In the next chapter, you will learn more effective ways of moving the insertion point and editing text.

❷ Type the name of your work or school/training location and press `⏎Enter`.

❸ Type your city and state.

If you started this exercise in Normal view, your Word window should look similar to the one shown in Figure 1.9.

Don't be surprised if you see wavy red lines under your name or city. This just means that Word's automatic spelling checker is turned on and some of the words you entered are not included the program's standard dictionary. Word flags unrecognized words to help you spot misspellings.

Similarly, if you believe that you are typing letters in a certain order, but Word insists on displaying the letters in a different order, Word's AutoCorrect feature may be activated. This feature recognizes common typos and automatically corrects the text as you type. This is normally a very useful feature; however, if you live in a town named *Esle*, you'll find that AutoCorrect will attempt to change the name to *Else*.

Figure 1.9
The initial document in Word's Normal view. The pointer is resting on the Normal View button, which causes the ScreenTip to be displayed.

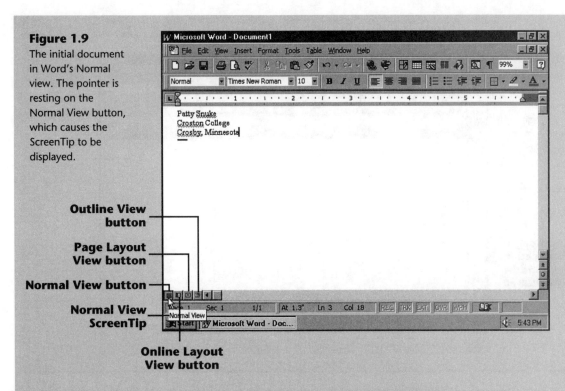

Outline View button

Page Layout View button

Normal View button

Normal View ScreenTip

Online Layout View button

You'll learn about each of these features, and how to turn them off and on, in the next chapter. For now, disregard Word's actions and use the text as it is entered on your screen.

You can change your view either by choosing the desired view from the **V**iew menu or by choosing one of the View buttons located at the left end of the horizontal scroll bar (refer again to Figure 1.9).

④ Change to Page Layout view now by choosing the Page Layout View button located at the left end of the horizontal scroll bar.

Your window should now look similar to the one in Figure 1.10, although your window may not currently display the horizontal and vertical rulers. (To display both rulers, when in the Page Layout view, choose **V**iew, **R**uler.)

⑤ Choose **V**iew, Onlin**e** Layout to see how you would work with your document in Online Layout view.

⑥ Choose **V**iew, **N**ormal to return your document to Normal view.

⑦ Leave the Word window open for the next exercise.

(continues)

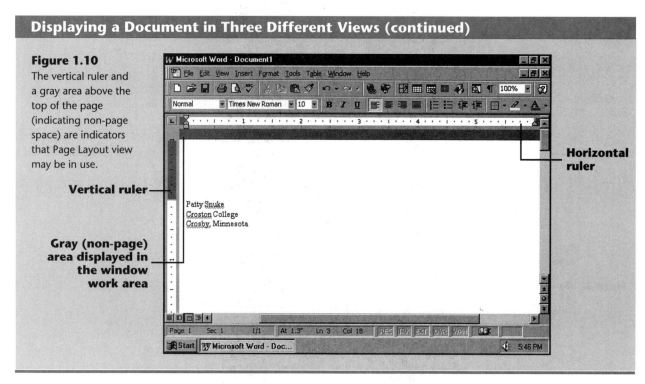

Displaying a Document in Three Different Views (continued)

Figure 1.10
The vertical ruler and a gray area above the top of the page (indicating non-page space) are indicators that Page Layout view may be in use.

Vertical ruler

Gray (non-page) area displayed in the window work area

Horizontal ruler

This exercise showed how quickly you can change views in Word. If you're sharing a computer with others, don't be surprised if you occasionally need to change the view of your Word window.

Objective 3: Create a New Document

The initial settings (font, font size, margins, and so on) in place when you start a new document are saved in a *template* file. When you give the command to create a new document, Word locates the default (or selected) template file and uses the settings in that file to establish the settings for your initial document.

Word contains several templates, each with different settings, and you can create additional templates of your own. If you base specific types of documents on templates, you don't have to define basic settings every time you start a new document; Word uses the settings in the template as a guideline for formatting the document. You can change the settings before you start typing or at any time while you are typing.

As you have already seen, you can begin typing text as soon as you start Word. The document that appears on-screen, *Document1*, is based on the Normal template. (The actual name of the template file is Normal.dot.) This is the template you will use for the majority of the exercises in this text. The Normal template includes the following settings:

- The Times New Roman font, with a font size of 10 points (one point equals approximately 1/72 of an inch)

- Left and right margins of 1.25 inches

- Top and bottom margins of 1 inch

- Single-spaced paragraphs, aligned flush with the left margin

- Tab stops set at every .5 inch

When you create a new document, it is displayed within a document window. Word enables you to have many documents open at one time. You can switch from document to document; however, only one document can be active at a time. You learn more about working with multiple documents in the next chapter. For now, complete the following exercise to see two ways to create new documents based on the Normal template.

Creating a New Document

The Word window displaying your name and location should still be open from the previous exercise. If you have just started the Word program, you are probably looking at a blank *Document1* Word window. In either case, follow these steps to open additional blank documents based on the Normal template:

1 Choose **F**ile, **N**ew.

The New dialog box is displayed (see Figure 1.11).

Figure 1.11
By default, the Blank Document icon is selected in the New dialog box.

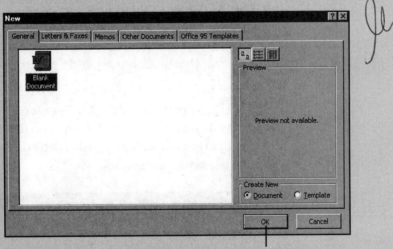

Click here to open a new blank document window.

2 Click OK to open a new blank document.

Word gives the temporary name *Document2* to the new document.

This is one way to open a new, blank document, but the most common method is to click the New button on the Standard toolbar.

 3 Click the New button on the Standard toolbar.

When you click the New button, Word automatically uses the Normal document template to create a new blank document.

4 Leave the Word window open for the next exercise.

Understanding Word Wrap

Normally, as you type characters in a document, they start at the left end of a line and progressively fill the line. As you near the right margin, if a word that you type is too long to fit on the line, Word places all the characters of that word at the left end of the next line. This feature, known as *word wrap*, makes it unnecessary for you to press the ⏎Enter key at the end of a line. Word wrap keeps your text within the margins and keeps all the characters of individual words together.

It is very important that you do not press ⏎Enter at the end of each line. Pressing ⏎Enter each time inserts unnecessary editing codes and makes it difficult for you to edit your work. Press ⏎Enter only when you want to make sure that the next character is placed on a new line, such as at the end of a paragraph or after each item in a list.

Typing Text in a Document

Typing text in a word processing program is much faster and easier than writing on paper or using a typewriter. With a word processing program, you can make changes quickly. If you change your mind about the structure of a sentence or the organization of a paragraph, you can easily insert, delete, or move text.

Entering Text

To enter text into a new document, follow these steps:

❶ In the open blank Word document displayed from the previous exercise, type the following paragraph. The paragraph is part of a letter you will work with in the next chapter. Be sure to use the word-wrap feature. Don't worry about typos at this time; just type the paragraph:

> **The primary focus, as always, is the customer. We will work in teams, using the Total Quality Service (TQS) approach. Each team will appoint a leader to record all the activities completed each month. The team leaders will then meet to coordinate all team activities.**

Note

With the advent of word processors for creating written documents, some traditional writing standards are changing. Throughout the exercises in this book, one space (rather than two) will be used to separate sentences. If you choose to use two spaces between sentences, you may notice that the line breaks in your document are slightly different from the ones shown in the illustrations.

Note

If your Word screen displays a paragraph symbol ¶ at the end of the paragraph, and if small, raised dots are displayed on-screen each time you press Spacebar, it indicates that the Show/Hide button is turned on. This button resembles a paragraph symbol and is usually positioned near the right end of the Standard

> toolbar. The symbols displayed on-screen when the Show/Hide button is activated can help you interpret what's happening on-screen; they will not be displayed when you print your document. For extra control when editing, many users prefer to leave these symbols turned on as they are fine-tuning their documents. To turn off the Show/Hide button and remove the symbols from your screen, simply click the Show/Hide button.

❷ Keep the Word window open for the next exercise.

Objective 4: Save a Document

After creating a document, you should save the document to disk for future use. You can save documents by choosing a command from the **F**ile menu or by choosing a button on the Standard toolbar. The **F**ile menu includes four commands for saving documents:

- **S**ave
- Save **A**s
- Save as **H**TML   *INTERNET! OR WORLD WIDE WEB!*
- V**e**rsions

Note

This text will focus on the use of the **S**ave and Save **A**s commands. The Save as **H**TML command is used when you want to save your document in a format so that it can be read on the World Wide Web. The V**e**rsions command enables a writer, or group of writers, to save multiple versions of the same document. Working with HTML documents and multiple versions is beyond the scope of this book.

Word offers one additional method for saving files that you can use when you have several documents open at the same time. To simultaneously save all the open documents, under the existing names, follow these steps:

1. Press ⬆Shift; then choose **F**ile to open the **F**ile menu.

2. Choose the Save All command (which has replaced the **S**ave command on the **F**ile menu).

Saving a New Document

To save your current document to your disk, follow these steps:

 ❶ Click the Save button on the Standard toolbar or choose File, Save **A**s.

(continues)

Saving a New Document (continued)

The Save As dialog box is displayed (see Figure 1.12).

Figure 1.12
Use the Save As dialog box to assign a file name and location to your document.

Click here to display a list of available storage locations.

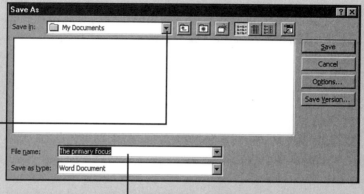

Enter the name of your file here.

❷ In the File **n**ame text box (where you see text highlighted in Figure 1.12), type **Sample Paragraph**.

As you type the new name, it automatically replaces the temporary name shown in the File **n**ame text box (*The primary focus*, in this example). One of the differences between Word 97 and versions of Word written for pre-Windows 95 operating systems is that file names can now be up to 255 characters in length and can include spaces. However, you cannot use the following characters in a file name: / \ : * ? " < > |.

Word automatically adds a .doc file extension to whatever file name you type. You might not be able to see the extension in Word, depending on whether the option to show extensions has been selected through Windows Explorer or the My Computer window. Contact your instructor or computer support person if you would like to change your current setting.

Note

The exercises in this text will direct you to save your files to the Student Disk in drive A. If you will be saving to a different location, modify the saving instructions as necessary. See your instructor if you have questions about where to save your file.

---

❸ Insert your Student Disk in drive A of your computer and select the appropriate storage location in the Save **in** drop-down list box.

To save the document to a drive or folder not originally displayed in the Save **in** drop-down list box:

- Click the down arrow at the end of the Save **in** box to display a list of available storage locations on your computer system.

- Scroll through the list if necessary and then click the drive letter or folder that corresponds to the location you want to save to. If your data drive is drive A, click 3 _ Floppy (A); if your data drive is drive B, click B; and so on.

4 Choose the **S**ave button to save the file to your disk.

The file is saved, and the Save As box is removed from the screen.

The name of your document should now be displayed in the Word window title bar. (Seeing the appropriate file name listed in the title bar is a quick way to make sure that you have saved the file.)

5 Keep the Word window and your Sample Paragraph.doc file open for the next exercise.

> ### Note
>
> If you are working on a document and choose the **Ex**it command from the **F**ile menu, or click the document Close button (X), Word prompts you to save any unsaved changes to the document before you exit the program.

When you are saving a *new* document, the Save As dialog box will be displayed whether you click the Save button on the Standard toolbar or choose the **F**ile menu's **S**ave or Save **A**s command. When you choose the Save **A**s command, the Save As dialog box is always displayed, even when you are working on a previously saved document. If you are editing an existing file and don't need to make any changes to how the file is to be saved, choose the Save button on the Standard toolbar, or choose **F**ile, **S**ave.

Objective 5: Preview and Print a Document

Before you print a document, you can preview it on-screen to check your document's content, formatting, and page layout. This helps ensure that when the document is printed you receive the results you expected. The typical way to preview a document is to activate Word's Print Preview feature. In the following exercise, you learn to use this feature as you prepare to print your document.

Previewing a New Document

To preview a document before you print it, follow these steps:

1 With the Paragraph Sample document still open on your screen, choose the Print Preview button on the Standard toolbar.

(continues)

The Print Preview window opens and displays your document, as shown in Figure 1.13. Word indicates you are using the Print Preview view by inserting the word *Preview* after the name of your document in the Word title bar.

> **Tip**
>
> For those who prefer to use the menu commands, choosing **F**ile, Print Pre**v**iew also displays the Print Preview window.

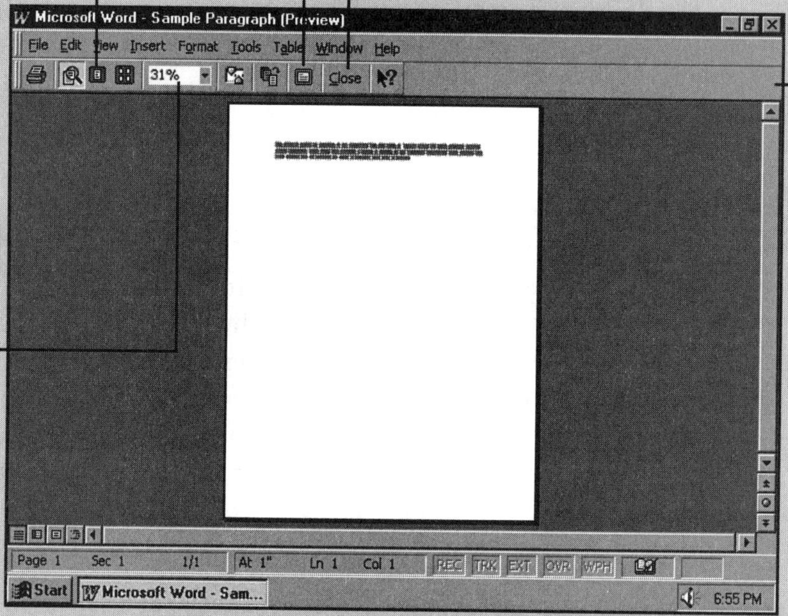

Figure 1.13
Initially, the Print Preview window displays the entire current page of your document. This is helpful for checking page layout, but makes it difficult to check content.

One Page button

Full Screen button

Close Preview button

Print Preview toolbar

Zoom button

When you first click on the Print Preview button, the document is reduced to around 31% so that the entire page can be displayed. However, you can quickly enlarge the size of the text in the Print Preview window. If your page is smaller than the one in Figure 1.13, choose the One Page button.

❷ Place your pointer on top of the lines representing your paragraph (notice that as you move the pointer onto the page, it changes into a magnifying glass) and click.

This quickly changes the Zoom setting to 100%. A disadvantage of this mode is that you may need to use the scroll bars to see your entire document.

Tip

Alternatively, you can change the magnification of your document by clicking the down arrow immediately to the right of the Zoom button to display a list of Zoom percentage choices and then choosing a new setting.

You learn about more features in the Print Preview window as you work through the text.

3 Click on your paragraph lines once more to return the Zoom percentage to its original setting.

Although you can print from the Print Preview window, close the window now by following the next step.

4 Click the Close button on the Print Preview toolbar (or press 🖰) to return to the Normal view of your document.

5 Keep the Sample Paragraph document displayed on your screen and move to the next exercise.

From most of the Word views, you can use either of two methods to print the active document:

- Click the Print button on the Standard toolbar, which sends the document to the default printer immediately. Although this method is fast and easy, it does not let you make any choices about how the document will be printed.

- Choose **File**, **Print**. This method enables you to make several choices about how the document will be printed.

Printing the Document

To print the Sample Paragraph document, follow these steps:

1 With the Sample Paragraph document displayed in the Normal view of the Word window, choose **File**, **Print** to display the Print dialog box (see Figure 1.14).

Word opens the Print dialog box, which provides you with a variety of printing options.

(continues)

Printing the Document (continued)

Figure 1.14
Use the Print dialog box to set printing options.

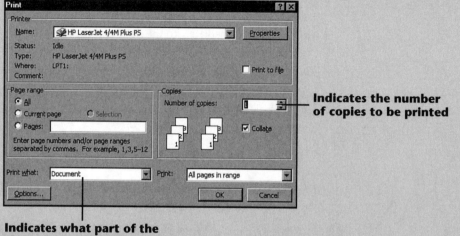

Indicates the number of copies to be printed

Indicates what part of the document will be printed

In Chapter 7 you learn to use many of the options presented in the Print dialog box. For now, just make sure that only one copy will be printed and the word *Document* is displayed in the Print **w**hat box. (If necessary, click the arrow at the end of the Print **w**hat drop-down list box and choose Document.)

❷ Choose OK to print the Sample Paragraph document.

❸ Leave the Sample Paragraph document displayed on your screen and move to the next exercise.

Objective 6: Close a Document

Now that your document has been saved and printed, you may close the document. Closing a document removes it from the computer's memory and frees that memory to hold new information, thus increasing the efficiency of your computer when dealing with additional documents. Also, when you close a document you no longer need, you remove the chance of accidentally changing it when you are working on other documents.

There are a number of ways to close a document, including

- Choosing the Close Window button (the X) on the far-right side of the menu bar of a maximized Word document window. Remember, the X button on the Word title bar closes the entire Word program.

- Choosing **F**ile, **C**lose.

- Double-clicking the Document Control menu icon.

- Choosing the Document Control menu icon, and then choosing **C**lose.

- Pressing Ctrl+F4 or Ctrl+W.

Closing Current Documents

If you have completed all the exercises from the beginning of this chapter in your current computing session, you have opened three document windows. (If you do not have three open documents, just modify the exercise to meet your situation.) In the following exercise, you will use three different procedures for closing those documents.

 ❶ In the Word window displaying the Sample Paragraph document, click the Close button on the far-right side of the menu bar.

If you have made no changes to your document since it was saved, the document will close and your screen should show a blank Document2 window. If changes were made (even if by accident), Word displays a message box asking whether you want to save the latest changes to your document. If this occurs, choose **No**.

 ❷ Close the blank Document2 window by choosing **F**ile, **C**lose.

❸ Close the Document1 window (the one containing your name and location) by pressing `Ctrl`+`F4`. When prompted to save the changes, choose **No**.

You may be surprised when the Word window changes and does not display a document window. Don't worry, you can always display a new document window by clicking the New button, or (as you learn in the next chapter) you can open an existing document from your disk.

❹ Keep the Word window open for the next exercise.

In the next objective, you learn about the Word Office Assistant and other aspects of the Word Help feature.

Objective 7: Access Help   SUNDAY 02/14/99

As you start to work with more complex documents, you may find that you need a little help to complete (or start) a procedure. Word's Help feature is designed to provide answers for almost any question you may have when using Word.

The Help feature in Word (and other Windows applications) is a sophisticated information system. If you have used Help in other Windows applications, you already know how valuable this feature is. However, you may not be familiar with the Office Assistant—the new animated Help feature included with the Microsoft Office 97 programs. This section provides a brief overview of the Help system, starting with the use of the Office Assistant.

Getting Help with the Office Assistant

The Office Assistant is an on-screen animated character (with sound) that can help you while you work. Some users prefer to keep a small Office Assistant window open on their desktop. Whenever the Office Assistant has a suggestion—designated by a light bulb displayed in the Office Assistant window—the suggestion will be displayed on the screen, or the user can just click on the light bulb to see the suggestion. Other users keep the Office Assistant window closed (to maximize the document content on-screen). When the Office Assistant is closed, just click the Office Assistant button (on the Standard toolbar) to open the window. In the following exercise, you learn how to display and use the Office Assistant (see Figure 1.15).

Figure 1.15
The animated paper clip Office Assistant.

Using the Office Assistant

1 In the open Word window (if you just completed the previous exercise, no document will be displayed in the window, and that's okay), choose the Office Assistant button on the Standard toolbar.

If you have problems... At this point, if you cannot start the Office Assistant, contact your instructor or computer support department for help.

Tip

When the Office Assistant has been activated on your computer system, you can also display the Office Assistant by pressing F1. If the Office Assistant has been turned off, pressing F1 opens the more traditional Help window.

The Office Assistant character is displayed in a small window (usually along the right side of your screen, refer to Figure 1.15). In the examples in this chapter, the Office Assistant appears as a paper clip. (The name of the paper clip character is *Clippit!*.) Later in this section, you learn the steps needed for changing the character (each character has its own name and personality) and customizing how the Office Assistant works.

2 If necessary, click the Office Assistant window to display its message box (see Figure 1.16).

Figure 1.16
The Office Assistant asks what you would like to do.

The Office Assistant is asking what you would like to do. If there already are some suggested topics displayed in your message box, disregard those topics for now and move to the next step.

❸ Type **tell me about the office assistant** in the What would you like to do? box; then choose **S**earch (or press ↵Enter).

If you have problems...   If the Office Assistant does not understand your statement or question, a message will be displayed that asks you to restate your topic.

The Office Assistant displays a list of topics relevant to the statement or question you entered in the What would you like to do? box (see Figure 1.17).

Figure 1.17
This message box displays a list of topics from which you can choose.

Click one of the round buttons to see the listed topic.

Click here to see latest tip.

Click here to display the Office Assistant dialog box.

Click here to close the message box.

> **What would you like to do?**
>
> ⬤ Get Help, tips, and messages through the Office Assistant
>
> ⬤ Get Help without the Office Assistant
>
> ⬤ Choose a different Office Assistant
>
> ⬤ Change the size of the Office Assistant
>
> ⬤ Hide or show the Office Assistant
>
> ▼ See more...
>
> [tell me about the office assistant]
>
> (⬤ **S**earch)
>
> (⬤ **T**ips)   (⬤ **O**ptions)   (⬤ **C**lose)

❹ Click the Get Help, tips, and messages through the Office Assistant option button to display a corresponding Help window (see Figure 1.18).

Click here to return to the previous Help topic.

Click here to display a shortcut menu of Help options.

Figure 1.18
The Word Help window on the selected topic.

Click here to return to the first Help window.

Button in Help window

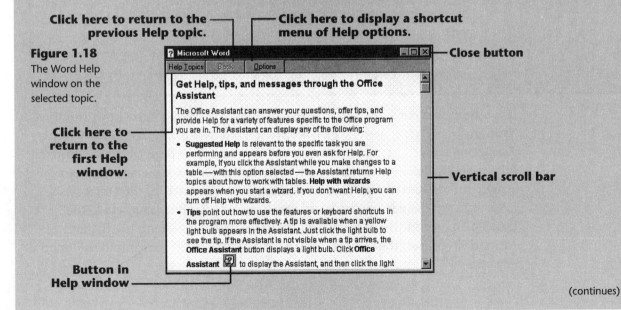

Close button

> **? Microsoft Word**   [_][□][X]
>
> Help **T**opics   Back   **O**ptions
>
> **Get Help, tips, and messages through the Office Assistant**
>
> The Office Assistant can answer your questions, offer tips, and provide Help for a variety of features specific to the Office program you are in. The Assistant can display any of the following:
>
> • **Suggested Help** is relevant to the specific task you are performing and appears before you even ask for Help. For example, if you click the Assistant while you make changes to a table—with this option selected—the Assistant returns Help topics about how to work with tables. **Help with wizards** appears when you start a wizard. If you don't want Help, you can turn off Help with wizards.
>
> • **Tips** point out how to use the features or keyboard shortcuts in the program more effectively. A tip is available when a yellow light bulb appears in the Assistant. Just click the light bulb to see the tip. If the Assistant is not visible when a tip arrives, the **Office Assistant** button displays a light bulb. Click **Office Assistant** to display the Assistant, and then click the light

Vertical scroll bar

(continues)

5 Read the information in the window (use the vertical scroll bar to scroll through the entire entry).

Notice that at the bottom of this (and most) Help windows, there is a section that provides a series of related topics. Click the button in front of a topic to move to the corresponding Help window.

6 Scroll back up in the document until you see the Office Assistant button displayed in the section on Tips.

When the Help text includes a button, clicking the button displays a short message about the button.

7 Click the button in the Help text to display its message. Then click in the Help window again to close the message box.

> **Note**
>
> When you see solid or dashed underlined words displayed in green inside a Help window, you can click these *hot words* or *hot phrases* to display additional Help information.
>
> Click on a solid underlined word to "jump" to the Help window for that topic. Click on a word with a dashed underline to view a definition of the term. To return to the Help window, click in the text area of the window, or press Esc or ↵Enter.

8 Close the Help window by choosing the Close button on the right side of the title bar.

9 Remove the picture of the Office Assistant by clicking the Close button in the window's title bar.

> **Note**
>
> You can also remove the Office Assistant window by right-clicking the character and choosing **H**ide Assistant.

10 Leave the Word window open for the next exercise.

If you want to change the Office Assistant character or customize how the Office Assistant works, display the Office Assistant window and click **O**ptions to display the **O**ptions page of the Office Assistant dialog box. This page lets you customize how the Office Assistant functions. Choosing the **G**allery tab enables you to change the Office Assistant character (and personality!). (If all the Office Assistants were not included when Word was installed, you'll need access to the install disk.) For further information about the Office Assistant, use the Office Assistant to consult the Help feature or ask your instructor or computer support department.

Getting Help Without the Office Assistant

The more conventional way of accessing Help is to open the **H**elp menu and choose one of its commands. Table 1.2 lists the function of each command on the **H**elp menu.

Table 1.2 The Help Menu	
Command	**Function**
Microsoft Word **H**elp	Displays the Office Assistant.
Contents and Index	Displays the Contents and Index page of the Help feature.
What's **T**his?	Turns on the Help pointer (a black question mark attached to the arrow pointer). When this function is active, click any menu command or window element to see a pop-up box describing the function of the element. Pressing (✦Shift)+(F1) also activates the Help pointer.
Microsoft on the **W**eb	Displays a list of options that can be completed through the use of the Microsoft Internet Explorer and connecting to the World Wide Web.
Word**P**erfect Help	Activates the Word Help feature to enable the user to learn the Word equivalents for WordPerfect commands.
About Microsoft Word	Displays the Word version number, copyright and legal notifications, user and organization's name, software serial number, and information about your computer and operating system.

Using the Help Window

To practice using the Help window, follow these steps:

1 In the open Word window, choose the New button on the Standard toolbar to open a blank document. Choose **H**elp, **C**ontents and Index to display the Help Topics: Microsoft Word window shown in Figure 1.19. If necessary, click the Contents Tab to display the Contents page.

The Help Topics: Microsoft Word window provides three tabs to assist you in getting the help you need. The Contents tab provides a list of topics that can be further subdivided into more specific topics. The Index tab provides index-style listings for specific topics. The Find tab can help you search for specific words or phrases within the Help text and then enables you to display information on those topics.

(continues)

Contents tab

Figure 1.19
Click any item in
the Help
Contents page
to access more
information on
that subject.

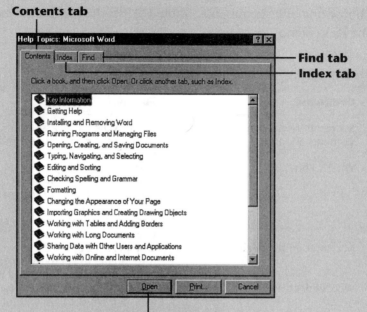

Find tab
Index tab

Click here to display information about the selected item.

Note

In the Help Contents page, *book* icons represent general topics. Double-click a
book icon to display a submenu for the topic. *Page* icons represent specific topics.
Double-click a page icon to display Help information about the selected topic.

❷ Double-click the Typing, Navigating, and Selecting book icon to open the
topic's submenu. (You can also open the submenu by clicking on the Typing, Navigating, and Selecting book icon once to select it, and then choosing the **O**pen button.)

❸ Double-click the book icon in front of the Typing topic to open the Typing
submenu.

The page icons inside the Typing submenu indicate that double-clicking on
one of these icons displays specific information about the topic.

❹ Double-click the Type over existing text topic to display the Help window
on that topic.

❺ Read the information displayed in the window.

You can simply read the information, or you can print the information by
choosing the Print command from the shortcut menu that is displayed
when you choose the **O**ptions button.

Some Help topics include a Show Me button. Clicking this button activates the steps needed to make changes to the way you are working. Word will not actually make the change, but will demonstrate or complete the initial steps needed to make the change.

6 Click the Show Me button in the Help window to see a demonstration of the steps listed in the window.

The demonstration stops before the final action is taken. Typically a message box is displayed explaining the step about to be completed.

7 You do not need to make this change now, so choose the Cancel button to return to the main Word window.

Sometimes you want help on a particular topic. Help enables you to search for the information you need.

Using the Index Tab

The Index tab in the Help Topics: Microsoft Word window displays help according to letters or words entered in the **T**ype the first few letters of the word you're looking for text box. To use the Index tab, follow these steps:

1 Choose **H**elp, **C**ontents and Index.

The Help Topics: Microsoft Word window is displayed.

2 Click the Index tab to display the Help Index page (see Figure 1.20).

Figure 1.20
The Index page of the Help window.

For this exercise, you want to display the Help information on nonprinting characters. As you will soon see, when you enter text in the **T**ype the first few letters of the word you're looking for text box, the Index list scrolls according to the text you enter.

(continues)

Using the Index Tab (continued)

❸ Type **non** in the text box.

If the Nonprinting characters topic is not already selected, continue typing some of the topic's name or use the scroll bar to display the nonprinting characters topic; then click on it once to select it.

❹ Click the **D**isplay button to display the topic's information.

Read the information. Pay close attention to the last sentence in the tip at the end of the text. You will use this feature quite often as you work through the text.

❺ To exit Word Help, click the Close button in the upper-right corner of the dialog box. Leave the Word window open for the next exercise.

The Find function of the Help feature enables you to search for particular words or phrases found in the text of the Help topics. Use this feature when you can't determine the name of the topic for which you are searching. The *first* time you choose the Find tab, the Find Setup Wizard (an automated program) is displayed. Read the instructions and click the appropriate buttons to set up the necessary database to enable you to use this feature. After the database is established, just type in the text box the word or phrase you want to search for. Then choose the appropriate button to display a listing of all the Help topics that include the word or phrase you entered.

Getting Help in the Word Window

Sometimes, you want to get help on a window element before you choose a command or click a toolbar button. Start by pressing ⬆Shift+F1 to change the regular pointer to the What's This? pointer (the Help pointer—an arrow-and-question-mark pointer).

When the Help pointer is activated and you click a menu command or toolbar button, Word displays information about the command or toolbar button instead of actually executing the command or completing an action.

If you activate the Help pointer and then decide that you don't want to use it, press Esc. The pointer returns to its normal shape.

Getting Help on a Dialog Box

Most Word dialog boxes have a Help button. The Help button is the one displaying a question mark in the upper-right corner of a dialog box. Click this button to display the arrow-and-question-mark pointer, and then click the area of the dialog box where you require help.

Objective 8: Exit Word

When you complete your Word session, it is important to exit the program properly to safeguard your program and documents.

Just as there are a number of ways to close a Word document, there are many ways to exit (close) the Word program, including

- Choosing the Close (X) button on the far-right side of the title bar of the Word document window

- Choosing **F**ile, **C**lose

- Double-clicking the Application Control menu icon

- Choosing the Application Control menu icon and then choosing **C**lose

- Pressing Alt+F4

Exiting Word

Now practice exiting the Word program. In the open Word window, choose the Close button on the far-right side of the Word title bar.

If there are any open documents with changes that have not been saved, a message box will be displayed to see if you want to save the files before exiting. If a message box is displayed, choose the appropriate response.

After the Word window is closed, you are returned to either the Windows desktop or another open program (such as Microsoft Excel).

Chapter Summary

This chapter helped familiarize you with Word's basic functions. You learned the basics of starting Word, creating a new document, entering text, saving a document, printing a document, closing a document, accessing Help, and exiting Word. You used both the mouse and keyboard to activate commands from the menu bar and toolbars.

In the next chapter, you learn to open and edit documents.

If you have completed your work for this computer session, make sure that you properly exit all open programs. Then use the Windows Sh**u**t Down command to exit safely from Windows. To test your knowledge of the material covered in this chapter, answer the questions in the Checking Your Skills section immediately following this summary. Then complete the exercises in the Applying Your Skills section at the end of the chapter.

Checking Your Skills

True/False

For each of the following, circle *T* or *F* to indicate whether the statement is true or false.

T (F) **1.** Microcomputers are most commonly used to complete word processing tasks.

(T) F **2.** The default Word window displays the Standard and Formatting toolbars.

(T) F **3.** Clicking a button on the toolbar usually saves keystrokes.

(T) F **4.** You can use the Standard toolbar to open a new blank document.

(T) F **5.** If you choose Exit before saving your work, Word warns you and gives you the opportunity to save the file.

(T) F **6.** You can access the Office Assistant by choosing a button on the Standard toolbar.

(T) F **7.** When the Help pointer is displayed, you can click a window element to see a description of its function.

(T) F **8.** You can simultaneously have numerous Word documents (each within its own document window) open within your Word window.

(T) F **9.** You can use the Open dialog box to assign a file name to your document and to specify the drive and folder to which you want to save it.

T (F) **10.** Closing a file is the same thing as closing Word.

Multiple Choice

In the blank provided, write the letter of the correct answer for each of the following questions.

1. If the word that you type is too long to fit on the line, Word places all the characters of that word at the left end of the next line, using the _____.

(a.) word-wrap feature

b. margin-release feature

c. automatic formatting

d. default settings

e. hard return

2. Which one of the following does *not* appear in the initial Word window? _____

a. the Drawing toolbar

b. menu bar

c. scroll bars

d. the Standard toolbar

(e.) status bar

3. Which tab(s) are not found in the Help Topics: Microsoft Word window? _____

(a.) Answer Wizard

b. Index

c. Find

d. Contents

e. B and C

4. When the Help window is opened, which tab should be clicked to display a list of basic Word features? _____

(a.) Contents

b. Find

c. Help

d. Answer Wizard

e. Save

1

5. The commands for initiating the document saving process appear in the ____c____ menu.

    a. **S**ave

    b. **E**dit

    c. **F**ile

    d. **U**tilities

    e. **F**ormat

6. Which Word view is designed to show you on-screen how your document will look when it is printed? ____a____

    a. Print Preview

    b. Normal

    c. Master Document

    d. Online Page Layout

    e. Zoom

7. The flashing vertical bar in the work area of the Word window is known as the _____.

    a. cursor position

    b. insertion point

    c. keyboard position

    d. button location

    e. mouse icon

8. The yellow rectangle that displays the button's name when you point to a button on a toolbar is known as a _____.

    a. flag

    b. menu

    c. tool button

    d. ScreenTip

    e. Help

9. The animated character that is displayed on your screen to offer tips and suggestions is called the ____d____.

    a. Helper

    b. Tip

    c. Wizard

    d. Office Assistant

    e. Tip Wizard

10. When a toolbar is in the rectangular format within the document work area, it is known as a ____d____ toolbar.

    a. Standard

    b. fixed

    c. docked

    d. floating

    e. vertical

Fill in the Blank

In the blank provided, write the correct answer for each of the following questions.

1. When you click the ____open____ button on the Standard toolbar, a new blank document is displayed.

2. The bar at the bottom of the Word window that displays the page and section number, the insertion point position, and whether certain Word functions are activated is called the ____status bar____

3. In the default Word window, the ____horizontal ruler____ is displayed below the Formatting toolbar.

4. To display the Office Assistant by using the keyboard, press ____Shift + F1____.

5. In the File **n**ame text box of the Save As dialog box, you can type a name for the document that contains up to ____256____ characters.

6. When you start Word, the application opens a new document named ___Doc 1___.

7. In the Save As dialog box, click the __look in__ drop-down list arrow to see other locations where you may save your file.

8. Right-clicking a toolbar displays a list of available Word ___Commands___.

9. The Word program Close button is located in the __upper right__ corner of the Word window.

10. At the bottom and right side of the screen are the horizontal and vertical __scroll__ bars.

Applying Your Skills

Review Exercises

Exercise 1: Using Help

To become as efficient as possible using Word, you should familiarize yourself with various Word features.

1. Click **H**elp in the menu bar, and then choose **C**ontents and Index. Work through a topic of your choice in the Contents page.

2. Use the Index page to view the same topic you reviewed in step 1.

3. Use the Office Assistant to see whether you can display the same information you found when using the Contents or Index page of the Help window.

4. Create a one-paragraph document summarizing the information you learned in steps 1-3.

5. Save the document to your Student Disk as **Chapter 1 Help Exercise**.

6. Print your document and then close it.

Exercise 2: Creating a Business Letter

In this exercise, you create a business letter.

1. In a blank Word document, enter today's date on the first line and press ⏎Enter.

    If a yellow tip box (containing today's date) is displayed by the insertion point when you start to type today's date, the AutoComplete feature has been enabled. If the date is accurate, press ⏎Enter to let Word automatically complete the date. To reject the AutoComplete entry, just keep typing. Chapter 10 includes additional information on AutoComplete. Also, you may see Word insert superscript characters after the dates in the letter. Leave these changes in the document—you will learn more about this type of formatting in Chapter 4.

2. On the status bar, notice the "inch" position of the insertion point. Press ⏎Enter until the insertion point is approximately at the 2-inch mark (1.9 inches is acceptable), and then enter the recipient's name and address listed below. (In a business letter the recipient's name and address are typically placed about an inch below the current date.)

Mr. Tom Carron
Shore Lane
Allentown, PA 16057

3. Press ⏎Enter twice to create a blank line below the last line of the recipient's address; then type the greeting, text, and closing of the letter. The letter should be single-spaced. Press ⏎Enter twice between paragraphs. Press ⏎Enter about four times after typing *Sincerely,*.

Dear Mr. Carron:

The Jolly Company is proud to announce the opening of our new location on Boston Post Road. We have increased our staff for efficient operation of the new facility.

We are extending an invitation for you to visit the facility any Sunday next month, from 10:00 a.m. to 3:00 p.m. All sales personnel will be available to answer questions.

The new facility will allow us to have new extended hours: Monday through Friday from 8:00 a.m. to 8:00 p.m. and Saturday from 6:00 a.m. to 11:00 p.m. We look forward to seeing you.

Sincerely,

Anita Harte
Human Resources Coordinator

4. Save the document to your Student Disk as **Business 01**.

5. Print the document and then close it.

Note

Most business letters are printed on letterhead. To make room for the preprinted letterhead, you typically set a larger top margin for the document. (You learn to set margins in Chapter 6.) Alternatively, you can also place the insertion point at the beginning of the document and press ⏎Enter until the status bar indicates the insertion point is at the two-inch mark (or any other appropriate location on the document).

Exercise 3: Creating a Business Memo

In this exercise, you create and save a business memo.

When typing a memo, the first letters of the entries following *DATE:*, *TO:*, *FROM:*, and *SUBJECT:* should all start at the same line position. To accomplish this, press Tab⇥ once or twice (as needed) after entering *DATE:*, *TO:*, and *FROM:*. The first four lines of the memo are double-spaced, so press ⏎Enter twice after the DATE:, TO:, and FROM: entries. There are usually two blank lines inserted after the SUBJECT: entry, so press ⏎Enter three times after the SUBJECT: entry. Finally, the paragraphs are single-spaced, and a blank line separates each paragraph. (Press ⏎Enter twice at the end of each paragraph.)

1. Type the following memo entering today's date on the date line:

DATE:

TO: Advertising Committee Members

FROM: Adam Airhelm, Chairperson

SUBJECT: Change of date of meeting

The date of the next meeting has been changed to the 9th of next month. Our speakers cannot attend the meeting on the 2nd, and their presence is required. Also, the decision date has been moved to the end of the next month. My apologies for any inconvenience these delays may have caused.

If you cannot attend this meeting, please contact me immediately.

2. Save the file to your Student Disk as **Meeting 01**.

3. Print the document and then close it.

Exercise 4: Employee Guidelines

1. Use the Standard toolbar to open a new document and type the following text:

Employee Vacation and Personal Day Guidelines

  1. Employee must notify employer at least 48 hours before requested days.

  2. Employee must mark the designated area of the time sheet as V for vacation or P for personal day.

  3. Employee must verify coverage of work area when necessary.

  4. Employer will respond to the request from the employee within 24 hours of request.

2. Save the file to your Student Disk as **Employee Guidelines 01**.

3. Print the document and then close it.

Exercise 5: Using the Formatting Toolbar

In Chapter 4, you will learn a variety of ways to format the characters in your documents. As a preview of things to come, complete the following exercise where you learn to use the Formatting toolbar to bold, italicize, underline, and center text.

B **1.** Open a new blank Word document, click the Bold button on the Formatting toolbar and then type **This is bold**. Click the Bold button again to turn off the formatting and press Enter.

I **2.** Click the Italic button on the Formatting toolbar and then type **This is italic**. Click the Italic button again to turn off the formatting and press Enter.

3. Click the Underline button on the Formatting toolbar and then type **This is underlined**. Click the Underline button again to turn off the formatting and press ⏎Enter.

4. Click the Center button on the Formatting toolbar and then type **This is centered**. Press ⏎Enter.

5. Click the Bold, Italic, Underline, and Align Right buttons, and then type **Look how this appears**.

6. Save the file to your Student Disk as **Buttons 01**.

7. Print and close your document.

Continuing Projects

Project 1: Practice Using Word

Practice using Word by following these steps:

1. Open a new document using the Standard toolbar.

2. After reviewing the chapter, type the steps necessary for a fellow worker to complete the following Word procedures:

    a. Start Word

    b. Save a document

    c. Print a document

    d. Close a document

    e. Exit Word

3. Save the file to your Student Disk as **Steps 01**.

4. Use the Print button on the Standard toolbar to print the document; then close it.

Project 2: Deli-Mart

You work at the Deli-Mart Delicatessen, and you want to create a list of items (with descriptions and prices) that will eventually be formatted and used in a brochure for the business.

1. To begin this venture, open a blank document window and type the following items (Press Enter twice after each item name and description.):

    Memphis Melt

    Enjoy tuna, seafood, or chicken salad with melted cheese, served on the bread of your choice. 6.95

    The Beef Sensation

    Choice sirloin steak, sauteed with onions, peppers, and mushrooms, and served on a toasted roll. 8.95

    Natural Blend

    Stir-fried vegetables, served on a bed of rice or linguine. 7.95

2. Save the file to your Student Disk as **Menu 01**.

3. Print the file and then close it.

Project 3: The Marketing Connection

You work for The Marketing Connection Company. Your supervisor has asked you to create a company newsletter. The first step in planning the publication is to find out what is happening in the company. After sending notices to the various departments, making them aware of the newsletter and requesting any articles or advertisements to be included, you need to send the initial newsletter to clients.

1. Open a blank document window and type the following text:

   The Marketing Connection

   Many businesses spend millions of dollars to market their products, without any substantial success. The Marketing Connection is ready to work with your company in promoting your service and/or products.

   We have a marketing team of 100 employees who will meet with the various departments in your company to determine your needs. The first step is to evaluate your present marketing approach. You may need a complete restructuring or only minor modifications. We guarantee an increase in sales within the first six months of putting our plan to work.

   We hope that we have sparked your interest in our company and that you will read our monthly newsletter. Our newsletter includes the latest marketing offerings, scheduled events that are open to the public, lists of contributions made to charitable organizations, and much more.

2. Save the file to your Student Disk as **Market 01**.

3. Print the file and then close it.

CHAPTER 2

Editing Documents

In the course of your daily work, you will have certain documents that you use repeatedly. To use a document you previously created, you must first "open" the document. In this chapter, you learn how to open and make changes to existing documents.

You learn how to move the insertion point to the locations that you want to edit and how to select, delete, move, and copy text in the document. The chapter concludes by showing you how to work with multiple document windows and how to move and copy text between documents.

Objectives

By the time you finish this chapter, you will have learned to

1. Open an Existing Document
2. Move the Insertion Point
3. Insert and Delete Characters
4. Select Text
5. Move and Copy Text
6. Work with Multiple Documents

Objective 1: Open an Existing Document

In Chapter 1, you learned that when you start Word, a blank document, labeled Document1, opens on-screen. To enter text into the blank document, you simply start typing. To work on an existing document, however, you must first *open* that document.

Opening a Document

After the Word window is displayed, you can start the procedure for opening an existing document by choosing a menu command or toolbar button. Follow these steps to open an existing document from your Student Disk:

(continues)

Opening a Document (continued)

1 Start Word; then insert your Student Disk in drive A.

2 Click the Open button on the Standard toolbar.

Word displays the Open dialog box. By default, when you start Word and then display the Open dialog box, the My Documents folder is listed in the Look in drop-down list box. (Your system may be set up to view a different default location.)

The large list box in the center of the dialog box displays the folders and the Word files in the folder or drive identified in the Look in list box.

> ### Tip
>
> The drive or folder identified in the Look in list box may contain names of files created in programs other than Word. Most likely, these file names will not appear when you first display the Open dialog box. To display non-Word files in the Open dialog box, see the Note at the end of this section.

If your Student Disk files are saved in a different location than the default (in this case, drive A), you need to change the entry in the Look in list box.

3 Click the down arrow at the end of the Look in drop-down list box to display a list of storage locations on your computer. Then click the icon for drive A (or the appropriate location) to display your Student Disk files.

The Open dialog box should now look similar to the one shown in Figure 2.1.

Figure 2.1
Click the Open button on the toolbar to display the Open dialog box.

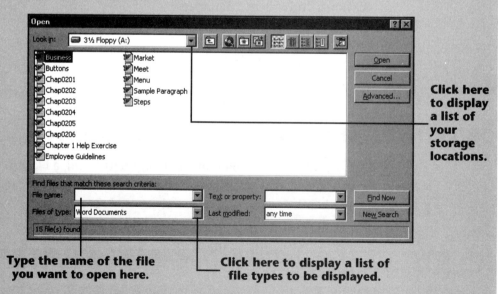

Click here to display a list of your storage locations.

Type the name of the file you want to open here.

Click here to display a list of file types to be displayed.

4 Locate the Chap0201 file listed in the large list box. If the file is not already selected (displayed in reverse video), click once on the icon preceding the file name to select the file.

> **Tip**
>
> When selecting a file, it is a good habit to practice clicking the icon immediately preceding the file name to select the file. As you will learn in Chapter 7, clicking the actual file name can lead to renaming a file or other file management functions.

If you prefer, you can also click in the File **n**ame list box to make it the active element in the dialog box and then type the name of the desired file into the box.

> **Tip**
>
> If the large list box is filled with files, but the one you need is not displayed, you may have to use the list box scroll bars to scroll through available files.

5 Choose **O**pen (or press ↵Enter).

The dialog box closes, and the document appears on-screen.

> **Tip**
>
> Instead of selecting the name of the document and choosing **O**pen, you can open the file by simply double-clicking the icon preceding the file name.

6 Briefly review the Chap0201 file; then close it by choosing the document Close button located on the right side of the menu bar. If a message is displayed asking you to save any changes, choose **N**o.

In Chapter 1, you learned you could display the Open dialog box by choosing **F**ile, **O**pen. However, the **F**ile menu also provides a quick way to immediately open one of the last files you viewed. By default, Word lists the last four files opened on your computer at the bottom of the **F**ile menu.

7 Choose **F**ile to open the **F**ile menu and locate the Chap0201 listing near the bottom of the menu.

8 Click this Chap0201 entry once to open the file again.

You will use this file throughout the chapter for practicing basic Word editing techniques. First, you should save this file now under a new name so that you can always go back to the original if you need to.

> **Tip**
>
> The Windows Start menu provides a shortcut for opening a file you recently worked with. Click the Start button on the taskbar to display the Start menu; then
>
> (continues)

Opening a Document (continued)

click **D**ocuments to see a list of recently saved files. (This list usually displays up to the last 15 files opened on the computer.) Click the name of the file you want to open, and Windows opens the chosen file inside the application used to create it.

9 Save the open Chap0201 file as **Sales 02** to your Student Disk.

10 Keep the file open for the next exercise.

Note

By default, when the Open dialog box is displayed, the entry in the Files of **t**ype drop-down list box is Word Documents (refer to Figure 2.1). (This list box is located near the bottom of the dialog box.) Also by default, when Word saves a document, a .doc extension is added to the end of the name of the file. Therefore, when you open the Open dialog box, only folders and files with a .doc extension—typically, only Word files and files created in the Windows WordPad program—will be displayed in the large list box.

To display all the files in the drive or folder identified in the Look **i**n list box, click the drop-down arrow at the end of the Files of **t**ype list box and choose All Files.

Objective 2: Move the Insertion Point

To edit text in a document, you first move the insertion point to the text that will be modified. Word provides many ways to use the mouse or the keyboard to move the insertion point.

Using the Mouse to Move the Insertion Point

To use the mouse to move the insertion point to a particular on-screen location, position the mouse pointer where you want the insertion point to be and then click the left mouse button. If you want to move the insertion point to a part of the document not currently displayed in the window, use the scroll bars to display that part of the document.

In general, a scroll bar consists of a beginning and an ending scroll arrow, the bar between the beginning and ending arrows, and the scroll box. The position of the scroll box in the vertical scroll bar indicates the position of the text in the window relative to the beginning and the end of the document. The position of the scroll box in the horizontal scroll bar indicates the position of the text in the window relative to the left and right margins.

When you create a new Word document, or open an existing one, you initially view the beginning of the document. The scroll box in the vertical scroll bar is located at the top of the scroll bar. The scroll box in the horizontal scroll bar is typically located at the left side of the scroll bar.

Scrolling in a Document

To practice using the scroll bars to move around in the Sales 02 document, follow these steps:

If you have problems...
If one or both scroll bars are not displayed in your Word window, the option to display the scroll bars may have been turned off. To turn the scroll bars back on, choose **T**ools, **O**ptions to display the Options dialog box. Click the View tab, and then click to insert a check mark in the check box for the Hori**z**ontal and/or **V**ertical scroll bar options; then choose OK.

---

1 In the open Sales 02 document (displayed in Normal view) point to the scroll box on the vertical scroll bar. Hold down the left mouse button and drag the box three inches down toward the ending (the down) scroll arrow; then release the mouse button.

> ### Tip
>
> When you drag the scroll box along the vertical scroll bar of a multiple-page document, page numbers are displayed next to the scroll box as the box is dragged along the scroll bar. When you see the page number you are looking for, just release the mouse button.

When you released the mouse button, the beginning paragraphs of the document scrolled out the top of the window work area. The specific lines of text remaining on your screen depend on the location of the scroll box on the scroll bar.

> ### Caution
>
> Scrolling through the document lets you see the document contents; however, the insertion point does not move until you click a new location in the document. If you scroll to a new location and then start typing, the new characters will be displayed at the insertion point, not in the text currently displayed in the Word window.

2 Rest the tip of the pointer on the up scroll arrow; then hold down the mouse button until you scroll to the top of your document.

This technique works fine for scrolling through short documents. For longer documents, however, you may prefer to move through the file by dragging the scroll box.

(continues)

Scrolling in a Document (continued)

> **Tip**
>
> Clicking the up or down scroll arrow moves you through the document one line at a time.

3 Click the area between the scroll box and the down arrow.

Clicking between the scroll box and the up or down arrow moves you through the document one screen at a time.

4 Leave Sales 02 document open for the next exercise.

You have not yet moved the insertion point. After you scroll to display the desired content in the window, you must place the mouse pointer in the desired document location and click the left mouse button to position the insertion point at the new location.

Examining the Buttons on the Vertical Scroll Bar

Both the vertical and horizontal scroll bars have a few extra buttons attached to them. In Chapter 1, you learned that the buttons on the left end of the horizontal scroll bar enable you to change your view of the document. The buttons at the bottom of the vertical scroll bar enable you to move quickly through a long document. Clicking the double-headed, upward-pointing arrow enables you to move up to the previous page of your document. Clicking the double-headed downward-pointing arrow enables you to move down to the next page of your document.

Instead of moving to the next or previous page, you can change the function of the double-headed arrows by clicking the Select Browse Object button (located between the double-headed arrow buttons on the vertical scroll bar). Clicking this middle button opens a selection box that enables you to choose different document elements (such as graphics or section headings) that you can move to each time you click one of the double-headed arrows.

Using the Keyboard to Move the Insertion Point

Using the keyboard to move the insertion point is often faster than using the mouse, particularly in large documents. Table 2.1 lists key combinations for moving the insertion point.

Table 2.1 Moving the Insertion Point with the Keyboard

Key Combination	Effect
←	Moves the insertion point one character to the left.
→	Moves the insertion point one character to the right.
↑	Moves the insertion point up one line.
↓	Moves the insertion point down one line.

Key Combination	Effect
Home	Moves the insertion point to the beginning of the line.
End	Moves the insertion point to the end of the line.
PgUp	Moves the insertion point up by the height of one window.
PgDn	Moves the insertion point down by the height of one window.
Ctrl+Home	Moves the insertion point to the beginning of the document.
Ctrl+End	Moves the insertion point to the end of the document.
Ctrl+←	Moves the insertion point to the beginning of the current word or one word to the left.
Ctrl+→	Moves the insertion point to the beginning of the next word.
Ctrl+↑	Moves the insertion point to the beginning of the current paragraph. If the insertion point is already at the beginning of a paragraph, moves the insertion point to the beginning of the preceding paragraph.
Ctrl+↓	Moves the insertion point to the beginning of the following paragraph.
Ctrl+PgUp	Moves the insertion point to the top of the preceding page.
Ctrl+PgDn	Moves the insertion point to the top of the next page.
Alt+Ctrl+PgUp	Moves the insertion point to the top of the current window.
Alt+Ctrl+PgDn	Moves the insertion point to the bottom of the current window.

From the current insertion point location, you can return to any of the three most recent insertion point positions. To do this, press ◆Shift+F5 one, two, or three times. If you press ◆Shift+F5 a fourth time, the insertion point returns to the location where it was before you first pressed ◆Shift+F5.

Note

When you save a document, Word stores the last three insertion-point positions. When you reopen the document, you can press ◆Shift+F5 once, twice, or three times to move directly to those positions.

Later in this chapter, you will have the chance to practice using key combinations to move the insertion point to various document locations. Don't try to memorize all the key combinations. As you work with Word, you will eventually memorize the key combinations that help you work in the manner most effective for you.

One final way to move the insertion point is to work with the Find, Replace, and Go To tabs in the Find and Replace dialog box. These features are examined in the first section of Chapter 3.

Objective 3: Insert and Delete Characters

Insert mode
A mode in which characters you type move existing characters to the right and down.

Overtype mode
A mode in which the characters you type replace existing characters.

In this section, you learn how to use the *Insert* and *Overtype modes*, work with simple text deletions, and use Word's automatic spelling and grammar checker.

Understanding Insert and Overtype Modes

When you first open a Word document and start typing, Word is in Insert mode. In this mode, Word inserts the characters that you type to the left of the insertion point, and text on the right side of the insertion point moves to the right. If this movement causes words to move beyond the right margin, word wrap moves those words to the next line. In the status bar, when OVR (an abbreviation for *overtype*) is dimmed, Word is in Insert mode. When in Overtype mode, your typing replaces the existing character at the insertion point. Most people prefer to work in the Insert mode.

The fastest way to switch to Overtype mode is to double-click the OVR marker on the status bar. You can also activate the Overtype mode by choosing **T**ools, **O**ptions to display the Options dialog box, clicking the Edit tab, choosing the **O**vertype mode option, and clicking OK.

Note

In previous versions of Word, Insert could be used to switch between Insert and Overtype modes. However, this option proved frustrating for many experienced Windows users who used the old ♦Shift+Insert shortcut command to paste Clipboard information. In this version of Word, Microsoft has removed the "toggling" function from Insert.

Adding Text to the Document

Suppose that after you review the Sales 02 document, you realize that another paragraph needs to be added to it. You can add text to the document by following these steps:

❶ In the open Sales 02 document, move the insertion point to the end of the third paragraph (the one ending with ...*this issue as soon as possible.*).

❷ Press ↵Enter twice.

❸ Type the next paragraph as it appears. (The paragraph includes some intentional misspellings and grammar errors.) Make sure that you are in Insert mode (the OVR indicator in the status bar is dimmed) so that you will not remove any of the existing characters.

> **It has been brought to our attention that the TQS concept is being presented to you as an acccepted plan of action. We would like to confirm that we are trying this method and will revert to others if it is not accepted by all personnel. Let's give the approach a try. We may find some posetive tips to use with our alrady successful work.**

> **Note**
>
> If Word's automatic spelling and grammar checker is activated, you will notice that as you type, Word inserts a wavy red underline beneath words not found in the selected Word dictionaries. A wavy green line is placed under phrases that may contain potential grammar errors. If you make a common typo, such as *teh* for *the*, and Word's AutoCorrect feature is turned on, you may see Word automatically correct your mistake.

4 Your document should now look similar to the one in Figure 2.2.

Figure 2.2
The new text has been added to the document.

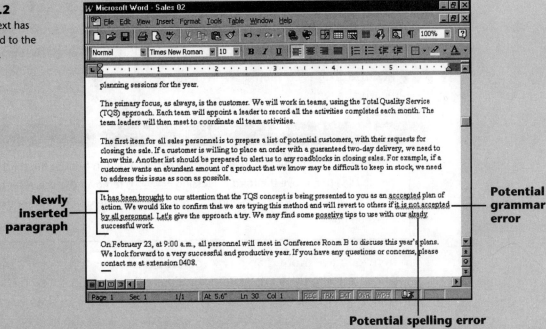

Newly inserted paragraph

Potential grammar error

Potential spelling error

5 Save the changes to your Sales 02 document and leave it on the screen for the next exercise.

You are now ready to correct the errors in the paragraph you just entered. Start by correcting the spelling errors (words that are underlined by a wavy red line). If you typed the paragraph as it appears in the text, the paragraph will contain three misspelled words. If you have more, no problem, just use the following techniques to correct all the spelling and grammar errors in the new paragraph.

> **Note**
>
> If your new paragraph does not display any wavy red or green underlining, some of the default settings for the automatic spelling and grammar features may have been changed. To reset these features, choose **T**ools, **O**ptions (to display the Options dialog box), and
>
> *(continues)*

then click the Spelling & Grammar tab. If the Check **s**pelling as you type or Check **g**rammar as you type check boxes are blank, activate the features by clicking their corresponding check boxes. If the Hide **s**pelling errors in this document and/or the Hide grammatical **e**rrors in this document check boxes are marked, clear the option(s). Then click OK to close the dialog box.

Correcting Simple Errors

To practice correcting simple errors in your document, follow these steps:

1 In the newly added paragraph in the Sales 02 document, place the mouse pointer after the third *c* in *acccepted*. Then click the mouse button to anchor the insertion point in its new location.

2 Press ⎆Backspace to remove the *c* located to the left of the insertion point.

When the error is corrected, Word removes the wavy red underline from beneath the word.

> ### Note
>
> In step 2, you could also have placed the insertion point in front of the third *c* and pressed Del to remove the third *c*. Pressing ⎆Backspace removes the character to the left of the insertion point. Pressing Del erases the character to the right of the insertion point.

When you have more than a few adjacent characters to erase, it's easier to select all the characters first and then delete the selected characters by pressing one key. You'll learn more about selecting text in the next objective; for now, we'll get back to correcting the typos in the new paragraph.

3 Move the insertion point immediately in front of the first *e* in *posetive*.

4 Double-click the OVR indicator in the status bar to turn on Overtype mode. (If your double-click was successful, the OVR letters will be displayed in black rather than gray.) Then type the letter **i** to correct the typo.

Note that when you are in Overtype mode, the character to the right of the insertion point is erased when you press a key on the keyboard.

5 Change back to Insert mode by double-clicking the OVR indicator in the status bar. (The black OVR letters should now be gray.)

6 Right-click the mouse on the misspelled *alrady* found in the last sentence of the new paragraph.

When you right-click a word displaying a wavy red underline, a shortcut spelling menu is displayed, as shown in Figure 2.3.

If you have problems...   If you do not see the Spelling shortcut menu displayed in Figure 2.3, the pointer may not have been placed on the unrecognized word when you right-clicked. Press Esc to close the menu, place the pointer on the unrecognized word, and try right-clicking again. If you still can't display the spelling shortcut menu, contact your instructor or network administrator for help.

Figure 2.3
Right-click on a word with a wavy red underline to display the spelling shortcut menu.

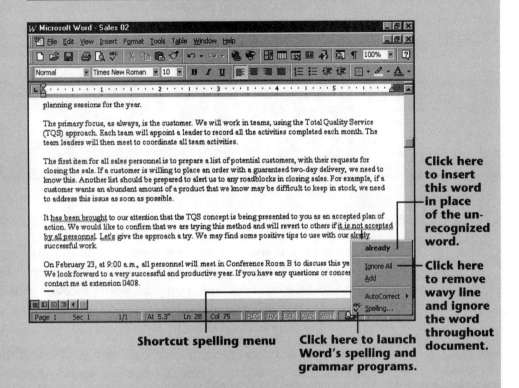

Click here to insert this word in place of the unrecognized word.

Click here to remove wavy line and ignore the word throughout document.

Shortcut spelling menu

Click here to launch Word's spelling and grammar programs.

When choosing a command from a shortcut menu, you can usually left-click or right-click the desired shortcut menu command.

❼ Click on *already* (the correct spelling of the word) at the top of the shortcut menu to insert the correct spelling and close the shortcut menu.

The automatic grammar checker works similarly to the automatic spelling checker. The grammar checker flags potential grammar errors by displaying a wavy green underline beneath questionable phrases.

❽ At the beginning of the newly added paragraph, right-click in the middle of the phrase *has been brought* to display the grammar shortcut menu.

You may not always want to change a word or phrase flagged by Word. In this case, you are satisfied with the sentence as it was entered.

❾ Choose the Ignore Sentence command in the grammar shortcut menu to remove the wavy green underline from the phrase.

❿ Right-click the *it is not accepted by all personnel* phrase and read Word's suggestion.

This time you want to accept Word's suggestion.

(continues)

Correcting Simple Errors (continued)

⓫ Choose the *all personnel do not accept it* item in the shortcut menu to insert it in place of the phrase in question.

Sometimes, making one change can lead to others. Note that Word has again flagged the words near the end of the sentence. However, at this point you are satisfied with the existing text.

⓬ Right-click the remaining phrases displayed with a wavy green underline and ignore Word's suggestions. (Ignoring the suggestions removes the wavy green underlines.)

⓭ Save the revisions to the Sales 02 document and keep the file open for the next exercise.

Objective 4: Select Text

Like many people, you may find it is easier to type an initial draft of a document on your word processor than to write it out using a pen or pencil. Upon proofreading the draft document on your word processor, you may decide to rearrange some paragraphs or use the italic or bold character attribute to emphasize a word or phrase. This is easy to do in Word.

Select
To highlight a specific part of a document. The highlighted portion will be affected by the next program action.

When modifying existing text, the basic concept is *select* and then do. This means that you first identify the characters you want to modify in your document (by selecting them), and then you use the appropriate Word feature to modify the selected characters.

You select characters by using the mouse or the keyboard. However, your Word file contains more than just the letters and numbers in your document. Your document is also filled with nonprinting characters. When you select text, it is important to know what printing and nonprinting characters you are selecting.

Displaying Nonprinting Characters

When you press most keyboard keys, your screen displays the corresponding character, and when the time comes for printing, the printer prints those characters. This is not the case for all keys, however.

Nonprinting characters
Keys, such as ⏎Enter and Tab⇄, that do not display or print a character.

When you press ⏎Enter, Tab⇄, or Spacebar, the insertion point moves on-screen without displaying a character. These keys are known as *nonprinting characters*.

Sometimes, you need to know which nonprinting characters are causing the insertion point to move. If a line contains a blank area, for example, you may need to know whether a tab caused the space or the Spacebar was pressed several times.

 Word displays special symbols to represent nonprinting characters. Position the mouse pointer on the Show/Hide ¶ button on the Standard toolbar and click. The nonprinting characters are now displayed in your window (see Figure 2.4).

Figure 2.4
This screen shows nonprinting characters for spaces and hard returns.

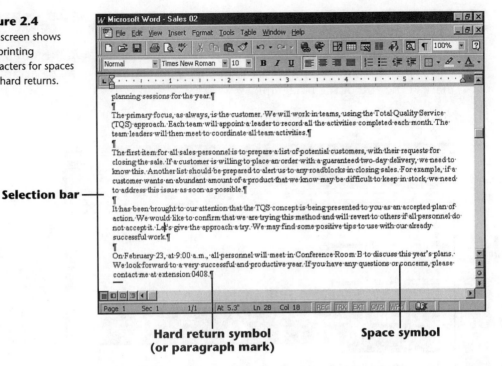

Selection bar ————

**Hard return symbol
(or paragraph mark)**

Space symbol

To hide nonprinting characters, click the Show/Hide ¶ button again.

If you have problems... If your document is displaying nonprinting characters and nothing happens when you click the Show/Hide ¶ button to turn off the nonprinting characters, various options may be activated in the Nonprinting Characters section of the View tab in the Options dialog box. Choose **T**ools, **O**ptions, click the View tab, clear the check boxes in the Nonprinting Characters section, and choose OK.

Selection bar
An unmarked region between the first characters in each line and the left border in the window work area. The selection bar is used to select text with the mouse.

Selecting Text with the Mouse

When you select text with the mouse, you can use the *selection bar*—an area at the left edge of the work area. The selection bar (refer again to Figure 2.4) is not marked in any way, but when you position the mouse pointer in the selection bar, the pointer appears as an arrow pointing up and slightly to the right.

Using the Mouse to Select Text

You can select text in a number of ways using the mouse. Table 2.2 at the end of this section details the various techniques. To practice some of these methods, follow these steps:

 1 In the open Sales 02 document displayed in your Word window, click the Show/Hide ¶ button to display the document's nonprinting characters.

The nonprinting characters should be displayed.

(continues)

❷ Place the pointer in front of the first letter in the first paragraph (beginning *Last year was very…*) and diagonally drag the pointer just past the paragraph mark at the end of the paragraph.

Your document should look similar to the one shown in Figure 2.5.

Figure 2.5
Selected text is usually displayed with white characters on a black background. Unselected text is displayed with black characters on a white background.

Selected text —

Selection bar —

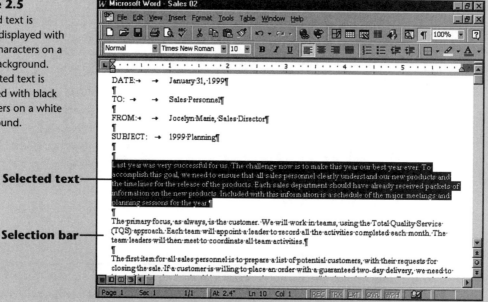

If the background colors for your screen have been changed in Windows, your screen may show regular and selected text in other color combinations.

Tip

It is recommended that you keep the Show/Hide ¶ button turned on whenever you select text. Remember that a paragraph can consist of a blank line, one line of characters, or many lines of characters.

If an entire word becomes selected when you drag the pointer through the first part of the word, the option to select an entire word (instead of just the part of the word that was actually selected) is active. To turn off this option (so that you can select only a portion of a word) choose **T**ools, **O**ptions, click the Edit tab, clear the When selecting, automatically select the entire **w**ord check box, and choose OK.

Caution

If you accidentally press a key while text is selected, the character pressed will replace the entire selection. There are many ways to correct this mistake. For now, either choose **E**dit, **U**ndo Typing to reinsert the deleted text, or, if necessary, close your document without saving changes and then reopen it. In a few pages, you'll learn to use the Undo and Redo commands.

❸ Place the pointer in the selection bar next to the second paragraph (the one beginning *The primary focus...*) and double-click the mouse to select the paragraph (see Figure 2.6).

Figure 2.6
When you double-click next to a line in the selection bar, the entire paragraph, including the line and the paragraph mark at the end of the paragraph, is selected.

Pointer in the selection bar

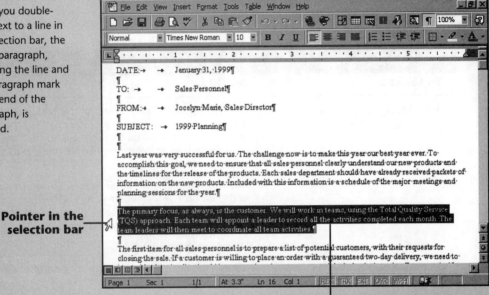

Selected paragraph and paragraph mark

Note

The paragraph mark that ends each paragraph contains the paragraph formatting (alignment, indents, tabs, and so on) for the entire paragraph.

If you delete a paragraph mark between two paragraphs, the second paragraph becomes part of the first. What was the second paragraph then takes on the formatting of the first paragraph.

As you have just seen, to "deselect" text, just click elsewhere in your document.

Now complete a few "clicking" exercises within your document to see quick ways to select a word, sentence, or paragraph.

❹ In the third paragraph (the one beginning with *The first item...*) double-click the word *item* (the third word on the first line) to select it.

❺ Press and hold down ⌃Ctrl while you click anywhere in the first sentence of the third paragraph to select the entire sentence.

(continues)

6 In the third paragraph, triple-click the word *for* (the fourth word in the first line) to select the entire paragraph.

7 Turn off the selection by clicking once on another word in the document.

8 Leave the Sales 02 document open for the next exercise.

In the previous exercise, you experimented with some ways to select text with the mouse. Table 2.2 includes additional techniques for using the mouse to select text.

Table 2.2   Selecting Text with the Mouse

To Select...	Do This...
Any block of text	Point to the beginning or end of the text, hold down the mouse button, drag the pointer to the other end of the text that you want to select, and then release the mouse button. Word highlights the text as you select it. Alternatively, click the beginning or end of the text and then press ⬆Shift while you click the other end of the text that you want to select. Word highlights the text when you click the second time.
A word	Double-click the word.
A line	Click in the selection bar at the left end of the line.
Multiple lines	Point to the selection bar at the left end of the first or last line. Then hold down the mouse button and drag the mouse pointer down or up the selection bar. Release the mouse button when the last desired line is highlighted.
A sentence	Press Ctrl while you click anywhere in the sentence.
A paragraph	Double-click the selection bar to the left of the paragraph. Or, triple-click anywhere within the paragraph.
Several adjacent paragraphs	Double-click the selection bar to the left of the first or last paragraph that you want to select, thereby selecting that paragraph. Then press ⬆Shift while you click the selection bar to the left of the paragraph at the other end of the range. Word highlights the paragraphs when you click the second time.
A document	Triple-click the selection bar, or press Ctrl while you click the selection bar.

Selecting Text with the Keyboard

To select text with the keyboard, you use techniques similar to the techniques for moving the insertion point with the keyboard, as detailed in Table 2.1 earlier in this chapter. In many cases, you simply add ⬆Shift to the key combination that you use to move the insertion point. Table 2.3 provides the most commonly used keyboard techniques for selecting text.

Table 2.3 Selecting Text with the Keyboard

Key Combination	Effect
⬆Shift+Home	Selects to the beginning of the line.
⬆Shift+End	Selects to the end of the line.
⬆Shift+←	Selects one character to the left.
⬆Shift+→	Selects one character to the right.
Ctrl+⬆Shift+←	Selects to the beginning of the word.
Ctrl+⬆Shift+→	Selects to the end of the word.
⬆Shift+↑	Selects to the same horizontal position in the preceding line.
⬆Shift+↓	Selects to the same horizontal position in the next line.
Ctrl+⬆Shift+↑	Selects to the beginning of the paragraph.
Ctrl+⬆Shift+↓	Selects to the end of the paragraph.
⬆Shift+PgUp	Selects one window of lines from the insertion point up.
⬆Shift+PgDn	Selects one window of lines from the insertion point down.
Ctrl+⬆Shift+Home	Selects to the beginning of the document.
Ctrl+⬆Shift+End	Selects to the end of the document.
Ctrl+A	Selects the entire document. (You also can press Ctrl+5 in the numeric keypad, when the NumLock is turned off.)

To use the keyboard to deselect the selected text, press any arrow key.

Using the Keyboard to Select Text

To experiment with some keyboard commands for selecting text, follow these steps:

1 In the open Sales 02 document, press Ctrl+Home to move the insertion point to the top of the document.

2 Press Ctrl+End to move to the end of the document.

3 Scroll up the document until you can see the entire third paragraph (the one beginning with *The first item...*) in the window work area; then place the insertion point in the middle of the paragraph.

4 Press and hold ⬆Shift while you press End, and then release both keys to select text from the insertion point to the end of the line.

5 Press ← to turn off the selection; then press ⬆Shift+Home to select text from the insertion point to the beginning of that line.

(continues)

Using the Keyboard to Select Text (continued)

Tip

When it is necessary to select just one or two characters in a document, many Word users find it is easier and more precise to use the ⬆Shift+⬅ or ⬆Shift+➡ instead of dragging over one or two characters with the mouse.

❻ Experiment with any other key combinations or mouse movements for selecting text. Then leave the document open for the next exercise.

Extending a Selection

With Word, you can select any amount of text by extending a selection. Most text selections are of words or sentences; but sometimes you want to select multiple paragraphs. You can use the Extend Selection feature (represented by the EXT indicator in the status bar) to select more than one paragraph when you click the mouse. To use the Extend Selection feature, you would follow these steps:

1. Place the insertion point at the beginning of the area you want to select.

2. Double-click the EXT indicator on the status bar.

   The indicator turns black to show that Extend Selection is active.

3. Click after the last character you want to select to complete the selection procedure.

As soon as you perform an operation on the selection, Word turns off the Extend Selection feature automatically. You can turn off the Extend Selection feature yourself by pressing Esc or double-clicking the EXT indicator in the status bar. When you turn off the Extend Selection feature, the selected text remains selected.

The Extend Selection feature can also be turned on by pressing F8. Pressing F8 twice selects the current word. Pressing F8 three times selects the current sentence. Pressing F8 four times selects the current paragraph. Pressing F8 five times selects the entire document. To return the selected text to the preceding increment, press ⬆Shift+F8.

Tip

If you find that large amounts of text are selected when you single-click the mouse or press an arrow key in your document, the Extend Selection feature may have been activated. Remember to check the EXT indicator in the status bar, and if you need to turn off the feature, just press Esc.

Deleting Many Characters at the Same Time

A quick way to delete a block of characters is to select the characters and then press either [Del] or [◂Backspace]. Table 2.4 provides a list of the specific key combinations you can use to delete characters, words, or phrases located near the insertion point.

Table 2.4 Deleting Text	
Key Combination	**Effect**
[◂Backspace]	Deletes the selected text or deletes one character to the left of the insertion point.
[Ctrl] + [◂Backspace]	Deletes one word to the left of the insertion point.
[Del]	Deletes the selected text or deletes one character to the right of the insertion point.
[Ctrl] + [Del]	Deletes one word to the right of the insertion point.
[Ctrl] + [X]	Deletes the selected text and places it on the Clipboard.

Undoing Your Mistakes

Everyone makes mistakes. Word's Undo command makes it easy for you to "undo" almost any of your editing actions. Earlier versions of Word limited the number of steps to be undone to 100 or fewer, but that limit has been removed in the current version of Word. You will find a few commands, however, that can't be undone (for example, saving or closing a file), so it's best to undo an action as soon as you realize you made a mistake.

What if you thought you made a mistake, so you used the Undo command to undo your action; then you realize it wasn't a mistake after all? Just use the Redo command to "undo your undo."

You can access the Undo and Redo buttons on the Standard toolbar, or you can use the **U**ndo and **R**edo commands at the top of the **E**dit menu. (Depending on your actions, the **R**edo command is sometimes listed as **R**epeat.)

The first time you click the Standard toolbar Undo button, Word undoes your most recent action; the next time you click Undo, Word undoes the action immediately before that. You can continue choosing the button to undo earlier actions.

The button to the right of the Undo button is the Redo button. Word remembers a sequence of redo actions as well as a sequence of undo actions. If you delete three different sections of text and then undo all three actions, Word remembers those actions and enables you to redo everything you just undid.

A drop-down arrow is attached to the right side of the Undo and Redo buttons. Clicking a drop-down arrow opens a list of actions that can be either undone or redone. Choosing an action from the middle of one of the drop-down lists will either undo or redo all the steps taken since you completed the chosen action in the list.

Note

A significant difference exists between the Undo and Redo drop-down lists. Whereas the Undo list is always available, the Redo list is available only immediately after you have undone actions. If you take any action (such as typing text) after undoing actions, you cannot redo those actions.

Undoing and Redoing Deletions

To practice selecting and deleting text, as well as using the Undo and Redo commands, follow these steps:

1 In the open Sales 02 Document, press Ctrl+Home to move the insertion point to the top of the document.

2 Select the first paragraph (the one beginning with *Last year was very...*)

3 Press Del to erase the paragraph.

4 Move the insertion point in front of the word *Conference* in the first line of the last paragraph; then delete the word *Conference* by pressing Ctrl+Del.

5 Hold down Shift and press ↑ four times to select a block of text.

6 Press Backspace to erase the block.

Note that the arrow in the Undo key is blue (showing that there are actions that may be undone), but the arrow in the Redo button is gray. The gray arrow indicates that because no steps have been undone, there are no steps to redo.

 7 Click the drop-down arrow immediately following the Undo button to display a list of your three edits; then press Esc to close the list.

8 Click the Undo button to restore the last deletion back to the window.

Notice that the arrow in the Redo button is now blue, indicating that it can now be used to redo an action.

 9 Click the Redo button to once again remove the block of text that was just restored.

10 Click the Undo button three times to restore all three deletions; then click the Redo button three times to delete all three selections again.

11 Close the Sales 02 document without saving the changes. Leave the Word window open for the next exercise.

Objective 5: Move and Copy Text

One of the benefits of using Word is the ease with which you can move and copy text (or any selected content) within your documents. You don't have to plan sentences, paragraphs, or even documents in detail before you start; just type as thoughts come into your mind. Later, you can polish your work by moving or copying words, sentences, and paragraphs.

Moving text means removing the text from its current position and placing it in a new position. *Copying text* means making a duplicate of the desired text and placing the duplicate in a new location. When you copy text, the original text remains in its current location.

As with most Word actions, there are several ways to move and copy text. Here are the five most common methods for moving and copying selected text:

- Using the Cut, Copy, and Paste buttons on the Standard toolbar
- Using the Cu**t**, **C**opy, and **P**aste commands from the **E**dit menu
- Using the Cu**t**, **C**opy, and **P**aste commands from the document shortcut menu
- Using the keyboard shortcut keys for cutting, copying, and pasting
- Using the drag-and-drop procedure available in Word and many other Windows-based applications

It is good to become familiar with each of these methods. Then you can use whichever method is appropriate for your current situation. Although you will most frequently want to move/copy selections within a document, you can also use each method to move/copy selections from Word documents into documents created by many other Windows applications.

Clipboard
A temporary storage area for selected text, graphics, sound clips, and video clips.

When you use the cut and copy selections, you make use of the Windows *Clipboard*.

The Clipboard is a Windows-controlled temporary storage area used during the move or copy process. You can select anything (text, graphics, sound clips, video clips, and so on) in a document and put it on the Clipboard. Then you can copy the contents of the Clipboard to a different place in the same document or to another document.

When you cut text, you remove it from your document and place it on the Clipboard. By contrast, when you copy text, that text remains in your document, and a copy of it goes onto the Clipboard.

The Clipboard can contain only one item at a time, but that item can be almost any size. When you move or copy a selection to the Clipboard, that selection replaces whatever was previously on the Clipboard. The selection that goes onto the Clipboard stays there until you cut or copy something else to the Clipboard or until you turn off your computer.

In the following exercises, you use the Clipboard to temporarily store selected text as you move and copy the paragraphs in your Sales 02 document.

Using the Standard Toolbar to Move and Copy Text

When using the Standard toolbar to move a selection, you use the Cut and Paste buttons. When copying a selection, you use the Copy and Paste buttons. To learn to use all three buttons, follow these steps:

1 Open the Sales 02 document from your Student Disk. Display the nonprinting characters if they are not already visible on-screen.

Displaying the paragraph symbols on-screen helps you to see exactly what text you are selecting.

2 Select paragraph four (which begins *It has been brought...*). In your selection, include the paragraph mark at the end of paragraph four and the paragraph mark on the blank line following paragraph four.

3 Click the Cut button on the Standard toolbar.

Word removes the selected text from the document and places it on the Clipboard.

4 Place the insertion point in front of the first character in paragraph three, which begins *The first item....*

5 Click the Paste button on the Standard toolbar.

The Paste command instructs Word to insert a copy of the text on the Clipboard into the document (beginning at the current location of the insertion point, see Figure 2.7). Because you included the paragraph marks in your selection, notice that a blank line between paragraphs was retained, and no extra blank line remains where the paragraph was removed.

Notice also that some phrases in the paragraph may again be flagged with a wavy green underline. Disregard the markings while you complete the moving and copying exercises in this chapter.

Figure 2.7
The text is moved to the new location.

The "cut" text has been "pasted" into a new location.

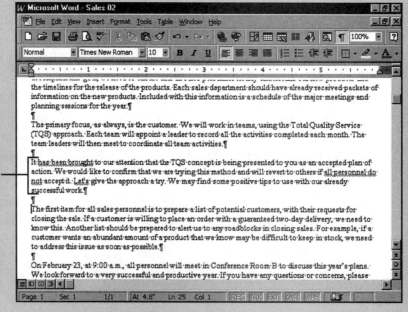

6 Select paragraph four of the Sales 02 document, which begins, *The first item....* In your selection, include the paragraph mark at the end of the paragraph and the paragraph mark on the blank line following paragraph four.

7 Click the Copy button on the Standard toolbar.

Word leaves the selected text in the document and places it on the Clipboard.

8 Place the insertion point in front of the first character in paragraph three, which begins *It has been brought....*

9 Click the Paste button on the Standard toolbar.

At the insertion point, Word pastes a copy of the text that is on the Clipboard (see Figure 2.8).

Figure 2.8
The Sales 02 document now has the same paragraph in two locations.

The copied text ——

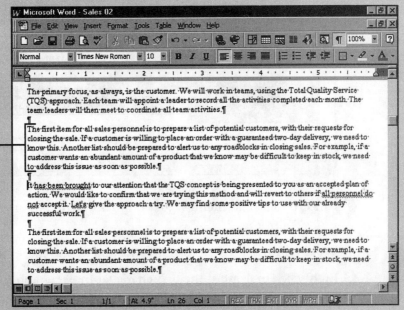

10 Save the Sales 02 document with the changes you have made. Leave the document open for the next exercise.

You just learned how to move and copy text to the Clipboard by using the Standard toolbar buttons. In the following exercise, you move and copy text using a Word shortcut menu.

Using a Shortcut Menu for Rearranging Text

In an earlier exercise, you worked with the shortcut menus for the spelling and grammar programs. You can also access a shortcut menu to cut, copy, and paste text. A shortcut menu is typically displayed when you right-click an item in the Word window. The commands displayed on a shortcut menu depend on the element clicked and your current operation.

Using the Shortcut Menu to Move Text

To use a shortcut menu to move text, follow these steps:

1 In the open Sales 02 document, select paragraph three, which begins with the first occurrence of *The first item....* In your selection, include the paragraph mark at the end of the paragraph and the paragraph mark on the blank line following the paragraph.

2 Right-click the selected text to display the shortcut menu (see Figure 2.9).

Figure 2.9
Right-clicking a selection displays a shortcut menu.

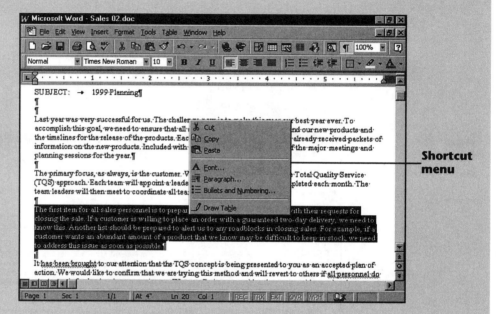

Shortcut menu

3 Click the shortcut menu's **Cut** command (with either the left or right mouse button).

Word removes the text from the document and places it on the Clipboard.

4 Right-click in front of the first character in paragraph four, which begins *The first item...,* to place the insertion point at the beginning of the paragraph and to open the shortcut menu.

5 Choose **P**aste from the shortcut menu.

At the insertion point, Word pastes a copy of the text that is on the Clipboard (see Figure 2.10). You should now have two instances of the paragraph beginning *The first item...* displayed consecutively.

6 Save the changes made to the Sales 02 document and leave it open for the next exercise.

Figure 2.10
The duplicate paragraph has been moved to a new location.

The moved text ——

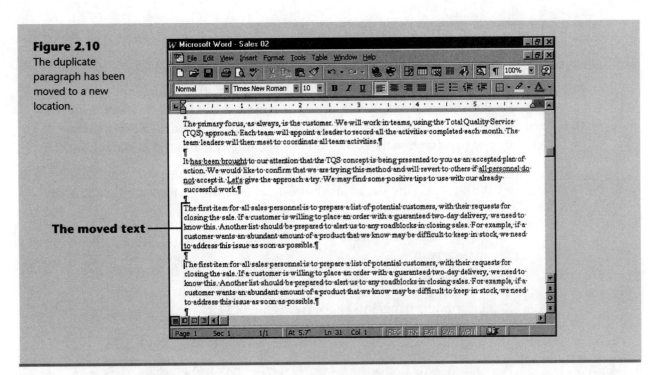

To copy text, you choose **C**opy, rather than Cu**t**, from the shortcut menu in step 3.

If you prefer to use the keyboard to select text, you may prefer to use the keyboard to cut, copy, and paste text. Table 2.5 lists the shortcut key combinations for cutting, copying, and pasting selections.

Table 2.5   Shortcut Keys for Cutting, Copying, and Pasting Text

Key Combination	Effect
Ctrl+X	Cuts the selection to the Clipboard
Ctrl+C	Copies the selection to the Clipboard
Ctrl+V	Pastes the selection on the Clipboard at the insertion point

Dragging and Dropping Text

You can use the mouse to "drag" text to a new location. After the insertion point is in the desired position, you "drop" the text at the insertion point by releasing the mouse button. The drag-and-drop procedure can be used for moving or copying a selection.

When you drag a selection past a window border, the document can scroll quite quickly, possibly causing confusion as to your exact location in the document. Therefore, for best results when using the drag-and-drop procedure, both the original location of the selection and the destination location (where the "drop" will occur) should be on-screen at the same time. When moving or copying a selection from one part of a document to a location one or more screens away, most people prefer to use the cut (or copy) and paste procedures provided by the toolbar buttons or program menus.

Dragging and Dropping Text

To use the mouse to move text by dragging it, follow these steps:

1. In the open Sales 02 document, scroll through the document until the first three paragraphs are clearly displayed in the window. Select paragraph three, which begins with *It has been brought....* In your selection, include the paragraph mark at the end of the paragraph and the paragraph mark on the blank line following the paragraph.

2. Without clicking the mouse button, position the mouse pointer anywhere within the selected text.

When you move the mouse pointer to the selected text, the pointer becomes an arrow.

3. Hold down the left mouse button.

The pointer changes its shape (see Figure 2.11).

Figure 2.11
The mouse pointer changes to include a dotted insertion point and an arrow with a box attached to it.

The drag-and-drop mouse pointer

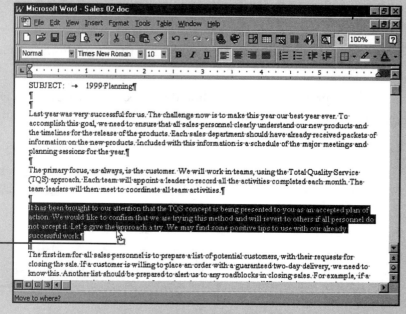

4. Drag the mouse pointer (specifically the dotted insertion point) to just before the first character in paragraph two, which begins with *The primary focus....* Then release the mouse button.

The text is moved from its preceding position to the new one.

To copy a selection using the drag-and-drop technique, hold down Ctrl until after you release the mouse button.

5. Select paragraph two, which begins with *It has been brought....* In your selection, include the paragraph mark at the end of the paragraph and the paragraph mark on the blank line following the paragraph.

6. Position the mouse pointer anywhere within the selected text.

7 Hold down the left mouse button and hold down Ctrl.

The pointer changes to look similar to the drag-and-drop "move" pointer; however, a plus symbol is now displayed over the lower-right corner of the box attached to the end of the arrow. The plus symbol indicates the drag-and-drop "copy" pointer is active.

8 Drag the mouse pointer to just before the first character in paragraph one, which begins with *Last year was*…. Release the mouse button and *then* release Ctrl.

The selected paragraph is copied in front of the original first paragraph.

9 Close the Sales 02 document without saving the changes.

Objective 6: Work with More Than One Document

Active window
The window containing the document on which you are currently working.

In Word, you work with documents in windows. You can open several documents at the same time, each in its own window. By default, Word maximizes the document window so that only one open window is visible at a time. The *active window* is the window in which you are currently working and in which the insertion point is displayed. Any editing action that you take affects only the active document.

When you have two or more documents open at the same time, you can easily copy or move text between them. You also can refer to information in one document while you work with another document.

When you want to open more than one document, open the first document, and then repeat the same steps to open the second. If the documents are not maximized, their windows are stacked on top of one another so that only the most recently opened document is completely visible; you can see only the edges of the other documents. If the documents are maximized, only the most recently opened one is visible.

Each document is independent; you can work in any document without affecting the other open documents. You can, however, move and copy text between documents by using the Clipboard.

> **Tip**
>
> There is another way to open two (or more) existing documents if they are in the same drive or folder. Display the appropriate list of files in the Open dialog box, press Ctrl, and click on each document you want to open; then choose the Open button. Word opens each of the selected documents in its own document window.

Working with Different Documents at the Same Time

To practice working with more than one document, follow these steps:

1 In your open Word window, close any document windows that are currently open. Then click the New button on the Standard toolbar to open a new document.

2 Type your first and last name on the first line of the new document, press ⏎Enter, type your city and state on the next line, and press ⏎Enter twice.

3 Select the entire contents of your new document by choosing **Edit, Select All** (or by pressing Ctrl+A).

4 Copy the selection to the Clipboard.

5 Open the Sales 02 document and move to the end of the document by pressing Ctrl+End.

6 Press ⏎Enter twice; then paste the selection from the Clipboard into the Sales 02 document.

7 Select the last full paragraph of the Sales 02 document, the one beginning with *On February 23,....* In your selection, include the paragraph mark at the end of the paragraph and the paragraph mark on the blank line following the paragraph.

8 Copy your selection to the Clipboard.

9 Open the **W**indow menu.

The open menu is shown in Figure 2.12. Don't worry if the files listed don't exactly match the ones in the figure.

10 Select your new document (Document2 in Figure 2.12).

That document becomes visible on your screen.

11 Move to the end of your new document and paste the selection into the document.

Figure 2.12
A list of the open documents appears at the bottom of the Window menu.

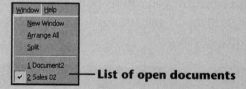 ——— **List of open documents**

12 Press Ctrl+Home to move the insertion point to the top of your new document.

13 Leave both documents open for the next exercise.

Working with Different Documents in the Same Screen

To make two or more documents visible on-screen at the same time, follow these steps:

1 With both your new document and the Sales 02 document open from the previous exercise, choose **W**indow, **A**rrange All.

The Word window work area splits into two windows (see Figure 2.13).

Figure 2.13
In this example, two documents are shown in separate windows within the Word window.

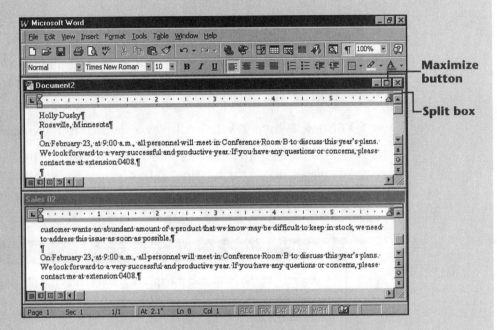

The active window has the brighter title bar. To make the other document active, click inside that document's window.

2 Click in the lower window to make it active.

Although the window is now active, you may need to click in the window again to locate the insertion point.

3 Activate and then close the new document window without saving the changes.

4 Maximize the Sales 02 document window and leave it open for the next exercise.

Note

When you choose the **A**rrange All command, Word divides the screen into as many windows as necessary to display all the open documents. If four documents are open, for example, Word divides the space in the Word window into four windows, with each open document occupying one window. Working in small windows is difficult. Do not choose the **A**rrange All command when many documents are open unless you need to see all the open documents on one screen.

Working with One Document in Two Panes

Panes
Portions of a window.

To view and work in two parts of the active document at the same time, you can divide the document window into two *panes*. You can scroll and work in each pane independently. This feature is particularly useful when you want to move or copy text between distant parts of a long document. You can split the screen into two panes and view the source text in one pane and the destination area in the other pane.

To split the screen into panes and work in two areas of one document, follow these steps:

1 Make sure that the open Sales 02 document is maximized (if necessary, click the Maximize button in the upper-right corner of the screen). Then move the insertion point to the top of the document.

2 Choose **W**indow, **S**plit to display a split bar in the center of the work area.

The mouse pointer changes to a double horizontal line, with an up arrow displayed above the top line and a down arrow displayed below the bottom line. The pointer is attached to the split bar; the bar moves up and down in a corresponding manner to your mouse movements.

> ### Tip
>
> If you accidentally activated the split bar, you can turn it off by pressing Esc. When the pointer is attached to the split bar, choosing the **W**indow menu name also removes the bar.

When the work area is a single pane, you can also activate the split bar by using the split box, which is located immediately above the up scroll arrow button on the vertical scroll bar (refer to Figure 2.13). Just drag the split box into the desired location in your window and then release the mouse button.

When the pointer is resting on the split bar, it changes to a double-headed arrow. To quickly create two equal panes, double-click the split box.

3 Position the split bar immediately below the first paragraph, which begins *Last year was…* and click the mouse button to anchor the split bar in place (see Figure 2.14).

Notice that each pane has a ruler and vertical scroll bar. Moving the scroll box on the horizontal scroll bar scrolls both windows simultaneously to the left or right.

The active pane displays the insertion point.

4 To make the inactive pane active, click anywhere inside the inactive pane or press F6.

5 Press F6 to switch back to the other pane.

Figure 2.14
The same document displayed in two window panes.

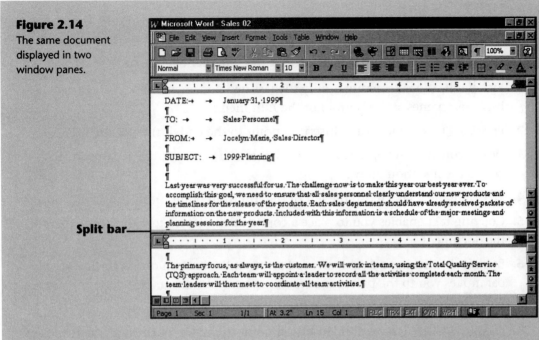

Split bar

Notice the insertion point has moved to the other pane.

After the split bar is displayed, the size of the panes can still be changed. To do this, rest the pointer on the split bar. When the pointer rests on the split bar, it changes shape, and the ScreenTip *Resize* is displayed by the pointer. Then drag the bar to the desired work area location.

6 To remove the split bar, double-click it or choose **W**indow, Remove **S**plit to display only one pane in the work area.

7 Close the Sales 02 document without saving any changes to it.

Chapter Summary

You have now gained a fundamental knowledge of some of the basic Word features. You now know how to move the insertion point, select text, move and copy selections, and work with different views and documents at the same time. In the next chapter, you learn to use some of Word's writing tools to help you further improve your documents.

If you have completed your work for this computer session, make sure that you properly exit all open programs. Then use the Windows Sh**u**t Down command to safely exit Windows. To test your knowledge of the material covered in this chapter, answer the questions in the Checking Your Skills section immediately following this summary. Then, complete the exercises in the Applying Your Skills section at the end of the chapter.

Checking Your Skills

True/False

For each of the following, circle *T* or *F* to indicate whether the statement is true or false.

T (F) **1.** By default, Word remembers only the last two documents that you opened and lists their names at the bottom of the **E**dit menu. 4–9

(T) F **2.** Pressing Ctrl+End moves the insertion point to the end of the document.

(T) F **3.** When you are viewing two panes of the same document, the active pane includes the insertion point.

T (F) **4.** To delete the character to the left of the insertion point, press the ↓.

(T) F **5.** Copying text enables you to place a copy of the selected text in another part of the document.

(T) F **6.** By default, clicking a double-headed arrow at the bottom of the vertical scroll bar moves you to the previous or next page of your document.

T (F) **7.** If you press F8 five times, the entire document will be selected.

(T) F **8.** Pressing Ctrl+Home moves the insertion point to the top of the document.

T (F) **9.** The position of the scroll box in the vertical scroll bar indicates the position of the text in the window relative to the top and bottom margins of the page.

(T) F **10.** In all cases, pressing Shift+Home selects all the characters between the insertion point and the top of the page.

Multiple Choice

In the blank provided, write the letter of the correct answer for each of the following questions.

1. In the Open dialog box, you can display a list of your system's storage locations by clicking the arrow attached to the end of the ___look-in___ drop-down list box.

   a. What's This?

   b. EXT

   c. Look **in**

   d. Save **in**

   e. File **type**

2. The shortcut key combination for pasting is ___e___.

   a. Ctrl+A

   b. Ctrl+Z

   c. Ctrl+X

   d. Ctrl+C

   e. Ctrl+V

3. The Windows-controlled temporary storage area used by your computer to store the latest cut or copied text is called the ___clipboard___.

   a. scrap

   b. heap

   c. pile

   d. glue board

   e. Clipboard

4. When you press Ctrl and click the left mouse button on a word in the document, the ___d___ is selected.

   a. entire document

   b. word

   c. paragraph

   d. current sentence

   e. top half of the document

5. To view two different panes of your current document, choose _____.

   a. **W**indow, Pan**e**

   b. **W**indow, **S**plit

   c. **W**indow, **T**wo

   d. **W**indow, **A**rrange All

   e. **W**indow, **D**ivide

6. To copy, instead of moving, when conducting a drag-and-drop procedure, keep the _CTRL_ key held down until you release the mouse button.

   a. Ctrl

   b. ↵Enter

   c. ⇧Shift

   d. Alt

   e. Spacebar

7. When the ___C___ mode is turned on, the character to the right of the insertion point will be replaced when a key is pressed on the keyboard.

   a. Edit

   b. Insert

   c. Overtype

   d. Extend

   e. Exclude

8. When nonprinting characters are displayed, the dot between words represents a(n) _space_

   a. comma

   b. semicolon

   c. space

   d. tab

   e. indent

9. You display the special symbols that represent nonprinting characters by clicking the _a_.

   a. Show/Hide ¶ button

   b. Open button

   c. Cut button

   d. Paste button

   e. View button

10. In the selection bar, if you double-click next to a line of text, you select the adjacent _a_.

   a. paragraph

   b. word

   c. line

   d. sentence

   e. page

Fill in the Blank

In the blank provided, write the correct answer for each of the following questions.

1. Word typically displays the four most recently opened documents in the _file_ menu.

2. In the status bar, when _the color_ is gray, Word is in Insert mode.

3. The first step in moving a block of text is to _select_ it.

4. _Copying_ text leaves the original text in its original location and places a duplicate block in another document location.

5. The menus that "pop up" when you right-click in the document are typically called _shortcuts_ menus.

6. When you use the window menu's _arrange all_ command, Word divides the screen into as many windows as necessary to display all the open Word documents.

7. The position of the scroll box in the _vertical_ scroll bar indicates the position of the text in the window relative to the beginning and the end of the document.

8. In _____ mode, Word inserts the characters that you type to the left of the insertion point, and text on the right side of the insertion point moves to the right.

9. When you select text with the mouse, you often use the _____, an area to the left of the text in the window work area.

10. The _____ mark contains information that controls the formatting of text in the preceding paragraph.

Applying Your Skills   _WORKING IN CLASS 2/16/99_

Review Exercises

Exercise 1: Adding Text to the Business Document

To practice adding text to a document, follow these steps:

1. Open the Chap0202 file from your Student Disk and immediately save the file back to your disk as **Business 02**.

2. Add the following text as the final paragraph before the closing (be sure to maintain one blank line above and below the new paragraph):

   A map and written directions are included. Refreshments will be served, and prizes will be given every hour. Please extend this invitation to other associates.

3. Save your revisions, and then print and close the file.

Exercise 2: Learning About the Microsoft IntelliMouse Pointing Device

To practice using Help, follow these steps:

1. Access the Help topic on the Microsoft IntelliMouse Pointing Device and review the topic's information.

2. Open a new document and enter your name on the first line. Then enter the phrase **Learning about the Microsoft IntelliMouse Pointing Device** on the next line and press (Enter) twice.

3. Create a one paragraph summary on the use of this pointing device. Be sure to identify the new "button" that makes using this mouse different from using a traditional mouse.

4. Save the file to your Student Disk as **IntelliMouse 02**.

5. Print and close your document.

Exercise 3: Moving Text

To practice moving text in a document, complete the following steps:

1. Open a new document; then type **one** and press (Enter).

2. Type **two** and press ⏎Enter. Continue this process until you have "numbered" lines one through ten of your document using the words, one, two, three, four, five, six, seven, eight, nine, and ten.

3. Use the mouse to drag and drop the words into alphabetical order. When you finish you should have one word on each line.

4. Save the document as **Alphabetical Numbers 02** to your Student Disk.   ✓

5. Print and close your document.

Exercise 4: Editing Text

To practice editing text, follow these steps:

1. Open the Chap0203 file from your Student Disk and immediately save the file back to your disk as **Employee Guidelines 02.**

2. Move guideline 3 to become guideline 2. If necessary, change the numbers so that the numbers in the list remain in numerical order. Make sure to keep one blank line between each guideline.

3. Add the fifth guideline listed below to the end of your document. (For this exercise, be sure to press ⏎Enter first to insert a blank line, type **5.**, insert one space, and then enter the guideline.)

> **5. If the employee cannot comply with the rules stated above, the employee must provide written notification to the employer within five (5) working days after receipt of guidelines.**

4. Save your revisions, and then print and close the file.   ✓

Exercise 5: Copying Text

To practice copying text within a document, follow these steps:

1. Open the Chap0204 file from your Student Disk and immediately save the file back to your disk as **Buttons 02**.

2. Move the insertion point to the end of the document and press ⏎Enter twice.

3. Copy each line of text (one line at a time) to a new location below the original text.

4. Save the revisions, and then print and close the file.

Continuing Projects

Project 1: Practice Using Word

Practice using Word by following these steps:

1. Open a new document window; then type the following text:

> **Schedule of Events**
>
> **February 28**
>
> **The planning committee will meet and discuss the fund-raisers to be accomplished for the next six months. Members will be assigned specific jobs.**
>
> **Refreshments will be donated by Dunkin' Donuts.**

March 6

The publications committee will meet and work on articles about up-coming events to be published in the local newspapers.

A representative will visit six restaurants and facilities to reserve the date. All information will be reviewed by the entire committee on April 3.

April 8

The publications committee will send letters to business organizations, requesting donations and support. Follow-up phone calls will be made.

2. Add the paragraph—and appropriate blank line(s)—that begins *Refreshments will be...* under the last paragraphs for the last two dates.

3. Use the automatic spelling and grammar checking features to correct the mistakes in your document. (For this exercise, ignore any grammar checker suggestions when the passive voice is indicated in the grammar checking shortcut menu.)

4. Save the file to your Student Disk as **Planning 02**.

5. Print and close the document.

Project 2: Deli-Mart

Continue developing the Deli-Mart menu by following these steps:

1. Open the Chap0205 file from your Student Disk and immediately save the file back to your disk as **Menu 02**.

2. Add the following entrees to the end of the Menu document. Be sure to press ⏎Enter twice after each item name and item description.

Sassy Burger

6-oz. sizzling burger with lettuce, tomato, and onion, served on a toasted roll. 6.95

Sarah's Blend

6-oz. chicken breast, stuffed with ham and Swiss cheese, served on a toasted roll. 8.95

Tom's Ketch

Stuffed filet of sole, served on a bed of rice with stir-fried vegetables. 8.95

3. Move the *Tom's Ketch* item name and description to the beginning of the document.

4. Type **Special of the Day** at the end of the document.

5. Delete *The Beef Sensation* item title and replace it with *Philly Delight*.

6. If necessary, activate the automatic spelling checker; then use the shortcut spelling menu to change *sauteed* to *sautéed*.

7. Move the *Memphis Melt* item and description to become the third menu entry.

8. Save the revisions; then print and close the file.

Project 3: The Marketing Connection

Continue working with The Marketing Connection newsletter by following these steps:

1. Open the Chap0206 file from your Student Disk and immediately save the file back to your disk as **Market 02**.

2. Type the following text after the last paragraph. Be sure to insert a blank line between all paragraphs.

> **Public Relations Group**
>
> **Our job is to contact businesses, both for-profit and not-for-profit, within the United States. Form letters are sent initially, and follow-up telephone calls are made. We find that five of every ten telephone calls result in at least a request for presentation of the materials, and of the five presentations, we have been able to capture two contracts. This is a start, but we want the 40 percent to grow to 50 percent, and so on. The newsletter can be one of the different methods offered to promote our new marketing service.**

3. Move the paragraph that begins *We hope that we have sparked...* to the end of the document.

4. Save the revisions, and then print and close the file.

5. Exit Word and Windows if you have completed your session at the computer.

2

CHAPTER 3

Proofing Your Work

In the last chapter, you learned to use the mouse or keyboard to move the insertion point to a particular document location. Then you learned to make simple edits in the document text. In this chapter, you learn to use the Find and Replace dialog box to find specific entries or locations in your document. This dialog box also enables you to select a specific entry and replace it with another entry with just a click of a button.

After becoming familiar with the Find and Replace commands, you learn to use some of Word's proofing tools. The spelling checker helps you quickly locate and correct your spelling errors. Besides checking the words in your document against Word's main dictionary, you can also check the words against your own custom dictionaries that you create through Word.

Typically, after you know that the text in a document is spelled correctly, you review your grammar. In this version of Word, the grammar checking and spelling checking programs are run simultaneously through the same dialog box. This chapter shows you how to work with both features so that you can work with the spelling and grammar checkers at the same time.

You also learn to use the thesaurus to help keep the wording in your document fresh and interesting. The chapter concludes by explaining how to use Word's AutoCorrect feature. After you learn to insert your common spelling errors (and the correct version of the word) into the AutoCorrect list, you empower Word to automatically correct your most common typing mistakes.

Objectives

By the time you finish this chapter, you will have learned to

1. Use the Find, Replace, and Go To Features
2. Check Your Spelling
3. Check Your Grammar
4. Use the Thesaurus
5. Use AutoCorrect to Prevent Mistakes

Objective 1: Use the Find, Replace, and Go To Features

Sometimes you need to move the insertion point to a particular document location, but you don't have the time to visually scan the entire document to find the desired word or phrase. When looking for a specific document entry, use the Find feature to move directly to the occurrence of that word or phrase. To activate the Find feature, choose **Edit, Find** to display the Fin**d** page of the Find and Replace dialog box.

Choose **Edit, Re**p**lace** to display the Re**p**lace page of the Find and Replace dialog box. Use this page of the dialog box not only to find a specific entry in your document, but also to replace the located entry with another entry. Besides finding and replacing text, you can also use this page to find and replace specific nonprinting characters in your document.

The third page of the Find and Replace dialog box is the **G**o To page. Use this page when you want to move the insertion point to a specific element (that is, a page, section, line, graphic, table, footnote, bookmark, and so on) within your document.

Complete the exercises in this section to learn how to work with all three pages of the Find and Replace dialog box.

Finding a Specific Text Entry

Follow the steps in this exercise to learn how to find a specific string of characters (letters, spaces, numbers, and so on) in a document.

❶ Start Word, insert your Student Disk in drive A, and then open the Chap0301 file from your disk. Immediately save the file back to your disk as **Sales 03**.

The Chap0301 file is similar to the file you worked with in the last chapter. However, some changes have been made to the document so that you can use it to learn about some of Word's proofing features. For the exercises in this section, disregard the spelling and grammar errors in the document.

❷ Make sure that the insertion point is at the top of the document.

❸ Choose **Edit, Find** (or press Ctrl+F).

Word displays the Fin**d** page of the Find and Replace dialog box (see Figure 3.1).

Figure 3.1
Use the Find and Replace dialog box to search for specific text.

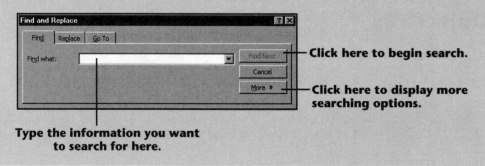

Type the information you want to search for here.

Click here to begin search.

Click here to display more searching options.

❹ In the Find what text box, type **team**.

As soon as you start typing, the previously disabled **F**ind Next button becomes enabled.

By default, the Find command locates every occurrence of the entry in the Fi**n**d what text box throughout the document. For example, if you entered *art* in the Fi**n**d what text box and then chose the **F**ind Next button, Word would stop on words like *artful* and *start* in addition to stopping on the word *art.*

❺ Choose the **F**ind Next button to move the insertion point to the first location of the *team* string of characters in the document.

Word first stops on the *team* character string inside the word *teams* in the second sentence of the second paragraph. (You may need to drag the dialog box to another location in the window to see the selected text. You drag a dialog box by placing the pointer on the title bar of the dialog box, holding down the left mouse button, moving the mouse to move the dialog box, and then releasing the mouse button.)

❻ Continue choosing the **F**ind Next button (and viewing the selected text in your document) until Word displays a message that the search is finished (see Figure 3.2). Choose OK to return to the Find and Replace dialog box.

> ### Tip
>
> You can end the Find procedure at any time by choosing the Cancel button or the dialog box Close button.

Note that you can search just part of a document by selecting the desired segment and then initiating the Find procedure.

Figure 3.2
Word displays this message box after completing the search.

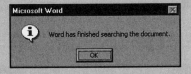

❼ Keep the Find and Replace dialog box displayed on top of your Sales 03 document for the next exercise.

Controlling the Search

You can take several actions to control Word's search of a document. You can broaden the Find procedure to include all forms of the word entered in the Fi**n**d what text box. Or, you can narrow the search parameters to help Word quickly find the exact information you want.

Display the additional Find options by choosing the **M**ore button in the Find page of the Find and Replace dialog box (see Figure 3.3).

Here are some options you have in searching a document:

- *Search only part of a document.* By default, Word searches an entire document. If you want to search only a specific part of a document, select that portion of the text before you open the Find and Replace dialog box.

- *Control the search direction.* By using the **S**earch drop-down list, you can control the direction of a search. By default, Word searches from the insertion point toward the end of the document. If you want to search from the insertion point toward the beginning of the document, choose the Up option.

- *Match the case.* By default, Word does not distinguish between uppercase and lowercase letters when it searches a document. If you want to find text that appears in an exact combination of uppercase and lowercase letters, choose the Match case check box. Word finds only those words in which the case of each character matches the case entered in the Find what text box.

- *Find whole words only.* To make a search even more efficient, you can choose the Find whole words only check box to find the information only when it appears as an entire word. If you create a document about animals and you tell Word to search for cat, for example, Word finds every occurrence of the consecutive letters c, a, and t: catalog, category, allocate, catch, and so on. If you choose the Find whole words only option, Word finds the specified text only when it appears as a separate word.

Wild-card characters
Characters that you can use to represent one or more other characters.

- *Use wild-card characters.* You can use the **U**se wildcards option to specify a word or phrase by using any of the numerous wild-card characters available to the Find feature. Two commonly used wild-card characters are the *?* (which represents any single character or no character) and the * (which represents any sequence of characters). This option is particularly useful when you don't know the exact spelling of the word that you want to find. (To see more information on this option, click the Help button—the question mark button—on the Find and Replace dialog box title bar; then click the **U**se wildcards option to view the related Help information.)

- *Find words that sound alike.* If you choose the Sounds like check box, Word finds words that sound like the word you entered in the Find what text box. If you ask Word to find *here*, for example, it also finds *hear.*

  This option is particularly helpful if you have a habit of typing *no* when you mean *know* and vice versa. After you finish your document, you can use either *no* or *know* as your search string and then choose the Sounds like option. Word finds every occurrence of both words, enabling you to double-check your usage.

- *Find all forms of the word.* If you choose the Find all word forms check box, Word finds all forms of the word you typed in the Find what check box. If you type *sit*, for example, Word finds also *sitting* and *sat.*

Note

You may choose only one of the **U**se wildcards, Sounds like, or Find all word forms options at a time. In addition, when you choose one of these options, the Match case and Find whole words only options are dimmed.

The expanded Find page in the Find and Replace dialog box includes three buttons along the bottom of the page:

- *The Format button.* Enables you to search for a font, paragraph format, tab format, language, frame format, or style. When this option is activated, Word displays the selected format below the entry in the Find what text box. (When this option is active, there does not need to be an entry in the Find what text box.)

- *The Special button.* Enables you to search for special codes (that is, paragraph marks, tabs, graphics, endnote marks, footnote marks, page breaks, section breaks, hyphens, spaces, and so on) in the document.

- *The No Formatting button.* Choosing this button deletes any codes displayed below the Find what text box from a previous Find procedure.

Using Find Options

Complete the following exercise to practice using some of the options in the Find page of the Find and Replace dialog box.

1 If the Find page of the Find and Replace dialog box is still displayed on top of the Sales 03 document from the previous exercise, move to the next step now. Otherwise, display the Sales 03 document; make sure that the insertion point is at the top of the document; then choose **E**dit, **F**ind.

2 If necessary, enter **team** into the Find what text box.

3 Also, if necessary, choose the **M**ore button to expand the Find page (see Figure 3.3).

Figure 3.3
The expanded Find page.

Additional Find options

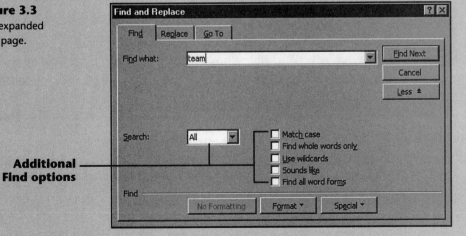

(continues)

Using Find Options (continued)

Tip

When searching for entries, if you don't need to choose any of the Find options and prefer to display the smaller Find page, choose the **L**ess button on the right side of the Find page.

4 Choose the Find whole words only option; then click **F**ind Next to move to the first occurrence of *team* in the document.

(Again, you may need to drag the dialog box to view the selected text.) Notice that this time the word *teams* was bypassed. Only the complete word *team* is highlighted.

5 Continue to choose the **F**ind Next button until you see the message that the search is completed. Then choose OK to return to the Find and Replace dialog box (and return the insertion point to the top of the document).

6 Enter **new** in the Find what text box.

This is the next term you are looking for. To test another option, try to find all the words that sound like *new*.

7 Choose the Sounds like option near the bottom of the Find page; then choose **F**ind Next.

Note

If you accidentally choose one of the last three Find options, but instead you wanted to choose one of the top two options (which have just be made unavailable), just choose the same lower option again to turn off the selection. (Turning off the selection of one of the three lower options enables you to choose one of the top two options.)

(Don't be too surprised when the first word selected is *now*.)

8 Continue the Find procedure until you see the message box stating that Word has finished the search; then choose OK to close the box.

9 Close the Find and Replace dialog box by choosing the Cancel button (or Close button in the dialog box title bar). Then leave the Sales 03 document open for the next exercise.

Replacing Text, Special Characters, or Formatting

When you use the Find command, Word highlights the first occurrence of the word or string of characters that you specify. You then can close the Find and Replace dialog box and start editing the selected text, or you can continue to look for more occurrences of the specified string of characters.

The Replace command works as an extension of Find. With Replace, you can find occurrences of specified character groups (or formatting codes) and replace each occurrence with another character group (or formatting codes).

Suppose that you create a document about cats and later decide that the material actually applies more to dogs. You can use Replace to change every occurrence of cat to dog. Unless you choose the Find whole words only option, however, you may not be pleased to find that every *catastrophe* becomes a *dogastrophe* and every *catalog* becomes a *dogalog*.

You can display the Replace page of the Find and Replace dialog box by any of the following methods:

- Choosing **E**dit, **R**eplace

- Pressing Ctrl+H

- Clicking the Replace tab if the Find and Replace dialog box is already displayed

3

Replacing Text

To find and replace text in the Sales 03 document, follow these steps:

❶ Position the insertion point at the beginning of the opened Sales 03 document.

❷ Choose **E**dit, **R**eplace.

The Replace page of the Find and Replace dialog box is displayed (see Figure 3.4).

Insert the entry to find here.

Figure 3.4
Use the Replace page to find and replace the entries you specify.

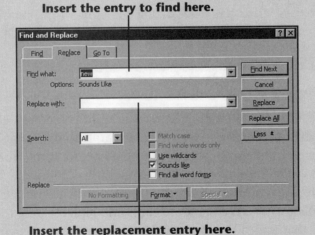

Insert the replacement entry here.

❸ Type **team** in the Find what text box.

❹ Press Tab↹ or click in the Replace with text box to move the insertion point there, and then type **group** (the replacement entry).

(continues)

Replacing Text (continued)

5 Turn off the Sounds like option (from the previous Find procedure).

6 Choose the **F**ind Next button to find the first occurrence of the text string *team* in the document.

You may need to move the Find and Replace dialog box to see the selected text.

7 Choose the **R**eplace button to replace the word *teams* with *groups* and move to the next occurrence of the *team* text string.

You know that there are a number of occurrences of *team* throughout the remainder of the document. Change all the remaining occurrences of *team* to *group* throughout the rest of the document by completing the next step.

8 Choose Replace **A**ll to have Word automatically replace all occurrences of *team* with *group*.

Note

If you use Replace **A**ll and find that you replaced more than you expected, you can choose the Undo button to undo the Replace All procedure that simultaneously entered all the replacements. You can also undo the changes by choosing **E**dit, **U**ndo AutoCorrect.

9 When Word displays the message of the number of replacements made, read the message; then choose OK to return to the Find and Replace dialog box.

10 Close the Find and Replace dialog box. Review the changes to your document, save the revisions, and then keep the Sales 03 file open for the next exercise.

There are two more important points to remember about the Replace command:

- *Matching the case of the replacement string.* If you do not choose the Matc**h** case option in the Replace page, Word attempts to set the case of characters in the replacement word to match the original word. If the word to be replaced appears at the beginning of a sentence that has an initial capital letter, for example, the replacement word is inserted with an initial capital as well. But if you choose Matc**h** case, Word finds and replaces only the words in your document that match the case of each character in the search string. In addition, the replacement word appears in your document exactly as the word was entered in the Replace with text box, without regard for the case of the characters in the word that was replaced.

- *Using spaces or no space as the replacement string.* If you want to replace a word with nothing (not even a space), leave the Replace with text box empty and make sure that no replacement format is specified. If you want to replace a word with one or more spaces, simply enter the desired number of spaces in the Replace with text box.

Move to Specific Locations with the Go To Page

The **G**o To page of the Find and Replace dialog box enables you to move the insertion point to a specific location within your document. After displaying the **G**o To page, you identify the document element you want to move to (for example, page 7, table 1, line 37, section 3, bookmark 4, and so on), and then choose the Go **T**o button to move directly to that document location.

You can display the **G**o To page of the Find and Replace dialog box by any of the following methods:

- Choosing **E**dit, **G**o To

- Pressing Ctrl+G

- Double-clicking the insertion point information in the status bar

- Clicking the **G**o To tab if the Find and Replace dialog box is already displayed

3

Moving to a Specific Location

Complete the following steps to learn how to use the Go To page of the Find and Replace dialog box.

1 In the open Sales 03 document, make sure that the insertion point is placed at the top of the document.

2 Choose **E**dit, **G**o To (or the method of your choice) to display the **G**o To page of the Find and Replace dialog box (see Figure 3.5).

Figure 3.5
Move directly to a specific location in your document by using the Go To page of the Find and Replace dialog box.

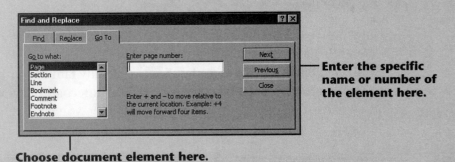

Enter the specific name or number of the element here.

Choose document element here.

As you can see in the **G**o to what list box, you can move to many types of locations: a page, section, line, bookmark, comment, footnote, field, table, graphic, heading, endnote, equation, or object.

In this exercise, you move to a specific line number in the document.

3 Choose the Line option in the **G**o to what list box.

The name of the center text box changes to correspond with the selection from the **G**o to what list box.

4 Type **15** in the **E**nter line number text box.

When you enter a value in this text box, the Ne**x**t button (on the upper-right side of the dialog box) changes to a Go **T**o button.

(continues)

Moving to a Specific Location (continued)

❺ Choose the Go **To** button now to move the insertion point to the beginning of line 15 in your document. (Line 15 is the blank line between the first and second paragraphs.)

The Ln 15 entry in the insertion point information (located in the second section of the status bar), indicates the insertion point is on line number 15.

❻ Close the Find and Replace dialog box and note that the insertion point is now active and located on line 15. Leave the Sales 03 document displayed in your Word window for the next exercise.

In the preceding exercise, instead of going to a line specified by its number, you can go forward or backward from the insertion point's current location by specifying a number of lines. To do this, type the plus sign (+) or minus sign (–) and a number in the **E**nter line number text box and choose Go **T**o (or press ⏎Enter). To move forward three lines in the document, for example, type **+3**; to move back four lines, type **–4**.

You can use the same technique to move to a specific page number (or up or down by a specific number of pages) in the current document. But first, you must select Page in the **Go** to what list box.

Objective 2: Check Your Spelling

Obviously, you should check the spelling in each document that you create. Presenting a document with misspelled words is one of the fastest ways to lose your credibility with your reader. You are already familiar with using Spell It, Word's automatic spelling checker that flags unrecognized words in your document with a wavy red underline. In this section, you learn to use the full spelling checker program and some of the options that come with the program.

Dictionary
An alphabetical list of words frequently used in documents. Word's main dictionary may not contain all the words used in your document, so Word also enables you to create custom dictionaries.

You can use the spelling checker to check a single selected word, a selected block of text, or an entire document. Word always checks the spellings in your document against the spelling of words in its main *dictionary*. In addition, you can instruct Word to compare words in your document with those in one or more of the custom dictionaries that you can create through Word.

The spelling checker checks the words in your document against the words in the selected dictionaries. If a string of characters is not in any of the selected dictionaries, the spelling checker highlights the string and gives you the option to make changes to the string, ignore the potential error, or add the character string ("legal" word or not) to one of the custom dictionaries.

Remember that the spelling checker checks only individual words, without regard to their context; the spelling checker does not attempt to alert you to errors such as typing *no* rather than *know*, *too* rather than *two*, *stationary* rather than *stationery*, and so on. Automated programs, like the spelling checker are helpful, but nothing can take the place of your careful proofreading of the document.

> **Note**
>
> As you will soon see, Word's spelling checker and grammar checker have been combined to work out of the same dialog box.

Detecting Unrecognized Words and Correcting Misspellings

You can start the spelling checker by any of the following methods:

- Clicking the Spelling and Grammar button in the Standard toolbar

- Choosing **T**ools, **S**pelling and Grammar from the menu

- Pressing F7

If you have problems... If you attempt to load the spelling checker and see a dialog box stating that Word cannot locate it, it may not have been loaded during the Word installation process. If you see this message, contact your instructor or network administrator for help.

Checking the Spelling in a Document

To practice using some of Word's tools for correcting potential spelling or grammar errors, follow these steps:

1 If the Sales 03 document is not displayed in your Word window, open the file now.

2 Make sure that the insertion point is at the beginning of the document; then scan the document for words or phrases underlined by wavy red or green lines.

Words displayed with a wavy underline have been flagged as either potential misspellings (wavy red underline) or potential grammar errors (wavy green underline).

If you have problems... If no wavy underlines appear under some of the words in the first and third paragraphs of this document, complete the following steps:

1. Choose **T**ools, **O**ptions to open the Options dialog box.

2. Choose the S**p**elling and Grammar tab.

3. Make sure that the Check s**p**elling as you type and the Check **g**rammar as you type check boxes are marked.

4. Make sure that the Hide **s**pelling errors in this document and Hide grammatical **e**rrors in this document check boxes are blank.

(continues)

Checking the Spelling in a Document (continued)

5. Choose OK to enable any changes you made to the Spelling and Grammar page.

If these steps still do not display wavy underlines below some of the words in the Sales 03 document, contact your instructor or network administrator for help.

Besides visually scanning your document, you can move quickly from one document error to the next by double-clicking the Spelling and Grammar Status button located on the right side of the status bar.

 ❸ Double-click the Spelling and Grammar Status button to move to the first error in the document.

When the error is selected, a shortcut menu is displayed offering different choices of action. For now, don't choose any of the shortcut options; instead, move to the next error.

❹ Double-click the Spelling and Grammar Status button again, to move to the next error and view the new shortcut menu.

The choices on the menu change depending on the potential error.

If you have problems...   If the Readability Statistics dialog box is displayed during any of the steps in this exercise, choose OK to close the box. Then, double-click the Spelling and Grammar Status button again to move to the next potential error. You learn about readability statistics later in the chapter.

❺ Continue to double-click the Spelling and Grammar Status button until you move back to the first error. Then press Esc to close the shortcut menu.

 ❻ Move the insertion point to the top of the document; then choose the Spelling and Grammar button on the Standard toolbar to start the spelling and grammar checking programs.

Word begins checking the document. When it finds the word *yeer*, the word is selected, and the Spelling and Grammar dialog box opens to offer replacement suggestions for *yeer* (see Figure 3.6).

Note

If your Spelling and Grammar dialog box does not display any suggestions, the command to display suggestions may have been turned off. To turn on this command, choose **T**ools, **O**ptions; click the Spelling and Grammar tab of the Options dialog box; and click the **Al**ways suggest corrections check box to mark the option. Then choose OK to enable your change.

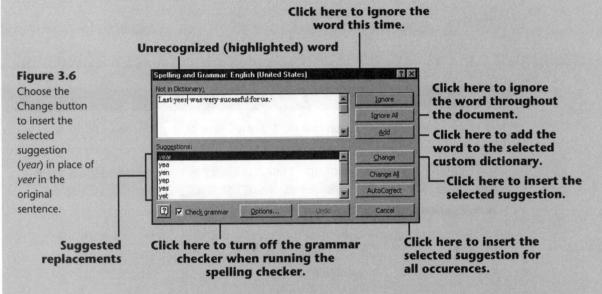

Click here to ignore the word this time.

Unrecognized (highlighted) word

Figure 3.6
Choose the Change button to insert the selected suggestion (*year*) in place of *yeer* in the original sentence.

Click here to ignore the word throughout the document.

Click here to add the word to the selected custom dictionary.

Click here to insert the selected suggestion.

Suggested replacements

Click here to turn off the grammar checker when running the spelling checker.

Click here to insert the selected suggestion for all occurences.

❼ Choose **C**hange to replace *yeer* with *year*; then note that the spelling program has caught another error.

Tip

Double-clicking a selected suggestion enters the suggestion into your document in place of the selected document text.

❽ Correct the next two errors in the paragraph (insert the words *successful* and *all* in the appropriate locations).

After correcting the third error, the Spelling and Grammar dialog box displays the next error; however, this time, no alternatives are listed in the Sugg**e**stions box.

A quick look at the highlighted error indicates that a space needs to be inserted between the words *Each* and *sales*. When no suggestions are offered, you can manually correct the error in the Not in Dictionary box and then click **C**hange; or click in the actual document (or press Ctrl+Tab) to move in the document, fix the error, and then click the Re**s**ume button in the dialog box to continue the checking of spelling.

(continues)

Checking the Spelling in a Document (continued)

9 Click the pointer between the *h* and *s* in the highlighted *Eachsales* text string in the Not in Dictionary text box, and press Spacebar once to insert a space; then choose the **C**hange button to insert the change into the document.

10 Make the correction for the last misspelling in the first paragraph: Change the text string *ination* to *information*; then close the Spelling and Grammar dialog box without taking action on the next error.

11 Save the changes to the Sales 03 document; then leave it open for the next exercise.

Note

You can click the Cancel button or press Esc at any time to stop the spelling checker.

To undo your last spelling change, click the Undo button in the Spelling and Grammar dialog box. To undo a number of the last spelling changes, use the Undo button on the Standard toolbar.

When the Spelling and Grammar dialog box indicates a repeated word, the **C**hange button becomes the Delete button. To delete one occurrence of the word, simply click the **D**elete button.

If you have special needs when proofing your document, you can customize how the spelling and grammar programs work, by choosing the **O**ptions button in the Spelling and Grammar dialog box. Then select the options that meet your situation.

Use of the AutoCorrect button in the Spelling and Grammar dialog box was not discussed in this section; however, it will be discussed in the AutoCorrect section, later in this chapter.

Working with Custom Dictionaries

Word's primary dictionary is the main dictionary. You can choose a main dictionary in one of many languages.

Although the main dictionary includes thousands of words, including common names, it probably does not contain every word that you may want to use, particularly if you work with material that includes specialized terminology. To solve this problem, Word enables you to create as many custom dictionaries as you want. Then you can select one or more of your custom dictionaries (up to ten at one time) to use when running the spelling checker.

Creating custom dictionaries for different subjects is a good idea. If you frequently create documents about computers and also documents about finances, for example, you may want to create two custom dictionaries to handle the terms specific to each subject. (The greater the number of custom dictionaries used in the spell checking process, the longer it takes Word to browse through all the word lists.)

Although you will not be asked to create a custom dictionary in any of the exercises in this text, you still may want to create one on your own. Complete the following steps to create a new custom dictionary:

1. Choose **T**ools, **O**ptions; then click the Spelling & Grammar tab.

2. Choose the **D**ictionaries button to display the Custom Dictionaries dialog box.

3. Choose the **N**ew button.

4. In the File **n**ame box, enter the name for the new dictionary file; end the name with a .DIC extension. (By default, the new dictionary will be saved in the C:\Program Files\Common Files\Microsoft Shared\Proof folder, unless you specify another location to store the dictionary.)

5. Choose **S**ave.

6. Close the Custom Dictionaries dialog box by choosing OK.

7. Close the Options dialog box by choosing OK in the Spelling & Grammar tab.

Although you cannot add words to the main dictionary, you can add words to your custom dictionaries. The following steps show you how easy it is to add words to a custom dictionary:

1. Run the spelling checker until it stops on an unrecognized word that you want to add to a custom dictionary.

2. Choose the **O**ptions button in the Spelling and Grammar dialog box to display the Spelling & Grammar page of the Options dialog box.

3. Choose a dictionary from the Custom **d**ictionary list in the Spelling & Grammar page; then click OK to return to the Spelling and Grammar dialog box.

4. Choose the **A**dd button in the Spelling and Grammar dialog box to add the highlighted word to the selected custom dictionary.

To add one or more custom dictionaries to the list of dictionaries Word uses when it runs the spelling checker, complete the following steps:

1. Display the Spelling & Grammar page of the Options dialog box (either by choosing **T**ools, **O**ptions, or by choosing the **O**ptions button in the Spelling and Grammar dialog box).

2. Choose the **D**ictionaries button to display the Custom Dictionaries dialog box.

3. Choose the desired custom dictionaries (insert a mark in the check box listed in front of each desired dictionary).

4. Choose OK to close the Custom Dictionaries dialog box.

5. Choose OK to close the Spelling & Grammar page of the Options dialog box.

You can edit, remove, or add a word in custom dictionary by completing the following:

1. Select the dictionary from the Custom Dictionaries dialog box.

2. Choose the **E**dit button in the dialog box.

3. Examine the alphabetical list of words included in the chosen dictionary; then edit, remove, or add words as necessary.

4. Save the revised file in the Text Only format (be sure to maintain the original file name and location in the saving process).

5. Close the dictionary file.

Note

Word automatically creates a custom.dic file the first time you run a spelling check. You can add words to the custom.dic file or create and name a new "customized" dictionary.

Objective 3: Check Your Grammar

Word's grammar checker helps you identify sentences that have questionable style or grammatical structure; it also suggests corrections for many grammatical errors. The grammar checker can check the grammar in all or part of a document. To check only part of a document, select the text that you want to check before you start the grammar checker.

The grammar checker and spelling checker run simultaneously through the Spelling and Grammar dialog box. In the preceding exercise, you worked with the spelling checker; in the next exercise, you focus on the use of the grammar checker. Both checkers function in the same way. In your everyday use of Word, you'll learn to use both the spelling and grammar checker at the same time.

Using the Grammar Checker

Complete the following exercise to practice using the basic steps needed to work with Word's grammar checker:

❶ If the Sales 03 document is not already displayed in your Word window, open the file now. (The spelling errors in the first paragraph should have already been corrected in an earlier exercise in this chapter.)

❷ Place the insertion point at the top of the document; then click the Spelling and Grammar button on the Standard toolbar to display the Spelling and Grammar dialog box and select the first potential grammar error in the document (see Figure 3.7).

Figure 3.7
The Spelling
and Grammar
dialog box.

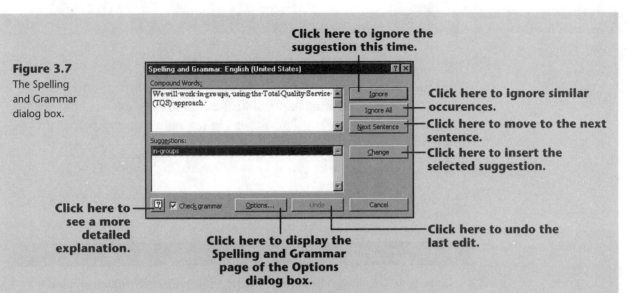

**Click here to ignore the
suggestion this time.**

**Click here to ignore similar
occurences.**

**Click here to move to the next
sentence.**

**Click here to insert the
selected suggestion.**

**Click here to
see a more
detailed
explanation.**

**Click here to display the
Spelling and Grammar
page of the Options
dialog box.**

**Click here to undo the
last edit.**

3 Choose the **I**gnore All button because this particular grammar rule does not affect your document.

The grammar checker then stops on the next questionable phrase. In this case, you want to accept the suggested change.

4 Read the information in the dialog box; then choose the **C**hange button to accept the *item for all sales personnel is* suggestion and insert it in place of the selected document text.

After accepting the change, the grammar checker then stops on the next questionable phrase.

5 Read the information in the dialog box, select the *a list* suggestion; then choose the **C**hange button to insert the suggestion. The next potential error then becomes selected.

6 Read the information in the dialog box; then change *knew* to *know*.

When you correct spelling and grammatical errors in a document, it is helpful to keep in mind the content of the document as you correct the errors. Traditionally, when checking for spelling and grammar errors, you would have to review your document twice—once for the spelling checker and once for the grammar checker. With Word's simultaneous spelling and grammar checking, you can focus on correcting both types of errors in just one pass of your document.

In step 6, you corrected a grammatical error. In the following step, without needing to load another program, Word takes you to the next error in the document—a spelling error.

(continues)

Using the Grammar Checker (continued)

7 Use the spelling program to change *Rom* to *Room*.

Word then displays a message that the spelling and grammar check is completed (or, if the Show **r**eadability statistics option is enabled on the Spelling & Grammar page of the Options dialog box, the Readability Statistics dialog box will be displayed). In either case, complete the next step.

8 Choose OK to close the box.

9 Save the revisions to your document; then leave the Sales 03 file open for the next exercise.

Note

As you have already seen, sometimes Word flags appropriately written phrases as potential grammar errors. This can slow down your proofing if you only need to check the spelling in the document. When using the Spelling and Grammar dialog box, you can turn off grammar checking by clearing the Chec**k** grammar check box located in the lower-left portion of the Spelling and Grammar dialog box.

Alternatively, you can choose **T**ools, **O**ptions, click the Spelling & Grammar tab, and then clear the Ch**e**ck grammar with spelling check box.

Personal Proofreading

At this point, you have used a spelling checker and a grammar checker to proof your document. However, what if you have entered an incorrectly spelled word in your custom dictionary? If a word with the incorrect spelling that is listed in your dictionary is also listed in your document, the spelling checker will not flag the word. What if you need to use slightly different grammar rules than the rules currently selected in the grammar checker?

Remember, automated programs can complement your proofing actions, but nothing can take the place of your final proofing of the document.

Completing the Final Editing

Although you used the spelling and grammar checker, you are not quite ready to save this document into its final form. Complete the following steps to learn of the errors the spelling and grammar checker missed.

1 In the open Sales 03 document, read the last sentence in the third paragraph to see whether the grammar checker may have missed an error.

You should be able to locate the *For example, if a customer wants a abundant amount...* phrase. Most people would rewrite the phrase.

② Change the phrase to read *wants an abundant....*

There is another error a few words later in the same sentence.

③ Delete the word *be* in the phrase *...is be difficult....*

④ Read the last sentence of the document and note that the word *contact* should be used in place of the word *context.* Make that change now.

⑤ Save the revisions to your document; then leave the file open for the next exercise.

The grammar checker enables you to choose one of five different writing styles to use during your grammar check. You may choose to use one writing style when writing for one particular audience and another writing style when writing for a different audience. Table 3.1 identifies each writing style and the rules applied for each style.

3

Table 3.1   The Grammar Checker Rule Groups

Writing Style	Rules Applied
Casual	Informal written communication rules are applied (the fewest number of rules).
Standard	Rules appropriate for written business communication.
Formal (all rules)	All grammar and style rules (except gender-specific words) are applied.
Technical	Rules for only technical communication are applied.
Custom	Rules that you design yourself are applied.

To change the rule group used by the grammar checker, perform the following steps:

1. Display the Spelling & Grammar page of the Options dialog box (by either choosing the **O**ptions button in the Spelling and Grammar dialog box, or choosing **T**ools, **O**ptions).

2. Choose the drop-down arrow at the end of the **W**riting style list box to display the list of rule groups.

3. Select the desired rule group.

4. Choose OK to close the Options dialog box and complete the change in rule groups.

To see the specific rules enforced in a rule group, follow these steps:

1. Display the Spelling & Grammar page of the Options dialog box.

2. Select the desired rule group.

3. Choose the Se**t**tings button to display the Grammar Settings dialog box.

4. Scroll through the list of rules to see which ones are enabled for that selected rule group.

Readability Statistics
Data analyzing how difficult a document is to read. The data includes word, character, paragraph, and sentence counts.

When you start checking grammar at a location other than the beginning of your document and you reach the end of the document, the grammar checker moves to the top of the document and continues the checking process.

Readability Statistics

Readability statistics can be used to determine how easy your writing is to read. (Most major newspapers are written at the eighth-grade level.) If you choose to display the readability statistics on one of your documents, you need to turn on the option in the Spelling & Grammar page of the Options dialog box. The statistics will then be displayed after the grammar is checked.

Displaying Readability Statistics

Complete the following exercise to display the readability statistics for the Sales 03 document.

1 If the Sales 03 document is not displayed in your Word window, open it now.

2 Choose **T**ools, **O**ptions to display the Options dialog box. If necessary, choose the Spelling & Grammar tab.

3 If the Show **r**eadability statistics check box is not already marked, choose the check box now to mark it.

4 Choose OK to close the Options dialog box.

5 Choose the Spelling and Grammar button.

Although there are probably no errors in your document, it may take a few moments for the Readability Statistics dialog box to be displayed (see Figure 3.8).

Figure 3.8
The Readability Statistics dialog box provides data about the reading level of the document.

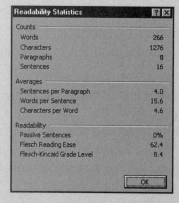

6 When you see the dialog box, the information in the Counts and Averages sections are self-explanatory. The following list defines the entries in the Readability section:

- *Passive Sentences* shows the percentage of sentences written in the passive, rather than active, voice.

- *Flesch Reading Ease* is based on the average number of words per sentence and the average number of syllables per 100 words. The higher the number, the easier the document is to read.

- *Flesch-Kincaid Grade Level* represents the educational grade level required for a reader to understand the sentence structure of the sentence.

7 Choose OK to close the dialog box; then leave the Sales 03 document open for the next exercise.

3

Objective 4: Use the Thesaurus

While you are creating or editing a document, you can use the thesaurus to find *synonyms*, *antonyms*, and related words for words that you use in your document.

Activating the Thesaurus

Synonyms
Words that have the same (or nearly the same) meanings as other words.

To use the thesaurus to find synonyms, antonyms, and related words, follow these steps:

1 Make sure that the Sales 03 document is displayed in your Word window.

The word *primary* is the second word in the second paragraph.

Antonyms
Words that mean the opposite (or nearly the opposite) of other words.

2 Click once on the word *primary* (it is not necessary to select the entire word); then choose **Tools**, **Language**, **Thesaurus** (or press ⬆Shift+F7).

Word selects the word and displays the Thesaurus dialog box (see Figure 3.9). The word *primary* is displayed in the Look**e**d Up text box. Meanings for the word appear in the **M**eanings list box, and synonyms appear in the Replace with **S**ynonym list box.

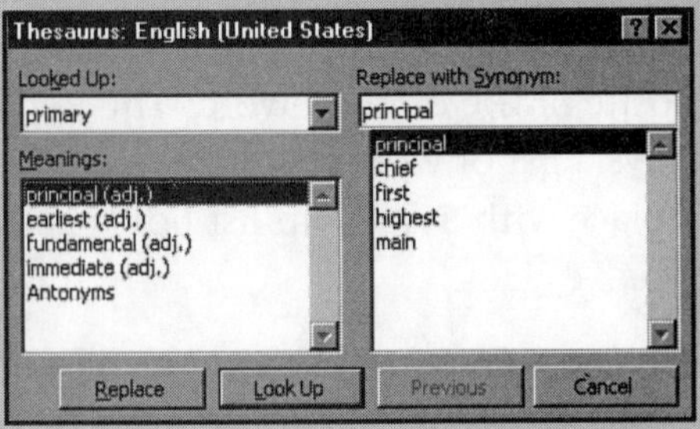

Figure 3.9
Word displays the selected word, a list of meanings, and a list of synonyms in the Thesaurus dialog box.

(continues)

3 Select *main* from the Replace with **S**ynonym list box; then choose **R**eplace to insert the word *main* in place of the selected word *primary* in your document. This will also close the Thesaurus dialog box.

4 Save your revisions to the Sales 03 document; then leave the file open for the next exercise.

Using Other Thesaurus Options

In the preceding exercise, you completed the standard steps for using the Thesaurus. However, the Thesaurus dialog box also includes options to:

- *Search for more possible synonyms by choosing a word in the Replace with **S**ynonym list box and then choosing the **L**ook Up button.* Word moves the word that you chose into the Loo**k**ed Up text box and displays the meanings and synonyms for the new word.

- *Search for even more synonyms by choosing a word in the **M**eanings list box.* Word displays a new list of synonyms in the Replace with **S**ynonym list box. If you choose a word in the Replace with **S**ynonym list box and then choose the **L**ook Up button, Word moves the word that you chose into the Loo**k**ed Up box and displays the meanings and synonyms for the new word.

> **Tip**
>
> Double-clicking a word in the **M**eanings or Replace with **S**ynonym list boxes inserts that word into the Loo**k**ed Up text box and refreshes the **M**eanings and Replace with **S**ynonym lists.

- *Display lists of antonyms or related words in the Thesaurus dialog box.* The entries Antonyms or Related Words may appear in the **M**eanings list box. If you choose either of these topics, the Replace with **S**ynonym list box changes to a Replace with **A**ntonym list box or a Replace with Related Word list box. The Replace with **A**ntonym list box displays a list of words that mean the opposite of the original word. The Replace with Related Word list box displays a list of words that are related to the original word. To return to the Replace with **S**ynonym list box, click any other word in the **M**eanings list box.

- *Type a word in the Replace with **S**ynonym text box.* When you click the **L**ook Up button, Word looks up the word that you typed. When you choose the **R**eplace button, Word replaces the selected word in the document with the word that you typed.

To cancel a Thesaurus operation and return to the document, click the Cancel button, click the Close button, or press (Esc).

> **Note**
>
> If Word cannot find a synonym for the word that you selected, the **M**eanings list box displays words that have similar spellings.

Objective 5: Use AutoCorrect to Prevent Mistakes

Most of us have fingers that don't always do what we want. People commonly type *adn* when they mean *and*, or *teh* rather than *the*. Word can detect and correct errors of this type automatically while you are typing, when the AutoCorrect feature is activated. In case you are wondering what to do if you really intend to type *adn* or *teh*, don't worry; you can turn off AutoCorrect by clearing the check box in front of the Replace **t**ext as you type option in the AutoCorrect dialog box.

When you install Word, AutoCorrect is initially enabled so that Word corrects certain spelling mistakes while you type. You can also use AutoCorrect to replace an abbreviation with its full phrase. For example, you can type *US* in your document and have AutoCorrect replace it with *United States*. As soon as you type **US** and press (Spacebar), *United States* is displayed in place of *US*.

After you type a string of characters and press the (Spacebar), (↵Enter), or a punctuation key, AutoCorrect checks the entered character string against its list of corrections to see whether the existing character string is to be replaced with a different character string.

Using AutoCorrect

To see how AutoCorrect automatically corrects a typo that already exists in the AutoCorrect list, follow these steps:

❶ If the Sales 03 file is not already open, open the file now.

❷ Choose **T**ools, **A**utoCorrect to display the AutoCorrect page of the Auto-Correct dialog box (see Figure 3.10).

(continues)

3

Using AutoCorrect (continued)

Figure 3.10
Use the AutoCorrect dialog box to specify several automatic corrections that Word can make as you type.

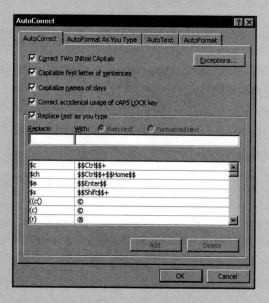

❸ Verify that all five check boxes at the top of the AutoCorrect page are checked. If any are not checked, select them now.

The lower half of the AutoCorrect page includes the Replace **t**ext as you type check box, the **R**eplace and **W**ith text boxes, and the list of the existing AutoCorrect entries. When typed into a document, the entry on the left side of the list will be replaced with the corresponding entry on the right side of the list after (Spacebar), (↵Enter), or a punctuation key is pressed on the keyboard.

❹ Use the vertical scroll bar to scroll through the list of existing AutoCorrect entries; then close the dialog box by choosing OK.

❺ Move the insertion point to the end of the document; then press (↵Enter) twice.

❻ Type **adn** and press (Spacebar).

Word should change *adn* to *And.* Pressing (Spacebar) activates AutoCorrect to recognize the three characters as an AutoCorrect list entry and then immediately correct the "mistake." In addition to correcting the spelling of *and,* the corrected word is capitalized because the Capitalize first letter of sentences option was turned on (see step 3 of this exercise).

❼ Open the AutoCorrect dialog box and scroll the list to find the *adn – and* entry; then close the dialog box.

❽ Leave the Sales 03 document open for the next exercise.

Editing the AutoCorrect List of Errors
At times, you may need to edit the paired entries in the AutoCorrect list. Complete the following exercise to practice modifying the entries in the AutoCorrect list.

Adding AutoCorrect Entries

To practice adding an entry to the AutoCorrect list, follow these steps:

1 With the Sales 03 file open in your Word window, open the AutoCorrect dialog box.

2 When you open the AutoCorrect page of the dialog box, the insertion point is placed in the **R**eplace text box. Enter **blnak** in the **R**eplace text box.

In this example, instead of typing *blank* you often type *blnak*, so you are adding an AutoCorrect entry to automatically have the character string *blnak* corrected to *blank* each time you enter it into a document.

3 Press Tab, or click in the **W**ith text box to move the insertion point; then type **blank** to indicate that *blank* is the AutoCorrect replacement whenever *blnak* is typed into one of your documents.

4 Click the Add button to insert your new entry into the list.

5 Choose OK to close the dialog box.

6 If necessary, move the insertion point just after the space following the word *And*—the last word in the Sales 03 document. Then type **blnak** and press Spacebar to see AutoCorrect in action.

Your "typo" should have been corrected.

Note

AutoCorrect entries affect only the character strings entered into a document after the AutoCorrect entry has been added to AutoCorrect corrections list. The AutoCorrect feature does not scan through existing text in an attempt to find existing text strings that need to be corrected.

Complete the next steps to see how you can use AutoCorrect to spell out an abbreviation.

7 Open the AutoCorrect dialog box.

8 In the **R**eplace text box, type the characters that you want to replace—for this example, type **TQS**.

You can type up to 31 characters and include spaces in the **R**eplace dialog box; however, the last character cannot be a space.

9 Press Tab to move to the **W**ith text box.

10 Type the replacement text—for this example, **Total Quality Service**.

Word allows you to use up to 255 characters in the **W**ith Text box. You can have spaces in the replacement text.

(continues)

Adding AutoCorrect Entries (continued)

⓫ Choose the Add button in the dialog box.

⓬ Choose OK to close the dialog box and put the changes into effect.

⓭ To confirm that this addition works properly in a document, move the insertion point past the space following the word *blank* at the end of the Sales 03 document; then type **TQS** (remember to use capital letters) and press Spacebar.

You should see the words *Total Quality Service* in place of *TQS*.

⓮ Leave the Sales 03 document open for the next exercise.

Although the following steps are not an exercise for you to complete, they do list an efficient way to add the corrections for your most common typos to the list of AutoCorrect corrections:

1. Type the first draft of your document.

2. Run the spelling checker through the Spelling and Grammar dialog box.

3. When the spelling checker stops on one of your common misspellings, select the correct word from the Suggestions list.

4. Choose the AutoCorrect button in the Spelling and Grammar dialog box to insert the typo and correct word as a paired entry in the AutoCorrect list of corrections. This step also makes the correction in your document.

5. Repeat steps 1–4 as needed.

Modifying and deleting AutoCorrect entries is also quite easy.

Editing and Deleting AutoCorrect Entries

To practice editing and deleting entries from the AutoCorrect list, follow these steps:

❶ With the Sales 03 document displayed in your Word window, open the AutoCorrect dialog box.

❷ Scroll to the *blnak – blank* entry and click on it once to select it.

The two words will be placed in the **R**eplace and **W**ith text boxes. This is the entry you will modify in the following steps.

❸ Change the word in the **W**ith box to your first name.

When you revise the entry in the **W**ith box, the **A**dd button in the lower-right portion of the AutoCorrect page changes to a Replace button.

❹ Choose the Replace button. When Word asks whether you want to redefine the selected entry, choose Yes; then choose OK to close the dialog box.

5 Move the insertion point to the end of the document, type **blnak** and press ⎡Spacebar⎤ to see your first name replace the *blnak* text string.

Now complete the following steps to remove an entry from the list.

6 Open the AutoCorrect dialog box and select the *blnak – your first name* entry again.

7 Choose Delete to remove the entry from the AutoCorrect list; then choose OK to close the dialog box.

8 Move the insertion point to the end of the document, enter **blnak**, and press ⎡Spacebar⎤ to see that the text string is flagged as an unrecognized word, but no AutoCorrect correction is made to the text.

9 Remove the *TQS – Total Quality Service* entry from the AutoCorrect list.

10 Close the Sales 03 file without saving your changes.

3

Chapter Summary

In this chapter, you learned how to use the Find, Replace, and Go To pages of the Find and Replace dialog box to move to specific locations in your document. You also learned that the Replace page enables you to find specified character strings and replace those characters with other characters. You also learned to use three document proofing tools: Word's spelling checker, grammar checker, and thesaurus. Finally, you learned how to use the AutoCorrect feature to immediately correct some of your common typing mistakes.

In Chapter 4, you learn how to format many of the characters in your document to enhance your document's appearance.

If you have completed your work for this computer session, make sure that you properly exit all open programs. Then use the Windows Sh**u**t Down command to safely exit Windows. If you want to continue, test your knowledge of the chapter's material by answering the questions in the Checking Your Skills section immediately following this summary. Then complete the exercises in the Applying Your Skills section at the end of the chapter.

Checking Your Skills

True/False

For each of the following, circle *T* or *F* to indicate whether the statement is true or false.

T F **1.** You can use the Find and Replace feature to find and replace one nonprinting character with another.

T F **2.** By default, the Word Find feature distinguishes between uppercase and lowercase letters when it searches a document.

(T) F **3.** The spelling checker checks individual words without regard to context.

T (F) **4.** The custom dictionary contains all the words in *Webster's* dictionary.

(T) F **5.** The grammar checker identifies sentences that have questionable style or grammatical structure.

(T) F **6.** When the spelling checker is active, it always checks the spelling in your document against the main dictionary.

T (F) **7.** If the spelling checker displays an unrecognized word with suggested changes, you should always click the Change All button.

(T) F **8.** The AutoCorrect feature can be set up to automatically capitalize the first letter in a sentence.

(T) F **9.** The Go To feature enables you to move to a specific line number in your document.

(T) F **10.** If you want, you can have up to ten custom dictionaries open when you use the spelling checker.

Multiple Choice

In the blank provided, write the letter of the correct answer for each of the following questions.

1. When using the Find page of the Find and Replace dialog box, choose the ___a___ option to find only those instances in which the capitalization matches the exact text that was entered in the Find what text box.

   a. Match case

   b. Control search

   c. Use wildcards

   d. Sounds like

   e. Find all word forms

2. When using the Find page of the Find and Replace dialog box, choose the ___c?___ option to enter part of the word you are searching for and a special symbol to represent the rest of the word.

   a. Match case

   b. Find whole words only

   c. Use wildcards

   d. Sounds like

   e. Find all word forms

3. If you choose the Sounds like option in the Find page of the Find and Replace dialog box, Word finds ___a___.

   a. *new* and *knew*

   b. *there* and *their*

   c. *can* and *could*

   d. *sew* and *so*

   e. a, b, and d

4. When using the spelling checker, to replace the highlighted word with the word that appears in the Suggestions list box, ___a___.

   a. choose the **Change** button

   b. choose the **Suggest** button

   c. choose the **Add** button

   d. choose the **Options** button

   e. choose the **Undo** button

5. When using the thesaurus, to replace one word with a word that is similar in meaning, click a word in the Replace with ___b___ list box.

    a. Meanings

    b. Synonym

    c. Related Word

    d. Antonym

    e. Looked up

6. A Word feature that locates a specific word or phrase within a document is ___c___.

    a. Search

    b. Locate

    c. Find

    d. Replace

    e. Look

7. The shortcut key combination for displaying the Go To page of the Find and Replace dialog box is ___a___.

    a. Ctrl+G

    b. Ctrl+F5

    c. Ctrl+F

    d. Ctrl+H

    e. Ctrl+Shift

8. As you type, when the word *teh* is automatically changed to *the*, and *adn* is changed to *and*, most likely, the ___c___ has been turned on.

    a. spelling checker

    b. grammar checker

    c. AutoCorrect feature

    d. Find and Replace feature

    e. Go To feature

9. You can do the following to the AutoCorrect list of entries. ___d___

    a. Add entries

    b. Modify entries

    c. Delete entries

    d. a, b, and c

    e. a and b, but not c

10. While creating or editing a document, you can use the thesaurus to find ___e___.

    a. synonyms

    b. antonyms

    c. related words

    d. homonyms

    e. a, b, and c

Fill in the Blank

In the blank provided, write the correct answer for each of the following questions.

1. When you use the Find feature, Word searches the entire document or the _first_ part of the document.

2. The _readability statistic_ dialog box displays the approximate grade level at which your document is written.

3. When using the Find feature, if you ask Word to find *here*, it also finds *hear* when you choose the _Sounds like_ option.

4. When you use the grammar checker, the _formal_ writing style contains the most grammar and style rules.

5. When you use the grammar checker, the _____Casual_____ rule group contains the least grammar and style rules.

6. To quickly move from one spelling or grammar error to the next, double-click the _____spelling_____ button on the status bar.

7. You can press _____Escape_____ at any time to stop the spelling checker.

8. When you create your own dictionary to be used in the spell checking process with Word's main dictionary, you are creating a _____custom_____ dictionary.

9. In the Thesaurus dialog box, the Replace with Antonym list box displays a list of words that mean the _____opposite_____ of the original word.

10. When the spelling checker stops on a double word entry, the **C**hange button changes to the _____ button.

Applying Your Skills

Review Exercises

Exercise 1: Using Find and the Spelling and Grammar Checkers

To use the Find feature and the spelling and grammar checkers, follow these steps:

1. Open the Chap0302 file from your Student Disk and immediately save the file back to your disk as **Business 03**.

2. Find all occurrences of *facility*. Add a line at the bottom of the document stating how many occurrences of *facility* you found in the document.

3. Run the spelling and grammar checkers and make any necessary corrections.

4. Save your revisions; then print and close the file.

Exercise 2: Using Find, Replace, and the Spelling and Grammar Checkers

To use Find, Replace, and the spelling and grammar checkers, follow these steps:

1. Open the Chap0303 file from your Student Disk and immediately save the file back to your disk as **Meeting 03**.

2. Replace all occurrences of *next month* with *February*.

3. Run the spelling and grammar checkers and make any necessary corrections. Then proofread one more time to catch the error(s) that the checking programs missed.

4. Save the revisions; then print and close the file.

Exercise 3: Using the Spelling and Grammar Checkers and the Thesaurus

To practice using the spelling and grammar checkers and the thesaurus, follow these steps:

1. Open the Chap0304 file from your Student Disk; then immediately save the file back to your disk as **Replace 03**.

2. Run the spelling and grammar checkers and make any necessary corrections. Proofread one more time to catch any remaining errors.

   3. Use the thesaurus to find and insert synonyms for *customer* and *appoint*.

   4. Save the revisions; then print and close the file.

Exercise 4: Using the Spelling and Grammar Checkers
To use the spelling and grammar checkers, follow these steps:

   1. Open the Chap0305 file from your Student Disk; then immediately save the file back to your disk as **Steps 03**.

   2. Add steps to the end of this document to explain how to use the Spelling and Grammar Checker dialog box to correct misspelled words and grammatical errors.

   3. Check the spelling and grammar in the document and make all necessary corrections.

   4. Save the revisions; then print and close the file.

Exercise 5: Using Find and Replace, and the Spelling and Grammar Checkers
To use Find, Replace, and the spelling and grammar checkers, follow these steps:

   1. Open the Chap0306 file from your Student Disk; then immediately save the file back to your disk as **Employee Guidelines 03**.

   2. Replace every occurrence of *employee* with *worker*.

   3. Run the spelling and grammar checkers and make any necessary corrections. Proofread one more time to catch any remaining errors.

   4. Save the revisions; then print and close the file.

Continuing Projects

Project 1: Practice Using Word
Practice using Word by following these steps:

   1. Open the Chap0307 file from your Student Disk; then immediately save the file back to your disk as **Planning 03**.

   2. Run the spelling and grammar checkers and make any necessary corrections. Proofread one more time to catch any remaining errors.

   3. Use the thesaurus to insert a synonym for the word *meet* in the first sentence under the *February 28* section of the document. Then insert another synonym for *meet* in the first sentence of the *March 6* section.

   4. Save your revisions; then print and close the file.

Project 2: Deli-Mart
Continue developing the Deli-Mart brochure by following these steps:

   1. Open the Chap0308 file from your Student Disk; then immediately save the file back to your disk as **Menu 03**.

   2. Use the thesaurus to insert synonyms for *bed* and *delight*.

   3. Run the spelling and grammar checkers and make any necessary corrections. Proofread one more time to catch any remaining errors.

   4. Save your revisions; then print and close the file.

Project 3: The Marketing Connection

Continue working with The Marketing Connection newsletter by following these steps:

1. Open the Chap0309 file from your Student Disk; then immediately save the file back to your disk as **Market 03**.

2. Run the spelling and grammar checkers and make any necessary corrections. Proofread one more time to catch any remaining errors.

3. Use the thesaurus to insert synonyms for *evaluate* and *guarantee*.

4. Use Find and Replace to find the word *contract* and replace it with *agreement*.

5. Save your revisions; then print and close the file.

6. Exit Word if you have completed your session at the computer.

Formatting Characters

4

Characters
Letters, numbers, punctuation marks, and symbols that appear in a document.

Font
A set of characters that have the same appearance (a typeface). Most typefaces are available in a variety of sizes and styles.

Word divides document formatting into three categories: *character* formatting, paragraph formatting, and page formatting. Each category enables you to affect the appearance of your document in many ways. This chapter covers character formatting.

In Word, you can affect the appearance of the document *characters* in many ways, including using bold type, italic, or underlining; changing the *font*, font style, font size, or font color; or using character effects (such as strikethrough, shadow, small caps, and so on). Along with changing the look of the standard keyboard characters, Word also enables you to insert characters into your document that do not appear on your keyboard.

Objectives

By the time you finish this chapter, you will have learned to

1. Bold, Italicize, and Underline Document Characters
2. Change Fonts, Font Sizes, Font Styles, and Effects
3. Copy Character Formatting
4. Insert Symbols and Special Characters

Note

To keep referencing simple, you will be instructed to save a file to your *Student Disk*. However, if you plan to complete all the assignments in this text, you will need a number of disks. Depending on the number of assignments you complete in the first three chapters, your first Student Disk may be too full to complete all the assignments in this chapter. Most likely, your instructor has already explained how to set up your student files to ensure that you have enough disk space to save an entire chapter's assignments on the same disk. However, if you try to save a file and see a message that there is not enough room left on your disk, don't hesitate to ask your instructor for help.

Objective 1: Bold, Italicize, and Underline Document Characters

Each time you open a new document, Word initially uses default settings for all aspects of character formatting. Up to this point, you have entered regular text (also referred to as *plain*, *normal*, or *roman*) into your documents. In this section, you learn to bold, italicize, and underline your existing characters. You also learn how to enable these formatting features and then add new (formatted) characters to your document.

> **Note**
>
> Some aspects of formatting are affected by the printer that you select to print your document. Before you begin formatting a document, make sure that the correct printer is selected. To do so, choose **F**ile, **P**rint to open the Print dialog box. The top portion of this dialog box states the name of the currently selected printer. If the correct name is displayed, click the Cancel button to close the dialog box. If the correct name is not displayed, refer to Chapter 7 for information about selecting a printer.

Boldfacing, Italicizing, and Underlining Characters

To practice applying bold, italics, and underline to characters, follow these steps:

❶ Start Word and open the Chap0401 file from your Student Disk; then immediately name the file **Sales 04** and save it back to your disk.

❷ Select the first sentence in the first paragraph (the one beginning with *Last year was...* by holding down Ctrl and clicking anywhere within the sentence.

The "Select, then Do" concept applies to formatting existing characters. In step 2, you selected the characters; in step 3 you complete the "Do" portion as you format the selected characters.

❸ Rest the pointer on the Bold button on the Formatting toolbar to see the corresponding ScreenTip; then click the Bold button to make the selected sentence bold.

In this exercise you will work with the Bold, Italic, and Underline buttons on the Formatting toolbar. Toolbar buttons are typically displayed in either the flat or pressed positions. If a button is in the flat position, the corresponding command is turned off. If the button is in the pressed position, the corresponding command is turned on. A flat toolbar button will appear in a raised position when you rest the pointer on it.

❹ In the second sentence of the first paragraph, click once on the word *challenge*.

When applying formatting to single words, you can either place the insertion point within the word or select the entire word and then apply the formatting.

5 Rest the pointer on the Italic button to see the ScreenTip; then choose the Italic button to place the word *challenge* in italic.

> ### Note
>
> After completing step 5, notice that the Formatting toolbar's Italic button is now pressed; however, the Bold button is not. The appearance of the buttons on the Formatting toolbar changes to correspond with the insertion point's position in the document.

6 Select the phrase *make this year our best year ever* at the end of the second sentence in the first paragraph. (Be careful that you don't select the period ending the sentence.)

7 Rest the pointer on the Underline button to see the ScreenTip; then choose the Underline button to underline the selection. Click in another document location to turn off the selection.

Your document should now look similar to the one in Figure 4.1

4

Figure 4.1
After selecting the desired text, you can quickly bold, italicize, or underline the text by using the buttons on the Formatting toolbar.

Italicized text

Bold text

Underlined text

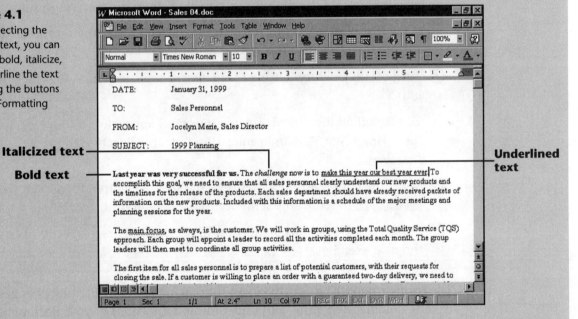

> ### Note
>
> When you use the Underline button on the Formatting toolbar to underline words in a selection, the spaces between the underline words are also underlined (see Figure 4.1). Later in this chapter you learn how to underline only the words in a selection.

You can apply a multitude of formatting combinations to the selected text.

(continues)

Boldfacing, Italicizing, and Underlining Characters (continued)

Tip

You can also bold, italicize, and underline selections using the keyboard shortcut keys. Press Ctrl+B to bold a selection. Press Ctrl+I to italicize a selection. Press Ctrl+U to underline a selection.

8 Select the italicized word *challenge* in the second sentence of the first paragraph by double-clicking it.

9 Display the italicized word in bold italics by choosing the Bold button.

You can choose the three buttons to change formatting individually or to apply combinations of formats. Note the Formatting toolbar, which displays the Bold and Italics buttons in the pressed position.

10 Select the first sentence in the first paragraph; then add underlining to it by choosing the Underline button.

You can turn off the bold, italic, or underlining format of selected characters by choosing the button(s) when they are in the pressed position.

11 If the first sentence is not still selected, select it now. Then turn off the underlining by choosing the Underline button.

12 Turn off the bold formatting of the first sentence by choosing the Bold button.

To turn off all the formatting in a selection, and return it to the default font (Times New Roman Regular 10-point, see Objective 2), press Ctrl+Spacebar.

13 Select the entire second sentence of the first paragraph; then press Ctrl+Spacebar to return the sentence to the default font.

14 Leave the Sales 04 document (now displaying only regular text) open for the next exercise.

The Formatting toolbar is convenient for making many formatting changes (including bolding, italicizing, and underlining) to portions of your document. However, the Font dialog box provides the most character formatting options. Continue with the next section to learn about the Font dialog box.

Objective 2: Change Fonts, Font Sizes, Font Styles, and Effects

This section introduces you to the use of the Font dialog box. This is one of the most powerful dialog boxes in Word because it can affect every character in your document.

In the first exercise, you learn to use the Font dialog box to format existing text.

Using Font Styles and Underlining Options

To practice using font styles and underlining options, follow these steps:

1 In the open Sales 04 document, select the entire second paragraph, the one beginning with *The main focus....*

2 Choose F**o**rmat, **F**ont to open the Font dialog box. If necessary, choose the Font tab to open the Font page of the dialog box (see Figure 4.2).

Tip

You also can open the Font dialog box by right-clicking anywhere in the text area of the screen and then choosing **F**ont in the shortcut menu. If you have already selected text, make sure to place the pointer within the selected text before you right-click or you will deselect the highlighted text.

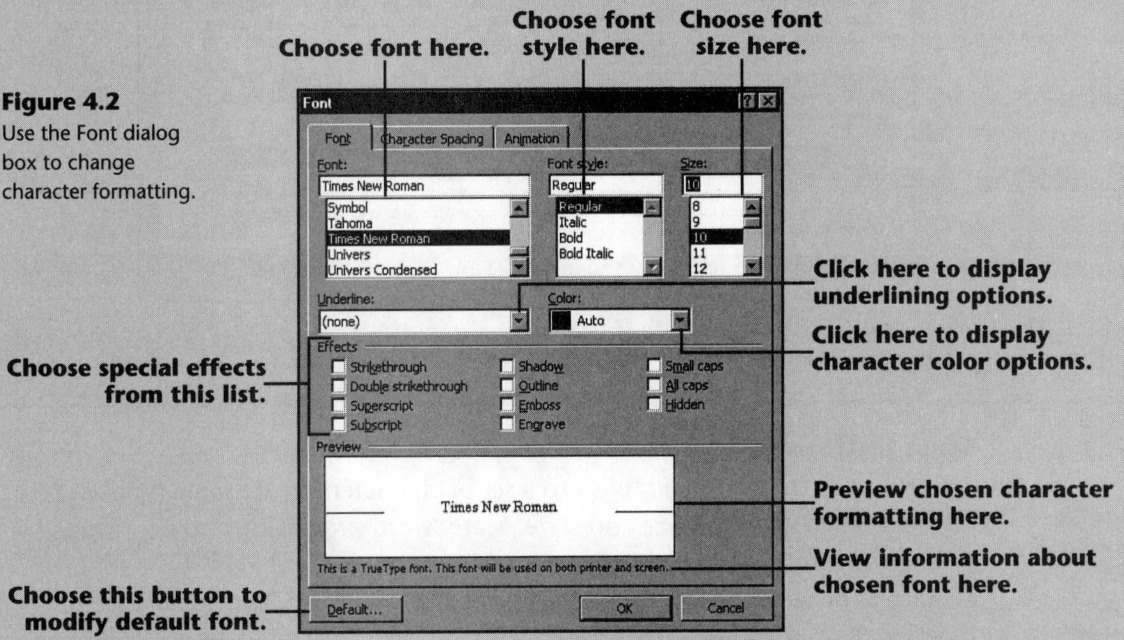

Figure 4.2
Use the Font dialog box to change character formatting.

Choose font here.

Choose font style here.

Choose font size here.

Click here to display underlining options.

Click here to display character color options.

Choose special effects from this list.

Preview chosen character formatting here.

View information about chosen font here.

Choose this button to modify default font.

3 Choose Bold Italic in the Font st**y**le box of the Font dialog box, noting the change in the Preview frame of the dialog box; then choose OK to format the selection in the Bold Italic font style and to close the dialog box. Click anywhere in the document to turn off the selection and view your formatting.

4 Select the first sentence of the third paragraph, the one beginning with *The first item...*; then open Fo**n**t page of the Font dialog box and click the drop-down arrow at the end of the **U**nderline list box.

5 When the list of underlining options is displayed, choose the Words only option, view the Preview frame to see the intended results, and then choose OK to format the selection and close the dialog box.

(continues)

Using Font Styles and Underlining Options (continued)

Your document should now look similar to the one in Figure 4.3. Notice that the spaces between the words are not underlined; however, the period at the end of the sentence is underlined. Because the default underline format was not used, the Underline button on the Formatting toolbar is not pressed.

Figure 4.3

Only the words in the selected sentence are underlined.

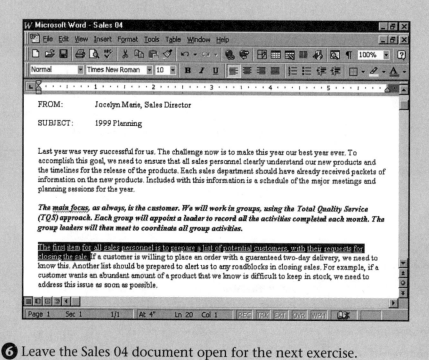

⑥ Leave the Sales 04 document open for the next exercise.

Changing Fonts, Font Sizes, and Effects

Point
A unit used to measure the size of typographic characters. One point is approximately 1/72 inch.

Traditionally, the word *font* refers to a set of characters of the same typeface, all of which have the same size and style. Many word processing and desktop publishing programs use the word font more broadly. In Word, a font is a set of characters of the same typeface, including all sizes and styles available for that typeface. Each font has a name, such as Times New Roman, Courier, or Symbol. To a traditional printer, Courier 12-point italic is a font. To Word, Courier is a font that contains characters in many sizes and in four font styles.

TrueType fonts
A type of font, included in Windows, Word, and many other software packages, where the same font-generating program used to create the font on the screen is used to create the font at the printer.

Windows (and, therefore, Word) supports fonts designed for various purposes. The TrueType fonts, supplied with Windows and Word, provide characters that appear on-screen almost exactly as they will appear when they are printed by laser printers, as well as by certain other types of printers. Because Word supports the WYSIWYG (what-you-see-is-what-you-get) screen display philosophy, the characters that you see on-screen very closely resemble the characters eventually printed on paper.

You probably also have access to some non-TrueType fonts. Some fonts, like the Roman and Script supplied with Windows, are designed for other purposes, such as use with a pen plotter. If you use a font that can be displayed on your screen but is not available to your printer, Windows instructs the printer to use an available font that most closely resembles the font displayed on your screen. However, when this happens, your printout may not look exactly like the document displayed in your Print Preview window. For this reason, many people prefer to use TrueType fonts, until they know exactly how their non-TrueType fonts will be printed.

As you work through the next few exercises, you will learn how Word identifies fonts as TrueType, printer, or screen fonts.

Scalable font
A font that can be enlarged or reduced to any size within a wide range without visual distortion.

TrueType fonts are scalable. In Word, you can specify font sizes ranging from 1 to 1,638 points in half-point increments (one point is equal to approximately 1/72 inch). This wide range of sizes is available if you are using most laser printers; it is more limited for other types of printers.

> **Note**
>
> Newspapers, magazines, and similar publications use 9-point to 12-point characters for most text, and 14-point or larger character sizes for headlines. You also can specify the space between lines in points.

In the following exercise, you learn to change the look of your characters by choosing from the various fonts, font sizes, colors, and effects that are available through the Font dialog box.

Working with Fonts, Font Sizes, and Effects

To practice working with fonts, font sizes, and effects, follow these steps:

1 In the open Sales 04 document, choose the first sentence in the last paragraph, the one beginning with *On February 23,....* Then open the Font dialog box by right-clicking on the selection to display the shortcut menu and choosing the Font command. Display the Font page if necessary.

> **Note**
>
> In step 1, if you held down Ctrl and clicked in the sentence, you may have been surprised when the entire sentence was not selected. This is because of the period at the end of *a.m.* in the first part of the sentence. In this case, because of the period in the first part of the sentence, Word actually views this sentence as two sentences.

Sometimes, to add emphasis to a statement, writers choose to format important information in a font or font size differently from the rest of the information in a document.

Note the sentence below the Preview box identifies the Times New Roman font as a TrueType font.

(continues)

4

Working with Fonts, Font Sizes, and Effects (continued)

❷ Change the font for the selected text by scrolling up through the list of fonts in the Font section and then selecting Arial. Note the change in the Preview box.

Arial is another TrueType font, as indicated in the sentence below the Preview box.

❸ Change the font size of the selected text by scrolling down through the options in the **S**ize list box and selecting 16. Again, note the change in the Preview box.

❹ Choose OK to format your selection in the new font and font size. When you return to the Word window, notice the change in the selected text and the changes in Font and Font Size boxes in the Formatting toolbar (see Figure 4.4).

Name of current font   Size of current font

Figure 4.4
The selected text is displayed in Arial Regular 16-point font.

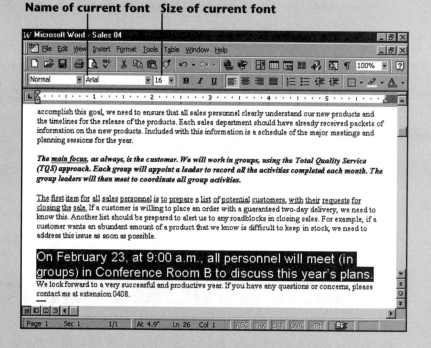

❺ Move the insertion point to the end of the document; then press ↵Enter twice.

So far, you have used the Formatting toolbar and the Fonts dialog box to change the formatting of existing characters in your document. If you want, you can set your character formatting first and then enter the characters into your document.

❻ Display the Font page of the Font dialog box; then change the font to Courier New and the font size to 18.

The Font dialog box provides many additional ways to enhance your text.

❼ In the Effects section, choose the **E**mboss check box (to mark it). View the change in the Preview frame; then choose OK.

> ### Note
>
> If you mark the wrong check box in the Effects section, choose the check box again to turn off the option. As you click in the various Effects check boxes, you'll see that some options can be used in combinations, whereas other options are mutually exclusive.

It looks as though nothing has happened because you did not have any text selected when you changed the character formatting.

8 Enter **This is the 18-point Courier New font with the Emboss effect.** Your new text should be displayed similarly to the text at the end of the document in Figure 4.5. Again, note the changes in the Formatting toolbar to reflect the changed font and font size at the insertion point.

Figure 4.5
The text at the bottom of the document shows the Emboss effect on text typed in the 18-point Courier New font.

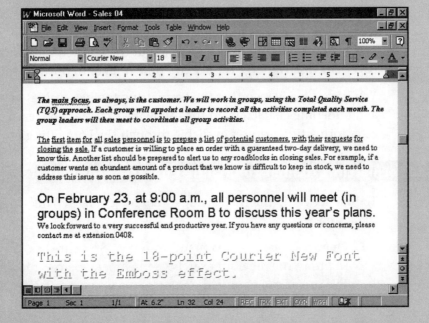

9 Make sure that the insertion point is at the end of the document; then press ⏎Enter twice.

10 Open the Fo**n**t page of the Font dialog box, make the necessary selections to change the font to the Century Schoolbook, Regular style, 18-point font. Then leave the Font dialog box open.

If you have problems... At any time throughout the use of this text, if the stated font, font size, or color is not available on your system, select a substitute that is available to you.

(continues)

Working with Fonts, Font Sizes, and Effects (continued)

11 Move to the Effects section and make only the Strikethrough and Small caps options active; then leave the Font dialog box open.

12 Change the color of the font to teal by clicking the arrow at the end of the **C**olor drop-down list box to display a list of available colors, and then clicking the teal color. View the proposed formatting in the Preview frame; then choose OK to return to your document.

13 Type **This is the Century Schoolbook, Regular style, 18-point font displayed in a teal color, with the Strikethrough and Small caps effects.** to see how your characters will be formatted.

14 Close the Sales 04 document without saving the changes. Leave the Word window open for the next exercise.

The advantage of using the Fo**nt** page of the Font dialog box to make character formatting changes is that most character formatting options, a Preview of the selected changes, and information about the selected font are all included in the page. The disadvantage is the extra time it takes to open the dialog box.

You have already seen that the Formatting toolbar enables you to bold, italicize, and underline characters. In the following exercise, you learn of additional character formatting features available through the Formatting toolbar.

Using the Formatting Toolbar to Change Character Formats

To practice using the Formatting toolbar to change character formats, follow these steps:

1 Open the Sales 04 document from your Student Disk. (If you are continuing from the previous exercise, remember, you can most likely open the **F**ile menu and choose the Sales 04 document from the list of recently opened documents.)

2 Select the first sentence of the first paragraph, the one beginning with *Last year was...*; then click the arrow at the end of the Font box on the Formatting toolbar to display the same list of available fonts you viewed in the Fonts dialog box.

The drop-down Font list has two sections. At the top of the Font list, you see the names of the fonts you have used most recently. A double underline follows these fonts, and then the names of all the fonts available on your computer are listed in alphabetical order. The double-T symbol to the left of some font names indicates that these fonts are TrueType fonts (see Figure 4.6).

Figure 4.6
The Font drop-down list box shows fonts available on your computer.

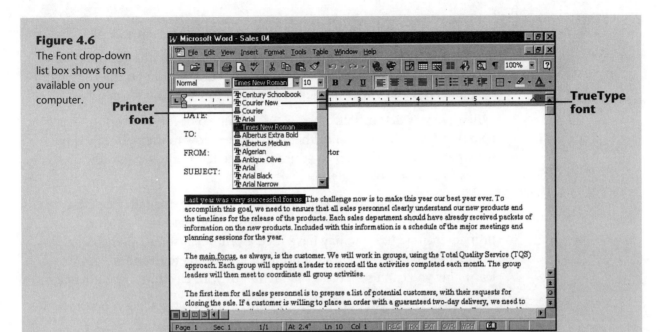

Printer font

TrueType font

Tip

If you want to select a font with a name that starts with a letter toward the end of the alphabet, type the first letter of the font's name. The Font list immediately scrolls to the first font name that starts with that letter. This technique can be much faster than scrolling through the entire list of names.

---

❸ If available, choose the Braggadocio font (if this font is not available, choose another one).

When you choose the new font, your selection is automatically updated. If you choose a font from this list, when no characters are selected, the chosen font is applied at the insertion point. The characters that you enter at this point appear in the chosen font.

❹ With the sentence still selected from the previous steps, change the size of the font for the first sentence to 16 by choosing 16 from the Font Size drop-down list. Again note the immediate update after selecting the new font size.

Tip

If you don't see the desired point size in the Font Size drop-down list, you can type the desired size (for example, 17.5) directly into the Font Size box and then press ⏎Enter.

(continues)

Using the Formatting Toolbar to Change Character Formats (continued)

5 With the sentence still selected from the previous steps, change the color of the selected text to red by choosing the Font color button on the Formatting toolbar. Then click outside the selection to view your formatting.

When Word is first installed, red is the default color for this button. If the color has been changed, click the drop-down arrow to the right of the button; then choose the red box—third from the left in the second row of colors—from the color palette.

As you look at your screen, you probably notice how the red characters stand out in your document. Similarly, when you have worked with printed documents, you may have used a yellow (or some other color) highlighter to mark important information. Complete the next steps to learn how you can use Word's highlighter in your electronic documents.

6 Choose the Highlight button on the Formatting toolbar to turn on the highlighter.

The Highlight button is now displayed in the pressed position. As you move the pointer into the work area, it changes to include the picture of a highlighter pen.

Tip

When a feature is activated that changes the shape of the pointer, you can still use the vertical and horizontal scroll bars in the normal manner.

7 Drag the pointer across the first sentence in the last paragraph, the one beginning with *On February 23...*, and then release the mouse button.

Tip

When the highlighter is active, you can use the same shortcuts for highlighting text as you used to select text.

The text you dragged across is highlighted, not selected, and the Highlight pointer remains active. At this point, you can continue to highlight any other pertinent section in your document. However, in this case, you are ready to deactivate the Highlight pointer.

Tip

Many e-mail users use Word to create their e-mail messages. Depending on the e-mail system in use, all character formatting features, including the use of color and highlighting, can enhance e-mail messages sent to others.

8 Choose the Highlight button in the Formatting toolbar to turn off the highlighter. Your document should now appear similar (except for the red and yellow colors) to the one in Figure 4.7.

Tip

If you prefer, you can use the highlighter by first selecting the characters to be highlighted and then clicking the Highlight button.

To change the color of the highlighting, click the button's drop-down arrow to display a palette of highlighting color choices; then click the desired color.

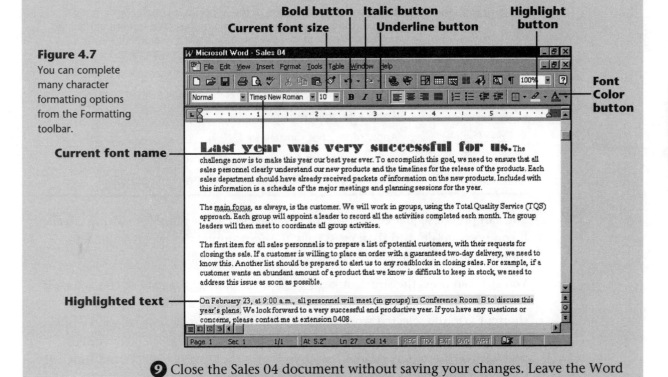

Figure 4.7
You can complete many character formatting options from the Formatting toolbar.

Current font name

Highlighted text

9 Close the Sales 04 document without saving your changes. Leave the Word window open for the next exercise.

The exercises you just completed focused on making character formatting changes through the use of the mouse. You can also use the keyboard to make many of these changes. Many, but not all, of the character shortcut keys work like toggle switches. This means that the first time you press the shortcut key combination the selected characters are changed; however, pressing the same key combination again changes the characters back to their original appearance. Table 4.1 lists the most commonly used character formatting shortcut key combinations.

Table 4.1 Character Formatting Shortcut Keys

Press these keys	To
Ctrl+B	Bold
Ctrl+I	Italic
Ctrl+U	Single underline (words and the spaces between them)
Ctrl+Spacebar	Restores the default character formatting
Ctrl+◆Shift+W	Word underline (underlines the words but not the spaces between them)
Ctrl+◆Shift+D	Double underline (words and the spaces between them)
Ctrl+◆Shift+A	Display in All caps
Ctrl+◆Shift+K	Display in Small caps
Ctrl+◆Shift+H	Hides selected characters (If the nonprinting characters are displayed, the hidden characters remain on-screen but are underlined with a dotted underline. If the nonprinting characters are not displayed, the hidden text is removed from the screen.)
Ctrl+[	Decrease the font size by 1 point
Ctrl+]	Increase the font size by 1 point
Ctrl+=	Apply subscript formatting
Ctrl+◆Shift++	Apply superscript formatting
Ctrl+◆Shift+F	Activates the Font text box in the Formatting toolbar
Ctrl+◆Shift+P	Activates the Font Size text box in the Formatting toolbar

You can press a sequence of shortcut keys to add two or more formatting effects. If you press Ctrl+B and then press Ctrl+I, for example, the selected characters (or the characters you type next) appear in bold and italic.

You also can press the shortcut key ◆Shift+F3 to change the case of characters. If you start with a selection of all lowercase letters, the first time you press the shortcut key, the selected words appear with only the first letters of each word capitalized. The second time you press the shortcut key, the selected words appear with all characters capitalized. If you press the shortcut key a third time, all the characters revert to their original lowercase state.

If you start with words initially entered in all uppercase letters, pressing the shortcut key once switches all uppercase to all lowercase. Pressing the shortcut key again sets only the first character of the selected text to uppercase; pressing it a third time makes all characters uppercase.

Note

Word also uses two automatic features to help you control the errant appearance of capital letters in your document. When activated, the Correct TWo INitial CApitals command in the AutoCorrect dialog box automatically corrects a word if it starts with two capital letters, instead of one—for example, *THis* is automatically changed to *This* when the command is activated.

Also found in the AutoCorrect dialog box is the Correct accidental use of the cAPS **L**OCK key command. When this command is activated, accidental use of the Caps Lock key—such as *cAPS LOCK* instead of *Caps Lock*—is automatically corrected.

Character Spacing

Fonts can be divided into two broad categories: *monospaced* (or nonproportional) fonts and *proportional* fonts. When you use monospaced fonts (like Courier New), each character takes up the same amount of space across the page.

When using proportional fonts (like Times New Roman), the amount of space a character occupies varies from character to character. To give the document a professional appearance, certain letters, such as *i*, occupy noticeably less space than others. TrueType font files (and some other types of font files) include information about character spacing. Word can use this information to optimize character spacing. The apparent excessive space between certain pairs of characters is more obvious for larger font sizes. By default, Word applies automatic *kerning* (the adjusting of the space between characters) for characters 10 points or larger. You can change the minimum font size at which Word applies kerning and work with other character spacing options through the Character Spacing page of the Fonts dialog box.

Working with the Default Font

Each time you open a new document and start typing, Word uses a preselected font, font size, and type style. Collectively, these elements are called the *default font*.

When you installed Word on your computer, the default font probably was Times New Roman, the default font size probably was 10 point, and the default style probably was Regular. If you are satisfied with the font, size, and style that you normally use, you will want to keep those settings. But if you normally use the Arial font and prefer a 12-point font size, you can easily change the default values to meet your needs. Then you don't have to change the font every time you start a new document.

Caution

The following steps are provided to explain how to change the default font; however, if you are working in a computer lab or sharing a computer with another worker, it is recommended that you do not change the default font settings unless all computer users are in agreement.

To change the default font:

1. Display the Font page of the Font dialog box.
2. Enter the desired settings.
3. Choose the **D**efault button to display a message box asking whether you want to change the default font to the settings you entered in step 2.
4. Choose **Y**es to confirm your action.

After you change the default font, your new blank documents will use the new default font settings.

Objective 3: Copy Character Formatting

So far, you have learned to add and remove individual character formatting options through the use of the Formatting toolbar and the Font page of the Font dialog box. You have learned that you can remove all character formatting from a selection by pressing Ctrl+Spacebar.

Sometimes, though, instead of removing character formatting, you want to copy the character formatting (not the characters) from one portion of your document to another. The following exercise shows you how to quickly accomplish this task through the use of the Word Format Painter.

Using the Format Painter

To practice using the Format Painter, follow these steps:

❶ Open the Sales 04 document from your Student Disk.

❷ Place the first sentence of the third paragraph, the one beginning with *The first item...* in the Bookman Old Style Regular 18-point font, with the Double strikethrough effect. Then keep the newly formatted sentence selected for the next step.

 ❸ Choose the Format Painter button on the Standard toolbar.

When you move the pointer into the work area, it changes to the Format Painter pointer (a small paintbrush attached to the I-beam).

❹ Drag the pointer over the phrase *Total Quality Service (TQS)* in the second sentence of the second paragraph; then release the mouse button.

The affected text changes to the new format, the Format Painter button returns to its flat (not active) position, and the pointer returns to its normal shape. Your document should look similar to the one in Figure 4.8.

❺ Place the first sentence of the first paragraph, the one beginning with *Last year was...* in italics.

 When you want to copy a format to several blocks of text, you can keep the Format Painter active by double-clicking the button on the Standard toolbar.

❻ Double-click the Format Painter.

❼ Drag the Format Painter pointer across the first sentence in the second paragraph, the one beginning with *The main focus...*; then release the mouse button.

Figure 4.8
Part of the document has been painted with the character format from another part of the document.

The "painted" characters

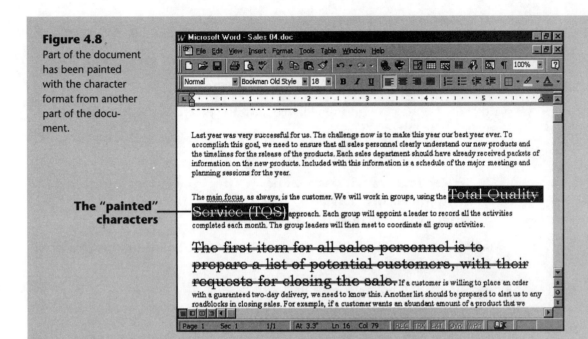

When the mouse button is released, the format of the affected text is changed; however, the Format Painter pointer remains on-screen, and the Format Painter button remains pressed on the Standard toolbar.

8 Hold down the Ctrl key, place the Format Painter pointer in the second sentence of the second paragraph (the one already containing some new formatting from earlier steps in this exercise), and click the left mouse button to paint the entire sentence.

The entire sentence is now formatted in the Times New Roman Italic 10-point font: the previous character formatting was removed when the new format was painted onto the characters. Now turn off the Format Painter.

9 Choose the Format Painter button (or press Esc) to turn off the Format Painter.

10 Close the Sales 04 document without saving the changes. Leave the Word window open for the next exercise.

Objective 4: Insert Symbols and Special Characters

Eventually, you may need to add a character into your document that is not on your keyboard. Characters like ©, ®, ™, and ☺ are already entered in the default AutoCorrect list of entries; these symbols are easy to add, after you know the pairing of the keystrokes to the symbols. In the following exercise, you learn to enter some of the symbols in the AutoCorrect list into your document.

The Symbol dialog box provides access to hundreds of symbols that are not in the default AutoCorrect list. The following exercise also shows you how to insert characters through the Symbol dialog box.

Inserting Symbols and Special Characters

To practice inserting symbols and special characters, follow these steps:

1 Open the Sales 04 document from your Student Disk.

2 Move the insertion point immediately past the period at the end of the second paragraph.

In steps 3–5 you enter the following sentence:

> **Group leaders will receive new office computers (equipped with Microsoft® Office 97 and the new Microsoft IntelliMouse®) to expedite this process.**

Make sure to complete each of the three steps to learn how to insert the two symbols in the sentence.

3 Press the Spacebar once and type all the characters through the *t* in Microsoft.

Because the AutoCorrect list already includes an entry for the ® symbol, open the AutoCorrect dialog box and review the symbol paired entries located at the top of the list; then close the dialog box and return to your document.

4 Type **(r)** and watch Word automatically change (r) to the ® immediately after the word *Microsoft*; then press Spacebar once and continue typing until you have entered the last *e* in *IntelliMouse*.

5 Open the AutoCorrect dialog box and look up the characters you need to enter to display the ™ symbol; then close the dialog box. Enter the appropriate characters to display the ™ symbol immediately after IntelliMouse; close the parenthetical phrase by typing the **)** and then complete the rest of the sentence.

Your document should now look similar to the one in Figure 4.9.

6 Save the change to your Sales 04 document; then leave the document open for the next steps.

Tip

The default AutoCorrect list includes the entry of pressing the key combination of *(c)* to display © (copyright) symbol. But what if you are trying to start a line with *(c)* as part of a list? Enter **keep the insertion point immediately to the right of the © symbol when it appears; then press** ⬅Backspace **to change the © symbol back to (c)**. If this technique does not work for you, you may need to temporarily turn off the **R**eplace text as you type option in the AutoCorrect dialog box.

7 Move to the end of the Sales 04 document; then press ↵Enter twice.

You can use the pages of the Symbol dialog box to insert symbols or special characters that are not yet included in your AutoCorrect list.

Figure 4.9
The new sentence contains characters not found on the keyboard.

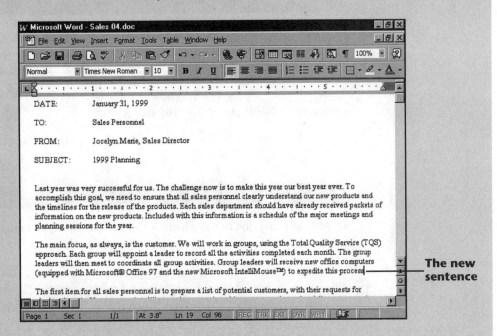

Figure 4.9
The new sentence contains characters not found on the keyboard.

The new sentence

4

❽ Choose **I**nsert, **S**ymbol to open the Symbol dialog box. If necessary, choose the **S**ymbols tab (see Figure 4.10).

Figure 4.10
The Symbol dialog box.

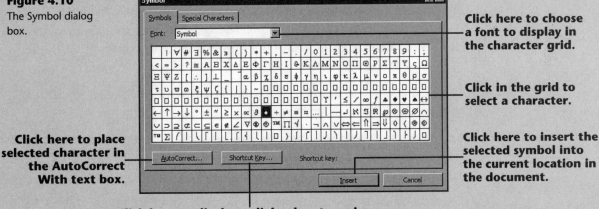

Click here to choose a font to display in the character grid.

Click in the grid to select a character.

Click here to place selected character in the AutoCorrect With text box.

Click here to insert the selected symbol into the current location in the document.

Click here to display a dialog box to assign a keyboard shortcut key for displaying the symbol.

❾ Click the arrow at the end of the **F**ont drop-down list box; then choose the Wingdings font to display those characters in the character grid. Next, view some of the characters from other listed fonts. Finally, redisplay the Symbol font characters.

(continues)

Inserting Symbols and Special Characters (continued)

Tip

To see a magnified view of a symbol, just click on it once. After an item is magnified, you may use the arrow keys to move the "magnifier" to other available symbols.

10 Locate the ♣, ♦, ♥, and ♠ symbols near the right end of the fifth row of characters. Select the ♣ by clicking it once.

11 Insert the ♣ into your document by choosing the **In**sert button. Then close the dialog box and view your results.

Tip

After inserting one or more items into your document, you may also be able to close the Symbol dialog box by pressing (Spacebar).

12 Press (Spacebar) once; then insert the ♦ by opening the Symbol dialog box and double-clicking the ♦ symbol. Close the dialog box to view your results. Then insert the ♥ and ♠ symbols. (Make sure to place a space between each symbol you insert.)

13 Press (Spacebar) once; then open the Symbol dialog box and display the S**pe**cial Characters page.

The S**p**ecial Characters page contains a number of special characters along with the key combinations to be pressed to display the special character. Note especially the entries for the © and ®. You will insert both of these characters in the following steps.

14 Choose the entry to display the ® (registered) symbol; then choose **In**sert to place the entry in your document.

15 Close the dialog box and press the (Spacebar) once. With the insertion point at the end of your document, press (Ctrl)+(Alt)+(C) to display the © symbol at the insertion point.

16 Close the Sales 04 document without saving your changes.

To create an AutoCorrect entry for a specific symbol, just select the symbol, choose the **A**utoCorrect button in the Symbol dialog box to display the AutoCorrect dialog box, enter your desired character string for the symbol in the **R**eplace box, and choose **A**dd. To create a shortcut key combination for a selected symbol, choose the Shortcut **K**ey combination and complete the necessary entries in the Custom Keyboard dialog box.

Chapter Summary

You made a number of formatting changes to the characters in the Sales 04 document. However, you did not save most of the changes because the exercises in this chapter were primarily designed to only show you different ways of formatting characters. Although changing the format of a few key portions of text draws attention to those sections, too many formats may confuse the reader. A document including too many formats may actually distract the reader from concentrating on the document's message.

At this point, you should be fairly comfortable working with the character formatting options provided through the Formatting toolbar and the Font page of the Font dialog box.

In Chapter 5, you work with margins, tabs, indents, line and paragraph spacing control, and many other features associated with paragraph formatting.

If you have completed your work for this computer session, make sure that you properly exit all open programs. Then use the Windows Shut Down command to safely exit Windows. If you want to continue, test your knowledge of the chapter's material by answering the questions in the Checking Your Skills section immediately following this summary. Then complete the exercises in the Applying Your Skills section at the end of the chapter.

Checking Your Skills

True/False

For each of the following, circle *T* or *F* to indicate whether the statement is true or false.

T   F   **1.** As used in Word, a font is a set of characters with the same typeface, including all sizes and styles available for that typeface.

T   F   **2.** The ActiveType fonts supplied with Windows and Word provide characters that appear on-screen differently from the way that the fonts will print.

T   F   **3.** TrueType fonts are scalable, which means that you can display and print each font in a wide range of sizes with minimal, or no, distortion.

T   F   **4.** You can press a sequence of shortcut keys to add two or more styles or effects to the selected characters.

T   F   **5.** The default font is the preselected font each time you open a new document and start typing.

T   F   **6.** You can copy the formatting of characters without copying the characters themselves.

T   F   **7.** You can insert special characters from the Symbol dialog box or from the keyboard.

T   F   **8.** Pressing Ctrl+Spacebar increases the font size by 1 point.

T   F   **9.** If you press Ctrl+U when no character is selected, the next character you enter from the keyboard will be underlined.

T   F   **10.** When you select three consecutive words and then click the Underline button, only the words are underlined, not the spaces between the words.

Multiple Choice

In the blank provided, write the letter of the correct answer for each of the following questions.

1. Which type of character formatting is usually not added to selected text through choosing a button on the Formatting toolbar? _____

  a. Bold

  b. Strikethrough

  c. Italic

  d. Subscript

  e. Both b and d

2. To change the font for a word in the document, you must _____.

  a. place the insertion point before the first letter of the word and then select the font

  b. select the entire word, and then select the font

  c. select the desired font and then select the text

  d. select the desired font and click the word once

  e. place the insertion point at the end of the word and select the font

3. Which of the following cannot be selected from the Formatting toolbar? _____

  a. Font

  b. Font Size

  c. Font Color

  d. Display all letters in lowercase

  e. All of the above can be selected from the Formatting toolbar.

4. The shortcut key combination for underlining only the words (not the spaces) in a selection is _____.

  a. Ctrl+U

  b. Ctrl+Shift+U

  c. Shift+U

  d. Ctrl+Shift+W

  e. None of the above

5. To copy the formatting of characters without copying the characters themselves, use the _____ button.

  a. Format Selection

  b. Format Painter

  c. Format Toolbar

  d. Copy

  e. Drawing

6. Word divides formatting into which three categories? _____

  a. Character, paragraph, and sentence formatting

  b. Character, sentence, and page formatting

  c. Sentence, page, and paragraph formatting

  d. Character, paragraph, and page formatting

  e. Word, paragraph, and page formatting

7. When viewing the Font dialog box, the terms Regular, Bold, Italic, and Bold Italic are considered to be _____.

 a. Standard toolbar

 b. fonts

 c. font styles

 d. effects

 e. special characters

8. To insert a character from the Symbols page of the Symbol dialog box into your document, _____.

 a. select the symbol; then choose Insert

 b. drag the symbol from the dialog box into the document

 c. double-click the desired symbol

 d. a and c

 e. a, b, and c

9. To boldface a word, you can _____.

 a. select the text and then choose the Bold button

 b. click in the word, and then choose the Bold button

 c. select the word and press Ctrl+B

 d. click in the word and press Ctrl+B

 e. all of the above

10. Probably the fastest way to increase the font size of selected text by one point is to _____.

 a. choose the next larger size from the drop-down Font Size list in Formatting toolbar

 b. choose the next larger size from the Size list in the Font dialog box

 c. click the Zoom button

 d. press Ctrl+[

 e. press Ctrl+]

Fill in the Blank

In the blank provided, write the correct answer for each of the following questions.

1. _____ fonts use the same program to generate the font displayed on the screen and at the printer.

2. The _____ dialog box is the most important dialog box to use when formatting characters.

3. The _____ enables you to "paint" a character format from one part of the document onto the characters in another part of the document.

4. Press _____ to remove all character formatting and display the selected characters in the default font.

5. One way to remove bold, italic, or underline formatting from selected text is to choose the B, I, or U buttons on the _____ toolbar.

6. The AutoCorrect list of entries can include words, phrases, and _____ to be displayed in the document when the appropriate shortcut keys are pressed.

7. Although the Font dialog box provides the greatest number of options, using the Formatting toolbar or the _____ usually is faster than using the dialog box.

8. The Format Painter button is located on the _____ toolbar.

9. One way to turn off the Format Painter is to press the _____ key.

10. If you press Ctrl+⬆Shift+F, the current _____ name is highlighted in the Formatting toolbar.

Applying Your Skills

Review Exercises

Exercise 1: Applying Font Styles

To review the process of applying formats before you type the text, open a new document and then follow these steps:

1. Start with a blank Word document and type the title **Font and Font Sizes** in a 12-point Times New Roman font, bold and underline the title, and press ⏎Enter twice.

2. Create the following document. Apply the necessary formatting changes before you enter each line of text.

This is 10-point Times New Roman.

This is bold, 10-point Times New Roman.

This is italic, 10-point Times New Roman.

```
This is 12-point Courier New.
This is bold, 12-point Courier New.
This is italic, 12-point Courier New.
```

This is 14-point Arial.

This is bold, 14-point Arial.

This is italic, 14-point Arial.

3. Save the file to your Student Disk as **Fonts and Font Sizes**, print the file, and then close it.

Exercise 2: Learning about Animation

Use your character formatting knowledge and Word Help to learn how to add animation to your character formatting.

1. Open the Animation page of the Font dialog box and review the page content.

2. Use the Help button to learn about the various features available on this page.

3. Use the Office Assistant, or the Help Contents or Help Index pages, to display additional information on the animation feature.

4. On a blank document enter your first and last name in the Courier New, Regular, 14-point font and assign the Marching Black Ants animated effect to your name.

5. Save the file to your Student Disk as **MBA Name**, print the file, and then close it.

Exercise 3: Changing Fonts in the Planning Document
To practice changing fonts, follow these steps:

1. Open the Chap0402 file from your Student Disk; then immediately save the file as **Planning 04** back to your disk.

2. Select the first date (February 28).

3. Change the font to Times New Roman, Bold, 14-point.

4. Repeat steps 2 and 3 for the *March 6* and *April 8* date headings. (Hint: Use the Format Painter.)

5. Save your revisions; then print and close the file.

Exercise 4: Changing Font Sizes and Copying Formatting
To check your skills in changing font sizes and copying formatting, follow these steps:

1. Open the Chap0403 file from your Student Disk; then immediately save the file as **Employee Guidelines 04** back to your disk.

2. Change the font size for the heading to 16 points and the font size for item 1 to 14 points.

3. Copy the font size 14 format to the last item.

4. Change the font for the entire document to Arial.

5. Save your revisions; then print and close the file.

Exercise 5: Applying Font Styles and Sizes
To review what you have learned about changing fonts and font sizes, follow these steps:

1. Open the Chap0404 file from your Student Disk; then immediately save the file back to your disk as **Steps 04**.

2. Add general steps for changing fonts and font sizes, and then format these steps in the Arial 12-point font.

3. Place the insertion point at the end of the last step you entered in the previous step and make sure that no text is selected. Press Ctrl+Spacebar to change back to the default font and then press ↵Enter twice.

4. Explain at least one method you can use to apply bold, italic, and underlining.

5. When you type the words bold, italic, and underlining, actually format each of these words with the corresponding attribute.

6. Save the revisions; then print and close the file.

Continuing Projects
Project 1: Practice in Using Word
To practice using character formatting, follow these steps:

1. Open the Chap0405 file from your Student Disk; then save the file back to your disk as **Meeting 04**.

2. In the top part of the memo, bold *DATE:*, *TO:*, *FROM:*, and *SUBJECT:*.

3. In one procedure, change all the characters in the last sentence to uppercase.

4. Save the revisions; then print and close the file.

Project 2: Deli-Mart

Continue your work on the catalog for Deli-Mart by following these steps:

1. Open the Chap0406 file from your Student Disk; then save the file back to your disk as **Menu 04**.

2. Select the first item name; then change the font size to 13 points and the font style to bold.

3. Copy the format of the first item name to all the menu item names.

4. Select the first item description; then change the font size to 11 points and the font style to italic.

5. Copy the format of the first item description to all the menu item descriptions.

6. Save the revisions; then print and close the file.

Project 3: The Marketing Connection

Continue your work on the newsletter for Marketing Connection by following these steps:

1. Open the Chap0407 file from your Student Disk; then save the file back to your disk as **Market 04**.

2. Change the font for the headings (The Marketing Connection and Public Relations Group) to 16-point Arial.

3. Underline *complete restructuring* and *minor modifications* in the second paragraph.

4. Boldface *40 percent*, *50 percent*, and *60 percent* in the third paragraph.

5. Place *millions* (the fourth word in the first sentence) in italics. Then copy the italicized format from *millions* to the words *for-profit* and *not-for-profit* in the third paragraph.

6. Save the revisions; then print and close the file.

CHAPTER 5

Formatting Lines and Paragraphs

In Chapter 4, you learned how to enhance the appearance of text by using character formatting. In this chapter, you learn to work with a variety of procedures for formatting paragraphs, including aligning paragraphs, setting tabs, indenting paragraphs, changing the spacing between lines and paragraphs, controlling hyphenation options, and creating bulleted and numbered lists.

Objectives

By the time you finish this chapter, you will have learned to

1. Align Paragraphs
2. Set Tabs
3. Indent Paragraphs
4. Control Line Spacing
5. Control Line Breaks
6. Create Bulleted and Numbered Lists

Note

As you learn to adjust the look of your paragraphs, you may also want to know how to change your page margins. (Changing your margins typically affects the width of all the paragraphs in your document.) Word considers the changing of margins to be a page formatting function. Therefore, setting margins is covered in the next chapter. If you can't wait that long, take a look at Objective 1, "Set Margins," in Chapter 6.

Objective 1: Align Paragraphs

The word *paragraph* has a more specific meaning in Word than it does in ordinary usage. Word defines a paragraph as any amount of text or graphics followed by a paragraph mark (¶). (The paragraph mark appears on-screen if you have chosen to display nonprinting characters.) You can also create a blank paragraph—typically shown as a blank line that contains only a paragraph mark.

You can format a paragraph before you begin typing, or you can format an existing paragraph. To format existing paragraphs, you must first select the desired paragraphs. However, if you are formatting just one paragraph, you need only to place the insertion point within that paragraph. After you enter paragraph formatting commands, they apply to the current, or all selected, paragraphs. Word stores all paragraph formatting in the paragraph mark at the end of each paragraph.

When you reach the end of a formatted paragraph and press ⏎Enter, you carry the formatting from that paragraph into the new paragraph. If you delete a paragraph mark, you delete all the paragraph formatting information that it contains.

By default, paragraphs in Word documents are aligned against the left margin. However, you can also align your paragraph contents to the right margin, center paragraphs, or justify the paragraph content to stretch between the left and right margins. You may use the Formatting toolbar, the keyboard, or the Paragraph dialog box to set paragraph alignment.

As you will see as you work through the exercises in this chapter, the Formatting toolbar and keyboard give you quick access to paragraph formatting commands. However, the Paragraph dialog box includes the most paragraph formatting options, and it also provides a Preview frame so that you can see how your selected options will look before you invoke the commands.

Using the Formatting Toolbar to Set Paragraph Alignment

To use the Formatting toolbar to align paragraphs, follow these steps:

❶ Start Word; then open the Chap0501 file from your Student Disk. Then immediately save the file back to your disk as **Memory and Storage**.

This is a file you will use to practice several paragraph formatting techniques. The first formatting change to be made is to complete character and paragraph formatting of the title line.

❷ Display the nonprinting characters; then select the entire *Memory and Storage* title line, including the paragraph symbol. Bold the title and change the font size to 12 points. Leave the title line selected for the next step.

You will now center the title line. (Remember, although it's just one line, the title line ends with a ¶, so Word treats the title line as a paragraph.)

 ❸ Look at the four paragraph alignment buttons on the Formatting toolbar.

Obviously, a paragraph can only be displayed in one type of alignment at a time. Because the title line paragraph is in the default alignment, the Align Left button is pressed, while, respectively, the Center, Align Right, and Justify buttons are in the flat position.

4 With the title still selected, choose the Center button on the Formatting toolbar; then press the ⟨End⟩ key to move the insertion point to the end of the title line and deselect the text.

If you are not careful, when you change the alignment for one paragraph, you may be surprised at the alignment of subsequent new paragraphs you enter.

5 Press ⟨⏎Enter⟩ once and note the location of the ¶ on the new line.

Because you are still using the Center paragraph alignment, the blank paragraph you just created will center any characters entered into it.

6 On the newly created line below the title, type your first and last name. Note that your name is centered across the page and that the format from the title line was carried down through your name.

 7 Left-align this new line (paragraph) by choosing the Align Left button on the Formatting toolbar.

8 Delete the characters in your name, but keep the blank line in place to separate the title from the rest of the document.

9 Select the next section heading (*MEMORY*); then press ⟨⬆Shift⟩+⟨F3⟩ until only the first *M* in memory is displayed as a capital letter (this is called *title case*).

10 Bold, center, and change the section title font size to 11 points. Finally, insert a blank line below the section heading.

> ## Note
>
> When you complete your formatting of the various titles, don't worry if you see a black mark in the left margin on a document or section title line. Similarly, if you see a new entry in the first box (the Style box) on the Formatting toolbar that reads *Title*, *Heading*, and so on, simply ignore that information for the present time. Some of Word's automated formatting features dealing with "styles" may be activated. You'll learn more about styles later in the text.

11 Select the next section heading (*STORAGE*) and format it the same way you formatted the *Memory* heading. Make sure to insert one blank line below the *Storage* heading.

(continues)

5

Using the Formatting Toolbar to Set Paragraph Alignment (continued)

⓬ Select the next section heading (*SIZES OF COMMON ITEMS PLACED IN FILES*), bold the selection and modify the characters to read **Sizes of Common Items Placed in Files**. (If you use the Shift+F3 method, you still may have to do a little additional editing.)

This is one of the times you want to see more of your document than you can view through the Normal Word window.

⓭ Place the insertion point at the top of the document; then choose **V**iew, F**u**ll Screen to display the Full Screen view of your document. Your screen should look similar to the one in Figure 5.1.

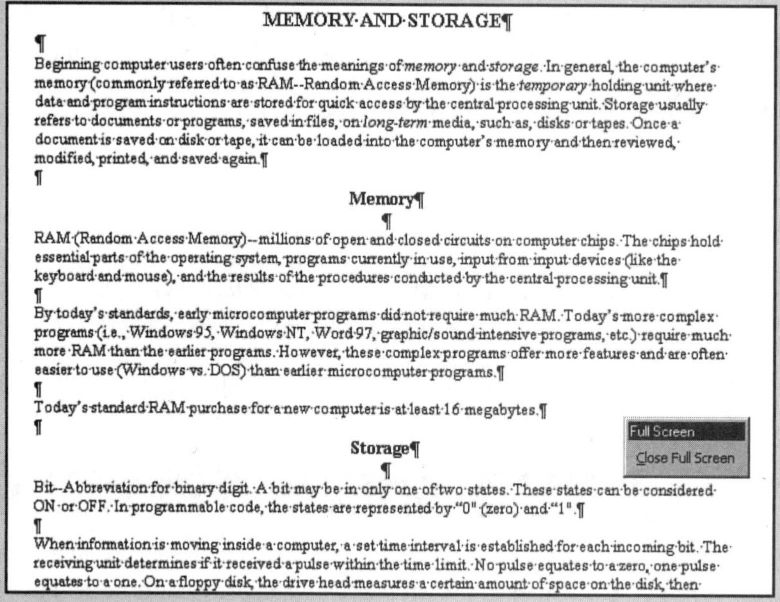

MEMORY AND STORAGE¶

¶

Beginning computer users often confuse the meanings of *memory* and *storage*. In general, the computer's memory (commonly referred to as RAM--Random Access Memory) is the *temporary* holding unit where data and program instructions are stored for quick access by the central processing unit. Storage usually refers to documents or programs, saved in files, on *long-term* media, such as, disks or tapes. Once a document is saved on disk or tape, it can be loaded into the computer's memory and then reviewed, modified, printed, and saved again.¶

¶

Memory¶

¶

RAM (Random Access Memory)--millions of open and closed circuits on computer chips. The chips hold essential parts of the operating system, programs currently in use, input from input devices (like the keyboard and mouse), and the results of the procedures conducted by the central processing unit.¶

¶

By today's standards, early microcomputer programs did not require much RAM. Today's more complex programs (i.e., Windows 95, Windows NT, Word 97, graphic/sound intensive programs, etc.) require much more RAM than the earlier programs. However, these complex programs offer more features and are often easier to use (Windows vs. DOS) than earlier microcomputer programs.¶

¶

Today's standard RAM purchase for a new computer is at least 16 megabytes.¶

¶

Storage¶

¶

Bit--Abbreviation for binary digit. A bit may be in only one of two states. These states can be considered ON or OFF. In programmable code, the states are represented by "0" (zero) and "1".¶

¶

When information is moving inside a computer, a set time interval is established for each incoming bit. The receiving unit determines if it received a pulse within the time limit. No pulse equates to a zero, one pulse equates to a one. On a floppy disk, the drive head measures a certain amount of space on the disk, then

Figure 5.1
Full Screen view of the beginning of the Memory and Storage document.

⓮ Review your document; if necessary, drag the Full Screen box to another screen location. Then return to the Normal view by choosing the **C**lose Full Screen command in the Full Screen box (or press Esc).

⓯ In the open Memory and Storage document, place the insertion point anywhere within the first paragraph below the title, the one beginning with *Beginning computer users....*

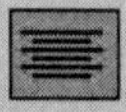

⓰ Center each line in the paragraph by choosing the Center button on the Formatting toolbar.

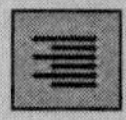

⓱ Place the insertion point in the first paragraph under the *Memory* heading, the one beginning with *RAM (Random Access Memory)...*; then right-align each line in the paragraph by choosing the Align Right button.

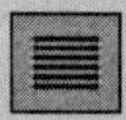

⓲ Place the insertion point in the second paragraph under the *Memory* heading, the one beginning with *By today's standards...*; then justify the paragraph lines by choosing the Justify button.

Note

When a paragraph is justified, spacing is entered into the lines to stretch each line's characters to the margins. However, in most cases, the last line of the paragraph does not include enough characters to fill the space between margins. When this happens, the last line is actually displayed in the Align Left format.

19 Place the insertion point at the top of your document; then choose **V**iew, F**u**ll Screen to display your document in Full Screen view. Your document should now look similar to the one in Figure 5.2.

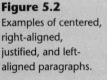

Figure 5.2
Examples of centered, right-aligned, justified, and left-aligned paragraphs.

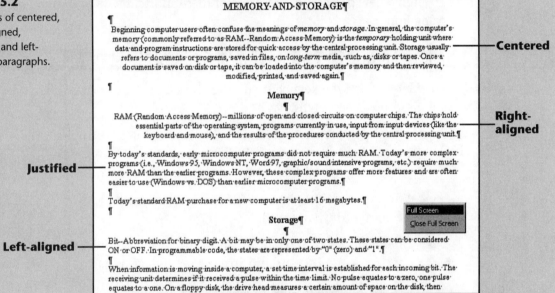

The first paragraph of text is center-aligned: each line is centered on the page so that both margins are ragged. The second paragraph of text is right-aligned: all lines end at the right margin, and the left margin is ragged. The third paragraph of text is justified: Word automatically adjusts the space between words so that all lines, except the last, start and end at the margins. The remaining paragraphs of text are left-aligned: all lines start at the left margin, and the right margin is ragged.

20 Choose the Close Full Screen command; then save the changes to the Memory and Storage file. Keep the file open for the next exercise.

When the insertion point is in a single paragraph, or when a single paragraph is selected, the toolbar alignment button indicates that paragraph's alignment by displaying a lighter shade of gray as if the button had been pressed. If two or more paragraphs having different alignments are selected, all four alignment buttons will appear in the flat position and will be a darker shade of gray.

Using the Keyboard to Set Paragraph Alignment

You can change paragraph alignment from the keyboard. Place the insertion point in the desired paragraph or select one or more paragraphs; then press one of the following key combinations:

Key Combination	Alignment
Ctrl+L	Left
Ctrl+E	Center
Ctrl+R	Right
Ctrl+J	Justify

To align a new paragraph, press one of these shortcut keys and then type the paragraph.

Using the Keyboard and the Paragraph Dialog Box to Set Paragraph Alignment

To practice using the keyboard and the Paragraph dialog box to align paragraphs, follow these steps:

❶ In the open Memory and Storage document, place the insertion point in the (centered) first paragraph that begins *Beginning computer users...*; then press Ctrl+R to right align the lines in the paragraph.

❷ With the insertion point still in the first paragraph, press Ctrl+J to justify the lines in the paragraph.

❸ Choose Format, Paragraph to display the Paragraph dialog box (see Figure 5.3; choose the Indents and Spacing tab if necessary).

Figure 5.3
The Alignment drop-down list box in the upper-left corner of the Indents and Spacing page shows the current alignment.

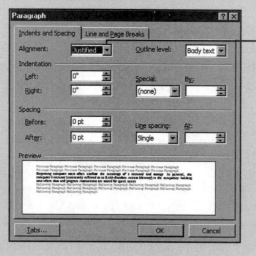

Click here to display a list of paragraph alignment options.

❹ Click the arrow at the end of the Alignment drop-down list box, choose Left, and then choose OK.

The dialog box closes, and the paragraph is left-aligned.

❺ Use the Formatting toolbar, keyboard, or Paragraph dialog box to return all the multiple-line paragraphs to left-alignment. Leave the document and section titles in their current format.

❻ Save the changes to the Memory and Storage document; then close it. Keep the Word window open for the next exercise.

Objective 2: Set Tabs

One way to place items at specific locations across a line is to use tabs. Setting tab stops, versus repeated presses of the Spacebar, can help ensure that your content will be displayed in the desired manner. Many experienced word processor users believe that if you have to press the Spacebar more than twice, you should set a tab stop to ensure that the characters in your document will be properly aligned.

Word has two types of tabs: default tabs and custom tabs. Although Word does not display default tab positions in the horizontal ruler, default tabs are set at half-inch intervals whenever you start a new document, and these tabs apply to every paragraph in a document. Default tabs are always left-aligned. When you press Tab and then type, the text that you type starts at the tab position and flows toward the right margin.

Custom tabs are tabs that you actually place in the document. A custom tab is applied to the paragraphs selected when you create the tab. If you are working in a paragraph that includes a custom tab and you press ↵Enter to create a new paragraph, the new paragraph will also contain the custom tab. You can place custom tabs wherever you want, but Word deletes all default tabs to the left of a custom tab. Five custom tab styles are available to you: left, centered, right, decimal, and bar.

Tab Alignment	Description
Left	Text starts at the tab position.
Center	Text is centered on the tab position.
Right	Text ends at the tab position.
Decimal	Decimal points (periods) align at the tab position.
Bar	A vertical line is inserted at the tab position.

The positions of the tabs you set (your custom tabs) are displayed in the horizontal ruler, with different symbols indicating each type of alignment (see Figure 5.4).

Notice that the "zero mark" of the ruler—in the default window, the location where the First Line Indent, the Hanging Indent, and Left Indent markers are positioned—starts at the left margin. The white space on the ruler indicates the amount of space between the left and right margins. The Right Indent marker is usually located on the right margin marker, although it can be moved inside or outside of the margin marker. The space between the right margin and the edge of the paper is represented by the dark gray shading at the right end of the ruler. (Depending on your display setting, you may need to use the horizontal scroll bar to view the right end of the ruler.)

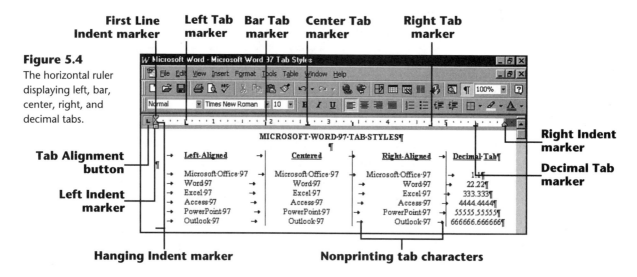

Figure 5.4
The horizontal ruler displaying left, bar, center, right, and decimal tabs.

You can fill the space at the left of a custom tab stop with dots, dashes, or underscore characters (these are known as *leaders* or *leader characters*). Leaders are commonly found in items like a table of contents for a book.

You can set and delete custom tabs and change tab alignment by using the Tabs dialog box or the horizontal ruler and the mouse.

Note

Microsoft Word is a full-featured program. Many times, Word "guesses" what you are trying to do, and then uses an automated feature to format your document. Occasionally, these automated features may actually slow you down or confuse you. Word makes available a Tab as Indent editing option that, when active, may replace a tab character that you insert from the keyboard, with a paragraph indent command. To give you maximum control while you learn to format paragraphs, it is recommended that you turn off this option.

Turn off the Tab as Indent option by choosing **T**ools, **O**ptions; clicking the Edit tab; clearing the Tabs and backspace set left **i**ndent option; and then choosing OK. After you are comfortable working with tabs and indents, you may want to reactivate this option.

Using the Tabs Dialog Box to Set Tabs

In this exercise, you create the tab table displayed in Figure 5.4. Most text is displayed in the Times New Roman Regular 10-point font. The title and columns headings are bolded.

1 Open a new blank document in your Word window; display the nonprinting characters; and then, using the default font, type

MICROSOFT WORD 97 TAB STYLES. Center and bold the title, deselect the text, press ⏎Enter twice, and then left align the current line.

❷ Choose Fo**r**mat, **T**abs to display the Tabs dialog box (see Figure 5.5).

Figure 5.5
Use the Tabs dialog box to set or clear tab settings and to choose leader characters.

At this point, you will set the tab positions for the headings. Note that although the title of the last heading is Decimal Tab, the heading itself consists of text. Therefore, when setting the tab for this heading, a center tab (not a decimal tab) will be used.

❸ Enter **.5** in the **T**ab stop position box, verify that the Left Alignment option is selected (change to **L**eft if necessary), verify that the **1** None Leader option is selected (change to **1** None if necessary), and then choose the **S**et button.

This sets a left tab one-half inch inside the left margin. Note the 0.5" has been entered into the list box below the **T**ab stop position text box. Now you are ready to enter the remaining tabs.

❹ Enter **1.9** for the **T**ab stop position, choose the **B**ar option, and then choose **S**et to insert a bar tab at 1.9" inside the left margin.

Tip

Remember, when you set your own custom tabs, you remove all the default tabs (set for every half-inch) to the left of your custom tab.

---

❺ Set a Center tab at the 2.63" mark.

❻ Set a Bar tab at the 3.4" mark.

❼ Set a Right tab at the 4.75" mark.

❽ Set a Bar tab at the 5" mark.

❾ Set a Center tab at the 5.5" mark.

❿ Choose OK to complete the tab insertion process and close the Tabs dialog box.

(continues)

Using the Tabs Dialog Box to Set Tabs (continued)

Note the tab markers on the horizontal ruler and the bar tabs already inserted on the current document line. You are now ready to enter the headings. The insertion point should still be two lines below the title, and the bold formatting feature should still be active.

> **Note**
>
> If the horizontal ruler is not displayed on your screen, choose **V**iew, **R**uler to display the ruler.

11 Press Tab⇆, enter **Left-Aligned** and then press Tab⇆ once; enter **Centered** and press Tab⇆ once; enter **Right-Aligned** and press Tab⇆ once; enter **Decimal Tab**, turn off the Bold button, and then press ⏎Enter twice.

12 Select the line with the column headings; then press ⬆Shift+Ctrl+W to underline only the words in the column headings line.

13 Save the document to your Student Disk as **Microsoft Word 97 Tab Styles**; then keep the document open for the next exercise.

You have now entered the tab stops and column headings for your table. Notice that the tab settings were inserted also into the new paragraphs (currently, just blank lines) when you pressed ⏎Enter twice after creating the Decimal Tab heading. In the next exercise, you will change an existing tab setting by using the options in the Tabs dialog box.

Changing Tab Settings in the Tabs Dialog Box

To use the Tabs dialog box to alter a tab setting, do these steps:

1 In the open Microsoft Word 97 Tab Styles document, right-click the mouse on the second blank line below the column headings to place the insertion point at that location and open the shortcut menu.

2 Choose **P**aragraph to open the Paragraph dialog box; then choose the **T**abs button to open the Tabs dialog box. (There are numerous ways to open the Tabs dialog box.)

3 In the **T**ab stop list position list box, select the 5.5" listing and note that the **C**enter Alignment option is selected. Change this alignment to **D**ecimal; then choose **S**et to reset the tab and choose OK to return to the document.

Note the slight change in the tab marker at the 5.5" mark on the ruler.

You just reset a tab. You can use a similar technique to clear a tab: Open the Tabs dialog box, select the tab you want to remove, choose the Cl**ear** button, and then choose OK.

4 Press (Tab⁵) once and enter **Microsoft Office 97** under the Left Aligned column heading. Press (Tab⁵) once and enter **Microsoft Office 97** under the Centered column heading. Press (Tab⁵) once and enter **Microsoft Office 97** under the Right Aligned heading. Press (Tab⁵) once and enter **1.1** under the Decimal Tab heading. Press (↵Enter) once to move the insertion point to the next line.

5 Repeat step 4 entering **Word 97** in the first three columns and **22.22** in the Decimal Tab column. Press (↵Enter) once.

6 Repeat step 4 entering **Excel 97** in the first three columns and **333.333** in the Decimal Tab column. Press (↵Enter) once.

7 Repeat step 4 entering **Access 97** in the first three columns and **4444.4444** in the Decimal Tab column. Press (↵Enter) once.

8 Repeat step 4 entering **PowerPoint 97** in the first three columns and **55555.55555** in the Decimal Tab column. Press (↵Enter) once.

9 Repeat step 4 entering **Outlook 97** in the first three columns and **666666.666666** in the Decimal Tab column. Keep the insertion point at the end of this line.

10 Save your file. Then keep it open for the next exercise.

The Tab dialog box provides the greatest amount of control for setting tabs. However, many users are willing to give up a little control to use the faster technique of setting left, center, right, and decimal tabs from the ruler.

Using the Mouse and Ruler to Set, Move, and Remove Tabs

To see how you can use the mouse and the ruler to set, move, and remove tabs, follow these steps:

1 With the insertion point at the end of your table from the previous exercise, press (↵Enter) twice.

Note that the tab markers from the previous one-line paragraphs are still displayed on the ruler. You could remove the marks by opening the Tabs dialog box and choosing the Clear **A**ll command, but in this exercise you use the mouse and the ruler to clear the tab settings.

2 To remove the first tab marker, place the tip of the pointer on the Left Tab marker at the .5" location on the ruler, drag the marker into the document, and then release the mouse button.

The tab marker should have been removed from the window.

3 Use this technique to remove all the tab marks on the ruler.

When you complete this step, the ruler should be clear of tab marks. This reactivates the default tabs at every half-inch across the page.

(continues)

Using the Mouse and Ruler to Set, Move, and Remove Tabs (continued)

4 Use the mouse to place the insertion point in the middle of the table and note how the tab markers are still active in that part of the document.

5 Use the up and down arrow keys to move the insertion point throughout the lines of your document and note the changes in the tab markers on the ruler to correspond with the current location of the insertion point.

6 Move to the end of your document (there should be no custom tabs set at this location) and make sure that the Tab Alignment button is displaying the Left Tab symbol (refer to Figure 5.4). Then move the tip of the pointer just below the 1.5-inch tick mark on the ruler and click the mouse button to insert a left tab at that location.

7 Press [Tab] once; then type **Word 97**. Click the Tab Alignment button once to change the symbol to a center tab and click just below the 2.5" mark on the ruler.

> ### Note
>
> Each time you click the Tab Alignment button, the symbol changes, rotating through left, center, right, and decimal alignment tab markers.

8 Press [Tab] once to move to the newly inserted center tab and type **PowerPoint 97**. Then click the Tab Alignment button once to change the symbol to a right tab and click just below the 5.5" mark on the ruler.

9 Press [Tab] once and type **Excel 97**.

In this case, the spacing between the entries does not look attractive, so you will use the mouse and ruler to move the tab stops to create a more attractive layout. Typically, when you display items spaced across a line, you try to balance the amount of white space between the entries.

10 With your insertion point still in the last line, drag the Left Tab marker to the 1" mark on the ruler. As you drag, notice the dotted line that extends into the document window—this is a guide to show you exactly where the tab will be when you release the mouse button. Release the mouse button and note that the first entry moves back on the line. Then, drag the Right Tab marker to the 4" mark to move the Excel 97 entry closer to the other entries.

The spacing between the items has improved. Now use this technique to impact some of the lines in the body of the first table you created.

11 Select the *Word 97*, *Excel 97*, and *Access 97* lines of the table at the top of your document.

In the following steps, you adjust only part of your table. Sometimes working with only a few lines of a table can result in distorting your columns and making the table hard to read. (Don't worry; you won't save these changes.)

⑫ Remove all the bar tabs in the selected text by dragging the Bar Tab markers off the ruler.

⑬ Drag the Center and the Right Tab markers one inch to the left.

⑭ Move your insertion point below your table to turn off the selection and view your results. Your document may look similar to Figure 5.6.

Figure 5.6
Selecting only part of a table and then moving tabs can make your table difficult to read.

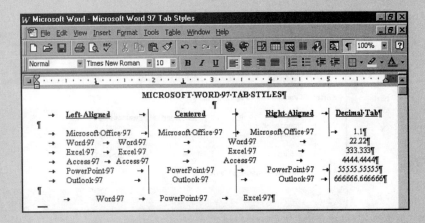

⑮ Close your document, without saving the changes. Keep your Word window open for the next exercise.

When using tabs and creating a table of entries, some Word users prefer to enter all the information for the table first, and then set tabs to format the lines. This approach can be effective, but you must remember to enter only *one* tab between entries when you first type the information (no matter how bad it initially looks). Complete the following exercise to practice this approach and learn how to insert a dot leader tab into a table.

Using Tabs to Format Existing Paragraphs

To format an existing paragraph and insert dot leaders, do these steps:

❶ Open the Memory and Storage document and scroll down about two-thirds of the first page to display the group of lines listed under the sentence *Common computer information storage units are described in the following table.*

In the following steps you use some of the techniques from the previous exercises to format tables to look like the ones in Figure 5.7.

❷ **a.** Select the entire block of six lines; then, using the tab marks in the ruler in Figure 5.7 as a guide, set left, center, and right tabs in the appropriate locations.

b. Select the column heading lines, bold the characters, and then press ⬆Shift+Ctrl+W to underline the words on the line.

(continues)

Using Tabs to Format Existing Paragraphs (continued)

Figure 5.7
The two tables to be formatted in the Memory and Storage document.

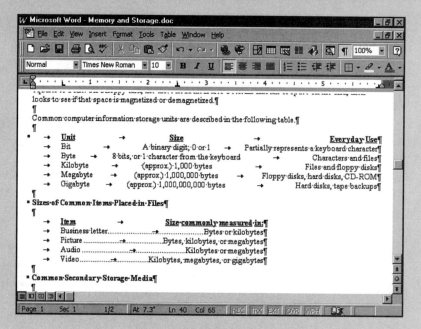

❸ Select the lines in the table below the *Sizes of Common Items Placed in Files* heading.

   a. Set the appropriate left and right tabs so that the table appears similar to the corresponding table in Figure 5.7

   b. Select the column heading lines, bold the characters, and then press ⇧Shift+Ctrl+W to underline the words on the line.

❹ Select the last four lines in the second table; then open the Tabs dialog box.

❺ In the **T**ab stop position list box, select your second tab (the right tab), choose the 2...... option in the Leader section of the dialog box, and then choose OK to insert the dot leader characters (the dots) leading into the second item on each of the last four lines of the table.

❻ Click outside your selection to turn off the highlighting and view your results. Save your revisions to the Memory and Storage document. Leave the document open for the next exercise.

If two or more paragraphs, with different custom tab settings, are selected, the tab markers in the ruler will be displayed in a gray shade.

When you have two or more paragraphs selected and you open the Tabs dialog box, the box lists only the tab positions that apply to all the selected paragraphs. Each paragraph may have other tabs set.

One final note about the ruler: By default, Word displays rulers calibrated in inches and measurements in inches. You can choose centimeters, points, or picas (one pica equals about 12 points) rather than inches. To change the unit of measurement, choose **T**ools, **O**ptions; choose the General tab; click the arrow at the end of the **M**easurement units drop-down list box; select the desired unit of measurement; and then choose OK.

Objective 3: Indent Paragraphs

You can indent paragraphs by moving their Left and Right Indent markers toward the center of the page. You can even extend paragraphs into the margins. Using Word, you can create a variety of indents, including hanging indents.

You can change paragraph indentation by using any one of the following methods:

- The Formatting toolbar
- The horizontal ruler and the mouse
- The keyboard shortcuts
- The Paragraph dialog box

Using the Formatting Toolbar and the Keyboard to Change Indentation

By using the indentation buttons in the Formatting toolbar, you can indent the left edge of paragraphs to default or custom tab positions, or change the indentation of paragraphs already indented. As with many of the Word commands, you can also indent paragraphs with keyboard shortcut key combinations.

By now, you already know that pressing the ⎯Tab⎯ key at the beginning of a paragraph indents the first line to the first tab stop position. However, you may not be aware of fast ways to indent all the lines in a paragraph. Complete the following exercise to practice using the Formatting toolbar, and the keyboard, to change the indentation of your paragraphs.

5

Indenting Paragraphs

Practice changing the indentation of paragraphs by using the Formatting toolbar and the keyboard.

1 In the open Memory and Storage document, place the insertion point in the first paragraph, the one beginning with *Beginning computer users....*

 2 Choose the Increase Indent button from the Formatting toolbar to indent the entire left side of the paragraph one-half inch toward the center of the window (see Figure 5.8).

The paragraph is indented to the first tab (in this case the default tab at .5" was used). Note that the First Line Indent, Hanging Indent, and Left Indent markers have moved to the .5" mark on the ruler.

If you were to click the Increase Indent button again, the paragraph would be indented to the next tab (in this case, to the one-inch mark).

 3 Choose the Decrease Indent button to decrease the indent of the current paragraph (the left edge of the paragraph is returned against the left margin).

(continues)

Indenting Paragraphs (continued)

Figure 5.8

Notice that the indent markers on the left side of the ruler have moved to the half-inch mark.

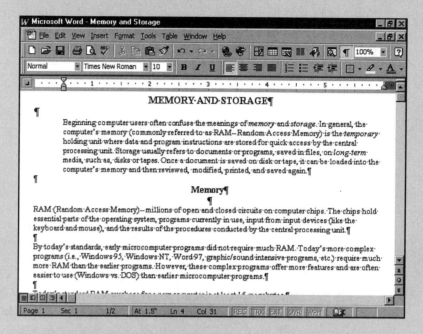

4 With the paragraph returned to its original position, press Ctrl+M to indent the paragraph to the first tab stop. Then press Ctrl+M a second time to indent the left side of the paragraph to the next tab stop.

5 To use the keyboard to move the indent back one tab, press ⬆Shift+Ctrl+M. Press ⬆Shift+Ctrl+M again to return the left side of the paragraph against the left margin.

A hanging indent is one where the left side of the first line of a paragraph looks as if it "hangs" beyond the left edge of the paragraph. Hanging indents are commonly used for creating numbered lists or entries in bibliographies.

6 Format the first paragraph as a hanging indent by pressing Ctrl+T (see Figure 5.9).

Note the position of the First Line Indent marker, the Hanging Indent marker, and the Left Indent marker when the insertion point is inside a paragraph formatted with a hanging indent. If you press Ctrl+T again, all lines except the first paragraph line would be indented to the second tab stop.

Tip

The hanging indent is often used when you are typing out a number of steps in a procedure. Type the first step number, press Tab⬄ once, enter the text for the first step, and then format the paragraph with a hanging indent. If the text is longer than one line, it will wrap neatly below the text in the first line. Press ⏎Enter to bring the hanging indent format into the next paragraph you create and continue entering your steps.

First Line Indent marker

Figure 5.9
All lines are indented
except the first one
when a paragraph is
formatted with a
hanging indent.

**Hanging
Indent
marker**

**Left Indent
marker**

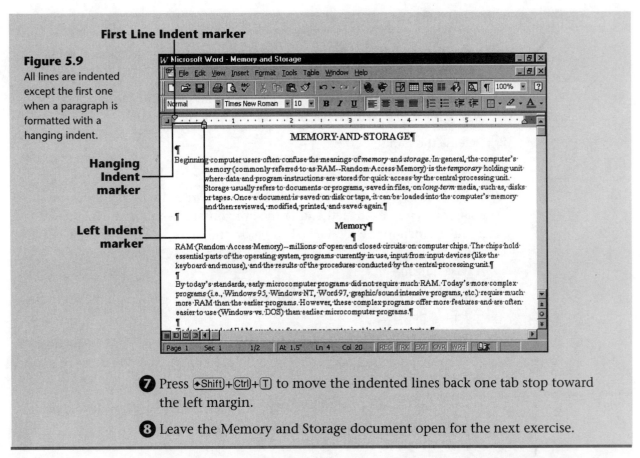

⓻ Press ⟨⬆Shift⟩+⟨Ctrl⟩+⟨T⟩ to move the indented lines back one tab stop toward
the left margin.

⓼ Leave the Memory and Storage document open for the next exercise.

In the preceding exercise, you indented only the paragraph containing the insertion point. You also can select a block of paragraphs and use the same commands to increase or decrease the indent of the selected paragraphs.

Using the Ruler and the Mouse to Indent Paragraphs

You can indent a paragraph by dragging indentation markers in the ruler. Using
this method, you can indent the following elements:

- The first line of a paragraph
- The left side of a paragraph
- The right side of a paragraph

In the following exercise, you work directly with the indent markers to affect the
look of the selected paragraphs.

Indenting Paragraphs with the Ruler and the Mouse

To use the mouse and tab markers on the ruler to indent paragraphs, do these
steps:

❶ In the open Memory and Storage document, select the first two paragraphs
under the *Memory* section, the ones beginning with *RAM—Random Access
Memory...* and *By today's standards....*

(continues)

Indenting Paragraphs with the Ruler and the Mouse (continued)

2 Point to the Right Indent marker at the right end of the horizontal ruler, and drag the marker about an inch to the left.

As you drag, a dotted vertical line moves in the same direction to show you where the indent will be placed in the document.

3 Release the mouse button.

The right edge of the selected paragraphs moves to the indented position.

4 Point to the Hanging Indent marker—the one with the triangular shape that points up—at the left end of the horizontal ruler, drag the marker about an inch to the right (the box below the triangular marker—the left indent marker—will move with the triangular marker), and release the mouse button.

The left edge of all lines except the first line of each paragraph moves to the indented position.

5 Point to the First Line Indent marker on the top at the left end of the horizontal ruler, drag the marker about an inch to the right, and release the mouse button.

The left edge of the first lines of the paragraphs move to the indented position (see Figure 5.10).

First Line Indent marker   **Hanging Indent marker**

Figure 5.10
The two selected paragraphs are indented. Notice the positions of the indent markers in the ruler.

Left Indent marker

Right Indent marker

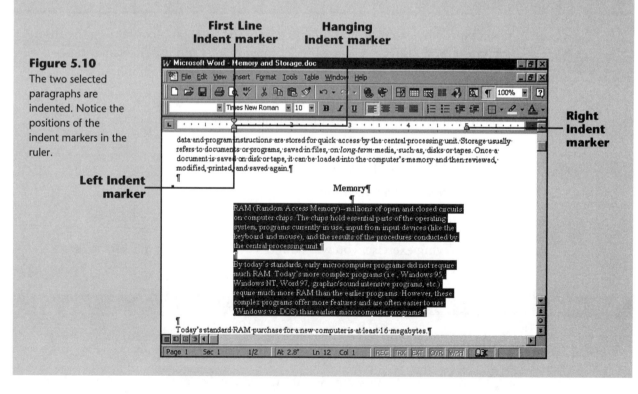

Note

To drag both the Hanging Indent marker and the First Line Indent marker at the same time, drag the Left Indent marker (the box below the triangular markers) to the desired location.

6 Click outside the selection to deselect the paragraphs. Then keep the Memory and Storage document open for the next exercise.

To extend the right edge of a paragraph into the right margin, drag the Right Indent marker in the ruler into the margin.

To extend the left edge of a paragraph into the left margin drag the Left Indent Marker over the Tab Alignment button, and wait until the left margin area is displayed on the ruler; then drag the Left Indent Marker to the desired ruler location.

Tip

To see the left margin area on the ruler more quickly, press and hold down (⬆Shift) while you click the left scroll arrow in the horizontal scroll bar.

 Another way to quickly view the left margin on the ruler is to change to the Page Layout view by choosing **V**iew, **P**age Layout or by clicking the Page Layout View button.

Using the Paragraph Dialog Box to Indent Paragraphs

Using the Paragraph dialog box, you can set indentations to precise measurements that you cannot obtain by dragging in the ruler. Before you open the Paragraph dialog box, however, you must place the insertion point in the paragraph you want to indent, or select multiple paragraphs.

To open the Paragraph dialog box, choose F**o**rmat, **P**aragraph. Alternatively, you can display the Paragraph dialog box by right-clicking in the single paragraph (or selected paragraphs) and then choose **P**aragraph from the shortcut menu. If necessary, click the **I**ndents and Spacing tab to display that page of the dialog box (see Figure 5.11).

While you work with the Paragraph dialog box, the Preview box indicates the effects of the choices you make.

You can set indentation measurements by clicking the arrows at the right of the **L**eft or **R**ight text boxes or by typing measurements in those boxes. Positive numbers move the indentation toward the center of the document; negative numbers move the indentation into the margins. Although Word displays abbreviations for measurement units in the text boxes, you don't have to type an abbreviation unless you want to use a measurement unit other than the default.

5

Figure 5.11
Using the Indents
and Spacing tab,
you can indent
from the left or
right margins or
create special
indentations.

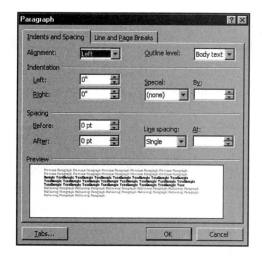

The measurement in the **L**eft text box defines the left indentation for all lines in
the selected paragraph. To set the indentation of the first line of a paragraph at a
different position from the indentation of the remaining lines, open the **S**pecial
drop-down list (see Figure 5.12).

Figure 5.12
Use the Special
drop-down list to
define an indenta-
tion for the first line
of a paragraph.

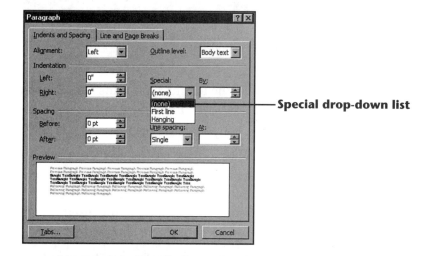

Special drop-down list

Indenting the First Lines of Paragraphs to the Right

To use the Paragraph dialog box to indent the first line of a paragraph, do these
steps:

❶ In the open Memory and Storage document, place the insertion point at
the beginning of the first paragraph, the one beginning with *Beginning computer users....*

❷ Choose F**o**rmat, **P**aragraph to display the Paragraph dialog box (if necessary
choose the **I**ndents and Spacing tab).

❸ Open the **S**pecial drop-down list and choose First Line.

❹ Click the arrows in the B**y** text box to increase the indentation of the first
line to 1.5, or select the entry in the B**y** text box and type 1.5.

Word allows only positive numbers in the **S**pecial drop-down list.

⑤ Choose OK to close the dialog box and to put into effect the first line indentation value you just specified.

To use the Paragraph dialog box to change the first paragraph to a hanging indent, follow the next steps.

⑥ Keep the insertion point in the first paragraph, and choose F**o**rmat, **P**aragraph to open the Paragraph dialog box.

⑦ Open the **S**pecial drop-down list and choose Hanging.

⑧ Click the arrows in the B**y** box to decrease the distance that the first line hangs over the remainder of the paragraph to 1, or select the current entry in the B**y** text box and type 1.

⑨ Choose OK to close the dialog box and to put into effect the hanging indent value you just specified.

The first line should now begin one inch to the left of successive lines in the paragraph.

⑩ Close the Memory and Storage document without saving the changes. Keep the Word window open for the next exercise.

Objective 4: Control Line Spacing

Paragraph formatting enables you to control line spacing within paragraphs and between paragraphs. In each case, you can specify spacing in terms of lines or specific measurements.

By default, Word uses single-line spacing, in which the spacing between lines is determined by the size of the characters in the line. If a line contains characters of various sizes, the largest character in the line determines the line spacing. The default line spacing is a little larger than the size of the font to allow a little space between lines.

Using the Keyboard to Set Line Spacing

To set line spacing, place the insertion point in the desired paragraph, or select one or more paragraphs; then press one of the following shortcut keys:

Key Combination	Line Spacing
Ctrl+1	Single
Ctrl+5	One and one-half
Ctrl+2	Double

Using the Keyboard and Paragraph Dialog Box to Set Line Spacing Within Paragraphs

To use the keyboard and the Paragraph dialog box to set line spacing in paragraphs, follow these steps:

1 Open the Memory and Storage document from your Student Disk and select the first two paragraphs under the *Memory* section, the ones beginning with *RAM—Random Access Memory... and By today's standards....* Be sure to include the paragraph marker below each paragraph in your selection.

2 Press Ctrl+2 to double-space the selected text.

3 Press Ctrl+5 to set the line spacing at one and one-half lines.

4 Press Ctrl+1 to return the selected text to single spacing.

5 Keep the paragraphs selected and choose Format, **P**aragraph to display the Paragraph dialog box.

If necessary, click the **I**ndents and Spacing tab to display that section of the dialog box.

Figure 5.13
The Line Spacing drop-down list offers six line spacing options.

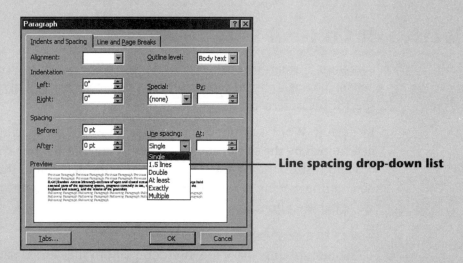

Line spacing drop-down list

6 Open the Li**n**e Spacing drop-down list (see Figure 5.13).

You can choose any of the following options:

- *Single*. Lines are spaced according to the height of the largest character in each line.

- *1.5 lines*. Lines are spaced at one and one-half times the height of the single line space.

- *Double*. Lines are spaced at double the height of the single line space.

- *At least*. Lines are spaced at the distance set in the **At** text box, or more, if required, to accommodate larger characters.

- *Exactly*. Lines are spaced at exactly the distance set in the **At** text box, even if this space is not large enough to show complete characters.

- *Multiple*. Lines are spaced at a multiple of the size of the largest character in each line.

7 Choose Double from the Line Spacing drop-down list.

8 Choose OK to close the dialog box and double-space the selected paragraphs.

9 Open the Paragraph dialog box and change the Line spacing option back to single; then choose OK to return to your document and apply that spacing to the selected paragraphs.

> **Note**
>
> When you choose At Least, Exactly, or Multiple, you must specify a value in the **At** text box. Experiment by using various values. Remember to choose OK to close the dialog box and see the changes in the selected paragraphs.

10 Keep the Memory and Storage document open for the next exercise.

Setting the Space Between Paragraphs

This book uses extra space (a blank line) between paragraphs to make the text easier to read; you may want to format your documents similarly. If you use a typewriter, you probably are accustomed to pressing the carriage-return key to create a space (blank line) between paragraphs. In Word, you can use the same method to create extra spaces between paragraphs if you are working with a single-page document. When you use this method in multiple-page documents, however, you may have problems. When you edit paragraphs, for example, the last line of a paragraph may be at the bottom of a page. This creates an inconsistent blank line at the top of the next page.

To prevent this extra blank line problem, you can format each paragraph to include space after it. Word automatically ignores this extra space if it comes at the top of a page, so you eliminate the possibility that pages will start with a blank line.

Formatting paragraphs with extra space before them works similarly. In this case, Word ignores the blank space before a paragraph if that paragraph is at the top of a page.

You can set the space between paragraphs from the Paragraph dialog box. Use the **B**efore or Aft**e**r text boxes (or both) to define the space before or after selected paragraphs (see Figure 5.13 from the preceding exercise). Word displays the space in points. If you type or select a number, Word interprets that number as points. You can specify the spacing in another unit of measurement by adding the abbreviation for the unit of measurement, such as *in* for inches, after the number.

After you set the spacing between paragraphs, choose OK to apply the spacing to the selected paragraphs.

Another way to set a space between paragraphs is to select a paragraph and then press Ctrl+0 (zero). This shortcut key adds a 12-point space ($^1/_6$ of an inch) above the first line of the paragraph.

Inserting Space Between Paragraphs

To insert space between paragraphs, follow these steps:

1 In the open Memory and Storage document, delete the blank line between the *Memory* section heading and the first paragraph of the section—the one beginning with *RAM (Random Access Memory)....*

2 Delete the remaining blank lines in the *Memory* section; then select only the paragraphs in the *Memory* section. Your selection should start at the beginning of the *RAM (Random Access Memory)....* sentence and end with the paragraph mark following the sentence that ends with ...*at least 16 megabytes.*

3 Press Ctrl+0 (zero) to add a 12-point space above each selected paragraph.

If you were to press Ctrl+0 again, the 12-point space would be removed because this command works like a toggle switch for inserting or removing a 12-point space above selected paragraphs.

4 With the text still selected, open the Paragraph dialog box, change the value in the **B**efore box to **0** (zero), and enter **12** in the Aft**e**r box. Then choose OK to close the box and format the selected paragraphs.

As you can see, this time the 12-point space was added below each selected paragraph.

5 Close the Memory and Storage document without saving your changes, but leave the Word window open for the next exercise.

Using the Paragraph Dialog Box Line and Page Breaks Options

The Line and **P**age Breaks page of the Paragraph dialog box provides additional ways to control paragraph formatting. Two major formatting errors that can be avoided by using the options on this page include:

- Displaying only the first line of a paragraph at the bottom of a page, or only the last line of a paragraph at the top of a page

- Splitting a small table over two pages

The Line and **P**age Breaks page of the Paragraph dialog box is displayed in Figure 5.14. There are six options on this page. The four Pagination options control the way in which Word separates documents into pages. When no Pagination option is selected, Word simply creates a new page whenever the current page is full.

Figure 5.14
The Line and Page Breaks page of the Paragraph dialog box contains six options that you can enable or disable.

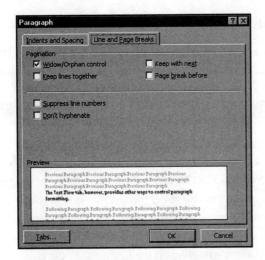

The functions of the six options in the Line and **P**age Breaks page of the Paragraph dialog box are listed as follows:

Option	Function
Widow/Orphan control	Prevents the first line of a paragraph from appearing at the bottom of a page, and prevents the last line of a paragraph from appearing at the top of a page. To prevent either of these circumstances, Word moves the last line of a page to the next page, when necessary.
Keep lines together	Prevents a page break within a paragraph.
Keep with ne**x**t	Prevents a page break between the selected paragraph and the next paragraph.
Page **b**reak before	Always places the paragraph at the top of a new page.
Suppress line numbers	With line numbering selected, omits selected paragraphs from the line-numbering sequence.
Don't hyphenate	Excludes selected paragraphs from automatic hyphenation.

The Keep with ne**x**t option is particularly useful for keeping headings and their subsequent paragraphs together. Apply this option to each heading and initial paragraph for the section to prevent the possibility that a heading will occur at the bottom of a page, with the text below that heading starting on the next page.

The preceding information was presented here to make you aware of some of the options affecting the placement of paragraphs on the page. In the next chapter you complete an exercise where you will apply some of these options to your current document.

Remove Paragraph Formatting

To simplify your work, Word enables you to remove formatting quickly. To remove all paragraph formatting from a paragraph, select it and press Ctrl+Q.

Objective 5: Control Line Breaks

By default, Word uses word wrap to avoid breaking a word over two lines. However, if you want, you can display hyphenated words in your documents. Hyphens serve two purposes in written English:

- Hyphens join words, as in *side-by-side*.

- Hyphens divide words, enabling you to start a long word at the right end of one line and continue that word at the left end of the next line.

Note

Don't confuse a hyphen (-) with a dash (—). On a typewriter, one key serves both purposes, but this isn't the case in Word. Use the hyphen key on the keyboard for the two purposes defined in the preceding list. To create an *en dash* to use in a range of numbers, such as in "pages 1–15," you can press Ctrl+- (on the numeric keypad). This creates a dash longer than a hyphen. To create an even longer dash, known as an *em dash*, to indicate a pause or break in a sentence, you can press Ctrl+◆Shift+-. The appearance and length of these dashes will vary depending on the font you are using.

Using Hyphens in a Document

When you are typing a document, you should type only the hyphens that join words, such as in *forget-me-not*. Normally, you should avoid trying to break a word at the end of a line by typing a hyphen and then continuing the word at the beginning of the next line; leave that for Word to do automatically.

Word offers three types of hyphens you can use when you don't want to use Word's automatic hyphenation feature:

- *Normal.* A normal hyphen acts almost like any other keyboard character. The only difference is that a word wrap occurs immediately after a normal hyphen located close to the right margin. Press - (the regular hyphen key) to add a normal hyphen to your text.

- *Optional.* Use this type of hyphen to join words that can be split between lines. If an entire word that contains an optional hyphen fits on a line, the hyphen is not displayed or printed. If the word occurs at the right end of the line, Word splits the word at the optional hyphen, which is displayed and printed. Press Ctrl+- to include an optional hyphen in your text.

- *Nonbreaking.* Use this type of hyphen to join words that should not be split between lines. Press Ctrl+◆Shift+- to include a nonbreaking hyphen in your text.

Figure 5.15 shows the interaction among the three types of hyphens and also shows how word wrap occurs.

Note

Don't get the nonbreaking hyphen confused with the nonbreaking space. A nonbreaking space is used when you don't want a series of characters, (like June 13, 1999) to be broken over two lines. To insert a nonbreaking space between words, instead of pressing Spacebar, press Ctrl+◆Shift+Spacebar.

Figure 5.15
This figure shows the three types of hyphenation: normal, non-breaking, and optional.

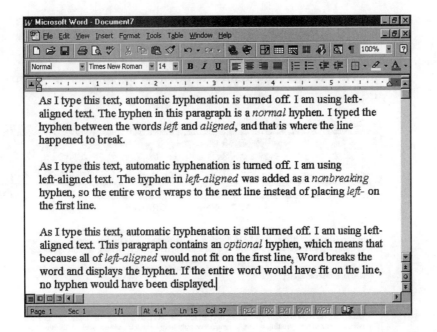

When you decide to include hyphenation in your document, Word makes it easy with its automatic hyphenation feature.

Hyphenating a Document Automatically

To practice using automatic hyphenation, follow these steps:

1 Open the Memory and Storage document from your Student Disk.

2 Choose **T**ools, **L**anguage, **H**yphenation to display the Hyphenation dialog box (see Figure 5.16).

Figure 5.16
Use the Hyphenation dialog box to select automatic hyphenation and to specify hyphenation parameters.

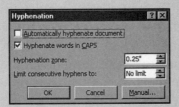

3 Click the **A**utomatically hyphenate document check box to turn on automatic hyphenation.

4 Check to see whether the Hyphenate Words in **C**APS check box is marked; if it is, clear the box to turn off the option.

5 Change the value in the Hyphenation **z**one box to **.1** and specify **3** in the **L**imit consecutive hyphens to box.

6 Choose OK to return to your document. You may need to wait a few seconds to see the results of the automatic hyphenation.

(continues)

5

Hyphenating a Document Automatically (continued)

You should be able to find some hyphenated text at the end of some of the lines in the first paragraph and other paragraphs in the document (see Figure 5.17).

Figure 5.17
The document displays some hyphenated text.

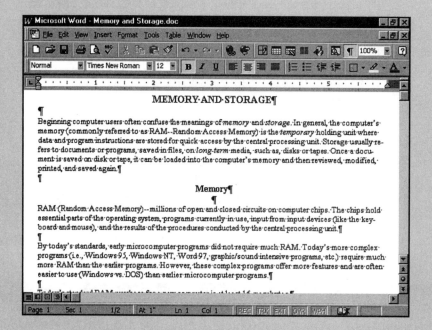

❼ Don't save your changes, but keep the Memory and Storage document open for the next exercise.

The *hyphenation zone* is the distance between the word at the end of a line and the right margin (where Word tries to hyphenate words). (In other words, you instruct Word to use the hyphenation feature to try to fill each line to within a certain distance of the right margin.) A narrow hyphenation zone tends to reduce the raggedness of the document's right margin, but it will increase the number of hyphenated words in the document. A wide zone reduces the number of hyphenated words because Word knows the point where it can wrap an entire word to the next line

After you turn on automatic hyphenation, Word adjusts hyphenation as you type and edit text.

Hyphenating a Document Manually

Instead of using automatic hyphenation, you can use a manual setting in which Word suggests places where hyphenation is possible; then you can accept or reject each suggestion. To use manual hyphenation, follow these steps:

❶ In the open Memory and Storage document, place the insertion point at the top of the document.

❷ Choose **T**ools, **L**anguage, **H**yphenation to display the Hyphenation dialog box.

3 Choose the **A**utomatically hyphenate document check box to turn *off* the automatic hyphenation you turned on in the preceding exercise.

4 Click the **M**anual button.

Word analyzes the document. When it reaches a place where hyphenation is possible, Word displays the Manual Hyphenation dialog box (see Figure 5.18).

> **Note**
>
> When Word is using this feature, the Word window is automatically changed to Page Layout view. When the hyphenation process is complete, Word returns the window to the previous view.

Figure 5.18
Word offers a hyphenation suggestion.

5 Note where the flashing box appears over the hyphen. To accept the location suggested by Word, choose **Y**es. Or you can click where you want to hyphenate the displayed word and then click **Y**es. To reject hyphenation, choose **N**o.

To stop the hyphenation process, choose Cancel.

For this exercise, choose **Y**es for each proposed hyphenation. When the message box stating that the hyphenation is complete is displayed, choose OK.

6 Close the Memory and Storage document without saving your changes.

Automatic hyphenation normally applies to an entire document, but you can exclude specific paragraphs from hyphenation.

If you use the automatic hyphenation feature to hyphenate your document and then change your mind about hyphenating certain paragraphs (or the entire document), you can remove the hyphenation from specific paragraphs by completing the following steps:

1. Select the desired paragraph(s).

2. Choose F**o**rmat, **P**aragraph, and choose the Line and **P**age Breaks page.

3. Choose the **D**on't hyphenate check box to mark it.

4. Choose OK to turn off the hyphenation for the selected paragraph(s).

Objective 6: Create Bulleted and Numbered Lists

Many types of documents contain lists. To make it easy for readers to see the individual items in the list, you can put each item in a separate line.

To add more emphasis to items and to indicate clearly where each item begins when some items occupy more than one line, place a marker, known as a *bullet*, at the beginning of each item.

Using a bullet to mark the beginning of each item implies that the order of the items has no particular significance. In cases in which the order is important, you can number the items rather than use bullets—when you are listing the steps in a procedure, for example, or when you are listing priorities.

Word can add bullets or numbers to a list automatically.

Creating Bulleted or Numbered Lists

To create a bulleted list, follow these steps:

1 Open the Memory and Storage document from your Student Disk; then place the insertion point at the end of the document.

2 Press ⏎Enter once to create a blank line between the insertion point and the last line of text. (You should now see two paragraph symbols at the left margin below the last paragraph, with the insertion point just before the last paragraph symbol.) Then type the following list of storage devices. (Press ⏎Enter after typing each entry.)

Floppy disk
Hard disk
CD-ROM
Tape backup

 3 Select the items you just entered, including the last paragraph mark under the *Tape backup* entry; then choose the Bullets button on the Formatting toolbar. Now click outside the entries to deselect the text.

Bullets are added to the selected entries; however, a bullet is not added to the last line (see Figure 5.19). When you select a group of paragraphs, including some blank lines, only the paragraphs that contain items to be printed (text, graphics, and so on) are bulleted. No bullets are assigned to blank lines.

If you make a mistake or change your mind, you can undo bulleting or numbering by choosing the Undo button or by choosing **E**dit, **U**ndo.

Tip

To choose a different bullet shape, choose **F**ormat, Bullets and **N**umbering; then, if necessary, choose the **B**ulleted tab, choose the desired bullet style, and choose OK.

When using the Numbering feature, you can change the number format by choosing the **N**umbered page of this dialog box, choosing the desired format, and then choosing OK.

If you don't like the supplied format, you can create your own by choosing the Cus**t**omize button in the dialog box.

Figure 5.19
Using the Bullets button, you can add bullets to your document quite easily.

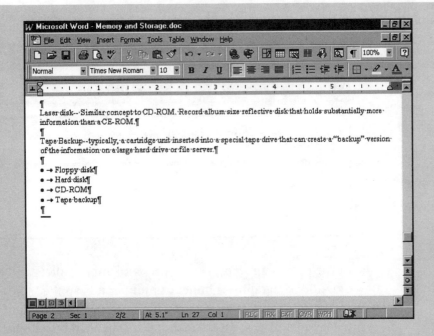

④ Move the insertion point to the last line of the document and type **Laser disk**. Note that as you type the entry, it appears as a normal entry.

⑤ Delete the term *Laser disk* that you just entered, place the insertion point at the end of the *Tape backup* line, and then press ⏎Enter once.

Note that when the insertion point is in a bulleted paragraph and ⏎Enter is pressed, the bulleted format is carried into the new paragraph.

⑥ Now enter **Laser disk** on the new bulleted line.

> **Tip**
>
> If you accidentally bring down the bulleted format to a new line that you want to keep in a normal format, just press ⬅Backspace to remove the bullet format and start typing.

⑦ Select the five bulleted entries at the end of the document; then choose the Numbering button on the Formatting toolbar to number the items 1–5.

⑧ Select the third item (*CD-ROM*) by clicking in the appropriate location in the selection bar; then drag the selection immediately in front of the *F* in the first item (*Floppy disk*) and release the mouse button.

The numbers remained in place, but the order of the items was changed (see Figure 5.20).

(continues)

Creating Bulleted or Numbered Lists (continued)

Figure 5.20

The order of numbered items can be easily rearranged when you use the drag-and-drop technique.

The third item is now the first.

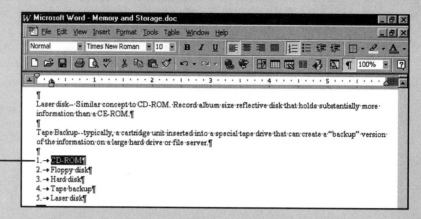

In the preceding steps, you saw how to apply bullets and numbering to one-line paragraphs. A bullet or number was applied to each selected line. In the following steps, you apply numbering to a block of multiple-line paragraphs (where each paragraph is separated by a blank line).

9 Scroll toward the top of the second page of the Memory and Storage document until you see the *3.5" high density disks are the preferred type...* one-line paragraph. Select a block of paragraphs, starting with this line, through the two-line *Tape Backup...* paragraph.

Tip

For precise selection of a block of text that may not all be displayed on the screen at the same time, place the insertion point at the beginning of the block, hold down ⬆Shift, and then use the arrow keys to highlight all the desired lines. Alternatively, you can place the insertion point at the desired starting position, press F8, and then use the arrow keys to select the desired text.

10 Choose the Numbering button to number the selected paragraphs.

Note that the paragraphs are now numbered, but the blank lines between the paragraphs are not. Each multiple-line paragraph is displayed in hanging indent format (see Figure 5.21).

11 Click in the document to turn off the selection; then leave the Memory and Storage document open for the next exercise.

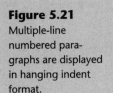

Figure 5.21
Multiple-line
numbered para-
graphs are displayed
in hanging indent
format.

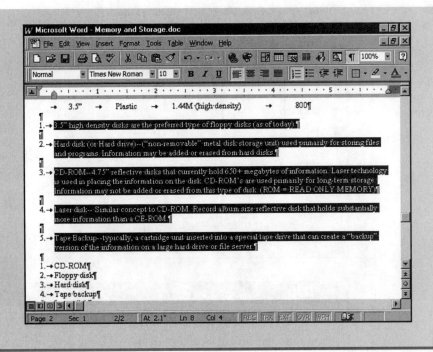

In the next exercise, you learn to use automatic numbering on a multiple-level
list.

Creating a Multiple-Level Numbered List

❶ In the Memory and Storage document, place the insertion point at the end
of the document, press ⏎Enter twice, type **Storage Media**, then press
⏎Enter once.

In an earlier exercise in this chapter you may have turned off a formating option
that we need to activate now.

❷ Choose **T**ools, **O**ptions to display the Options dialog box; then click the
Edit tab to display the Edit options.

❸ Make sure the Tabs and backspace set left **i**ndent option is active (if necessary, select the option to place a check in the check box), then choose OK
to close the dialog box.

❹ Choose **F**ormat, Bullets and **N**umbering, to open the Bullets and Numbering dialog box. Choose the **O**utline Numbered page (see Figure 5.22).

5

Creating a Multiple-Level Numbered List (continued)

Figure 5.22

Choose your desired numbering scheme from this page of the Bullets and Numbering dialog box.

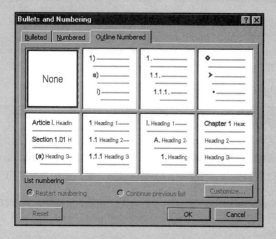

Tip

Another way to open the Bullets and Numbering dialog box is to right-click in the appropriate document location and choose the Bullets and **N**umbering command from the shortcut menu.

5 Choose the second option in the first row (the *1) a) i) option)*; then choose OK to return to your document.

When you return to your document, the current line now begins with *1)* and includes a hanging indent at the .25 inches.

6 Type **Removable Units** and press ⏎Enter once to move to the next line.

The new line starts with the 2), however, you need to add some "sub-points" to the *1) Removable Units* entry. Complete the next step to change the *2)* at the beginning of the line to *a)*.

7 Press Tab⇆ once to keep the insertion point on the same line but change the beginning of the current line to *a)*.

8 Type **Floppy Disks**, press ⏎Enter, type **CD-ROMs**, and press ⏎Enter.

On the new line you need to enter a new major point. Complete the next step to change the beginning of the current line from *c)* to *2)*.

9 Press ⇧Shift+Tab⇆ to change the beginning of the current line from *c)* to *2)*, then type **Fixed Units** and press ⏎Enter.

10 Press Tab⇆ once to begin the current line with *a)*, then type **Hard Drives**, press ⏎Enter, and type **Network Drives**.

11 As you look at your new list, you realize you need to add *Tape Backup Cartridges* as the second sub-point under the *Removable Units* heading.

12 Place the insertion point immediately following the *Floppy Disks* item; then press ⏎Enter once to create a new (already indented) line and change the CD-ROMs entry to sub-point *c)* under item *1)*.

⓭ Enter **Tape Backup Cartridges** to complete your list.

⓮ Review your list, save the changes to the Memory and Storage document; then close the file.

Chapter Summary

This chapter contained information about aligning and indenting paragraphs, setting tabs, controlling line spacing, controlling line breaks, and creating bulleted and numbered lists. Although you learned many formatting features in this chapter, you may find that you use only certain ones in your daily work.

In the next chapter, you learn to use Word features to help you format the pages of your document, including changing margins, adjusting page size, adding headers and footers, and using other page-layout techniques.

If you have completed your work for this computer session, make sure that you properly exit all open programs. Then use the Windows Sh**u**t Down command to safely exit Windows. To test your knowledge of the material covered in this chapter, answer the questions in the Checking Your Skills section immediately following this summary. Then complete the exercises in the Applying Your Skills section at the end of the chapter.

Checking Your Skills

True/False

For each of the following, circle *T* or *F* to indicate whether the statement is true or false.

T   F   **1.** The Formatting toolbar includes four paragraph alignment options: Align Left, Center, Align Right, and Justify.

T   F   **2.** Default tabs apply only to the first and last paragraphs of a document.

T   F   **3.** The only way to indent paragraphs is to drag their left and right indent markers on the ruler toward the center of the page.

T   F   **4.** You can align paragraphs using the ruler, the Paragraph dialog box, and the Standard toolbar.

T   F   **5.** When you choose to hyphenate a document manually, Word displays the potential hyphen for the word and enables you to approve, or change the location of, the hyphen.

T   F   **6.** Word stores all paragraph formatting in the paragraph mark at the end of the paragraph.

T   F   **7.** You can change the distance between default tabs, but you cannot change custom tabs.

T   F   **8.** The measurement of the **L**eft text box in the Paragraph dialog box always defines the left indentation for all lines in the selected paragraph from the edge of the paper.

T   F   **9.** The Widow/Orphan **c**ontrol option, in the Line and **P**age Breaks page of the Paragraph dialog box, prevents the first line of a paragraph from appearing at the top of a page and prevents the last line of a paragraph from appearing at the bottom of a page.

T   F   **10.** Word does not provide the option for a multiple-level list when using the Bullets and **N**umbering dialog box.

Multiple Choice

In the blank provided, write the letter of the correct answer for each of the following questions.

1. The Word feature that enables you to apply the most formatting to a paragraph is the _____.

    a. Tabs dialog box

    b. Horizontal ruler

    c. Paragraph dialog box

    d. Text Flow dialog box

    e. Hyphenation dialog box

2. You can set and delete custom tabs and change tab alignment by using _____.

    a. the horizontal ruler and the mouse

    b. the Tabs dialog box

    c. the Paragraph dialog box

    d. the Formatting toolbar

    e. a and b

3. You can use the keyboard to indent the left side of a paragraph by pressing _____.

    a. Ctrl+I

    b. Ctrl+N

    c. Ctrl+M

    d. Ctrl+T

    e. Ctrl+L

4. The option that is *not* available in the Line and **P**age Breaks page of the Paragraph dialog box is _____.

    a. Widow/Orphan **c**ontrol

    b. Cle**a**r all tabs

    c. Page **b**reak before

    d. Keep with next

    e. **D**on't hyphenate

5. To add more emphasis to separate items and to indicate clearly where each item begins when some items occupy more than one line, you should add a marker, known as a(n) _____.

    a. asterisk

    b. dash

    c. equal sign

    d. bullet

    e. double asterisk

6. A tab that applies only to the paragraphs that are selected when you create the tab is a _____ tab.

    a. left

    b. decimal

    c. custom

    d. default

    e. right

7. Word's default tabs are set every _____ across the page.

    a. inch

    b. two inches

    c. half-inch

    d. quarter-inch

    e. inch and one-half

8. Lines spaced at twice the height of the single line space are said to use _____ spacing.

    a. double

    b. single

    c. 1.5

    d. at least

    e. multiple

9. Which hyphen can you manually insert in your document? _____

    a. Normal

    b. Nonbreaking

    c. Optional

    d. Outside

    e. a, b, and c

10. Which shortcut key combination centers the paragraph containing the insertion point? _____

    a. Ctrl+C

    b. Ctrl+E

    c. Ctrl+N

    d. Ctrl+T

    e. Ctrl+R

Fill in the Blank

In the blank provided, write the correct answer for each of the following questions.

1. The _____ dialog box provides the "most complete" way to format paragraphs because it includes most of the paragraph-formatting options.

2. When you indent paragraphs, the indentation takes place from the left or right _____.

3. The _____ button increases paragraph indentation by moving the left edge of paragraphs to the right.

4. If two or more paragraphs with different alignments are selected, all four _____ buttons are in the flat position on the Formatting toolbar.

5. The _____ zone is a set distance left of the right margin that helps determine how closely hyphenated words will be displayed next to the right margin.

6. To move a custom tab in the ruler, _____ it to the right or left.

7. Pressing Ctrl+0 either adds or removes a _____ space from the top of the selected paragraphs.

8. The shortcut key combination to double-space selected text is _____.

9. The **S**pecial box in the Paragraph dialog box controls the formatting of the _____ of the selected paragraph.

10. On the ruler, you can choose the type of tab you want to insert by clicking the _____ button.

5

Applying Your Skills

Review Exercises

Exercise 1: Indenting Paragraphs

Practice indenting paragraphs by following these steps:

1. Open the Chap0502 document from your Student Disk; then immediately save the document back to your disk as **Business 05**.

2. Center the first paragraph under the salutation.

3. Create a hanging indent for the second paragraph.

4. Right-align the third paragraph.

5. Indent the fourth paragraph one inch from both the left and right margins.

6. Locate the time ranges listed in paragraphs two and three. If a time is split over two lines (for example, if *3:00* is at the end of one line and *p.m.* is listed at the beginning of the next line), replace the space immediately in front of the *p.m.* or *a.m.* with a nonbreaking space. (Hint: refer to the second *note* in Objective 5: Control Line Breaks for help.)

7. Save the revision; then print and close your file.

Exercise 2: Using Custom Tabs

In the following exercise, you format the document title and use custom tabs to create a table. Follow these steps:

1. Open the Chap0503 document from your Student Disk; then immediately save the document back to your disk as **Planning 05**.

2. Place the title in a Times New Roman Bold 17-point font and center it.

3. Move to the end of the document; then create the new heading **Upcoming Summer Events**. Format the new heading in the same format as the existing date headings.

4. Add the appropriate spacing below the new heading and then enter the following table. Format the heading characters as shown. Use tabs of .5 left, 1.5 left, 3.25 center, and 4.5 center tab for the Fee heading, 4.5 decimal tab for the dollar amounts.

Date	Fundraiser	Time	Fee
06/02	Bake Sale	9:00 a.m. - 4:00 p.m.	$0.00
07/01	Movie Night	8:00 p.m.-11:00 p.m.	$20.00
08/01	Craft Fair	9:00 a.m. - 6:00 p.m.	$15.00

5. Save the revisions; then print and close the file.

Exercise 3: Double-Spacing a Document

Practice double-spacing a whole document by following these steps:

1. Open the Chap0504 document from your Student Disk; then immediately save the document back to your disk as **Fonts and Font Sizes 05**.

2. Double-space the entire document.

3. Save the revisions; then print and close the file.

Exercise 4: Creating Space and a Numbered List

To practice inserting a space below a paragraph and creating a numbered list, follow these steps:

1. Open a new document.

2. Use the options in the Paragraph dialog box to automatically insert a 6-point space below every paragraph.

3. Type the following chapter titles, making sure to press ⏎Enter only once after completing each entry:

   Word 97 SmartStart Contents:
   Getting Started
   Editing Documents
   Proofing Your Work
   Formatting Characters
   Formatting Paragraphs
   Formatting Pages

4. Format the chapter titles as a numbered list.

5. Save the file to your Student Disk as **Content 05**; then print and close the file.

Exercise 5: Manipulating the Items in a List

To practice moving items in a numbered list, follow these steps:

1. Open the Chap0505 document from your Student Disk; then immediately save the document back to your disk as **Employee Guidelines 05**.

2. Use the Numbering button on the Formatting toolbar to assign a number to each guideline.

3. Use the drag-and-drop procedure to rearrange the guidelines from shortest to longest. (Hint: Make sure to select the guideline *and* the paragraph mark immediately below the selected guideline when you use the drag-and-drop procedure. The *Worker must verify coverage of work area when necessary.* guideline will be the first one.)

4. Save the revisions; then print and close your file.

Continuing Projects

Project 1: Practice Using Word

You have been asked to write an article about how colleges and high schools communicate with one another to facilitate the students' college-search process.

1. Start with a blank document; then create the following three-level outline. Make sure that all first-level headings are next to the left margin:

   Orientation at the High School

   Fall Orientation

   Spring Orientation

> **College Fairs**
>> **Fall College Fairs**
>>> **October at Hale School**
>>> **November at Civic Center**
>> **Spring College Fairs**
>>> **March at University**
>>> **May at Civic Center**
> **Testing**
>> **Dates**
>>> **December**
>>> **May**
>> **Courses**
>>> **Private**
>>> **Public**

2. Place the outline in the I., A., 1. format (the third option in the second row of the Outline Numbered page of the Paragraphs and Numbering dialog box).

3. Save the file to your Student Disk as **College 05**; then print and close the file.

Project 2: Deli-Mart

Continue your work on the catalog for Deli-Mart by following these steps:

1. Open the Chap0506 document from your Student Disk; then immediately save the document back to your disk as **Menu 05**.

2. Add two blank lines to the top of the document; then type the company name, **Deli-Mart International,** on the top line of the document. Format the name in the Times New Roman Bold Italic 16-point font.

3. Center the title.

4. Place the insertion point on the blank line just below the title, press `↵Enter` once, change the font size to 11 points, (turn off the Bold button if necessary), and type the following opening paragraphs:

> **Enjoy lunch at our site or yours. Next time you are in, take back one of our menus. To order daily lunches for your company just call with your order and we will deliver it.**
>
> **To order by phone:**
>
> 1.   **Select the desired items from the menu.**
> 2.   **Have the menu items numbers available.**
> 3.   **Call 1-800-DEL-MART**

5. Press ⏎Enter twice after entering the phone number to create appropriate line spacing.

6. Set a left tab at the 2-inch mark on each line that lists the name of a menu item. On the lines that include a menu item name, enter a menu number consisting of the first letter of the name of the item and a three-digit number at the 3-inch mark. (For example, the menu number for Tom's Ketch could be T123.)

7. Save the revisions; then print and close your file.

Project 3: The Marketing Connection

Continue your work on the newsletter for The Marketing Connection by following these steps:

1. Open the Chap0507 document from your Student Disk; then immediately save the document back to your disk as **Market 05**.

2. Use the keyboard shortcut to center the headings *The Marketing Connection* and *Public Relations Department*.

3. Use the keyboard shortcut to double-space the first paragraph under the *The Marketing Connection* heading.

4. Use the keyboard shortcut to create a hanging indent for the second paragraph under the *The Marketing Connection* heading.

5. Use the keyboard shortcut to justify the first paragraph under the *Public Relations Department* heading.

6. Save the revisions; then print and close the file.

5

CHAPTER 6

Formatting Pages

Orientation
The placement of text and graphics on the page—vertical or horizontal.

Headers
Text that appears at the top of each page.

In Chapters 4 and 5, you worked with formatting features for characters and paragraphs. In this chapter, you learn how to use formatting features to enhance the appearance of your document pages. Specifically, you learn how to set margins, paper size, and *orientation*; insert page breaks; format in the Print Preview window; format sections; create *headers* and *footers*; use page numbering; and work with *footnotes* and *endnotes*.

Objectives

Footers
Text that appears at the bottom of each page.

Footnotes
Reference text that appears at the bottom of the page containing the corresponding reference mark.

By the time you finish this chapter, you will have learned to

1. Set Margins

2. Choose Paper Size and Orientation

3. Control Page Breaks

4. Format a Document in the Print Preview Window

5. Divide a Document into Sections

6. Create Headers and Footers

7. Create Footnotes and Endnotes

Objective 1: Set Margins

Endnotes
Reference text or comments that appear at the end of a document, or end of a section.

Gutter
An extra margin at the inside edge of facing pages to allow space for binding.

When you first open a document, Word utilizes default page formats that include:

- Left and right margins of 1.25 inch ✓
- Top and bottom margins of 1 inch ✓
- Headers placed 0.5 inch from the top of the page ✓
- Footers placed 0.5 inch from the bottom of the page ✓
- No *gutter* (indicated by a setting of 0 inch)

Note

The defaults that you see may be different from these settings if the values were changed during installation, if another user changed them, or if your particular printer requires specific page settings.

You can set margins for both new and existing documents. By changing the margin settings, you can affect the document's length, improve the clarity of the document, or leave room for binding the document. You can always use the **M**argins page of the Page Setup dialog box to change margins. In addition, in the Word views that display margin markers on the rulers, margins can be changed by dragging the margin markers to new ruler locations.

In the following exercise, you learn to set margins by using the Page Setup dialog box.

Using the Page Setup Dialog Box to Set Margins

To use the Page Setup dialog box to set margins, follow these steps:

1 Open the Chap0601 file from your Student Disk; then immediately save the file back to your disk as **Report**. Make sure that you are using Normal view; then scroll through document.

In Normal view, a dotted line spanning the width of the document window represents a page break.

2 Click in the line of text beginning with *Table of floppy disks...* immediately above the page break dotted line; then look at the information in the status bar.

The left side of the status bar indicates that you are looking at Page 1, Section 1, of a two-page document. The next portion of the status bar indicates that the insertion point is near the 9.7-inch mark on the page (if your current unit of measurement is inches).

3 Move the insertion point to the line immediately below the dotted line and note the change in the information on the left side of the status bar. (The status bar should indicate that the insertion point is on line 1 of page 2 of the document.)

4 Choose **F**ile, Page Set**u**p.

The Page Setup dialog box is displayed. If necessary, click the **M**argins tab to display the options on the **M**argin page (see Figure 6.1).

5 Change the values in the **T**op, **B**ottom, **L**eft, and R**igh**t text boxes to 2, 2, 1.5, and 1.5, respectively.

To change margins values, you can enter the desired value directly into the text box, or use the spinner arrows at the end of a text box to adjust the existing value. Clicking an increase or decrease arrow changes the existing value by one-tenth of an inch. Pointing to an arrow and holding down the mouse button quickly increases or decreases the existing value. As you change the margins, the document in the Preview frame changes to reflect the new settings.

Figure 6.1

The Margins page of the Page Setup dialog box displays the current margin values.

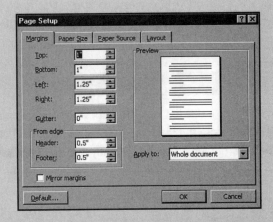

6 At this time, do not change any of the other settings in the **M**argins page.

7 Choose OK to apply the new margins to your document. Then scroll through the document and note that the pages break differently after the margins have been changed.

8 Keep the Report document open for the next exercise.

6

In the **M**argins page of the Page Setup dialog box, you also find the following options:

- *Apply to.* By default, Word applies your margin changes to the entire document. Later in this chapter, in Objective 5, you learn how to divide your document into sections and use different margins in each section.

- *Mirror Margins.* When you choose this option, the Le**f**t text box in the Margins section of the dialog box changes to **In**side, and the Ri**g**ht text box changes to **O**utside. This option enables you to specify separate inside and outside margins when you intend to print your document on both sides of the page and bind it. You can achieve the same result by specifying left and right margins together with a gutter margin.

- *Default.* Click this button if you want to apply the Page Setup settings to the current document and to save them as default values to apply to new documents.

> **Note**
>
> The Page Setup dialog box is divided into four pages—**M**argins, Paper **S**ize, **P**aper Source, and **L**ayout. When you choose the dialog box **D**efault button, your changes in all four pages of the dialog box (not just the page currently displayed) are saved as the defaults.

Objective 2: Choose Paper Size and Orientation

Word enables you to select the paper size and orientation of a document. The default paper size is a standard business letter: 8.5 by 11 inches. You can change the paper size easily if your document is larger or smaller. The default orientation is portrait orientation (where the page height is greater than the page width), but you can print in landscape orientation (where the page width is greater than the page height) if you want your document to print across the page.

Changing the Paper Size and Orientation

To alter the paper size and orientation, follow these steps:

1 In the open Report document, move the insertion point to the top of the document. Then choose **F**ile, Page Set**u**p to display the Page Setup dialog box.

2 Click the Paper **S**ize tab to display the paper size and orientation options (see Figure 6.2). Note the current settings.

Figure 6.2
Use the Paper Size tab to choose among standard paper sizes, to define custom paper sizes, and to choose page orientation.

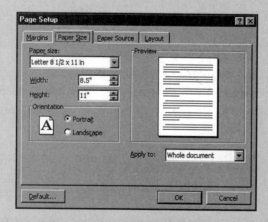

3 Click on the arrow at the end of the Pape**r** size drop-down list box to display a list of paper sizes. Note the list also includes envelope sizes.

4 Choose a new paper size and note that the entries in the **W**idth, H**e**ight, and Preview boxes change to correspond with the newly selected paper size.

(If you choose the "custom" option, you need to enter values in the **W**idth and H**e**ight boxes.)

5 Choose the Letter 8 1/2 x 11 in option (it's at the top of the drop-down list) to return to the standard Pape**r** size setting.

> ### Caution
>
> One of the leading causes of printer malfunction is the printer not having access to the selected paper size when the printing process begins. (Many printers also have trouble printing envelopes.) Make sure to change back to the paper size that was displayed when you opened the Paper **S**ize page.

6 Loca**t**e the Orientation section of the page; then choose Land**sc**ape and note the change in the Preview frame.

7 Choose OK to apply the new orientation to the Report document.

 8 To see the overall effect of your changes, choose the Print Preview button on the Standard toolbar; then use the *vertical* scroll bar in the Print Preview window to see all pages of your document.

Remember, to enlarge the size of the document in the window, either increase the Zoom setting, or click in the document.

9 After reviewing your changes, click the **C**lose button on the Print Preview toolbar to close the Preview window.

10 Open the Paper **S**ize page of the Page Setup dialog box again and change the Orientation back to Portrait; then keep the dialog box open and move to the next step.

11 Click the **M**argins tab, and then change the margins back to their original settings. (Change the top and bottom margins to 1 inch; change the left and right margins to 1.25 inches.)

12 Choose OK to close the dialog box and return your document to its original settings. Then review the changes to the document through the Print Preview window again.

As you can see, you can change the settings in two or more pages of a dialog box at one time. In this case, the changes you made to two pages in the Page Setup dialog box were activated when you chose OK.

13 Save your current version of the Report document and keep it open for the next exercise.

6

Objective 3: Control Page Breaks

Pagination
The way in which Word separates your document into pages.

Soft page break
A page break that Word inserts after calculating that the page cannot display the next character or graphic.

Hard page break
A break that you insert into a document to force Word to begin a new page.

When you format documents, you often need to control how the pages break throughout the document. (This is also referred to as *pagination*.)

Setting and Removing Page Breaks

Word automatically starts a new page whenever the current page is full, based on the settings for page size, margins, font sizes, the document text, line spacing, pagination options, and other relevant factors. When a page is full, Word inserts a *soft page break* into the document. As you edit or move text, Word continually recalculates the amount of text on each page and moves soft page breaks accordingly.

In some documents, you may want to begin a new page in a specific location. To do so, you insert a *hard page break*. Hard and soft page breaks differ in two ways:

- Word inserts soft page breaks automatically, but you must insert hard page breaks manually.

- You cannot delete a soft page break, but you can delete a hard page break.

> **Note**
>
> In most cases, when you insert a hard page break, the soft page break that Word placed at the (former) bottom of the page is either removed or relocated.

You can insert and delete hard page breaks with a menu command or by using the keyboard. Complete the following exercise to gain practice in working with hard page breaks.

Inserting and Removing Hard Page Breaks

To insert and remove hard page breaks, do the following steps:

1 In the open Report document, place the insertion point immediately in front of the *Memory* heading located near the top of the first page.

2 Choose **Insert**, **B**reak to display the Break dialog box. By default, the **P**age break option is selected in the Insert section (see Figure 6.3).

Figure 6.3
The Break dialog box.

3 Choose OK to insert a hard page break immediately above the current line.

The hard page break is represented by the dotted line (that includes the term *Page Break*) displayed above the *Memory* heading. Note that the insertion point is positioned below the page break and that the status bar indicates that the insertion point is now on page two of the document.

4 Choose the Print Preview button; then scroll through and view the pages of your document in the Print Preview window.

5 Close the Print Preview window by choosing the **C**lose button on the Print Preview toolbar (or by pressing Esc) and return to the Normal view of your document.

You may find it is necessary to create page breaks in specific locations in your documents. Using the menu is one way to add page breaks, but another way is to use the keyboard for this task.

6 Place the insertion point immediately in front of the *Storage* heading (located a few paragraphs below the *Memory* heading); then press Ctrl+↵Enter.

Word inserts a hard page break into the document immediately above the insertion point. The insertion point is now located on page three of the document.

Whichever method you use, the hard page break is shown in your document (when in Normal View) as a single dotted line across the page with the words *Page Break* at the line's center. This line does not appear when you print your document.

Depending on the location of your insertion point, you can press either Del or ←Backspace to remove a hard page break.

7 Make sure that your insertion point is still immediately in front of the *Storage* heading; then press ←Backspace once to remove the hard page break you just entered.

8 Click the hard page break dotted line immediately above the *Memory* heading; then press Del to remove the hard page break.

9 Choose the Print Preview button to view your document once more. It should be back into its original two-page format.

10 Close the Print Preview window by choosing the **C**lose button on the Print Preview toolbar, or by pressing Esc.

11 To ensure a consistent starting point for the next exercise, close the Report document now, without saving your changes. Leave Word open for the next exercise.

Using Pagination Options in the Paragraph Dialog Box

In the preceding chapter, you were introduced to the Line and **P**age Breaks page of the Paragraph dialog box. In the following exercise, you learn to use some of the options in this dialog box page to control where Word enters soft page breaks.

Keeping Lines Together

To keep lines together, follow these steps:

1 Open the Report document from your Student Disk. Turn on the display of the nonprinting characters, and then move the insertion point near the bottom of the first page.

2 Under the *Common Secondary Storage Media* heading, select the short paragraph, which begins with *Floppy Disks—removable...*, and the blank line below the paragraph; then delete the three selected lines.

Most likely, you now have part of a table at the bottom of your first page and the other part at the top of the second. If this is not the case, delete or insert enough document lines so that the table on 3.5-inch and 5.25-inch disks is split over two pages.

3 Select the group of lines, starting with the sentence located just above the table—the one beginning with *Table of floppy disks...*—and including the last line of the table (the line listing the 3.5-inch high-density disk).

4 Choose Format, Paragraph, and then, if necessary, choose the Line and Page Breaks tab to display that page.

5 In the Pagination section, place a mark in the Keep with next check box; then choose OK.

The page break should move to immediately above the *Table of floppy disks...* sentence. However, another error has occurred: a section title is left alone at the bottom of the first page while the accompanying text is displayed at the top of the next.

6 Select the block of lines starting with the *Common Secondary Storage Media* heading down through the last line of the disk table. Open the Line and Page Breaks page of the Paragraph dialog box, choose the Keep with next option for the new selection, and then choose OK.

The entire *Common Secondary Storage Media* portion of the document should now be placed on the second page.

7 Close the Report document without saving the changes; then open the File menu and click the Report file listing (near the bottom of the menu) to quickly reopen the file.

In the following steps, you rearrange the document to demonstrate the use of the Widow/Orphan protection option, which prevents a single line of a multiple-line paragraph from being displayed as a *widow* at the top, or as an *orphan* at the bottom, of a page.

8 Press Ctrl+A to select the entire document.

9 Choose Format, Paragraph to open the Paragraph dialog box; if necessary, display the Line and Page Breaks page.

10 Clear all the check boxes in all options (if some check boxes show a shaded gray check mark, you will need to click twice to remove the mark); then choose OK.

11 With the entire document still selected, press `Ctrl`+`2` to double-space the document; then click in the document to turn off the selection.

12 Scroll the window to display the last part of page 1, the page break, and the first lines of page 2.

13 Delete the blank line below the *Storage* heading and note that the first line of the paragraph *When information is moving...* moves from the top of the second page to the bottom of the first page.

It is standard practice to avoid displaying a single line of a paragraph, by itself, at the top or bottom of a page.

When a paragraph must be split between two pages, activating the **W**idow/ Orphan control option directs Word to place at least two lines of a paragraph at the top or bottom of a page.

14 Select the entire document (press `Ctrl`+`A`), open the Paragraph dialog box to the Line and **P**age Breaks page, choose the **W**idow/Orphan control option (to activate the command), and then choose OK.

Word relocates the soft page break to prohibit a single line of a paragraph from being displayed at the top or bottom of a page.

15 Click anywhere in the work area to turn off the selection; do not save the changes, but keep the three-page Report document open for the next exercise.

Objective 4: Format a Document in the Print Preview Window

Up to this point, you have probably been using the Print Preview window to make a final check of your document before it is printed. If you saw that changes were needed, you may have closed the Print Preview window and returned to Normal view to complete your edits. Although the Print Preview window is not designed to handle major document modifications, you can make many revisions while viewing your document in this window. The Print Preview window provides access to many of the Word menu commands, and offers some unique features to help you complete your work. Complete the following exercise to see new ways to use the Print Preview window.

Formatting in Print Preview

To use the Print Preview window for formatting, follow these steps:

1 Place the insertion point at the top of the opened, three-page, double-spaced Report document. (If your Report document is not open, open it now and double-space the entire document.)

2 Choose the Print Preview button from the Standard toolbar (or choose **File**, Print Pre**v**iew) to display the document in the Print Preview window.

> **Note**
>
> If the horizontal and vertical rulers are not displayed in your Print Preview window, choose the View Ruler button on the Print Preview toolbar (or choose **V**iew, **R**uler) to display both rulers.

Most of the time when you are working in Word, you see only a few paragraphs on your screen at one time. Similarly, when you open the Print Preview window, you usually see the page layout of just the current page of your document. However, you can see the general layout of numerous pages at the same time.

3 Rest the pointer on the Multiple Pages button on the Print Preview toolbar to display its ScreenTip; then choose the button to display a small grid immediately below the button.

Each cell in the grid represents a page that can be displayed in the Print Preview window. You determine the number of pages to be displayed (and hence, the size of each page) by either moving or dragging the pointer across the desired number of cells. If the grid does not include enough cells to represent all the pages you need to see, you can increase the grid size by dragging the pointer past the right side of the grid. By default, the grid will extend up to six cells across by two rows deep—representing 12 pages that can be displayed simultaeously in the Print Preview window.

4 Starting with the first cell in the upper-left corner of the grid, drag across the first three cells in the top row; then release the mouse button to display (small) images of all three pages of the document. (Alternatively, you can point and click on the third cell in the first row to achieve the same results.)

Your window should look similar to the one in Figure 6.4.

> **Note**
>
> When displaying more than one page in the Print Preview window, the horizontal ruler is displayed above only one page at a time. To move the horizontal ruler above a particular page, just click that page. You learn more about working with the Print Preview rulers later in this exercise.

Figure 6.4
The Print Preview window displaying three pages of a document.

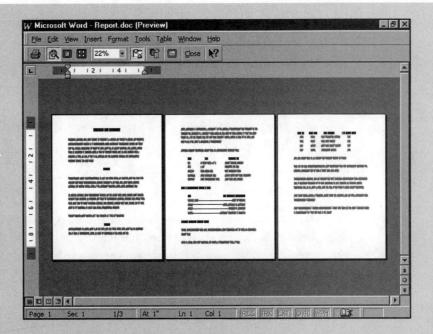

You know that you can move the magnifying glass pointer into a document page and then click to enlarge the page. However, you also can change the pointer to an *I-beam* pointer and then complete editing or formatting procedures inside your document.

5 Rest the pointer on the depressed Magnifier button on the Print Preview toolbar to see its corresponding ScreenTip; then choose the button and move the pointer into the middle of the first page of your document.

The shape of the pointer now appears as an I-beam. Although the print may be impossible to read, you can see what the basic page layouts consist of and the location of the topic headings.

6 Place the pointer in front of the *Memory* heading located about one-third of a page down from the top of the first page; then click the mouse button to place the insertion point in front of the heading.

7 Enter a hard page break at this location by choosing **I**nsert, **B**reak to display the Break dialog box (if necessary), selecting the **P**age break option, and then choosing OK.

Your document should now consist of four pages. Verify this by checking the document paging information in the left half of the status bar.

> **Note**
>
> By default, Word calculates pagination in the *background*—that is, whenever you pause while typing or editing. Background repagination uses some memory. If you experience memory problems, you may want to turn off this option. This option is located in the General page of the Options dialog box. To display the Options dialog box, choose **T**ools, **O**ptions.

(continues)

Formatting in Print Preview (continued)

 8 Display all four pages in the Print Preview window by choosing the Multiple Pages button on the Print Preview toolbar, pointing on the second cell in the second row, and then clicking the mouse button.

 9 Choose the One Page button on the Print Preview toolbar to display only one page (the one containing the insertion point, in this case, page 2) in the Print Preview window.

10 Click the arrow at the end of the Zoom button to display a list of Zoom options; then choose 75%.

This enables you to see almost all the entire page width across your window. Verify that you can edit the characters in your document from the Print Preview window by completing the next step.

11 Use the selection bar to select the first paragraph under the *Memory* heading, the one beginning with *RAM (Random Access Memory…)* then press Ctrl+U to underline the selection. (Although the Formatting toolbar is not displayed, you can still use the shortcut keys and dialog boxes to complete formatting procedures.)

By dragging the margin markers on the vertical and horizontal rulers, you can change the margins of a document when it is displayed in the Print Preview window. A ruler margin marker is shown as a light gray line between the white (document) part of the ruler and the dark gray (margin) part of the ruler. When the pointer is resting on a margin marker, it changes to a black double-headed arrow. The direction along the ruler that you drag the arrow determines the dimension of the margin.

Press Alt *while* you are dragging a margin marker to display the dimension of the margin in the ruler. The dimension changes as you drag the marker. When you establish the desired margin, release the mouse button first; then release Alt.

12 Rest the pointer on the top margin marker in the vertical toolbar, press the mouse button, and then press Alt. Drag the pointer (and margin marker) down until you establish a two-inch top margin (see Figure 6.5).

Tip

The advantage of pressing Alt when dragging margin markers is that you see the exact dimension of the margin you are creating. To determine your margin size when dragging a margin marker without pressing Alt, read the ruler markings at the end of ruler where you are making the margin adjustment.

13 Release the mouse button now (then release Alt) to create a 2-inch top margin for all the pages in your document.

Figure 6.5
You can change the document margins by dragging the margin markers to a new location along the vertical or horizontal rulers.

Black, double-headed arrow on top of the margin marker

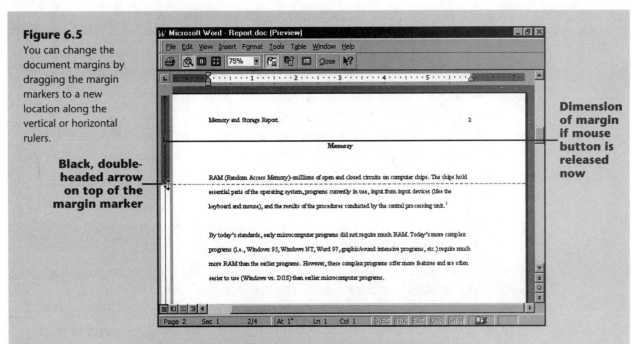

Dimension of margin if mouse button is released now

🄬 Choose the Multiple Pages button; then drag the pointer across the top three cells in the grid. Keep moving the mouse until you drag past the right edge of the third cell to expand the grid width to four cells. Then release the mouse to display the first four pages of the document.

Note the 2-inch margin at the top of each page. If you want to change the left or right margin for each page, you would use a similar technique to work with the horizontal ruler.

🄫 Return the document to its original 1-inch top margin by choosing **E**dit, **U**ndo formatting. Then leave the document open in the Print Preview window for the next exercise.

6

Earlier, you learned how to use the Widow/Orphan control to stop a single line of a paragraph from being displayed by itself at the top or bottom of a page. Sometimes, you create a multiple-page document where the last few lines are displayed at the top of the last page. Choosing the Print Preview window's Shrink to Fit option slightly reduces the size of some fonts used in the document. (The margins remain the same.) Using slightly smaller fonts increases the number of characters that may be displayed on each line of the document. This in turn usually results in a document being printed in fewer pages.

Shrinking the Document to Fit in Fewer Pages

To use the Shrink to Fit feature, complete the following steps:

❶ With the open four-page Report document displayed in the Print Preview window, choose the Shrink to Fit button on the Print Preview toolbar and note the change in the Print Preview window.

(continues)

Shrinking the Document to Fit in Fewer Pages (continued)

Choosing this button reduces the document to three pages while maintaining the hard page break between pages one and two that you inserted in the previous exercise.

In the original document, the size of the title font was 12 points, the *Memory* and *Storage* headings were displayed in an 11-point font, and regular text was displayed in a 10-point font.

❷ Close the Print Preview window; then move the insertion point into the text and note the new size of the text font.

❸ Move the insertion point into the title and headings and note the new sizes of the title and headings fonts.

❹ Close the Report document without saving the changes. Leave the Word window open for the next exercise.

At this point, you know how to change the top margin of all the pages in your document. However, what if you need to change the margins of only one page in a multiple-page document? Similarly, in an earlier exercise you learned to change the orientation of the pages in a document from portrait to landscape; what if you want only one page in your document to print in landscape orientation? At times like these, you need to divide your documents into sections. You learn about sections in the next objective.

Objective 5: Divide a Document into Sections

Setting margins, page orientation, and page numbering, and creating headers and footers, are examples of page-level formatting procedures. When working in a document where you need some pages to use one set of page-level formats, and another group of pages to use different page-level formats, you need to break the document into sections. Each document section can contain its own collection of page-level format settings.

A common example of a document requiring sections is a report where the title page needs to be formatted differently from the rest of the document. In most reports, the majority of the pages include page numbers, headers, and footers; however, these items are usually not included in a title page.

To break a document into sections, insert a section break wherever you want a new section to begin. You can have as many sections as you want within a document. In the following exercise, you create a title page for the Report document. Because the new title page requires a different format from the rest of the pages in the document, you insert a section break to separate the title page from the rest of the document pages. In later exercises, when working with page numbers and headers and footers, you will insert additional section breaks into the document.

Creating a Vertically Centered Report Title Page

Title pages for reports are usually vertically centered to ensure the same amount of white space appears above and below the top and bottom lines of text on the title page. Vertical centering replaces the need to press ⏎Enter a number of times to center the content of the page.

❶ Open the Report document from your Student Disk and make sure that the insertion point is at the top of the document.

Note that the insertion point is placed in a document location where the text is already bolded, the font size is 12 points, and the paragraph alignment is centered. This is important because you are about to add some new text to the document, and you should be aware that the present character and paragraph formatting is different from what is used in regular document text.

In the following steps, you create the title page for the Report document. There are many ways to format a title page. In the following steps, you use a commonly accepted title page format. However, feel free to modify the following steps if you use a different format for your work documents, or if your instructor requires a different format.

❷ Press ⏎Enter once; then move the insertion point back to the top of the document. Turn off the Bold button and return the font size to 10 points. (Keep the paragraph centered.)

❸ Type **MEMORY AND STORAGE**; then press ⏎Enter 15 times.

❹ Type **An internal report submitted by**, press ⏎Enter twice, type your first and last names, and then press ⏎Enter 15 times.

Word includes a date feature that enables you to insert a code into a document to display the date on your computer system's calendar when your document is printed. In the following step, you learn one way to insert this code into your document.

❺ Choose **I**nsert, Date and **T**ime to display the Date and Time dialog box.

This dialog box includes the various formats in which the date and time can be displayed in your document.

❻ Choose the third date option (the name of the month, date, and four-digit year), make sure that the **U**pdate automatically check box is marked, and then choose OK to close the dialog box and insert the date code into your title page.

❼ Choose **I**nsert, **B**reak to display the Break dialog box.

The Section breaks portion of the dialog box displays four types of section breaks:

(continues)

6

Creating a Vertically Centered Report Title Page (continued)

- *Next page.* The text after the break starts at the beginning of a new page.

- *Continuous.* The text after the break continues on the same page as the text before the break.

- *Even page.* The text after the break starts at the beginning of the next even-numbered page.

- *Odd page.* The text after the break starts at the beginning of the next odd-numbered page.

> **Note**
>
> To accomplish the goals of this chapter, you will exclusively use the **N**ext page section break in the chapter exercises. In later chapters, you will have the chance to work with other types of section breaks.

8 Choose the **N**ext page option in the *Section breaks* portion of the dialog box; then choose OK to close the dialog box and insert the section break following the date.

Word starts a new section at the position of the insertion point. A non-printing double line appears across the screen. The words *Section Break (Next Page)* appear in this line, indicating where one section ends and that the next section begins on the next page.

9 Delete the blank line immediately below the section break; then press the ⬆ key once to return to the title page section of the document.

Your Word window should look similar to the one in Figure 6.6.

Figure 6.6
The title page is created as a separate section from the rest of the document.

Section break that serves also as a page break

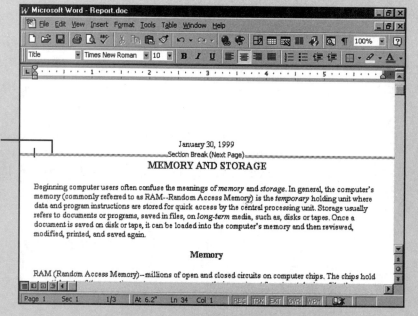

⑩ Choose the Print Preview button to display the title page of your document; if necessary, choose the One Page button.

Note the unequal amount of white space above and below the last lines of text on this page.

⑪ With the Print Preview window still open, choose **F**ile, Page Set**u**p to display the Page Setup dialog box.

⑫ If necessary, choose the **L**ayout tab to display the **L**ayout page; then click the arrow at the end of the **V**ertical alignment drop-down list box to display a list of choices of vertical alignment—Top, Center, Justified.

These choices affect all the pages in the current section. Note that Apply to text box displays the this section option, and the status bar indicates that the insertion point is currently in the first section by its listing of *Sec 1* on the left side of the bar.

⑬ Choose Center from the list; then choose OK to close the dialog box and vertically center the contents of each page within the current section (in this case, just the title page) between the top and bottom page margins.

⑭ Scroll through the next pages (the pages in Section 2) and note that the last document page is not vertically centered.

⑮ Close the Print Preview window. Save your changes to the Report document; then leave it open for the next exercise.

Deleting a Section Break

Word stores all section formatting in the section break. If you delete a section break, the preceding text assumes the formatting of the following section.

To delete a section break, position the insertion point in the double line and press Del. Alternatively, you can position the insertion point immediately after the section break and press ⦅⬅Backspace⦆.

Numbering Pages

Word automatically keeps track of the number of pages in a document. As you work in a document, you can see the current page number in the status bar. To display page numbers on your printouts, you must first insert them into the document. Word inserts page numbers into the page header or footer. (In very general terms, a *header* is information printed within the top margin of a page; a *footer* is information printed within the bottom margin. The next objective provides more information on headers and footers.)

Word provides two methods for inserting page numbers into the document:

- The Page Number dialog box, which is displayed when you choose **I**nsert, Page N**u**mbers

- The Header and Footer toolbar, which is displayed when you choose **V**iew, **H**eader and Footer

6

In this section, you learn how to place page numbers in a document by using the Page Numbers dialog box. From this dialog box, you can choose the position, alignment, and format of the page numbers. By default, Word places an Arabic number (1, 2, 3, and so on) in a footer on the right side of the page.

In the objective following this section, you learn to insert many different types of entries (including page numbers) into headers and footers by using the Header and Footer toolbar.

Inserting Page Numbers

To insert page numbers in your document, follow these steps:

1 In the open Report document, place the insertion point at the top of the document.

2 Choose **Insert**, Page N**u**mbers.

The Page Numbers dialog box is displayed (see Figure 6.7).

Figure 6.7
Use the Page Numbers dialog box to choose the position, alignment, and format of page numbers.

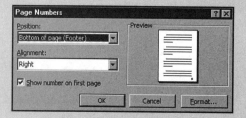

3 Choose Top of Page (Header) from the **P**osition drop-down list to place the page numbers at the top of the page.

4 Open the **A**lignment drop-down list to see the alignment choices; then choose Right to place the page numbers about .5 inches down from the top edge of the page and 1.25 inches in from the right edge of the page.

Note

The Left, Center, and Right options are relative to the left and right margins; the Inside and Outside options are relative to the inside binding and outside edges of pages that will be bound.

5 Clear the **S**how number on first page check box to deselect that option so that no page number will appear on the first page.

6 Choose OK to insert page numbers on all pages except the first.

Don't be surprised when your Word view changes to Page Layout view. Page numbers are not displayed on-screen in Normal view. They are displayed in Page Layout view and Print Preview.

7 Choose the Print Preview button to open the Print Preview window, and then display the first page by itself. Use the scroll arrows on the vertical scroll bar to scroll through the three pages of your document and verify that the page numbers in the upper-right corner of pages two and three are displayed.

Note

While in Page Layout view, if you increase the Zoom setting so that you can read the text, you may note that while the document text is displayed in black, the page number appears in a gray shading. The page number actually is placed in a page header. When the document text is active, header and footer entries are inactive (and thus displayed in a gray shade). In the next objective, you learn to activate the header and footer portions of your document.

 8 Change back to Normal view by choosing the Normal View button in the set of buttons attached to the left end of the horizontal scroll bar.

9 Save the changes to the Report document and leave it open for the next exercise.

In the preceding exercise, you used the default number format in the Page Numbers dialog box. You may choose to use a different page number format by selecting one of the options in the Page Number Format dialog box (see Figure 6.8). To display this dialog box, open the Page Numbers dialog box and choose the **F**ormat button. When the Page Number Format dialog box is displayed, choose the drop-down arrow at the end of the Number **f**ormat text box to display a variety of numbering styles. Then choose the desired style, make any other needed changes in the dialog box, and choose OK to return to the Page Numbers dialog box. Choose OK to close the Page Numbers dialog box and apply the changes to your document.

Figure 6.8
The Page Number Format dialog box.

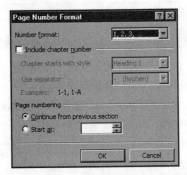

This dialog box also provides the option to include the current chapter number (if one exists) with your page number. In the dialog box Page numbering section, you must choose to either continue the page numbering from a previous section, or start the page numbering at the beginning of the current document section. (If you choose the second option, you also need to insert a number in the Start **a**t box.)

6

The typical format used in numbering the pages of a report includes these options:

- No page number assigned to the title page

- The first page of the actual report identified as page 1, but no page number printed on this page

- The second page of the actual report identified as page 2 with a page number near the top or bottom of the page

To change the page numbering you just entered in the Report document, complete the following exercise.

Changing the Page Numbers

Do these steps to change page numbers:

1 In the open Report document, place the insertion point in front of the main document title *Memory and Storage* at the beginning of section 2.

Before continuing with the next step, review the status bar information to ensure that the insertion point is placed in section 2.

2 Choose **Insert**, Page **Nu**mbers to display the Page Numbers dialog box.

Note

By default, when the Page Numbers dialog box is displayed, the **S**how numbers on first page check box is marked. In the previous exercise, when the insertion point was in the first section of the document and you displayed this dialog box, you cleared the **S**how numbers on first page check box. When you display the dialog box again by completing step 2, the option is active once again because the insertion point is now in the second section of the document.

Caution

Make sure that the entries in the **P**osition and **A**lignment boxes correspond with the position of the existing page numbers. If these entries do not correspond, your attempt to modify existing page numbers will actually insert page numbers into additional locations in the document.

3 Choose the **F**ormat button to display the Page Number Format dialog box.

4 Choose the Start **at** option and make sure that **1** is displayed in the Start **at** text box.

5 Choose OK to return to the Page Numbers dialog box.

6 Clear the check box in front of the **S**how number on first page command; then choose OK to close the Page Numbers dialog box and complete the page numbering changes.

7 Change the zoom setting to page width; then scroll through the pages in the document and note that only the last page (listed as page 2) displays a page number.

8 Return to Normal view of your document, save the changes, and then leave the file open for the next exercise.

You have learned how to insert page numbers into headers and footers; however, headers and footers can contain a multitude of different entries. In the next section, you learn how to insert additional information into headers and footers.

Objective 6: Create Headers and Footers

You can add headers and footers to an existing document, or you can create headers and footers in a new document before that document contains any text.

Word provides a number of options for displaying headers and footers on the pages in your document. The same header and/or footer can appear on each page. You can omit or place a different header or footer on the first page of a document (or on the first page of a section of a document). You can also display one header or footer on odd-numbered pages and a different header or footer on even-numbered pages. Different odd-page and even-page headers and footers are useful when you print on two sides of the paper and bind your documents.

Headers and footers are not displayed in the Word Normal view; however, they are displayed in Page Layout and Print Preview views. To start working with headers and footers, choose **View**, **H**eader and Footer. When this command is chosen, four things happen:

- Word changes to Page Layout view if it is not already in use.

- A Header text box (also referred to as an editing box) is displayed near the top of the page in the window work area. The insertion point is located in the top-left corner of the box.

- The Header and Footer toolbar is displayed.

- The document text is dimmed to gray to show that the document text is currently inactive.

Word does not enable you to work with document text *while* you are working with headers and footers. The document text turns gray (that is, it is inactive) when the header and footer boxes are active. When the header and footer boxes are closed, the text returns to black (it's now active), and the headers and footers are displayed in gray to show that *they* are now inactive.

The Header and Footer toolbar has 13 buttons. As with other toolbar buttons, you can rest the pointer on any button to see the button's ScreenTip. For more information on a button, press ⚡Shift+F1 to display the Help pointer; then click on a button to see a brief description of its purpose. Table 6.1 provides a quick reference to the use of the Header and Footer toolbar buttons.

6

Table 6.1   Header and Footer Toolbar Buttons

Button	Name	Function
Insert AutoText ▾	Insert AutoText	Displays a list of AutoText entries and inserts the chosen entry into the header or footer.
[#]	Insert Page Number	Inserts page numbers into the header or footer; these page numbers are automatically updated when pages are added or deleted.
[+]	Insert Number of Pages	Inserts the total number of pages in the document; use in combination with the Page Number button and appropriate text to display entries like *Page 4 of 7* in headers or footers.
[#]	Format Page Number	Displays the Page Number Format dialog box to format page numbers.
[7]	Insert Date	Inserts a date field that displays the current date (according to your computer system) in the header or footer when the document is opened or printed.
[clock]	Insert Time	Inserts a time field that displays the current time (according to your computer system) in the header or footer when the document is opened or printed.
[book]	Page Setup	Opens the Page Setup dialog box so that you can modify various page settings.
[doc]	Show/Hide Document Text	Shows or hides the current document text while you work in the header or footer.
[pages]	Same as Previous	When activated, inserts the header or footer of the preceding section into the current section. When turned off, breaks the link between the header and footer in the preceding section.
[switch]	Switch Between Header and Footer	Switches from header box to footer box, and vice versa.
[prev]	Show Previous	Moves the insertion point to the preceding header or footer.
[next]	Show Next	Moves the insertion point to the next header or footer.
Close	Close	Closes the Header and Footer toolbar and editing boxes and returns the insertion point into the document.

By default, when the insertion point is in a header or footer text box, the horizontal ruler displays two tab stop settings: a Center Tab at the 3-inch mark and a Right Tab at the 6-inch mark. These settings make it easy for you to place three elements in a header or footer—one at the left, one at the center, and one at the right.

In the following exercise, you insert a header that is displayed on most, but not all, of the pages of a document.

Creating a Header or Footer

To create a header or footer, do these steps:

1 In the open Report document, select all lines of text on the last two pages of the three-page document.

2 Press Ctrl+2 to double-space the selected lines.

When you first create headers and footers, word applies them to all sections of your document, thus ensuring the same header and footer on each document page. However, the Layout page of the Page Setup dialog box provides options for creating odd page and even page headers and footers. A second option lets you create a different first page header and footer for each section of your document.

3 Click anywhere in section two to turn off the selection. Then choose **F**ile, Page Set**u**p, choose the **L**ayout tab if necessary; then check the Headers and Footers frame to see that the Different **o**dd and even check box is clear and if necessary put a check in the Different **f**irst page option check box (The different first page option may already be checked because you suppressed the page number on the first page of Section 2.)

4 Move the insertion point into the first section and then verify that the default header and footer options will be used. Make any changes necessary to ensure the Different odd and even check box is clear and the Different first page check box is marked. Then choose ok to close the dialog box.

5 Using the status bar as a guide, place the insertion point anywhere in the third page of the four-page document.

6 Choose **V**iew, **H**eader and Footer to change the document view to Page Layout view, and to display the document text in gray (it's currently inactive), the Header text box, and the Header and Footer toolbar.

7 Enter **Memory and Storage Report** along the left side of the header box (see Figure 6.9).

8 Use the down arrow in the vertical scroll bar to scroll down to the last page of the document to see the *Memory and Storage Report* header on the last page of the document.

Because the Different **f**irst page header and footer option is active for both sections, the header you inserted on the third page of the document should not appear on pages one and two.

9 Use the up arrow on the vertical scroll bar to view the tops of pages one and two of your document.

Verify that the header box is blank for the first two pages.

(continues)

6

Creating a Header or Footer (continued)

Figure 6.9
The Section 2 Header box and Header and Footer toolbar.

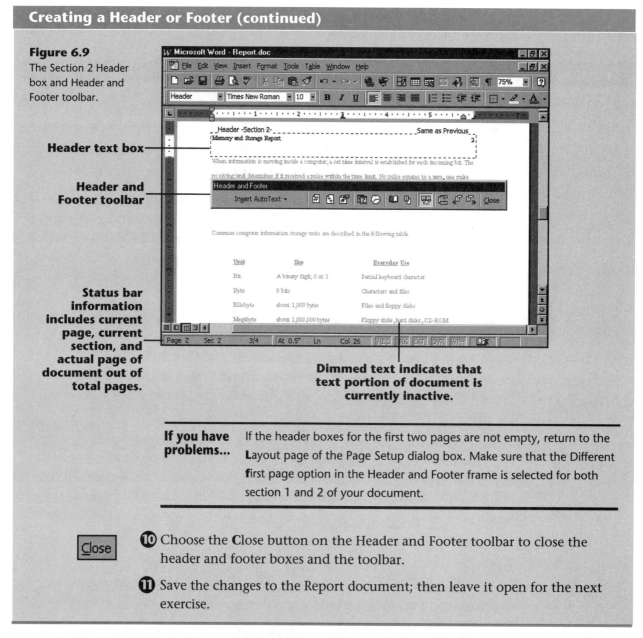

Header text box

Header and Footer toolbar

Status bar information includes current page, current section, and actual page of document out of total pages.

Dimmed text indicates that text portion of document is currently inactive.

If you have problems... If the header boxes for the first two pages are not empty, return to the **L**ayout page of the Page Setup dialog box. Make sure that the Different **f**irst page option in the Header and Footer frame is selected for both section 1 and 2 of your document.

🔟 Choose the **C**lose button on the Header and Footer toolbar to close the header and footer boxes and the toolbar.

⓫ Save the changes to the Report document; then leave it open for the next exercise.

After you insert a header or footer, you can edit and format the entry in the same way that you edit and format document text.

Editing a Header or Footer

To practice editing headers and footers, follow these steps:

❶ In the open Report document, place the insertion point anywhere in the third page; then choose **V**iew, **H**eader and Footer to display the Header and Footer toolbar and the header entry you made in the preceding exercise.

The insertion point is automatically placed in the page header.

❷ Select the phrase *Memory and Storage Report* and delete it.

3 Choose the Switch Between Header and Footer button on the Header and Footer toolbar to switch to the Footer -Section 2 box.

4 Press (Tab⇆) once to move the insertion point to the center tab position in the footer. Type **Report on Memory and Storage** and then bold the new footer entry and change its font size to 12 points.

Your window should look similar to the one in Figure 6.10.

Figure 6.10
The Section 2 Footer text box with a formatted entry.

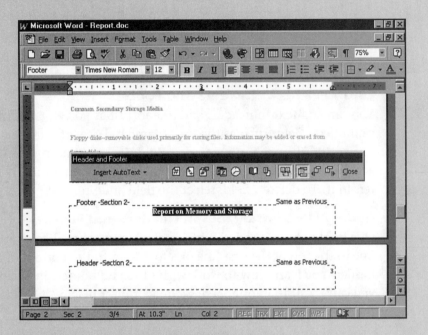

5 Use the up arrow in the vertical scroll bar to scroll to the First Page Footer – Section 2- box, which is located on the previous page. (The page you are scrolling to is the second of the four total pages in the document and is also the first page of Section 2.) Note that the new footer has not been placed in the footer box.

This is because the default Different **f**irst page Header and Footer option is active for section 2.

6 Choose the Page Setup button on the Header and Footer toolbar to display the **L**ayout page of the Page Setup dialog box.

7 Clear the check box in front of the Different **f**irst page option in the Headers and Footers section; then choose OK to return to your document.

8 Display the footer box on the second page (the page following the title page; this is also the first page of the Section 2). You should see that the *Report on Memory and Storage* footer is now also displayed on this page.

Because you did not change the Different **f**irst page option for the first section, there still should not be a footer on the first page of your document.

(continues)

Editing a Header or Footer (continued)

9 Scroll up to the first page of the document to verify that it does not contain a footer entry.

If the footer appears on the first page, open the **L**ayout page of the Page Setup dialog box and activate the Different **f**irst page option.

10 Choose the **C**lose button on the Header and Footer toolbar to close the header and footer boxes and the toolbar.

11 Close the Report document without saving the latest changes. Leave the Word window open for the next exercise.

Editing Fields in Headers and Footers

You can edit text in headers and footers just as you edit any other text, but you cannot edit fields such as the Page Number, Date, or Time. Each of these fields is one entity, although number, date, and time appear on-screen as separate characters. You can delete the entire field, but you cannot modify individual characters in it. To delete a field, select the field and press Del.

Adding Horizontal Lines in Headers and Footers

One final note on headers and footers. Many people like to attach a horizontal line to the top of the first line of a footer, or to the bottom of the last line of a header. You learn how to work with lines and borders in Chapter 11. However, if you can't wait that long, here's a quick tip for placing a horizontal line above the first line of a footer:

1. Place the insertion point in the first line of the footer.

2. Click the down arrow to the right of the Border button to display a list of lines and borders.

3. Choose the Top Border button in the grid (second from left in the first row).

Objective 7: Create Footnotes and Endnotes

Footnotes and endnotes are used to provide references for the information in the document. Numbers or symbols may be used to mark a footnote or endnote. The default footnote format in Word is an Arabic number (1, 2, 3,...) that has been formatted in superscript. Footnotes are displayed on the same page as their corresponding mark. Endnotes are displayed at the end of a section or at the end of a document. The default endnote format uses lowercase Roman numerals to identify each endnote. The same basic procedure is used for inserting a footnote or an endnote.

When you use the Footnote or Endnote feature, Word automatically formats the footnotes and endnotes for you. If you make a mistake when entering the note information, or if you want to change the format of the note, you can edit the notes at any time.

Inserting a Footnote

To insert a footnote, do these steps:

1 Open the Report document and make sure that the document is displayed in Normal view.

2 Place the insertion immediately following the period at the end of the first paragraph on the second page, the paragraph that ends with ...*modified, printed, and saved again.*

3 Chose **I**nsert, Foot**n**ote to display the Footnote and Endnote dialog box (see Figure 6.11).

Figure 6.11
The Footnote and
Endnote dialog box.

<table>
<tr><td colspan="2">Footnote and Endnote</td></tr>
<tr><td colspan="2">Insert</td></tr>
<tr><td>● Footnote</td><td>Bottom of page</td></tr>
<tr><td>○ Endnote</td><td>End of document</td></tr>
<tr><td colspan="2">Numbering</td></tr>
<tr><td>● AutoNumber</td><td>i, ii, iii, ...</td></tr>
<tr><td>○ Custom mark:</td><td></td></tr>
<tr><td colspan="2">Symbol...</td></tr>
<tr><td colspan="2">OK   Cancel   Options...</td></tr>
</table>

Tip

To insert a custom mark, start by choosing the **C**ustom mark option in the Numbering section. Then enter the desired mark directly into the text box. You may also choose the **S**ymbols button to display the Symbol dialog box, select the desired mark, and then choose OK to place the selected mark into the text box.

4 Make sure that the **F**ootnote option is selected in the Insert section, and that the **A**utoNumber option is selected in the Numbering section; then choose OK.

This step closes the dialog box, inserts a superscripted 1 at the insertion point, opens the Footnote pane in the lower half of the window work area, and places the insertion point immediately behind the corresponding superscripted 1.

5 Enter the following information in the Footnote frame:

Debbie Powers, *Computer Memory and Storage*, Holly Books, Indianapolis, 1997, p. 4.

Your window should now look similar to the one in Figure 6.12.

6 Choose the **C**lose button on the Footnote bar to close the footnote pane.

7 Choose the Print Preview button to view the footnote added to the bottom of the second page of the document.

(continues)

6

Inserting a Footnote (continued)

You also can view and insert footnotes from Page Layout view. The Footnote pane is not displayed in Page Layout view. Instead, the **F**ootnote command moves the insertion point directly into the footnote section at the bottom of the page.

Footnote markers may be moved or deleted.

Figure 6.12
The text for the first footnote is entered in the Footnote pane.

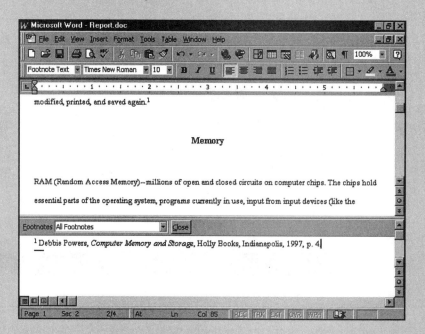

8 Return to Normal view; then (if it is not already there) place the insertion point immediately after the footnote marker in the first paragraph on the second page of the document.

9 Press **+Backspace** once to select the footnote marker; then choose the Cut button on the Standard toolbar to cut the selection to the Clipboard.

10 Move the insertion point to the end of the next paragraph, the one on RAM that ends with *...the central processing unit.*

11 Click the Paste button to complete the move of the footnote marker.

Note

You can also delete a footnote marker, and accompanying reference material by selecting the footnote marker and pressing **Del**. Alternatively, you can place the insertion point immediately after the footnote marker and press **+Backspace** twice.

12 Save the changes to the Report document and close the file.

Chapter Summary

This chapter focused on working with page formatting commands. You learned how to set margins, paper size, and orientation; insert page breaks; format in the Print Preview window; format sections; create headers and footers; use page numbering; and work with footnotes and endnotes.

If you have completed your work for this computer session, make sure that you properly exit all open programs. Then use the Windows Sh**u**t Down command to safely exit Windows. To test your knowledge of the material covered in this chapter, answer the questions in the Checking Your Skills section immediately following this summary. Then complete the exercises in the Applying Your Skills section at the end of the chapter.

Checking Your Skills

True/False

For each of the following, circle *T* or *F* to indicate whether the statement is true or false.

T (F)   **1.** The default left and right margin for Word documents is one inch. *IS 1.25 "*

(T) F   **2.** By default, Word starts a new page whenever the current page is full.

T (F)   **3.** A footer is the same thing as a footnote.

T F   **4.** Word stores all section formatting in the section break.

T (F)   **5.** The Page Setup dialog box is the only dialog box that can control where the pages break in a document.

(T) F   **6.** You can change the document margins in the Print Preview window without using a dialog box.

(T) F   **7.** The Print Preview window does not enable you to access most of the commands available from the menu bar.

(T) F   **8.** The Shrink to Fit option can usually reduce a two-and-one-quarter-page document to a two-page document by slightly reducing the size of the font(s) used in the document.

(T) F   **9.** Only two page orientations are available in Word: portrait and landscape.

T F   **10.** Probably the fastest way to enter a hard page break is to press Ctrl+H.

Multiple Choice

In the blanks provided, write the letter of the correct answer for each of the following questions.

1. The default top and bottom margin settings in Word are __*a*__.

    a. 1 inch for both

    b. 1.5 inches for both

    c. 1 inch and 2 inches

    d. 1.25 for both

    e. none of the above

2. Which Word element cannot be used to format part or all of a page in a Word document? _____

    a. Formatting toolbar

    b. Header and Footer toolbar

    c. Print Preview window

    d. Page Setup dialog box

    e. all of the above *can* be used in page formatting

6

3. When a page is full and you continue typing, Word inserts __c__.

    a. a hard page break

    b. a hard section break

    c. a soft page break

    d. a soft section break

    e. printer control characters

4. Click the __b__ Header and Footer toolbar button to move the insertion point to the next header or footer in a document that contains headers or footers in different sections of the document.

    a. Switch to Header and Footer

    b. Show Next

    c. Show Previous

    d. Same As Previous

    e. Show/Hide Document Text

5. Section header and footer options available through the Page Setup dialog box include which of the following? _____

    a. Different **f**irst page

    b. **I**dentical header and footer

    c. Different **o**dd and even

    d. a and b

    e. a and c

6. Which of the following is not a page in the Page Setup dialog box? __e__

    a. **L**ayout

    b. **H**eaders and Footers

    c. Paper **S**ize

    d. **M**argins

    e. **P**aper Source

7. When you use the default margins and display the header or footer text box, the horizontal ruler appears with which of the following tab settings? __e__

    a. a Left Tab at 1.25 inches in from the left edge of the page

    b. a Right Tab at the 6-inch mark on the ruler

    c. a Center Tab at the 3-inch mark on the ruler

    d. a and b

    e. a, b, and c

8. To delete a section break, position the insertion point on the double line representing the section break and press __d__.

    a. Esc

    b. Tab

    c. ↵Enter

    d. Del

    e. ←Backspace

9. The default Word footnote marker is an Arabic numeral displayed in _____.

    a. bold

    b. italic

    c. superscript

    d. subscript

    e. a font one size larger than the document text.

10. Extra space added to the inside edge of facing pages to allow space for binding describes a __c__.

    a. note space

    b. section break

    c. gutter

    d. soft space

    e. page break

Fill in the Blank

In the blank provided, write the correct answer for each of the following questions.

1. Page breaks and section breaks can be inserted from the _____ dialog box.

2. You set page orientation from the _____ page of the Page Setup dialog box.

3. Typically, headers consist of characters or graphics that are displayed in the _____ margin of a page.

4. Endnotes are displayed at the end of a document or the end of a *page*_____.

5. The Header and Footer toolbar enables you to insert time, date, and page number _____ into your headers and footers.

6. By default, footers are placed _____ inches from the bottom of the page.

7. As _____ size increases, the amount of room to display document information decreases.

8. You automatically create a _____ or _____ when you add page numbers to a document.

9. To set the vertical alignment of a page, use the **V**ertical alignment option in the _____ page of the Page Setup dialog box.

10. If the first page of your document is vertically centered, you must use _____ to enable other pages to not be displayed as vertically centered.

Applying Your Skills

Review Exercises

Exercise 1: Changing Margins and Page Orientation

To practice formatting margins and changing the page orientation, follow these steps:

1. Open the Chap0602 file from your Student Disk; then save the file back to your disk as **Meeting 06**.

2. Set the left and right margins at 2 inches.

3. Set the top and bottom margins at 2 inches.

4. Set the page orientation to landscape.

5. Save the revisions to the Meeting 06 file; then print and close the file.

Exercise 2: Creating Page Breaks and Inserting Page Numbers

To practice formatting margins and inserting page breaks, follow these steps:

1. Open the Chap0603 file from your Student Disk; then save the file back to your disk as **Planning 06**.

2. Set the top and bottom margins at 2.5 inches.

3. Create page breaks immediately in front of the *March 6*, *April 8*, and *Upcoming Summer Events* headings.

4. Insert a page number at the bottom of each page. The page number should be centered across the page.

5. Save the revisions to the Planning 06 file; print and then close the file.

Exercise 3: Vertically Centering Business Letters

Business letters are usually vertically centered on the page. To practice this technique, complete the following steps:

1. Open the Chap0604 file from your Student Disk; then save the file back to your disk as **Business 06**.

2. Preview the document in the Print Preview window to view its current page layout. Then keep the Print Preview window open during steps 3 and 4.

3. Vertically center the document using the technique discussed in the chapter. (Do not try to center the document by pressing ⏎Enter numerous times.)

4. While viewing your vertically centered document in the Print Preview window, save the revisions to the file and then print the file.

5. Close the Print Preview window; then close the document.

Exercise 4: Creating Headers and Footers

To practice using headers and footers and the Word Page Layout view, follow these steps:

1. Open the Chap0605 file from your Student Disk; then immediately save the file back to your disk as **Employee Guidelines 06**.

2. Display the document in Page Layout view; then use the horizontal and vertical rulers to change the left, right, top, and bottom margins to two inches. (Note: If you have trouble moving the margin marker to precisely the 2" mark, try increasing the Zoom percentage to 75%.)

3. Create a page break immediately in front of the fourth guideline. (Hint: Place the insertion point in front of the *W* in *Worker*—the first word in the fourth guideline; then create the page break.) Make sure that the first line of the second page is not a blank line.

4. On the first page of the document, create a footer that displays the phrase **Employee Guidelines** in italic on the left side of the footer and the current page number on the right side of the footer. (Hint: In the horizontal ruler, drag the Right Tab marker so that it is on top of the Right Indent marker.) This footer should not be displayed on the second page of the document.

5. On the second page of the document, create a header that displays the phrase **Worker Vacation and Personal Day Guidelines** in bold print in the center of the header box, and with the current page number on the right side of the footer. This header should not be displayed on the first page. (IIint: In the horizontal ruler, drag the Center Tab marker to the 2.25-inch mark on the ruler.)

6. Save the revisions to the Employee Guidelines 06 document; print and then close the document.

Exercise 5: Dividing a Document into Sections

To practice creating sections and using headers and footers, complete the following steps:

1. Open the Chap0606 file from your Student Disk; then save the file back to your disk as **Steps 06**.

2. Create a combined section and page break immediately in front of the *To close a document* heading. Then create another combined page and section break immediately in front of the *To change fonts* heading.

3. Set 3-inch top and bottom margins for the text in section 2. Do not change the margins in sections 1 and 3.

4. Enter the text **Steps 06** as a left-aligned header for pages 2 and 3. No header should be displayed on page 1.

5. Type the appropriate text and use the appropriate Header and Footer toolbar buttons to create a right-aligned footer on pages 2 and 3 that reads **Page X of Y** (where *X* is the current page number, and *Y* is the total number of pages in the document). No footer should be displayed on page 1.

6. Save the revisions to your Steps 06 document; then print and close the file.

Continuing Projects

Project 1: Practice Using Word

Practice formatting a report by completing the following steps.

1. Open Chap0607 from your Student Disk; then save the file back to your disk as **Computer Hardware Overview**.

2. Create a title page for the report similar to the one you made earlier in this chapter. Use for the title page font the same Times New Roman, Regular, 12-point font used in the body of the report. Assume that this is an internal report for the people in your department at work.

3. Place the title *Table of Popular Intel Microprocessors* and the table below it in a separate section.

4. Vertically center the section including the table.

5. Create a footer that prints on all pages except the title page, left-aligns the phrase **Computer Hardware Overview**, and right-aligns the page number.

6. Attach a horizontal line to the top of the footer line.

7. Save the revisions to the Computer Hardware Overview file; print the file and then close it.

Project 2: Deli-Mart

Continue your work on the Deli-Mart menu by following these steps:

1. Open the Chap0608 file from your Student Disk; then immediately save the file back to your disk as **Menu 06**.

2. Create a combined section break and page break in front of the first menu item name.

3. Display the second section in landscape orientation.

4. Create a footer that prints only on the second and third pages and places the text *Deli-Mart Menu Items* at the left side of the footer and the word *Page*, followed by the current page number, on the right side of the footer. Adjust the position of the Right Tab marker as needed.

5. Save the revisions to the Menu 06 file; then print and close the file.

Project 3: The Marketing Connection

Continue your work on the newsletter for The Marketing Connection. The corporation is considering a new format and wants this newsletter to include the new headings and paragraphs listed below. Follow these steps to make the proposed changes:

1. Open the Chap0609 file from your Student Disk; then immediately save the file as **Market 06**.

2. Move to the end of the document; press ⏎Enter twice; then type the following paragraphs at the end of the file:

   Sales

   The sales department has developed a team approach for marketing products. Each sales representative visits or contacts organizations in his or her territory. If an organization is interested in a site demonstration of a product, the salesperson provides a presentation package. For more information about our sales department, call (401) MAR-SALE.

   Tours

   Every Monday through Friday, THE MARKETING CONNECTION offers tours of the corporate facilities. The hours of operation are 9:00 a.m. to 9:00 p.m. We ask that the organization send groups of no more than three representatives to view the facilities. We feel that a small group provides for a more personal tour. For more information, call (401) MAR-TOUR.

   Travel

   THE MARKETING CONNECTION offers special travel packages to all clients. We have a four-person department that plans 1-day to 10-day trips. If you are feeling down and need a lift, come and visit us; our office is open weekdays from 10:00 a.m. to 6:00 p.m. You also can reach us at (401) MAR-TRAV.

3. Create a combined section and page break for each heading and accompanying paragraph.

4. Center each heading throughout the document and make sure that each heading is displayed in the 16-point Arial font.

5. Create a header for the odd pages that centers and bolds the phrase *Marketing Connection News* and right-aligns the current page number. This header should print on every page but the first page.

6. Create a header for the even pages that left-aligns the current page number and centers and bolds the following phrase: *Give us a call at (800) MAR-CONN.*

7. Save the revisions to the Market 06 document; then print and close your file.

CHAPTER 7

Managing and Printing Files

As you continue to work with Word, your collection of saved documents will continue to grow. Eventually, you may find it difficult to remember the contents of specific files, or even remember the names of specific documents.

Besides enabling you to process characters and graphics, Word also provides features that help you manage and print your files. In this chapter, you learn how to use Word's file management tools to view file information and to find, copy, move, rename, and delete files. You also learn how to insert entire files into other files. The chapter concludes with information about Word's most frequently used printing options.

Objectives

By the time you finish this chapter, you will have learned how to

1. View File Information
2. Manage Files
3. Find Files
4. Insert Files into Open Word Documents
5. Manage the Printing of Files

Objective 1: View File Information

So far, you have used the Open and Save As dialog boxes for their most important functions: opening and saving files. However, both dialog boxes also include a number of tools to help you view file information and manage your files.

In the following exercise, you learn to use some of the tools in the Open dialog box to view file information and preview a selected file *before* opening it into a document window.

Note

The Student Disk used when creating the figures for this chapter included files from Chapters 5, 6, and 7. Make sure that the disk you use for this exercise includes the student files for Chapter 7 and at least a few additional files. This will enable you to see the functions of Word's file management tools. Don't worry if your screen does not exactly match the illustrations in the text. The only files you will delete from the disk, during the file management activities, will be copies of existing files on the disk.

The exercises in this chapter were written under the assumption that the Student Disk is placed in the 3.5-inch floppy (A:) drive. If your files are stored in a different location, please make the necessary corrections as you work through the chapter activities.

Throughout this chapter, the phrase *items in the large list box* is used often to keep referencing simple. In these instances, the term *items* refers to the folders and files on the disk or folder listed in the Look in drop-down list box of the Open or Save As dialog box. The *large list box* refers to the list box occupying most of the middle of the Open and Save As dialog boxes.

Viewing File Lists and File Information

To view files and file information, follow these steps:

 ❶ Start Word, place your Student Disk in the appropriate disk drive; then choose the Open button on the Standard toolbar to display the Open dialog box. Change the entry in the Look in box to the drive containing your Student Disk.

The Open dialog box on your screen should look similar to the one displayed in Figure 7.1. The name of each file is listed in the large list box. (If your dialog box displays different types of information, it may be necessary to choose the List button—the fifth button from the right in the group of buttons located slightly below the dialog box title bar.) If you have more files than can fit into the list box, scroll bars are displayed to enable you to scroll to the file names that are not visible when you first open the dialog box.

Note

Word's default setting for the Open dialog box includes using the List mode to list the folders, and then the files, in alphabetical order.

After the List button is pressed in your Open dialog box, your files are probably displayed like those in Figure 7.1. However, you can change the amount of file information included in the Open dialog box.

Figure 7.1
The buttons in the Open dialog box can be used to determine how the files are listed.

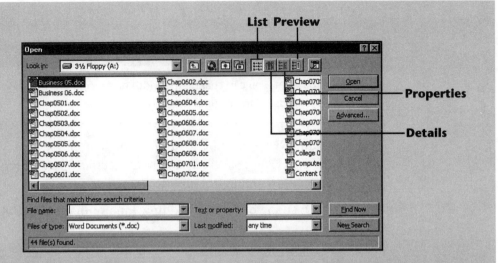

List Preview

Properties

Details

Note

The file names in Figure 7.1 display the three-character *doc* extension. As mentioned in an earlier chapter, you can choose to display or hide file extensions when listing your files. To change the listing of file extensions, open the Windows Explorer or My Computer window; choose **V**iew, **O**ptions; choose the View tab, and then mark or clear the Hide MS-DOS file **e**xtension for file types that are registered check box.

 ❷ Choose the Details button to display more information about each file.

At the top of the list box, note the headings above the information of the first file. Details mode includes the listing of the each item's name, file size of documents (in kilobytes—1 kilobyte equals 1,024 bytes), type of file, and the date and time it was either created or last modified (see Figure 7.2).

Files can be arranged by file name, size, type of document, or creation date/date of last modification. You change the order of the items by clicking a column heading. For example, to toggle between sorting the items in ascending or descending alphabetical order, click on the Name heading.

7

Figure 7.2
Choosing the Details button in the Open dialog box displays each file's name, size, type, and last modification date and time.

File information headings

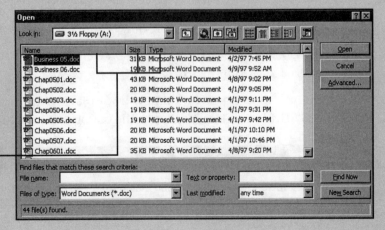

(continues)

Viewing File Lists and File Information (continued)

Tip

If you want, you can change the width of the columns by dragging the left or right border of the column heading box.

❸ Click the Name heading to arrange the item names in reverse alphabetical order (z–a). This is also referred to as *descending alphabetical order*. Then use the vertical scroll bar to scroll to the top of your list.

Your Open dialog box should now look similar to the one in Figure 7.3.

Figure 7.3
Choosing the Name heading changes the alphabetical listing of the items in the Open dialog box.

The names of the items are now in descending alphabetical order.

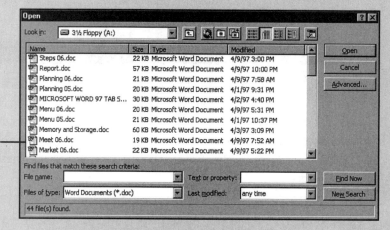

❹ Click the Name heading one more time to restore the listing to the ascending (a–z) alphabetical order format.

❺ Click the Size heading once to list the files from smallest to largest. Scroll through the list to see the new order.

❻ Click the Modified heading once to list the files from the earliest modified date to the most recent. Scroll through the list to see the new order.

❼ Click the Name heading once to return the listing to alphabetical order.

You can also split the large list box to display items in the storage location on the left side of the box and a preview of the selected file on the right side.

❽ In the Open dialog box, choose the Preview button; then select the Chap0701 file from the list.

Your Open dialog box should now be displaying the beginning of the Chap0701 file and look similar to the dialog box in Figure 7.4

Note

In the Preview frame of the Open dialog box, you can scroll through the contents of the selected document, by using the vertical scroll bar on the right side of the Preview frame.

Figure 7.4

Choosing the Preview button splits the list box to display items in the storage location on the left side and a preview of the beginning of the selected file on the right side.

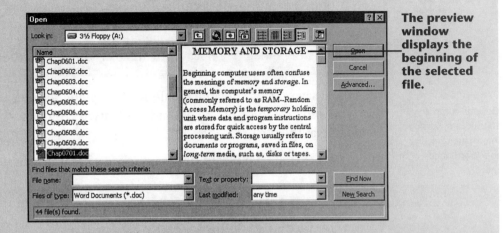

The preview window displays the beginning of the selected file.

You can also determine the contents displayed in the large list box by choosing to display only a certain type of file.

Different programs save files in different formats. For example, Word saves files in one format; Write (the Windows 3.1 word processor) saves files in a different format. (Write files are typically saved with a *wri* extension.) The listing in the Files of **t**ype box determines which items are displayed in the list box.

9 Click the arrow at the end of the Files of **t**ype list box to display a drop-down list of recognized file types.

The All Files (*.*) option is useful for displaying all the items on the storage device listed in the Look **i**n box. Most users prefer to display only a certain type of file in the list box to limit the number of items in the box. This makes it easier for you to find a particular file when scanning the list.

10 Choose the All Files (*.*) option; then look in the lower-left corner of the Open dialog box to see how many items are on your Student Disk.

Most likely, this will be the same number of items found when you use the default entry, Word Documents (*.doc).

11 Open the list again and choose Windows Write (*.wri).

The list box displays all items with a *wri* extension. If you have no files with a *wri* extension on your disk, the message in the bottom of the Open dialog box will show that no files were found.

12 Open the Files of **t**ype list box once more and choose the Word Documents (*.doc) option to redisplay your Word files in the dialog box.

Using the Preview option in the Open dialog box can be helpful, but it probably is an option you want to use sparingly. Leaving the Preview option active requires you to wait for Word to place the contents of the first file in the Open dialog box list into the computer's memory each time you display the Open dialog box. (This is necessary for the file to be displayed in the preview frame.) The dialog box information will be displayed more quickly when the dialog box only shows a list of item names or the details about the items in the list.

7

(continues)

Viewing File Lists and File Information (continued)

⓮ Choose the List button in the Open dialog box to change back to the default listing mode. Then leave the dialog box open for the next exercise.

Properties

General, summary, statistical, or version information relating to a Word document.

When you save a Word document, along with saving the characters and formatting, you also save information about the file itself. You view this information by looking at the file's *properties*.

In the next exercise, you learn two ways to view file properties.

Viewing File Properties

To view file properties, do these steps:

❶ With the Open dialog box displaying the list of items on your Student Disk, select the Chap0701 file; then choose the Properties button inside the dialog box.

Choosing the Properties button splits the list box in half. The right side of the box displays a short list of file properties for the selected file on the left side of the box. Your Open dialog box should look similar to the one in Figure 7.5

Figure 7.5

Displaying the short list of file properties in the Open dialog box.

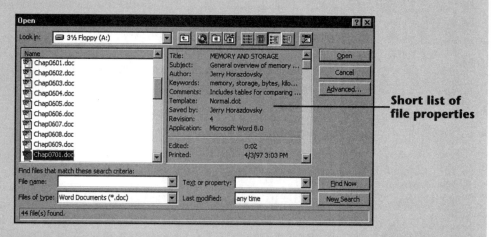

Short list of file properties

To view additional file information, display the Properties dialog box for the file. You can do this by choosing **File**, Properties when the file is open, or you can display the file's Properties dialog box from the Open dialog box.

❷ Right-click the Chap0701 file; then choose Properties from the shortcut menu.

The Chap0701 Properties dialog box is displayed; if necessary, choose the Summary tab (see Figure 7.6).

The Properties dialog box consists of five pages of information. In Figure 7.6, you see the Summary page.

Figure 7.6
Use the Summary page of the Properties dialog box to save relevant file information and attach it to the file.

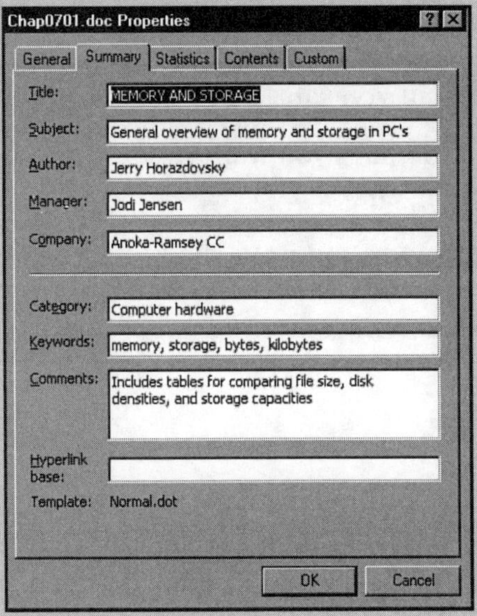

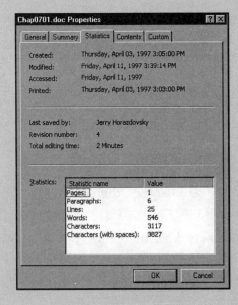

To enter summary information for an opened file, choose File, Properties to display the Properties dialog box; choose the Summary tab (if necessary); and then enter your desired information into the text boxes (up to 255 characters in each text box). If you are not sure of the purpose of a text box, choose the dialog box Help button (it looks like a ?); then click the box in question to see its purpose.

The unique information entered into the Summary page may be specified later as criteria when you search for particular files. (You learn how to use Word's search feature later in this chapter.)

❸ Choose the Statistics tab to see a statistical report on the file (see Figure 7.7).

Figure 7.7
Use the Statistics page to learn more about your document.

7

(continues)

Viewing File Properties (continued)

The Statistics page contains useful information about a document. You can view these statistics, but you can't edit them.

4 Choose any of the other tabs you want to see; then close the Properties dialog box by choosing OK.

5 Close the Open dialog box, but leave the Word window open for the next exercise.

Objective 2: Manage Files

Sometimes you need to work simultaneously with two or more files. Instead of opening the first file and then repeating a similar procedure to open each of the remaining files, you can use the Open dialog box to open at one time all the Word files you need. You learn how to do this in the first exercise in this section. In the second exercise, you work in the Save As dialog box to create a new folder on your disk. In the third exercise, you learn to use the Open dialog box to copy, move, rename, and delete files on your disk.

Opening, Closing, or Saving a Group of Files

To open and close groups of files, do the following steps:

1 Start this exercise with an open Word window and your Student Disk in the appropriate drive. Then display the Open dialog box and, if it is not already in use, choose the List button to display the items in List mode.

If necessary, change the entry in the Look in location to the location holding your student files.

The key to opening a group of files is to select all the desired files first, before choosing the Open button in the Open dialog box. You already know that clicking a file name selects one file. Holding down Ctrl or ◆Shift when clicking file names in the Open dialog box enables you to select as many files in the item list as you need.

2 Click the first file in the list box; then hold down ◆Shift and click the fourth file in the list.

The first four files should be selected (see Figure 7.8).

3 Note the names of the selected files; then choose the **O**pen button to open all four selected files at once.

All four files will be opened. Each file is opened in its own document window.

4 Choose the **W**indow command and note the listing of the four documents at the end of the menu.

Figure 7.8

Selecting the first file, pressing ⇧Shift, and then clicking the fourth file selects a group of four consecutive files in the Open dialog box.

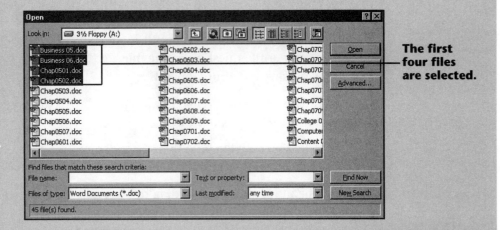

The first four files are selected.

⑤ Note the name of the currently displayed document; then choose from the lower part of the **W**indow menu a document name that does not display a check mark in front of it. (A check mark is placed in front of a document name to indicate the currently active document.)

⑥ Repeat steps 4 and 5 until you are satisfied that all the selected files are open.

Tip

Pressing Ctrl+F6 repeatedly is a quick way to cycle through the open files inside your Word window.

Just as you can open numerous files in one procedure, you can close or save numerous files in one procedure.

⑦ Press ⇧Shift and then open the **F**ile menu to see two new choices on the menu.

When you press ⇧Shift and then open the **F**ile menu, the **C**lose command is replaced by the **C**lose All command, and the **S**ave command is replaced by the Save A**ll** command.

If you are working with a number of open files and you want to keep all the modifications made to the open files, choose the Save A**ll** command to save simultaneously the changes to each open file. The file names will remain the same. If a new file has been created, Word asks you whether you want to save the changes to the new file. If you answer **Y**es, the Save As dialog box is displayed so that you can name and save the file.

For this example, you need to close just the open files.

⑧ Choose **F**ile, **C**lose All.

(continues)

7

Opening, Closing, or Saving a Group of Files (continued)

If no changes were made to the files, they all close. If changes have been made, answer the question in the message box about saving your changes; then close any remaining open files.

You can also draw a *selection box* around a consecutive group of files to be opened in the Open dialog box.

9 Open the Open dialog box; then place the mouse pointer about one-quarter inch to the right of the first file on the list.

10 Press the mouse button and drag the pointer down until it is even with the fourth file in the list. If the first four files are not already selected, drag the mouse to the left until the first four files are selected; then release the mouse button.

As you know, if you were to choose the **O**pen button, you would open all four selected files. Instead, complete the next step to turn off the selection of the four files.

11 Click the first of the four selected files to turn off the selection.

To select nonconsecutive files to open them simultaneously, select the first file, press and hold down Ctrl, and click each of the remaining files you want to open.

12 With the first file already selected, press and hold down Ctrl; then click the third and fifth files listed in the Open dialog box to select the first, third, and fifth files.

Again, if you chose **O**pen, all three selected files would be opened. Instead, complete the next step to close the dialog box and get ready for the next exercise.

13 Choose the Cancel button to close the Open dialog box. Leave the Word window open for the next exercise.

So far in this chapter, you have used the Open dialog box for file management activities. In the next exercise, you use the Save As box to add a folder to your Student Disk.

Creating a Folder from the Save As Dialog Box

To create a folder from the Save As dialog box, follow these steps:

1 If no blank or existing document is open in your Word window, choose the New button from the Standard toolbar to open a new blank document. (A document window must be open before you can access the Save As dialog box.)

2 Choose **F**ile, Save **A**s to display the Save As dialog box.

If necessary, change the storage location listed in the Save **in** box to the drive or folder holding your student files. Note that the Save As dialog box also includes List, Details, and Properties buttons, which function the same as in the Open dialog box.

❸ Make sure that the items are being displayed in List mode.

From the Word Save As dialog box, you can create a new folder in the drive or folder listed in the Save **in** box as easily as you can create a folder by using the Windows Explorer or My Computer windows.

❹ In the Save As dialog box, choose the Create New Folder button, located to the left of the List button, to display the New Folder dialog box (see Figure 7.9).

Figure 7.9
Enter the desired name for the new folder in the Name text box of the New Folder dialog box.

❺ Type **Chapter 7** in the **Name** text box; then choose OK to close the New Folder dialog box and create a new Chapter 7 folder on your Student Disk.

If you have problems...	If you see a message stating that you can't create the folder on your disk, make sure that the write-protection box on the disk is in the off position.

In the default settings, when the identified storage location in the Open or Save As dialog box includes folders and files, the items are listed in alphabetical order with all folders listed above the first file. If you are using the default setting, look for the Chapter 7 folder to be displayed above the first file in the list box.

❻ Choose Cancel to close the Save As dialog box. Leave the Word window open for the next exercise.

The steps in the next exercise may be completed from either the Open dialog box or the Save As dialog box. Both dialog boxes offer the capability to copy, move, rename, and delete items included in the large list box.

Completing File Management Activities from the Open Dialog Box

To move a file from one location to another, follow these steps:

❶ In the open Word window, display the Open dialog box.

If necessary, change the storage location in the Look **in** box to the drive or folder holding your student files and the Chapter 7 folder you created in the preceding exercise. Use List mode for displaying the items in the identified storage location.

(continues)

Completing File Management Activities from the Open Dialog Box (continued)

❷ Right-click the Chap0701 file to select the file and display the shortcut menu as shown in Figure 7.10.

Depending on how your system is set up, your shortcut menu may look somewhat different from the one in Figure 7.10.

Figure 7.10
The shortcut menu with the Open dialog box provides a variety of choices for working with the selected item.

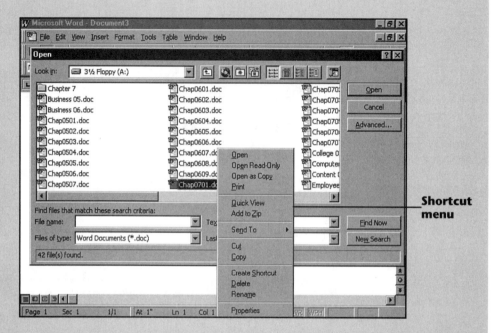

Shortcut menu

❸ Choose the Cut command from the Shortcut menu (you can left- or right-click the command).

The shortcut menu closes, but the Chap0701 file name is still displayed in the list box.

❹ Double-click the Chapter 7 folder at the top of the list box to open the folder and change the storage location in the Look **in** box to Chapter 7.

Note that no items are in the Chapter 7 folder.

❺ Right-click in the empty list box to display the shortcut menu; then click the **P**aste command to insert the Chap0701 file into the list box.

You may briefly see the Moving dialog box as you move the file from its current location into the Chapter 7 folder.

If you have problems... If you see an access denied, or cannot move message, make sure that the Chap0701 file is not open and that the write-protection option is not engaged on your Student Disk.

When you conduct file management procedures like the ones in these exercises, it is best to keep the selected file(s) closed until the management activities are completed.

6 Choose the Up One Level button, located to the right of the Look **in** drop-down arrow in the Open dialog box, to return the listing of your student files in the list box. Note that the Chap0701 file is no longer included on the list.

7 Open the Chapter 7 folder again.

In the preceding steps, you conducted a "cut-and-paste" procedure to move a file from one storage location to another. In the next steps, you use a similar procedure to copy a file.

8 In the Open dialog box displaying the contents of the Chapter 7 folder, right-click the Chap0701 file; then choose the **C**opy command.

9 Right-click in a blank area of the list box; then choose the Paste command to insert a copy of the Chap0701 file into the Chapter 7 folder (see Figure 7.11).

10 Right-click the Copy of Chap0701.doc file (your file name may not include the *doc* extension); then choose the Rena**m**e command to select the characters in the name of the selected file.

Figure 7.11
You can make a copy of a selected file by using the Copy and Paste shortcut commands.

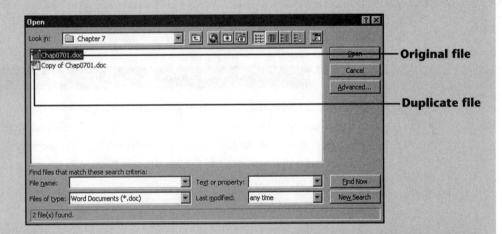

Tip

You can also select the characters in the file name by clicking once the file *name* (not the icon in front of the name), waiting a second or two, and then click the characters again. If you don't pause between clicks, Word thinks you are double-clicking a file and will attempt to open the file into a document window.

(continues)

Completing File Management Activities from the Open Dialog Box (continued)

You are now ready to rename the file. As soon as you press the first character on the keyboard, all the selected characters will be erased.

11 If the file names in your dialog box DO NOT include the three-character *doc* extension, type **Renamed file** as the name for the new file.

If the listing of your files DOES include the *doc* extension, type **Renamed file.doc**—if you don't add the *doc* extension, a message box is displayed warning that if you don't include the extension, the file may become unusable. The file also will not be displayed in the Open dialog box when the default entry Word Documents (*.doc) is listed in the Files of **t**ype drop-down list box.

12 Press ⏎Enter to complete the renaming process.

The list box should now include the Chap0701 and Renamed file items.

The shortcut menu also may be used to delete a selected item from the large list box.

13 Right-click the Renamed file entry in the list box to display the shortcut menu.

14 Choose **D**elete from the shortcut menu; then confirm the deletion by choosing **Y**es in the Confirm File Delete message box.

> **Note**
>
> If you had deleted a file from your hard drive instead of from your floppy disk, you would need to empty the Windows Recycle Bin to completely remove the file from your system. If the file is still in the Recycle Bin and you change your mind about the deletion, you can use the appropriate Recycle Bin commands to return the file to its preceding location.
>
> You do not have this option when you delete a file from a floppy disk. If you accidentally delete a file from your floppy disk, don't make any additional changes to the disk. Immediately ask your instructor or technical support person for help. A person familiar with file utility programs may be able to restore some or all of the deleted file if you haven't already saved new information to the disk space that previously held the deleted file.

 15 Choose the Up One Level button to return to the location holding the rest of your student files; then leave the Open dialog box open for the next exercise.

In another exercise in this chapter, you will move the Chap0701 file back with the other files and remove the Chapter 7 folder from your disk. However, leave the Chapter 7 file as it is now to learn how to add an item to the Favorites folder.

Objective 3: Find Files

As you continue to work with your computer system, you'll find that you use certain storage locations more often than others. You are already familiar with the tedious process of working (level-by-level) through the storage locations on your system to find a needed entry in the Look **in** box (Open dialog box) or the Save **in** box (Save As dialog box). Word's Favorites folder provides an alternative to this level-by-level searching. In the first exercise, you learn how to add an item to the Favorites folder.

Quickly moving to favorite storage locations is one way to help find your files. However, sometimes you just can't remember where you stored a file, and you don't have the time to look in each possible storage location. At times like these, use the find file options provided in the Open dialog box to help you quickly find the file in question. You learn to use these options in the last exercise in this section.

Adding an Item to the Favorites Folder

To add an item to the Favorites Folder, do these steps:

❶ If you are continuing from the preceding exercise, and the Open dialog box is already displayed in your Word window, go to step 2. If you are just starting again, display the Open dialog box; then change the entry in the Look **in** box so that your student files and the Chapter 7 folder are displayed in the large list box. (Most likely, this is the root directory of your Student Disk.)

❷ Select the Chapter 7 folder by clicking once the folder icon in front of the folder name.

 ❸ Choose the Add to Favorites button to display the options to either add the current entry (the entry in the Look **in** box) or the selected item (the Chapter 7 folder) to the Favorites list.

❹ Choose the **A**dd Selected Item to Favorites command to add the Chapter 7 file to the Favorites list.

> ### Note
>
> In this exercise, you added a folder from your Student Disk to the Favorites folder. This was done so that you could see how to complete this procedure. In normal use, you probably would add only a network or hard drive storage location to the Favorites folder.

 ❺ Choose the Look in Favorites button (in the Open dialog box) to see a list of frequently used storage locations on your system.

(continues)

7

Adding an Item to the Favorites Folder (continued)

Most likely you did not add all the locations you see displayed in the list box; however, you should be able to locate the Chapter 7 folder you added in the preceding steps. The curved arrow you see in the lower-left portion of the folder icon indicates that the listing is a shortcut to a location. Refer to your Windows documentation, or to your instructor or network administrator, to learn more about file or folder shortcuts.

6 Double-click the Chapter 7 folder in the large list box to open the folder and list its one file.

 7 Choose the Up One Level button to move up one storage level on your Student Disk and return the listing of the Chapter 7 folder and your student files in the list box. Leave the Open dialog box displayed and move to the next exercise.

Searching for Files

As long as you can remember some characteristic about a file you previously saved, there is a good possibility that you can locate the file through Word's file searching features. Complete the following exercise to learn a few ways to search for files.

Note

Word has an intricate and full-featured file searching function, including the advanced search feature that lets you expand your search locations to search the subfolders of the entry in the Look in box. The advanced search feature also lets you enter a number of characteristics about the file you are searching for to help limit the search. It is beyond the scope of this text to discuss advanced search options. Therefore, in the following first exercise, you return the Chap0701 file to the root directory of your Student Disk and delete the Chapter 7 folder. If you want additional information about using advanced file searching features, refer to the Word Help program, or contact your instructor or network administrator.

Removing an Item from the Favorites Folder

To remove an item from the Favorites Folder, do the following steps:

1 From the preceding exercise, the Open dialog box listing the files and folder on your Student Disk should still be displayed on your screen. If necessary, display the Open dialog box and place your Student Disk in the Look in location before moving to the next step.

2 Open the Chapter 7 folder, right-click the Chap0701 file icon, choose Cut from the shortcut menu, and then choose the Up One Level button to display a list of the rest of your student files. Choose **P**aste to paste the Chap0701 file back into the same location as the rest of your student files.

❸ Click once the folder in front of the Chapter 7 listing; then press ⒟ⓔⓛ to see a message asking you to confirm the deletion of the Chapter 7 folder. Choose **Y**es to confirm the deletion.

Now that you have removed the folder from your disk, you should also remove the Chapter 7 folder from the Favorites folder.

 ❹ Click the Look in Favorites button to display the list of Favorites storage locations, click the Chapter 7 folder once to select it, and press the ⒟ⓔⓛ key.

❺ Confirm the deletion by choosing **Y**es to close the dialog box and remove the Chapter 7 folder from the Favorites folder.

❻ Change the entry in the Look **i**n box back to the location holding your student files; then leave the Open dialog box displayed on your screen for the next exercise.

Your disk is now ready to complete the following file searching activities.

If you remember part of the name of the file you are looking for, you can enter the partial name and *wild-card* symbols to represent the rest of the file name. The two most frequently used wild cards are the asterisk (*) and the question mark (?). The asterisk represents any string of characters; the question mark represents any one character.

Complete the following exercise to practice a few different techniques for searching for files.

Searching for Files

To search for files, do the following steps:

❶ In the Open dialog box currently displaying the files on your Student Disk, enter **B*** in the File **n**ame box; then choose the **F**ind Now button (or press ↵Enter).

In the Open dialog box, Word displays a list of the files starting with the letter *B* in the list box (see Figure 7.12). If your disk does not contain any files starting with the letter *B*, repeat step 1 using a letter that does start the name of a file on your disk.

To clear the results of a search, choose the Ne**w** Search button.

❷ Return all the items to the list box by choosing the Ne**w** Search button.

Word also lets you search for a particular string of characters or text within a document.

❸ Enter **memory** in the Te**x**t or property text box; then choose **F**ind Now to display only the files that include the word *memory*. Your results may be similar to those in Figure 7.13.

7

(continues)

Searching for Files (continued)

Figure 7.12
The results of the search for the files that begin with the letter *B*.

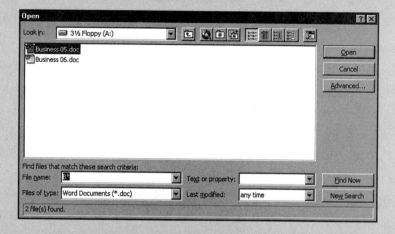

Figure 7.13
The results of searching for files that contain the word *memory*.

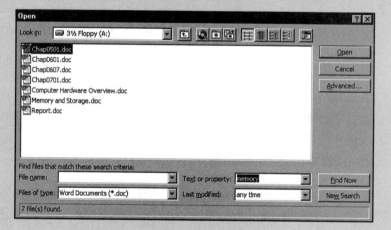

Depending on your system and the number of files on your disk, the search process may take a few minutes. During a search, the **F**ind Now button is replaced with a **S**top button. If you need to cancel a search in process, choose the **S**top button.

❹ Choose the Ne**w** Search button to return all your student files to the list box.

You can also search by specific file properties. Earlier in this chapter, you viewed the summary information for the Chap0701 file. One of the entries listed Jodi Jensen as your manager. You use that information in the next search.

❺ Enter **Jodi Jensen** in the Te**x**t or property box; then choose **F**ind Now.

The results of the search should just show the Chap0701 file in the list box. This demonstrates the advantage of using summary information, and of entering unique text or properties in the Te**x**t or property text box.

❻ Choose the Ne**w** Search button to restore all the files to the list box. Close the Open dialog box, but leave the Word window open for the next exercise.

It is not possible to cover all the ways to search for your files in the space pro-vided. However, if you know when you created the file for which you are look-ing, you may want to use the Last **m**odified drop-down list box to help narrow your search. Opening this list provides choices such as, yesterday, this week, last week, last month, and so on. Choosing one of these options alone may produce a small enough list of files so that you can find the file you need. Alternatively, you can limit your search further by combining an entry in the Last **m**odified box with entries in the File **n**ame or Te**x**t or property boxes.

Objective 4: Insert Files into Open Word Documents

Word offers three ways to insert information into a document. In earlier chap-ters, you learned about the first two methods: typing characters from the key-board and inserting information from the Clipboard. In this section, you learn the third method: inserting a file. You can insert files created by Word and many other applications into your Word documents. Complete the following exercise to insert the Chap0701 file into a new document.

Inserting a File into a Document

To insert a file into a document, follow these steps:

1 Your Word window, displaying a blank document, should still be open from the preceding exercise. Make sure that there are no open files from your disk; then move to step 2.

2 Type the following sentence: **The Chap0701 file is inserted below this sentence.** Then press ⏎Enter twice.

3 Choose Insert, Fi**l**e to display the Insert File dialog box.

The Insert File dialog box looks almost identical to the Open dialog box. It also serves a similar function; but when you choose a file from the Insert File dialog box, the chosen file is placed within the *current* (or existing) document window.

4 Select the Chap0701 file to insert. Then choose OK.

The file that you selected is inserted into your document at the insertion point.

5 Scroll to the top of your document to see the sentence you entered and the beginning of the inserted file.

6 Leave the file open so that it can be used in the next exercise where you examine some of the Word printing options.

7

Objective 5: Manage the Printing of Files

Previous chapters have indicated the importance of selecting the right printer before you do any character, paragraph, or page formatting. Word knows the capabilities of the selected printer and will offer you formatting options compatible only with that printer.

If you need to change the selection of your printer, the process is straightforward. Selecting a printer really is a matter of selecting a printer driver—usually a file on your hard disk. Word can use any printer driver installed in Windows 95. If you need to install a printer driver, however, you must click the Start button from the taskbar to display the Start menu, select **S**ettings, and then select **P**rinters to start the installation process. (If you need help installing your printer, review your printer and Windows 95 documentation, or see your instructor or technical support person.)

Displaying the Selected Printer

To display the printer that Word is prepared to use, follow these steps:

1 With the document from the preceding exercise displayed in your Word window, choose **F**ile, **P**rint to display the Print dialog box.

The name of the printer that Word currently is prepared to use is displayed in the **N**ame text box (see, for example, Figure 7.14).

Figure 7.14
The Name box of the Print dialog box shows which printer Word is prepared to use.

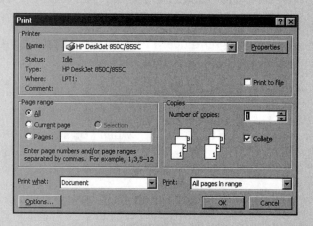

To select another printer that is already installed to work with your system, click the arrow at the end of the **N**ame drop-down list to display the additional printers from which you may choose. Then click the desired printer.

Before printing your current document, it is beneficial to review the other options available through the Print dialog box.

The Page range section enables you to choose to print all of your document (the default choice), the page where the insertion point is currently located, the current selected text, or specific pages of the document.

2 If the **A**ll option is not already selected in the Page range section, select it now.

The Copies section enables you to set the number of copies you need to print (the default setting is one).

Leaving the Collate box checked means that if you have a multiple-page document, all pages of the document will print once before any page prints a second time. For example, if you need to print ten copies of an eight-page report and choose the Collate option, the printer will print all eight pages of the report once before printing all eight pages a second time. You could soon pick up five collated copies of the report before the printer finishes printing the remaining five collated copies.

If instead you deselect the Collate box, the printer will produce in this example ten copies of the first page, followed by ten copies of the second page, and so on until all eight pages are printed. Afterward you will need to collate the reports manually before you can have ten copies of the report.

When the Collate check box is clear, your printer may complete the printing process a little more quickly; but if you choose Collate, what you save in collating time (usually) more than offsets what you lose in printing speed.

❸ Change the Number of copies setting to 2, and leave the Collate box checked.

❹ Click the arrow at the end of the Print what drop-down list box.

The majority of your print jobs will print just the pages of your document. Occasionally though, you may need to print specific document elements. In these cases, select exactly what needs to be printed by choosing an item from the Print what drop-down list.

❺ Click Document to close the Print what drop-down list.

❻ Click the arrow at the end of the Print drop-down list box to see its list options.

When Document is selected in the Print what box, the Print list box provides the option of printing all the pages in a range, or just the odd or even pages.

This option is useful when you are producing a document with printing on both sides of the paper, but your printer can print on only one side. After printing all the odd pages, you can stop the printing process, enter the odd pages (properly) back into the printer, and then issue the command to print the even pages. It may take a little practice, but this procedure can help you produce a document with printing on both sides of a sheet of paper.

❼ Make sure that the All pages in range option is selected; then choose OK to print two collated copies of your current two-page document.

❽ Verify that your printer produced two collated copies of the document; then close the document without saving it.

7

If you refer back to Figure 7.14, you'll see three elements included in the Print dialog box that were not discussed in the preceding exercise.

Checking the Print to file check box enables you to print a file to a floppy disk. This procedure is most commonly used when you need to use a printer not connected to the computer you are currently using. Printing the file to the disk actually creates a file (that you name and save) on your floppy disk. You can then take the disk to a computer that is connected to the desired printer and use a DOS print command to print the file—even if the other computer does not have access to Word.

Choosing the **P**roperties button in the Print dialog box opens the printer's Properties dialog box. The options in this dialog box let you change some of the most important settings (including print quality) that control the way your printer works with the *Windows* operating system. (Depending on how your computer system is configured, your printer's Properties dialog box may have one page, or it may include a number of pages.)

To change the *Word* printer options, choose the **O**ptions button in the Print dialog box. Choosing this button makes a number of useful options available to you, including:

- *Draft output.* Use this option when you are printing a preliminary copy of a report that contains a number of graphics—graphics slow down the printing process and consume a large amount of printer toner (or ink). Turn off this option before printing your final report.

- *Reverse print order.* Activating this option instructs your printer to print the last page of your document first. This is useful when your printer outputs the page with the printed side up.

- *Background printing.* This option enables you to keep working in Word while your document is printing.

If your printer uses more than one paper tray, you can change the default tray from the Printer options page. (If you need to control more than just the default printer tray, open the Page Setup dialog box and display the **P**aper Source page. This page lets you choose the tray for the first page of a document—such as the tray holding sheets displaying the company letterhead—and the tray for the remaining pages of a document.)

As you continue to work with Word, you will occasionally find a need to customize the way your printer operates. You can make these changes through the Print dialog box and the related dialog boxes that can be accessed from the Print dialog box. However, to just print one copy of the on-screen document, choosing the Print button on the Standard toolbar is still probably the preferred method.

Chapter Summary

The more you work with Word, the greater your need becomes for managing your files and your printing. In this chapter, you learned to use a number of procedures for viewing file information, working with groups of files simultaneously, organizing your files, searching for files, inserting files into other documents, and finally controlling your printing needs.

In the next chapter, you learn how to use Word's table feature to provide an alternative method to the use of tabs for presenting tables in your document.

If you have completed your work for this computer session, make sure that you properly exit all open programs. Then use the Windows Shut Down command to safely exit Windows. To test your knowledge of the material covered in this chapter, answer the questions in the Checking Your Skills section immediately following this summary. Then complete the exercises in the Applying Your Skills section at the end of the chapter.

Checking Your Skills

True/False

For each of the following, circle *T* or *F* to indicate whether the statement is true or false.

T   F   **1.** Summary information is saved as a separate file from your document.

T   F   **2.** Word can search for a file based on information inserted into the Summary page of the document's Properties dialog box.

T   F   **3.** When displaying the Save As dialog box, you can create a new folder inside the storage location listed in the Save **in** box.

T   F   **4.** In Word, you can insert one file inside of another.

T   F   **5.** Choose Pa**g**es in the Print dialog box to enable the printing of specific pages of the document.

T   F   **6.** The Favorites folder is designed to make your most frequently used storage locations easily available to you, in either the Open or Save As dialog boxes.

T   F   **7.** From the Open dialog box, you can view the contents of a document without opening the file into a document window.

T   F   **8.** Rather than type an entire file name, you can use the question mark wild-card character (?) to represent more than one omitted character, as in Ch?.DOC in the File **n**ame box.

T   F   **9.** The Print dialog box gives you the option to set the number of copies to be printed for the current document.

T   F   **10.** It is possible to search for a file you created yesterday, by displaying the term *Yesterday* in the Date **m**odified box of the Open dialog box and then choosing the **F**ind Now button.

7

Multiple Choice

In the blank provided, write the letter of the correct answer for each of the following questions.

1. When choosing the Details button in the Open dialog box, which heading does not appear in the large list box?_____

    a. Name

    b. Size

    c. Type

    d. Modified

    e. Last Printed

2. In Word you can search for a file based on which of the following criteria?_____

    a. when the file was created

    b. some or all of the file names

    c. key text or character entries in the file

    d. key property of the file

    e. You can use one or all of the above when searching for files.

3. To change both the first page default printer tray and the remaining pages printer tray, you need to display the_____.

    a. Print dialog box

    b. Printer Options dialog box

    c. Paper Size page of the Page Setup dialog box

    d. Paper Source page of the Page Setup dialog box

    e. Save as Printed dialog box

4. When your document is displayed in the Word window, to start the process for inserting a file from Word or another program, _____.

    a. choose Insert, File

    b. click the file from the View menu

    c. choose the file from the File menu

    d. choose the file from the Window menu

    e. choose Edit, File

5. To print only selected text in a document, click _____ in the Print dialog box.

    a. All

    b. Current page

    c. Pages

    d. Selection

    e. Full page

6. Choosing the Preview button in the Open dialog box results in the following changes to the large list box:_____.

    a. file details in the top half, preview of selected file in the bottom half

    b. file information in the left half, preview of selected file in the right half

    c. alternating views of a list of files and preview of selected document every ten seconds

    d. alternating views of a list of files and preview of selected document every three seconds

    e. preview of selected file in top half, file details in the bottom half

7. The Document Statistics dialog box provides a count for all of the following except _____.

    a. words

    b. pages

    c. lines

    d. characters

    e. phrases

8. Word can print certain special information when you select it from the _____.

    a. Print **h**ow drop-down list

    b. Print **w**hat drop-down list

    c. Print **w**here drop-down list

    d. Print **o**nly drop-down list

    e. Look **i**n drop-down list

9. To clear the results of a file search, choose the _____ button in the Open dialog box.

    a. **C**lear

    b. **F**ind Now

    c. Sum**m**ary

    d. Ne**w** Search

    e. **O**pen

10. The command to print the document in reverse order is found in the _____.

    a. Save As dialog box

    b. Printer Properties dialog box

    c. Page Setup dialog box

    d. Paper dialog box

    e. Print Options dialog box

Fill in the Blank

In the blank provided, write the correct answer for each of the following questions.

1. When conducting a file search, you can list words that identify important terms in the file in the _____ text box of the Open dialog box.

2. To view document statistics, open the _____ dialog box and click the Statistics tab.

3. The _____ print option can save on your printer resources when you are printing preliminary copies of a report.

4. To insert a file into a Word document, choose **Insert**, _____ to open the appropriate dialog box.

5. When you want to print a Word document on a printer connected to a computer other than the one you are using, you can print your document to a _____ on a disk.

6. To cancel a file search activity after it is started, choose the _____ button.

7. While in the Open or Save As dialog box, you can move and copy files via the _____ menus.

8. To display files in the Open or Save As dialog box from most recent to oldest, choose the _____ heading at the top of the large list box.

9. When you want to save all your open documents, under their existing names, using just one procedure, press _____; then choose **File**, **Save All**.

10. The option to enable you to use Word to edit a document while you are printing a Word document is called _____.

7

Applying Your Skills

Review Exercises

Exercise 1: Using Summary Information

To practice using the Summary Information feature, follow these steps:

1. Open the Chap0702 file from your Student Disk; then immediately save the file back to your disk as **Business 07**.

2. Type the subject of the document, your name, and one keyword or key term in the Summary page of the document's Properties dialog box.

3. Save the revisions to your file.

4. Open the Print dialog box, choose the **O**ptions button to display the printing options; then in the Include with document section, enable the Docu**m**ent properties command, and choose OK to return to the Print dialog box.

5. Print the document and the document properties.

6. Open the Print dialog box, choose **O**ptions to display the print options, and then deactivate the Docu**m**ent properties command in the Include with document section. Choose OK to close the dialog box displaying the print options. Finally, choose Close to close the Print dialog box without printing the file again.

7. Close the file.

Exercise 2: Finding Files

To practice finding all the files that start with the same first letter, follow these steps:

1. Click the Open button from the Standard toolbar.

2. Find all files on your Student Disk that have names beginning with the letter *S*. (If you have no files that begin with *S* choose an appropriate letter for your situation and repeat this step.)

3. Open the Chap0703 file from your Student Disk; then immediately save the file back to your disk as **Steps 07**.

4. Move to the end of the document; then add the steps for finding files that begin with the letter *S*.

5. Save the revisions to your file; then print and close your file.

Exercise 3: Searching for Files Containing Specific Text

To practice searching for a file containing specific text, follow these steps:

1. Conduct a search on your student files for all the files that include the word *vacation*.

2. Open the **Steps 07** document you created in Exercise 2 and add the steps at the bottom of the document on how to search for files containing specific text.

3. Save the revisions to the **Steps 07** file; then print and close the file.

Continuing Projects

Project 1: Practice Using Word

In the following exercise, practice using the shortcut menus in the Open dialog box.

1. Open the Open dialog box and display the files on your Student Disk.

2. Rename all the **Employee Guidelines** files to just **Guidelines** (make sure to include the number after the word *Guidelines*, as in *Guidelines 06*).

3. Make a copy of the Guidelines 06 file and name it **Guidelines for Employees**.

4. Delete the file you created in step 3.

5. Close the Open dialog box.

Project 2: Deli-Mart

Continue your work on the catalog for Deli-Mart by following these steps:

1. Open a new document.

2. Type the following:

   Weekend Entertainment

   Looking for a relaxing and fun night, enjoying a leisurely dinner? We are extending our hours and our menu to include a full dinner menu with live music Friday through Sunday until midnight. Call us at (800) 377-5577 for more information.

3. Press ⏎Enter twice to create a blank line between the paragraph you just entered and the text you are about to insert.

4. Insert the Chap0704 file into your new document at the insertion point.

5. Save the new document as **Menu 07** to your Student Disk.

6. Select the two paragraphs you typed; then cut and paste them to the second blank line below the 1 (800) DEL-MART telephone number in step 3 of the inserted document. Make sure to keep the pasted text within the first section in the document.

7. Format the paragraph you typed to match with the character format of the previous lines.

8. Save the revisions to your file, print, and then close the file.

Project 3: The Marketing Connection

Continue your work on the newsletter for The Marketing Connection by following these steps:

1. Open a new document.

2. Enter the following paragraphs:

   Deadline dates for summer and early fall publications:

   > **May 25**
   > **June 25**
   > **July 27**
   > **August 26**
   > **September 25**

7

3. Save the file to your Student Disk as **Dates**.

4. Open the Chap0705 file from your Student Disk.

5. Insert the Dates file at the end of the Public Relations Group section of the Chap0705 file.

6. Save the revisions to the file as **Market 07;** then print the pages in reverse order.

7. Close the file, Word, and Windows.

CHAPTER 8

Using Tables

Table
A method of organizing and displaying data in a collection of rows and columns.

Row
A horizontal line of cells. Word numbers rows consecutively from top to bottom.

Column
A vertical line of cells. Word names columns alphabetically from left to right.

Cell
The intersection of a row and a column in a table.

Tables are frequently used to present information in a brief, organized, easy-to-read manner. In addition to conveying information, inserting a table within a series of paragraphs makes the page layout a little more interesting for the reader. Each day, you probably view some type of information presented in a table format. Common uses of tables include television program listings, calendars, document glossaries, catalog price lists, and inventory forms.

In Chapter 5, you learned to space text across the page by using tabs. In this chapter, you learn to use Word's table features to display data in *rows* and *columns*. When working in a table, you enter and edit data in *cells*. A cell is the point where a row and column intersect. You can format the content of an individual cell, row, or column, or you can have Word do the formatting for you. You also can easily sort the data in alphabetical order and (in the case of numerical data) perform calculations within the table.

Objectives

By the time you finish this chapter, you will have learned to

1. Create a Simple Table
2. Enter Data in a Table
3. Insert and Delete Columns and Rows
4. Adjust Column Width and Row Height
5. Edit and Format Items in a Table
6. Add Borders and Shading to the Table
7. Enter Calculations into a Table
8. Create a Complex Table
9. Convert Text to Tables and Tables to Text

Objective 1: Create a Simple Table

Word provides three basic ways to create a table:

- Choose the Insert Table button, and drag the mouse through the pop-up grid representing potential rows and columns in a table.

- Choose the Tables and Borders button and actually draw the table in your document.

- Choose T**a**ble, **I**nsert Table to display the Insert Table dialog box; enter the desired number of rows and columns; and then choose OK.

In the initial exercise in this chapter, you create a table using the Insert Table button (the easiest way to create a table). In the second exercise, you create a table by using the **T**able menu. After you gain some experience working with tables, you'll have a chance to draw a table in your document—one of the new features in Word 97.

The first step in designing a table is determining what you want to display in it. The next step is to identify the number of columns and rows that you want to start with in your table. In most cases, you know the approximate number of columns needed, but you probably don't know how many rows you will need. That doesn't matter; just make your best guess, because you can change the number of rows and columns as you work.

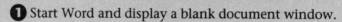
Creating a Table

To create a table, follow these steps:

1 Start Word and display a blank document window.

2 Check to see that the Show/Hide button on the Standard toolbar is pressed so that the nonprinting characters are visible. If the button is not pressed, choose it now so that the nonprinting characters will be displayed in the window work area.

3 Change the font to 16-point Arial, Bold. Then enter the following text and center it:

Jolly Fine Furniture Store Inventory Form

4 Place the insertion point at the end of the line and make sure that no text is selected. Turn off the bold feature, press ⏎Enter twice, left-align the current line, and return the font to the size of 10 points.

Most of the characters entered into this document will be entered in the Arial font, so leave the Arial font turned on.

5 Choose the Insert Table button in the Standard toolbar to display the table grid (see Figure 8.1).

> **Note**
>
> Make sure that no text is selected before you click the Insert Table button to create a table. If any text is selected, Word attempts to convert that text to a table.

Figure 8.1
A table grid is displayed when you click the Insert Table button.

6 Rest the pointer on a few cells in the table grid and notice that all cells to the left and above the cell the pointer is resting on are highlighted.

The highlighted cells indicate the number of rows and columns that will be placed inside a table if you click on the current cell. The bottom of the grid also displays the dimensions (in rows and columns) of the table to be placed in your document if you click on the cell where the pointer is resting.

7 Point on the cell in the table grid that highlights five columns and four rows, as shown in Figure 8.2.

Figure 8.2
In the table grid, five columns and four rows are highlighted.

8 Click the mouse button to display a 4 (row) by 5 (column) table outlined with *gridlines*.

> **Note**
>
> In previous versions of Word, users typically would place the pointer in the top-left cell, press the mouse button, drag across to the desired cell, and then release the mouse button to create the table.

If the table gridlines are not displayed in your document or they are displayed in a gray shade instead of a black shade, the gridlines will not be printed when the document is printed. To make sure that your table gridlines print when the document is printed, place the insertion point in the table; choose T**a**ble, Table Auto**F**ormat; activate the **B**orders option; choose OK to close the Table AutoFormat dialog box; choose T**a**ble to open the T**a**ble menu; and choose the Show **G**ridlines command at the bottom of the menu. (If the Hide **G**ridlines command is displayed in place of the Show **G**ridlines command, do not choose the Hide **G**ridlines command.)

8

(continues)

Figure 8.3 displays a table with gridlines. Notice that when the table is first displayed, the insertion point is positioned in the top-left cell inside the table.

Figure 8.3
A preliminary version
of a table.

Table column
marker

End-of-text marks

Gridlines

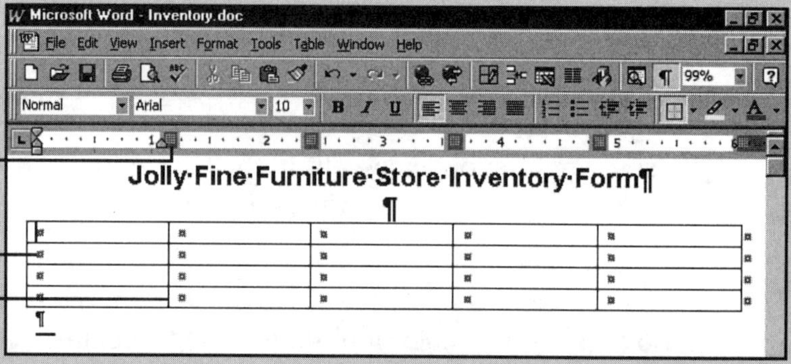

9 Type your first name in the cell in the top-left corner of the table.

To delete a word or phrase, you select the characters and then press Del. This technique removes the characters from inside a table; however, it will not remove a table from your document. To remove a table, you must first select it, and then delete its row, or cut the table to the Windows Clipboard.

10 Make sure that the insertion point is inside the table.

11 Choose T**a**ble, Select T**a**ble to select the entire table; then press Del.

The entire table should have been selected when you chose T**a**ble, Select T**a**ble; however, when you pressed Del, only your name was deleted. The table remained in your document.

12 Choose T**a**ble, Select T**a**ble to select the entire table; then choose T**a**ble, **D**elete Rows to delete the highlighted table.

> **Tip**
>
> You also can remove a table from a document by selecting the entire table and choosing the Cut button from the Standard toolbar, or choosing the Cu**t** command from the shortcut or **E**dit menu.

If you accidentally insert a table with incorrect dimensions, you can use this technique to remove the entire table. Later in this chapter, you learn to insert and delete rows and columns in your table.

13 Name this file **Inventory** and save it to your Student Disk. Then keep the file open for the next exercise.

In the next exercise, you use the T**a**ble menu to recreate your 4 × 5 table.

The default table created by using the Insert Table button on the Standard tool-bar divides the chosen number of columns equally between the left and right margins. When you insert a table into a document, the gridlines and table column markers in the horizontal ruler show the width of each column.

The usable width of each column is slightly less than the space between the vertical gridlines so that some blank space exists between columns to make the entries easier to read.

When you create a table and show the nonprinting characters, Word typically displays gridlines, end-of-text marks, end-of-row marks, spaces, tab marks, and paragraph marks. However, you can customize the display of the nonprinting characters by choosing **T**ools, **O**ptions to display the Options dialog box, choosing the View tab to access the nonprinting character options, and then activating or deactivating particular nonprinting character options.

Using the Insert Table Command to Create Tables

The Insert Table dialog box provides text boxes for entering the desired number of columns and rows for your new table. In addition, this dialog box enables you to set a precise width for all the columns in the table. To create a table using the Insert Table dialog box, follow these steps:

1 If necessary, display the Inventory file in your Word window; then position the insertion point at the end of the document.

2 Choose T**a**ble, **I**nsert Table.

The Insert Table dialog box appears (see Figure 8.4).

Figure 8.4
Use the Insert Table dialog box to specify the number of columns and rows that you want to include in a table.

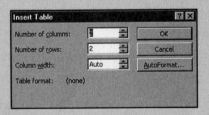

3 In the Number of **c**olumns text box, enter **5** (or click the up button at the end of the text box until the number 5 is displayed).

4 In the Number of **r**ows text box, enter **4**.

5 Accept Auto (the default) in the Column **w**idth text box to automatically display columns of equal width across the page.

If you wanted to set all columns to a specific width, you would place the desired width in this text box.

6 Choose OK to create the table.

Again, notice that the insertion point is originally positioned in the top-left cell in the table when it is first displayed in the document.

7 Save your changes to the Inventory document and keep it open for the next exercise.

8

Objective 2: Enter Data in a Table

As you have already learned, when working with tables, you enter data in cells. Cells typically contain text, numbers, or graphics. You can enter data by typing, importing from another application, or creating a drawing or chart within the cell. In the next exercise, you learn how to enter text and numbers in cells.

> **Note**
>
> When you are placing or editing data in a cell, pressing a keyboard key (except for Tab⇄ and ⬆Shift+Tab⇄) has the same effect as when you are working with normal text. When you press Tab⇄, you move to the next cell; when you press ⬆Shift+Tab⇄, you move to the preceding cell.

Entering Column Titles

Placing a column title in the top cell of each column helps the reader quickly understand the information presented in the table. To enter column titles in your table, follow these steps:

1 In the open Inventory document, place the insertion point in the top-left cell of the table.

The insertion point appears to the left of the end-of-text mark in that cell (if you have the nonprinting characters displayed).

2 Type **Item Number** in the top-left cell.

3 Press Tab⇄ to move to the second cell in the first row, or click anywhere in the second cell.

4 Type **Description** in this cell.

5 In the third column of the first row, type **Quantity**.

6 In the fourth column of the first row, type **Price**.

7 In the fifth column of the first row, type **Extended Price**.

Your table should look like Figure 8.5.

Figure 8.5
The first row of this table now contains titles for each column.

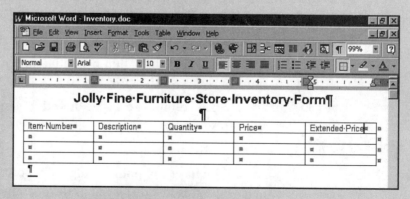

8 Save your changes and keep the Inventory document open.

You can enter additional data in the table in the same manner in which you entered column titles.

Table 8.1 lists the keyboard keys or key combinations you can use to quickly move the insertion point from one cell to another within your Word tables.

Table 8.1 Keyboard Keys for Moving the Insertion Point in Word Tables	
Key or Key Combination	**Action**
`Tab`	Moves to the next cell to the right. If already at right end of a row, moves to the first cell in the next row. If at right end of bottom row, creates new row and moves to the first cell.
`Shift`+`Tab`	Moves to the next cell to the left. If already at left end of row, moves to the last cell in the preceding row. No effect if at first cell of first row.
`→`	Within a cell, moves one character to the right. When the insertion point is at the right of the last character in a cell, moves to the next cell. When the insertion point is at the right of the last character in the bottom-right cell, moves the insertion point out of the table.
`←`	Within a cell, moves one character to the left. When the insertion point is at the left of the first character in a cell, moves to the preceding cell. When the insertion point is at the left of the first character in the top-left cell, moves the insertion point out of the table.
`↑`	Moves up one row. When the insertion point is in the first row, moves out of table.
`↓`	Moves down one row. When insertion point is in the last row, moves out of table.
`Alt`+`Home`	Moves to first cell in current row.
`Alt`+`End`	Moves to last cell in current row.
`Alt`+`PgUp`	Moves to top cell in current column.
`Alt`+`PgDn`	Moves to bottom cell in current column.

Entering Data in a Table

To enter additional data to your table, follow these steps:

1 In the open Inventory document, position the insertion point in the first cell of the second row of the table.

2 Type **KX245**.

3 Press `Tab` to move to the second cell of the second row, or click that cell.

4 Type **Brass table lamp**.

5 In the third cell of the second row, type **4**.

6 In the fourth cell of the second row, type **349.95**.

7 Press `Tab` twice to skip over the *Extended Price* column and move the insertion point to the first column of the third row.

(continues)

8

Entering Data in a Table (continued)

8 In the third and fourth rows, type the following data:

| PS444 | Oak end table with slide-out shelf | 5 | 359.99 |
| ZZ881 | Glass top table with brass pedestal | 2 | 895.00 |

When you finish entering the data, your table should look similar to the one in Figure 8.6.

Note

When you type more text than will fit within the width of the cell, Word wraps the text and starts a new line in the same cell. Later in this chapter, you learn how to adjust column widths. For now, let Word wrap your text as you type it. Don't be concerned if Word does not wrap your text exactly as shown in Figure 8.6.

Figure 8.6
The table with column headings and three rows of data entered.

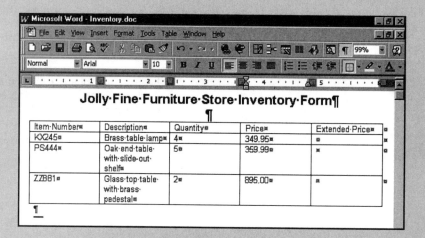

9 Save your changes and keep the Inventory document open.

It is a common practice to attach a caption, identifying or describing important information the reader is to see, above or below a table you insert in a document. Using Word's Caption dialog box, you can assign a number to the current table and display a caption (that you create) above or below the table. Later if you insert a new table, before or after the existing table, Word automatically updates the numbering for all the table captions in the document.

Attaching a Caption to the Table

To attach a caption to your table, follow these steps:

1 Make sure that the insertion point is placed within the table of the open Inventory document.

2 Choose **Insert**, **Caption** to display the Caption dialog box (see Figure 8.7).

Figure 8.7
Use the Caption dialog box to attach a caption to a table.

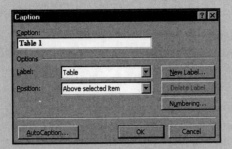

❸ In the **Caption** text box, enter **Table 1. Table lamps and end tables.**, choose Table (if necessary) in the drop-down **Label** list box, and choose Below selected item (if necessary) in the **Position** drop-down list box.

❹ Choose OK to close the Caption dialog box and insert the caption below your selected table.

If you have problems...	If the caption *Table {SEQ Table *ARABIC}. Table lamps and end tables.* is displayed below your table, the number *1* (that was to follow the first word *Table*) has been replaced with the corresponding Word SEQ field code. Field codes are instructions to Word to display certain characters on your screen. Usually, you only see the results of a field code, such as the number *1*. To display the results of field codes, instead of the actual codes, choose **T**ools, **O**ptions; select the View tab; clear the **F**ield Codes option; and then choose OK.

Objective 3: Insert and Delete Columns and Rows

When you create a table, you must make a preliminary choice regarding the number of columns and rows that you want to use in your table. However, after you start working with the table, you can easily change the number of columns and rows in the table. You can insert and delete columns and rows by using the Standard toolbar, shortcut menu, or the **T**able menu.

Word regards the contents of a cell as a paragraph. When you do any type of formatting in the table, from formatting existing characters to adding or deleting rows and columns, you must first select the cells, columns, or rows that you want to format.

8

Selecting a Cell and a Group of Cells

To practice selecting a cell and a group of cells within a table, follow these steps:

❶ In the open Inventory document, position the insertion point in the second cell of the first row of the table.

(continues)

Selecting a Cell and a Group of Cells (continued)

2 Move the mouse pointer to the left edge of the cell until the pointer changes to an arrow pointing up and angled to the right.

3 Click the mouse to select this cell (see Figure 8.8).

Figure 8.8
One cell in the table is selected.

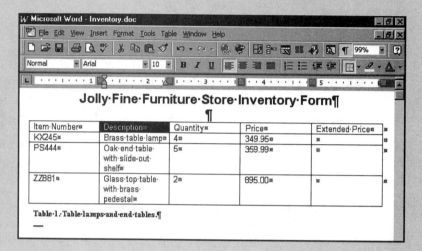

4 Move the mouse pointer to the right until it becomes an arrow pointing up and to the left; then click the mouse button to deselect the cell.

5 To select the group of cells beginning with the second cell in the second row and ending with the third cell in the third row, first select the second cell in the second row. Then, with the pointer still displayed as an arrow pointing up and to the right, press and hold down the left mouse button as you drag the mouse pointer to the right and down until the group of (four) cells is selected.

6 To deselect this group of cells, simply click another location in the table or document.

7 Keep the Inventory document open for the next exercise.

Along with selecting a cell or group of cells, you can also select one or multiple columns or rows. Sometimes, it is necessary to change the format of all the cells within a table; in this case, you need to select the entire table (all rows and columns) before you begin the format change. You already know how to select the entire table by choosing Table, Select Table. Complete the following exercise to learn ways to select table columns or rows.

Selecting a Column and a Row

To learn to select a column or a row, follow these steps:

1 In the open Inventory document, point to the horizontal gridline at the top of the first column in the table.

When you have the mouse pointer in the correct location for selecting an entire column, the pointer changes to a down arrow.

2 When the down arrow is visible, click to select the entire first column (see Figure 8.9).

Figure 8.9
When the pointer is displayed as a down arrow over a table column, click the mouse button to select the column.

Down arrow indicating column selection

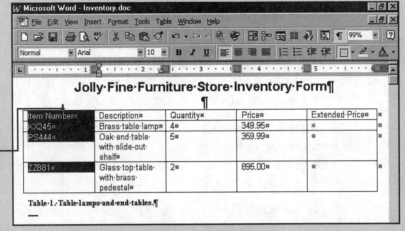

Note

To select two or more adjacent columns, point to the top of the first column, click, and drag to the right or left to include more columns. You cannot select nonadjacent columns.

3 To select the first row, point to the left of the row, outside the gridline. When you see the I-beam pointer change to an arrow pointing upward diagonally to the right, click to select the row.

Note

To select two or more adjacent rows, point to the first row, click, and then press and drag up or down to include more rows. You cannot select nonadjacent rows.

4 To select the entire table, place the insertion point anywhere in the table and press Alt+5. You must use the 5 on the numeric keypad and have NumLock turned off.

5 You haven't actually made any changes to the Inventory document, so leave the file open for the next exercise.

After you know how to select a part of a table, it's easy to insert or delete columns or rows.

Inserting Columns

To insert a column into your table, follow these steps:

❶ In the open Inventory document, select column 4 (the Price column) of the table.

When you insert a column, the new column is placed immediately in front of the selected column.

 ❷ Click the Insert Columns button in the Standard toolbar. You see an Insert Columns symbol on the button if a column is selected in the table, but you see an Insert Rows symbol on the same button if a row is selected. (Note that you see an Insert Cells symbol on the button if just a cell is selected.)

Alternatively, you also can choose **I**nsert Columns from either the **T**able menu or the shortcut menu. Again, a column needs to be selected before you see the option on either menu. (The table shortcut menu is displayed when you right-click a selection within the table.)

Word inserts the new column. All inserted columns have the same format, including width, as the selected column used in the two-step, column-insertion process. This is why the columns now seem to run through the right margin and off the page.

 ❸ Choose the Print Preview button to view the results of adding the extra column to the original table.

❹ Click the Close button to close the Print Preview window and return to Normal view.

❺ Keep the Inventory document open for the next exercise.

To add a column to the right side of the table, select all the end-of-row marks at the right side of the table; then click the Insert Columns button in the Standard toolbar.

Inserting Rows

To insert a row into your table, follow these steps:

❶ In the open Inventory document, select row 2 of the table.

When you insert a row, the new row is placed immediately above the selected row.

❷ Right-click in the selection to display the shortcut menu and choose the **I**nsert Rows command (or choose the Insert Rows button on the Standard toolbar, or choose **T**able, **I**nsert Rows from the menu).

Notice that the name of the (Insert) command changes, depending on whether you have selected a column, row, or cell.

Word inserts a new row.

Note

If you select two or more rows, Word inserts that number of rows, above the first selected row, when you choose the **I**nsert Rows command or click the Insert Rows button. Similarly, when working with columns, if you select two or more columns, Word inserts that number of columns, in front of the first selected column, when you choose the **I**nsert Columns command or click the Insert Columns button.

3 Keep the Inventory document open for the next exercise.

All inserted rows have the same format as the selected row (or the top row in a group of selected rows). To add a new row at the bottom of the table, place the insertion point in the bottom-right cell and press Tab↹. This row will have the same formatting as the preceding row.

Deleting Columns and Rows

Deleting columns and rows is similar to inserting columns and rows, in that both processes consist of two steps, and the first step of each is to select the appropriate columns or rows. To delete a selected column or row, you can choose to *cut* or *delete* the selection. Cut the selected item by using either the Cut button on the Standard toolbar or by choosing Cu**t** from the shortcut or **E**dit menus. Delete a selected row or column by using the **D**elete (*Rows* or *Columns*—depending on the selected item) command from the shortcut or T**a**ble menu.

Removing a cell isn't quite as simple. You can remove the *contents* of an individual cell, not the cell itself, by selecting the cell and then pressing Del (or by using the menus or Standard toolbar). To actually remove a cell from a table, however, you must choose T**a**ble, **D**elete Cells. When the Delete Cells dialog box is displayed, you have to choose how you want the space to be closed up after the cell has been removed.

Deleting Columns and Rows

To practice deleting columns and rows, follow these steps:

1 In the open Inventory file, select the new blank column that you inserted in an earlier exercise.

2 Choose T**a**ble, **D**elete Columns to delete the blank column.

3 Select the row that you inserted in the preceding tutorial.

4 Right-click in the selection; then choose **D**elete Rows from the shortcut menu to delete the blank row.

5 Save your changes and keep the Inventory document open.

8

Objective 4: Adjust Column Width and Row Height

You can change column widths quickly by dragging gridlines in the table, or table column markers in the ruler. In addition, you can use the Cell Height and Width dialog box to set column widths precisely. When using the Cell Height and Width dialog box, you can also change the space between columns and set row heights. When you change the width of columns, Word adjusts any word wrap within cells to suit the new column widths.

Changing Column Widths by Dragging Gridlines

To change a column width by dragging a table gridline, follow these steps:

1 In the open Inventory document, make sure that no cells are selected; then point to the gridline to the right of the second column in the table.

The mouse pointer changes to a double-headed arrow with a double rule in the center, as shown in Figure 8.10.

Figure 8.10
Dragging the vertical gridline to the right increases the width of the left column and decreases the width of the right column.

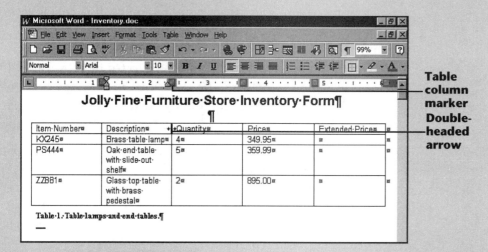

2 Click and drag to the right to increase the width of this column by about one-half inch.

Watch the corresponding table column marker in the vertical ruler to see how far you have moved the gridline.

The last two entries in the Description column (column 2) should now consist of two lines each, and the width of the Quantity column should have become narrower.

If you have problems...   If one or more cells were selected when you moved the gridline, it is possible that only the gridline for the selected cell(s) was changed. This would leave some cells in a column wider than other cells in the same column. If this happens, choose the Undo button to undo the change in gridline positions, deselect any selected cells, and then try dragging the gridline again.

---

3 Save your changes and keep the Inventory document open.

When you change the width of one column by dragging a column gridline, the overall width of the table remains the same. Only the columns on each side of the gridline being moved are affected. As one column becomes wider, the other becomes narrower.

You can modify the way Word changes column widths when you drag gridlines, by using any of the following methods:

- Hold down (⬆Shift) while you drag to the right to increase the width of a column. The columns to the right of the gridline maintain their current size; the table expands and moves toward the right edge of the page.

- Hold down (Ctrl) while you drag. This adjusts all columns to the right of the selected gridline equally. The table width does not change.

- Double-click a column border to adjust the column width to fit the widest cell entry in the column.

You also can adjust column margins by dragging the table column markers in the ruler.

- Drag a table column marker to the right to widen the current column. Columns to the right of the marker maintain their existing width, and the table expands toward the right edge of the paper.

- Hold down (⬆Shift) and drag a table column marker to the right to adjust the two columns' widths on either side of the marker. The other columns remained unchanged. The table width remains unchanged.

- Hold down (Ctrl) and drag a table column marker to the right to equally adjust all column widths to the right of the marker. The table width remains unchanged.

To display the width of columns in the ruler, point to any vertical gridline or table column marker, hold down (Alt), and then click or drag the mouse.

Setting Column Widths Precisely

You also can set the column width to a precise value by using the Cell Height and Width dialog box; follow these steps:

1 In the open Inventory file, place the insertion point in column two of the table.

2 Choose T**a**ble, Cell Height and **W**idth to display the Cell Height and Width dialog box.

3 If necessary, click the **C**olumn tab to display the column options (see Figure 8.11).

4 In the **W**idth of column 2 text box, type **1** or click the down arrow until 1 is displayed in the box.

(continues)

8

Setting Column Widths Precisely (continued)

Figure 8.11
The Column page of
the Cell Height and
Width dialog box
shows the width of
the column that
currently contains the
insertion point.

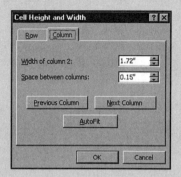

> **Note**
>
> To change the amount of space between columns, change the value in the **S**pace
> between columns text box. The value that you set affects the space between all
> columns. When you change the **S**pace between columns value, the overall width
> of the table changes.

5 Choose OK to redisplay the table with the new column 2 width.

You can see the new, shorter table is left-aligned, as it no longer stretches
between the left and right margins.

6 Do not save your changes, but leave the Inventory file open for the next
exercise.

> **Note**
>
> If you click the **A**utoFit button in the Cell Height and Width dialog box, Word adjusts col-
> umn widths automatically, according to the contents of the cells.

Changing Row Heights

By default, Word automatically adjusts row heights to accommodate the text in
the cells in each row, but you can change the row height to match your needs.
The height of individual rows, or the entire table, may be changed from the default settings. You may want to change the height of a row when you are working with column headings and want to make the first row taller than the other
rows to emphasize the headings.

To change the height of a row, you use the **R**ow page of the Cell Height and
Width dialog box. From the Height of rows drop-down list, you can choose one
of the following three options:

- *Auto.* Word automatically determines the height of each selected row.

- *At least.* Word sets each selected row to a specific height or more if the text
  requires more space.

- *Exactly*. Word sets each selected row to a specific height, even if this height does not provide enough space for all the text.

Changing Row Heights

To change the height of a row, follow these steps:

1 In the open Inventory document, select row 1 of the table.

2 Choose T**a**ble, Cell Height and **W**idth to display the Cell Height and Width dialog box.

3 If necessary, click the **R**ow tab to display the row options (see Figure 8.12).

Figure 8.12
You can change row height in the Row tab of the Cell Height and Width dialog box.

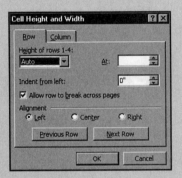

4 Choose At Least from the H**e**ight of row 1 drop-down list.

5 Enter **20** in the **A**t text box.

Note

If you choose Auto in the H**e**ight of Row drop-down list, the **A**t text box will not accept a value.

6 If you want to set the height for another row, click the **N**ext Row or **P**revious Row button, and repeat steps 4 and 5.

7 Choose OK to set the new height for row 1 in the table.

8 Save your changes and keep the Inventory document open.

Many times your table will not span the entire distance between the left and right margins. When this happens, you can choose to display your table as centered across the page, left-aligned, or right-aligned. These options are available through the Alignment section of the **R**ow page of the Cell Height and Width dialog box. The Alignment section also may be used to align individual rows on the page. Click the **L**eft button (the default) to align selected rows at the left page margin, the Cen**t**er button to center selected rows, or the Ri**g**ht button to align selected rows at the right page margin.

By default, text in a row splits across the page break when the row contains two or more lines. To prevent this from happening, click the Allow row to **b**reak across pages check box to remove the check mark.

8

Objective 5: Edit and Format Items in a Table

You can delete characters within a table by using (◆Backspace) and (Del), just as you do outside a table. If you select an entire row or column, pressing (◆Backspace) deletes only the text in the first cell of the row or column, leaving the first cell blank. Pressing (Del) deletes all text in the row or column, leaving all the cells empty.

To move or copy text within a table, you can click the Cut, Copy, and Paste buttons in the Standard toolbar, or choose the Cut, Copy, and Paste commands from the shortcut or **E**dit menus.

Word enables you to merge two or more cells together to create a cell that may be larger than others within the table. When working with larger cells, you may find it necessary to set a tab setting within the cell to enable you to place two types of entries in the cell. Complete the following exercise to learn how to accomplish these tasks and how to format existing text within a table.

Working with Table Cells: Formatting Text, Merging Cells, and Setting Tabs

To practice formatting existing text in a table, merge cells, and set tabs within cells, follow these steps:

1 In the open Inventory document, select the entire first row.

2 Use the Formatting toolbar to bold the selected characters and center the text within each cell. Then deselect the first row.

Your headings row should now look similar to the one in Figure 8.13.

Figure 8.13
You format text in a table the same way that you format text in a paragraph.

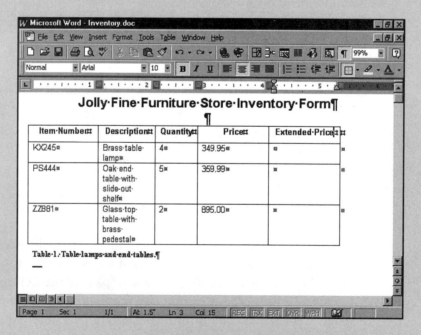

3 Place the insertion point in any cell in the first row and right-click the mouse to display the table shortcut menu.

4 Choose **I**nsert Rows to insert a new row at the top of the table.

The cells in the new first row have the same format as the cells in the original (now, second row).

5 Select the entire new first row and use the Formatting toolbar to turn off the Bold feature and left-align all cell entries. Leave the row selected for the next step.

To merge two or more cells, start by selecting the cells to be merged; then choose T**a**ble, **M**erge Cells.

6 Choose T**a**ble, **M**erge Cells to merge the five cells in the first row into one cell spanning the width of the table. Then click once in the new large cell to turn off the selection and view your results.

The top row of the table should now consist of one large cell.

Tip

To split a cell, select it; choose T**a**ble, S**p**lit Cells to display the Split Cells dialog box; choose the number of columns and rows that the selected cell is to be divided into; then choose OK and view your results.

A quick way to set a tab in a table cell is to use the Tab Indicator button and the horizontal ruler.

7 With the insertion point still in the first cell of the table, click the Tab Indicator button until the symbol for a Right Tab is displayed.

8 Position the pointer immediately below the 5-inch mark on the horizontal ruler and click to insert a right-align tab at the 5-inch mark.

9 Type **Table Lamps and End Tables**; then press Ctrl+Tab to move to the Right Tab stop.

10 Choose **I**nsert, Date and **T**ime to display the Date and Time dialog box, select the third date option, and then choose OK to insert today's date at the right side of the first cell.

Your table should now look similar to the one in Figure 8.14.

Within the next few exercises, you'll learn to complete other manual and automatic table formatting. Therefore, you do not need to save the current formatting changes.

8

(continues)

Working with Table Cells: Formatting Text, Merging Cells, and Setting Tabs (continued)

Figure 8.14

Word enables you to format existing text in the cells, merge and split cells, and use tab stops within the cells of your table.

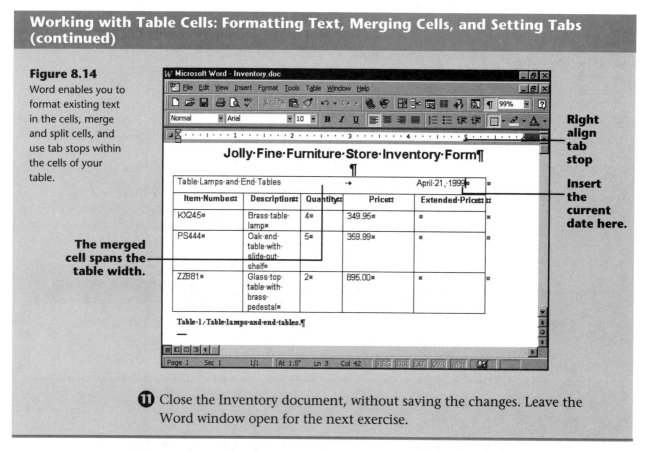

⓫ Close the Inventory document, without saving the changes. Leave the Word window open for the next exercise.

You can move columns or rows from one location in a table to another by dragging them or by using the Cut and Paste commands or buttons.

> **Note**
>
> Do not confuse moving rows and columns with moving text within a table. When you move text within a table, you move the contents of a cell. When you move rows and columns, you move both the cells and their contents.

Moving a Column by Dragging

To move a column by dragging it to a new location, follow these steps:

❶ Open the Inventory document. (If you just completed the preceding exercise, open the **F**ile menu and choose the Inventory file listing located in the list of files in the last section of the menu.)

❷ Select the third column (the Quantity column) in the table.

> **Note**
>
> When you move a row or column, be sure to select the entire row or column.

❸ Rest the pointer on the selected column, press the mouse button, and then drag the dashed insertion point pointer into column 4 (the Price column). Then release the mouse button.

Your table should look similar to the one shown in Figure 8.15.

Figure 8.15
The column in your table that was column 3 is now column 4.

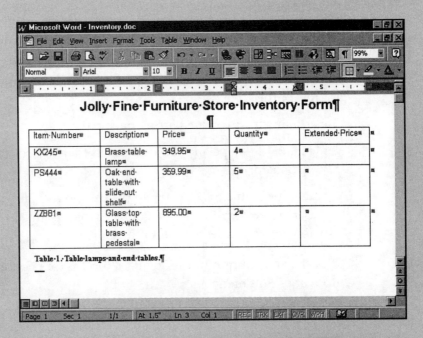

❹ Save your changes and keep the Inventory document open for the next exercise.

Note

Use the same steps to move rows by dragging. To copy columns or rows, instead of moving them, press and hold Ctrl while you drag. When you finish dragging the pointer to the desired location, make sure that you release the mouse button before you release Ctrl.

You also can move columns and rows—including the cell contents—by cutting and pasting.

Moving a Row by Cutting and Pasting

To move a row by using the Cut and Paste commands, follow these steps:

❶ In the open Inventory document, select row 2 of your table. Then right-click in the selected row and choose the **Insert Rows** command to insert a blank row following row 1.

❷ Type **Total** in the first cell of the blank row (row 2, column 1).

❸ Select the new (*Total*) row.

(continues)

Moving a Row by Cutting and Pasting (continued)

Be sure to select the entire row, including any end-of-text or end-of-row marks.

❹ Click the Cut button in the Standard toolbar (or choose Cut from the shortcut or **E**dit menu).

Word removes the entire row from the table.

❺ Position the insertion point in the ZZ881 cell entry (located at the bottom of the first column) to prepare to paste the cut row immediately above the last row of the table.

The area in which you are pasting must either:

- Match the shape and size of the cells that you cut or copied into the Clipboard; or

- Be expandable to allow for all the cells in the Clipboard to be pasted into a new location. (For example, avoid trying to paste an entire row into one selected cell in the table.)

❻ Click the Paste button in the Standard toolbar (or choose **P**aste from the shortcut or **E**dit menus).

The row is pasted into the new location.

If you have problems... If you pasted the Total row into the second through fifth cell of the ZZ881 row of your table, your last row may contain a combination of cells from the original last row and the new Total row. If this happened, choose the Undo button to undo the paste. Then click in the ZZ881 entry and paste the new Total row in place.

---

❼ Select the fifth row and cut it, so that *Total* is in the last row.

❽ Place the insertion point in the Total cell in the last row; then paste the cut row into the fourth row.

Word places the cut row back in the table in its new position. The Total row is now the fifth row (see Figure 8.16).

❾ Save your changes and keep the Inventory document open for the next exercise.

Note

You can move an entire table from one location in a document to another by cutting and pasting. Simply select the entire table and then cut and paste as usual.

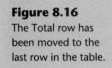

Figure 8.16
The Total row has been moved to the last row in the table.

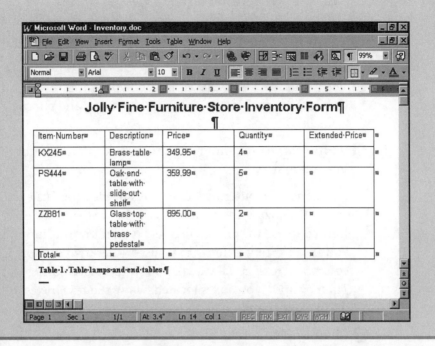

Sorting the Rows in a Table

Choosing T**a**ble, **S**ort displays the Sort dialog box, which enables you to sort the information within the table. To arrange the five rows of the table in alphabetical order, follow these steps:

1 In the open Inventory document, select the first column.

The first step in the sort procedure is to select the column on which your initial sorting of rows will be based. Your sort can be based on the entries of up to three columns. (Entire rows, not just the cells, in the selected columns are rearranged during a sort.)

2 Choose T**a**ble, **S**ort to display the Sort dialog box.

Figure 8.17
The Sort dialog box.

3 Select the Header ro**w** option (to activate the command) in the My list has section of the dialog box. (Enabling this option prevents the first row of the table—the header row—from being sorted into the remaining rows of the table.)

8

(continues)

❹ Verify that Column 1 is displayed in the **S**ort by box. If it is not, repeat steps 1 and 2.

❺ Verify that Text is displayed in the **T**ype text box. If it is not, choose the drop-down arrow at the end of the text box and choose Text from the options list.

❻ Verify that the **A**scending option is selected. If it is not, choose the **A**scending option now.

This concludes entering the settings needed for this exercise—where you are alphabetizing the table rows by the first entry in each row. If you wanted to use the entries in a second and third column, to create a second and third sorting criteria (to be used when two or more items in the first column were of equal value), you would place entries in the remaining Then by and Type boxes located below the text boxes in the **S**ort by section of the dialog box.

❼ Choose OK to conduct the sort.

Notice that, because of the alphabetical sorting, the Total row has now been placed above the ZZ881 row.

❽ Close the Inventory file without saving the changes. Leave the Word window open for the next exercise.

Sorting rows can make the listing of the information in a table easier to understand. Another way to clarify table information is to enhance certain portions of the table. In the next section, you learn to use borders and shading to enhance the appearance of your table.

Objective 6: Add Borders and Shading to the Table

By default, table gridlines appear as single, thin black lines that create the borders for each of the cells in the table. However, you can change the appearance of any border in your table (for example, you may prefer to make some lines thicker, or replace a single line with a double line). You also can turn off the gridlines, so that no borders will be displayed when you print your table. You also can add shading to emphasize sections of a table or to make a table easier to read.

The simplest way to add attractive borders and shading to a table is to have Word do it automatically. If you are not satisfied with the automatic borders and shading, you can modify what Word does or create your own borders and shading.

Adding Borders and Shading Automatically

Word includes 39 predetermined table formats. These formats consist of various combinations of borders and shading options. When you display the Table Auto-Format dialog box, you can choose any one of the 39 formats from the Formats list box. Three of these combinations provide three-dimensional effects. Most people find that the use of automatic formatting saves them a great deal of time.

To apply automatic borders and shading to your table, follow these steps:

❶ Open the Inventory document and place the insertion point anywhere within the table.

❷ Choose Table, Table AutoFormat.

The Table AutoFormat dialog box appears (see Figure 8.18).

❸ Choose Classic 1 from the Formats list box.

Figure 8.18
You can choose from among 39 combinations of borders and shading in the Table AutoFormat dialog box.

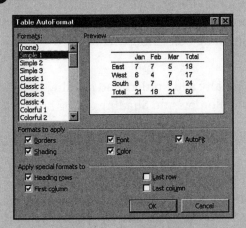

You can see what the format looks like in the Preview box.

❹ If they aren't already selected by default, click the **B**orders, **S**hading, **F**ont, **C**olor, and AutoF**i**t check boxes in the Formats to apply area.

❺ In the Apply special formats to area, make sure that the Heading **r**ows and First **c**olumn options are active.

❻ Choose OK to format your table.

It should now resemble the example in the Preview box.

❼ Choose T**a**ble, Table AutoF**o**rmat to once again display the Table AutoFormat dialog box.

❽ Try choosing a few additional table formats from the Formats list box and view the selected table format in the Preview box. When you find a format you like, choose OK to apply the format to your table. Repeat this step as often as you like.

(continues)

8

Adding Borders and Shading Automatically (continued)

> **Note**
>
> If you have access to a color printer, try some of the table formats with color enabled. You probably will be pleased by the results.

❾ Close the Inventory document without saving your changes. Leave the Word window open for the next exercise, where you learn to add borders and shading manually to the cells in your table.

If you are not quite satisfied with the results of the automatic table formatting, you can "fine-tune" the format of the table manually. Or, if you prefer, you can take charge of the entire formatting process by personally inserting your own border and shading options. To remove the formatting that results from the use of the Table AutoFormat dialog box, place the insertion point in the table, open the Table AutoFormat dialog box, choose *(none)* in the Formats list, and then choose OK.

The easiest way to manually add borders and shading to a table is to use the Borders toolbar and the Borders and Shading dialog box.

Adding Borders and Shading Manually to a Table

To apply borders and shading to your table manually, follow these steps:

❶ Open the Inventory document, place the insertion point in the table, and then choose T**a**ble, Select T**a**ble to select the entire table.

❷ Click the drop-down arrow immediately to the right of the Borders button on the Formatting toolbar to display the Borders toolbar. Then drag the blank toolbar title bar one-half inch down from the Formatting toolbar to display the "Borders" title in the Borders toolbar (see Figure 8.19)

Figure 8.19
The Borders toolbar.

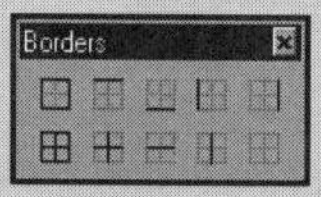

❸ Rest the pointer on each of the different buttons in the Borders toolbar and display each button's ScreenTip to learn the functions of the buttons.

❹ With the table still selected, choose the No Border button to remove all the gridlines from the table. Then click inside the table to turn off the selection and view your results.

❺ Close the Borders toolbar by choosing the Close button on the far right side of the title bar.

Another way to customize the gridlines in a table is to use the **B**orders page of the Borders and Shading dialog box.

6 With the insertion point still inside the table, choose F**o**rmat, **B**orders and Shading to display the Borders and Shading dialog box.

7 If necessary, choose the **B**orders page; then use the dialog box help button to learn the functions of the different parts of the **B**orders page.

8 Choose the **A**ll option in the Setting section; then preview the results in the Preview box and note that you will again be displaying gridlines throughout the table. (You also could have clicked each of the gridline buttons in the Preview frame to reinstate the various vertical and horizontal gridlines.)

You can see that, because this page of the dialog box provides options for setting the number of lines, the line color, and the line thickness, it provides even more formatting options for the gridlines than the Borders toolbar.

9 If necessary, use the St**y**le, **C**olor, and **W**idth drop-down list boxes to make your line selection a single, black (the *Auto* **C**olor setting), ½-point line; then choose OK to add the borders to your table.

The first and last rows of tables are often shaded to add emphasis to the titles (typically in the first row) and totals (typically in the last row) of a table.

10 Select the first row in the table; then choose F**o**rmat, **B**orders and Shading to display the Borders and Shading dialog box. Display the **S**hading page of the dialog box (see Figure 8.20).

The entry in the Apply to drop-down list box should now be Cell.

Figure 8.20
The Shading page of the Borders and Shading dialog box.

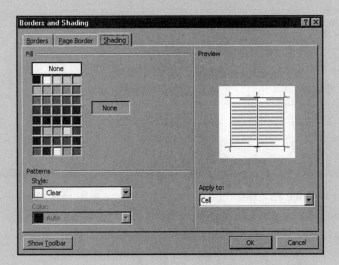

11 Choose the Gray—25% option (third box in the second row) in the Fill section.

Notice the change in the Patterns St**y**le box and the Preview box.

(continues)

Adding Borders and Shading Manually to a Table (continued)

⓬ Choose OK to apply the Gray—25% option to the selected row.

Tip

To apply shading to a color rather than to gray, choose a percentage of shading in the Style drop-down list of the Patterns section; then choose in the Color pop-up list the color you want shaded. View the result (a rough approximation) in the Preview box.

⓭ Select the last row of the table; then right-click in the selection to display the shortcut menu. Choose the Borders and Shading command to display the Borders and Shading dialog box; then apply the Gray—25% shading option to the last row of the table. Deselect the row. Your table should look similar to the one in Figure 8.21.

Figure 8.21
The table displaying the first and last rows with 25% gray shading.

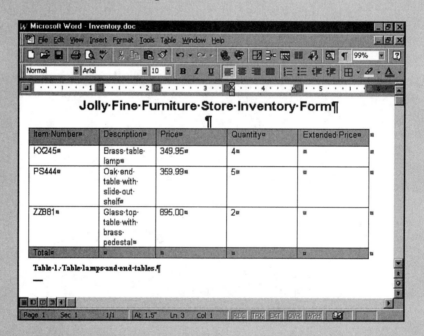

⓮ Save the changes to the Inventory document and leave it open for the next exercise.

As you will see in Chapter 11, you follow the same technique for adding borders and shading to paragraphs. The first step is to select the desired paragraph(s); then use a toolbar or the Borders and Shading dialog box to apply appropriate borders or shading to the selected paragraph(s).

Objective 7: Enter Calculations into a Table

Some tables contain numbers in particular cells that are calculated from the numbers in other cells. You can obtain these calculated numbers in three ways:

- Calculate the values manually or with a calculator, and then enter the values in the appropriate cells just as you would any other data.

- Prepare the table separately in a spreadsheet application, such as Microsoft Excel, and then import the table into your Word document or link the table to the document.

- Perform the calculations within the Word table.

When you are working with a small table and the calculations are simple, you may choose to use the first method. The second method is the only practical choice for large tables and complex calculations. The third method is a good choice when you have an average-size table, especially if it contains more than a few calculations. This section explains how to use the third method.

Formulas
Expressions that perform mathematical operations on data in cells in a table.

With Word, you can calculate values in a table. Word uses *formulas* to add, subtract, multiply, and divide numbers. Word also can calculate averages and percentages, as well as find minimum and maximum values. In this section, you learn to use Word's formulas features to add and to multiply values in the cells.

> **Note**
>
> If you are familiar with a spreadsheet application—such as Lotus 1-2-3, Microsoft Excel, or Borland Quattro Pro—you already know how to perform calculations within a Word table.

Adding Numbers in a Table

To add numbers in a column in your table, follow these steps:

❶ In the open Inventory document, place the insertion point in the empty cell at column 4, row 5 of the table.

❷ Choose Table, Formula to display the Formula dialog box (see Figure 8.22).

Figure 8.22
Use the Formula dialog box to define the calculation.

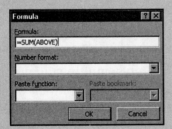

The Formula dialog box displays a suggested formula for a calculation in the Formula text box. Word guesses that you want to sum (add) numbers, because that is the most common type of calculation. Word also guesses that you want to sum numbers above the selected cell. You can, of course, enter other types of calculations and other cells on which to base the calculation.

(continues)

8

❸ Choose OK to accept the default calculation.

The calculated number is displayed in the cell in column 4, row 5 (see Figure 8.23).

Figure 8.23
The total for the Quantity column is displayed in the last cell of column 4.

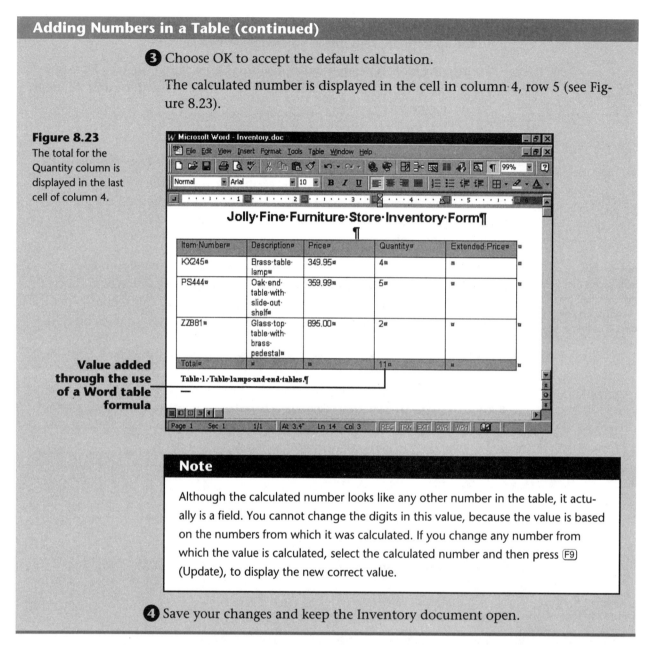

Value added through the use of a Word table formula

Note

Although the calculated number looks like any other number in the table, it actually is a field. You cannot change the digits in this value, because the value is based on the numbers from which it was calculated. If you change any number from which the value is calculated, select the calculated number and then press F9 (Update), to display the new correct value.

❹ Save your changes and keep the Inventory document open.

Adding numbers in a table is quite simple; multiplying numbers is a little more difficult because you must refer to cells in terms of their positions in the table. As in regular spreadsheet applications, Word names columns alphabetically from left to right: column one is A, column two is B, and so on. Rows are named numerically from top to bottom: the first row is 1, the second row is 2, and so on. Individual cells are named in terms of the column and row that contain them: the top-left cell is A1, the cell in the second column and second row is B2, and so on.

Multiplying Numbers in a Table

To multiply numbers in your table, follow these steps:

❶ In the open Inventory document, place the insertion point in the second cell in the fifth column.

This blank cell is cell E2. This is the cell that will display the result of multiplying the Price value in cell C2 by the Quantity value in cell D2.

❷ Choose Table, Formula to display the Formula dialog box.

When the dialog box opens, the insertion point is at the end of the text in the Formula text box.

❸ Press (◆Backspace) nine times to delete all but the equal sign (=) from the text box; you must leave the equal sign there to indicate the beginning of a formula.

❹ After the equal sign, type the formula **C2*D2** to define the calculation.

The *C* and *D* can be entered in either upper- or lowercase.

> **Tip**
>
> If the Formula dialog box covers the part of the table you need to see, drag the dialog box to a new screen location.

❺ Click the arrow at the end of the Number format drop-down list box to display a list of number formatting options.

❻ Select the $#,##0.00;($#,##0.00) format; then choose OK to enter the calculated value $1,399.80 in cell E2 (see Figure 8.24).

Figure 8.24
The value in cell E2 is the result of the value in cell C2 multiplied by the value in cell D2.

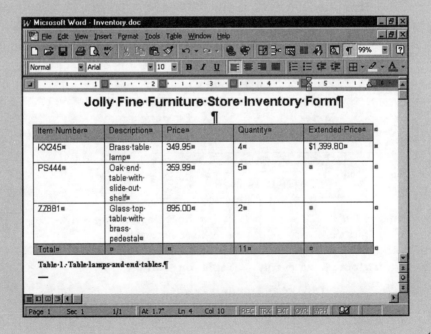

8

(continues)

Multiplying Numbers in a Table (continued)

7 Repeat the appropriate steps to place the correct values ($1,799.95 and $1,790.00, respectively) in cells E3 and E4.

8 Use the appropriate formula and format to display the total for the extended prices ($4,989.75) in cell E5.

9 Save your changes and keep the Inventory document open for the next exercise.

Objective 8: Create a Complex Table

Your current table in the Inventory document is considered a simple table because it is a rectangular block of cells, in which the cells in a column have the same width, and the cells in a row share the same height.

Word's new Draw table feature makes it easy to create complex tables; tables where all the cells in a column may consist of different widths and heights. In the following exercise, you learn to use the Draw Table feature to create a complex table.

Creating a Complex Table

To use the Draw Table feature to create a complex table, follow these steps:

1 Move the insertion point to the end of the Inventory document; then press ⏎Enter twice.

You will create a new table below your first one.

 2 Choose the Tables and Borders button from the Standard toolbar to change to Page Layout view and display the Tables and Borders toolbar that (by default) floats just inside your window work area. (See Figure 8.25 to learn the names/functions of the toolbar buttons.)

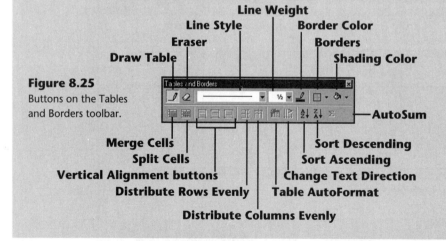

Figure 8.25
Buttons on the Tables and Borders toolbar.

> **Note**
>
> It is beyond the scope of this text to learn the functions of all the buttons on the Tables and Borders toolbar. However, you can see from Figure 8.25 that the Tables and Borders toolbar contains a number of features, many of which are accessible also from the Table menu, Borders toolbar, or Borders and Shading dialog box. If you like, you can display the Tables and Borders toolbar when you work on any simple or complex table.

3 Use the vertical scroll bar to scroll the entire work area downward until the insertion point is positioned slightly above the center of the Word window.

4 Verify that the Draw Table pointer (it looks like a pencil) is displayed when the pointer is moved into the window work area. If this pointer is not displayed, choose the Draw Table button (the first button on the left side) on the Tables and Borders toolbar.

5 Point on the insertion point; then press the mouse button and draw about four inches across the page and two inches down. Then release the mouse button.

This results in displaying a 4-inch wide by 2-inch high rectangle beneath the first table. The pointer still appears as a pencil to enable you to draw in your rows and columns.

In the next step, use the second table in Figure 8.26 as a guide for creating a complex table that includes columns of unequal width, and rows of unequal height.

As you will see, after you draw part of a line within the table, Word displays it as a dashed line and quickly completes drawing the line to the next cell or table border line. After the entire dashed line is displayed between the desired border lines, just release the mouse button to insert a solid line in place of the dashed line.

6 Draw three vertical lines within the second table to create four columns of unequal width; then draw two horizontal lines across the table to create three rows of different heights.

> **Tip**
>
> To erase the last line you drew, choose the Undo button on the Standard toolbar.

Your second table may now look similar to the one in Figure 8.26.

8

(continues)

Creating a Complex Table (continued)

Figure 8.26
You can use the Draw Table feature to draw your table in the document.

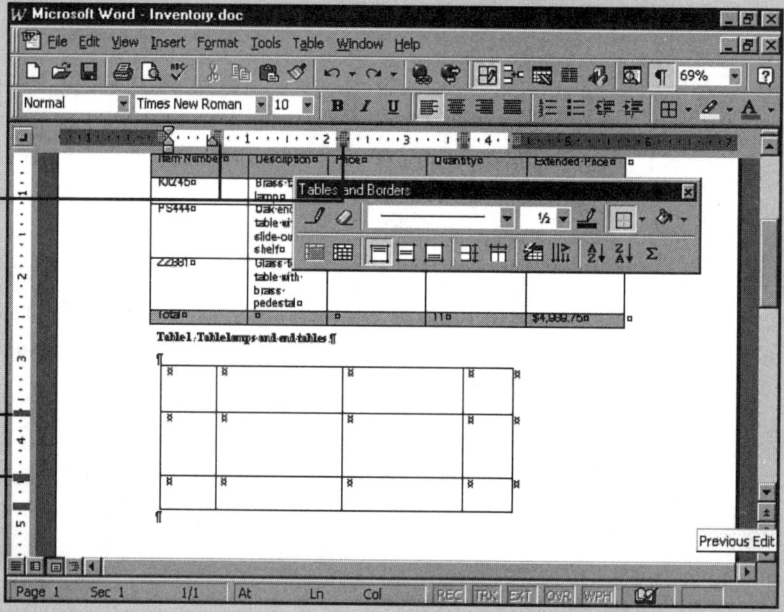

Move Table Column markers

Adjust Table Row markers

Tip

To move a gridline when displaying the Draw Table pointer, drag the Move Table Column markers (on the horizontal ruler) or the Adjust Table Row markers (on the vertical ruler) to the desired locations along the rulers.

7 Choose the Eraser button in the Tables and Borders Toolbar to change the pointer into an eraser.

8 To merge the first and second cells in the second column, drag the pointer across the horizontal line separating the two cells until the line is highlighted; then release the mouse button.

This action should erase the line separating the first and second cells and create a larger first cell in the second column. The insertion point is now placed in this cell.

9 Enter the text of your choice in any of the cells in the second table.

10 Continue to work with the Draw Table and Eraser buttons, or experiment with any of the other buttons in the Tables and Borders toolbar. Then close the toolbar by choosing the Close button on the far right side of the toolbar title bar.

11 Save the changes to the Inventory document; then leave the document open for the next exercise.

Objective 9: Convert Text to Tables and Tables to Text

Sometimes you create a section of a document and are not sure whether you should place the information in a table or just use tabs to space the information across the page. Word removes the pressure from this decision because it enables you to quickly change tabbed text into tables, and tables into tabbed text.

Converting Text to Tables and Tables to Text

To practice changing text to tables and tables to text, follow these steps:

1 Move the insertion point to the end of the open Inventory document; then press ⏎Enter twice.

If you have problems...   If your pointer has not been changed back to the regular *I-beam* pointer (for example, it still looks like a pencil or eraser from using the Tables and Borders toolbar), press Esc once.

This is the location where you will enter some tabbed text and then convert the text into a table.

2 Change back to Normal view if you prefer working in that view. Then enter the following three lines of text (the lines consist of the names of colors). Start each line at the left margin and be sure to insert only one tab between entries.

Red	**Blue**	**Yellow**	**Green**
Purple	**Tan**	**White**	**Black**
Brown	**Gold**	**Orange**	**Carnation Pink**

3 Use the selection bar to select all three lines of the colors.

4 Choose Table, Convert Text to Table to display the Convert Text to Table dialog box (see Figure 8.27).

Figure 8.27
The Convert Text to Table dialog box.

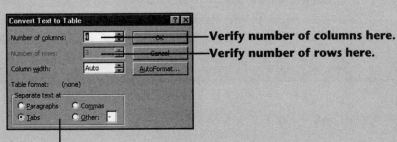

Verify number of columns here.
Verify number of rows here.

Choose mark for separating text into cells here.

8

5 After verifying that the selected options match those in Figure 8.27, choose OK to close the dialog box.

(continues)

Converting Text to Tables and Tables to Text (continued)

6 Click in the table to turn off the selection. The text should be displayed in a table format (see Figure 8.28).

> **Tip**
>
> You can also select your lines of text and quickly convert those lines into a table by choosing the Insert Table button on the Standard toolbar.

Figure 8.28
The selected text has been formatted into a simple table.

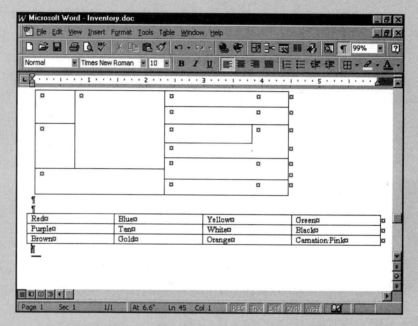

7 Select the entire table; then choose T**a**ble, Con**v**ert Table to Text to display the Convert Table to Text dialog box.

8 Accept the default choice of Tabs in the Separate text with section; then choose OK to close the dialog box and change the table back to tabbed data.

Notice that when the information is returned to the tabbed text format, the tab stop positions have been modified. The tabbed columns are now the same width as the cells were when the data was displayed in a table format.

9 Save the changes to the Inventory document; then close the file.

Chapter Summary

In this chapter, you learned to create simple and complex tables in your documents. You learned how to edit and format tables and how to perform mathematical calculations in Word tables. Finally, you learned to convert tabbed text into tables and tables into tabbed text. In the next chapter, you learn another time-saving skill: how to merge form letters, mailing labels, and envelopes to produce customized mass mailings.

If you have completed your work for this computer session, make sure that you properly exit all open programs. Then use the Windows Shut Down command to safely exit Windows. To test your knowledge of the material covered in this chapter, answer the questions in the Checking Your Skills section immediately following this summary. Then complete the exercises in the Applying Your Skills section at the end of the chapter.

Checking Your Skills

True/False

For each of the following, circle *T* or *F* to indicate whether the statement is true or false.

T   F   **1.** By default, the gridlines that identify the cell borders are dotted lines that are not printed.

T   F   **2.** In Word, it's easy to convert tabbed text into tables and tables into tabbed text.

T   F   **3.** When placing characters within the cells of a table, you must use Word's default font.

T   F   **4.** Before you can complete the movement of a row in a table, you must cut it out of the table and place it on the Windows Clipboard.

T   F   **5.** You display the Caption dialog box through the **C**aption command from the **T**able menu.

T   F   **6.** When you type more text than fits within the width of the cell, Word truncates the text.

T   F   **7.** Double-clicking on a gridline automatically adjusts the width of the column to the widest cell entry in the column.

T   F   **8.** To display the width of your table columns, press `⬆Shift` and then click on a vertical gridline or table column marker.

T   F   **9.** If you are not satisfied with the automatic borders and shading created by the Table Auto**F**ormat command in the **T**able menu, you can either modify what Word does or create your own borders and shading.

T   F   **10.** Word uses functions to add, subtract, multiply, and divide numbers.

Multiple Choice

In the blanks provided, write the letter of the correct answer for each of the following questions.

1. To move to the next cell to the right within a table, press _____.

     a. `⬆Shift`+`Tab⇄`

     b. `Tab⇄`

     c. `Ctrl`+`Tab⇄`

     d. `Alt`+`Tab⇄`

     e. `Spacebar`

2. You can insert and delete rows and columns in your table by using which of the following? _____

     a. the Standard toolbar

     b. the Formatting toolbar

     c. the appropriate menu bar commands

     d. the shortcut menu

     e. a, c, and d

8

3. Choosing _____ in the Cell Height and Width dialog box enables you to change the heights of selected cells to a specific measurement.

   a. Exactly

   b. Auto

   c. Alignment

   d. Allow Rows to Break

   e. Default

4. To delete just the contents of all cells in a selected row or column (leaving the selected row or column in the table), just _____.

   a. press Spacebar

   b. press Ctrl+Tab

   c. click the Cut button

   d. press Del

   e. c or d

5. To calculate the extended price of an item, using cell A8 to contain the price and cell C8 to contain the quantity, the formula would be _____.

   a. +A8×C8

   b. =SUM(A8+C8)

   c. =A8*C8

   d. =SUM(Across)

   e. =A8timesC8

6. If you want to use a spreadsheet program to set up a table and then use the data in Word, you would _____.

   a. create a drawing or chart within the cell

   b. import the spreadsheet from the spreadsheet program into a Word table

   c. retype the data from the other application

   d. copy the Word program into your spreadsheet program

   e. discover that Word cannot use data created in another application

7. When the insertion point is in the last cell of the last row of a table, pressing Tab _____.

   a. adds another cell to the right of the last cell in the table

   b. creates a new column

   c. moves the insertion point to the first cell in a new row

   d. moves the insertion point to the left

   e. moves the insertion point to the first cell in the first row

8. When you drag an interior vertical gridline of a table, the overall width of the table _____.

   a. doubles in size

   b. shrinks to half its size

   c. remains the same

   d. exceeds its limit

   e. increases to 1.5 times its size

9. Placing the insertion point within the table and then pressing (Alt)+ _____ selects the entire table.

    a. (F5)

    b. (A)

    c. (5) on the number pad (Num Lock must be off)

    d. (5) on the number pad (Num Lock must be on)

    e. (◆Backspace)

10. To add a column to the right side of a table, select all the end-of-row marks at the right side of the table and then click the _____ button in the Standard toolbar.

    a. Insert Rows

    b. Insert Columns

    c. Add Rows

    d. Add Columns

    e. Move Columns

Fill in the Blank

In the blanks provided, write the correct answer for each of the following questions.

1. The intersection of a row and a column in a table forms a(n)_____.

2. Before you can move a row or a column, you must first _____ it.

3. If you click _____ in the Column page of the Cell Height and Width dialog box, Word adjusts column widths automatically, according to the contents of the cells.

4. Click the _____ button to start the procedure for manually drawing a table into your document.

5. You can determine the position of an entire table across a page by using the _____ page of the Cell Height and Width dialog box.

6. If any text is selected before you click the _____ Table button to create a table, Word attempts to convert that text to a table.

7. An easy way to create a table where the cells within a column have different widths and heights is to _____ it in.

8. When you hold down (Ctrl) and drag an interior gridline to change the width of a column, columns to the _____ of the selected gridline are automatically resized in proportion to their original widths.

9. You can insert a caption above or below the selected table by using the _____ dialog box.

10. In a table, if you change any number from which a value is calculated, select the existing calculated value, and then press _____, to update calculated value to show the new correct amount.

8

Applying Your Skills

Review Exercises

Exercise 1: Creating a Two-Column Table

To practice creating a table, follow these steps:

1. Open a new document.

2. Create a four-row by two-column table that contains the the column headings *Terms* and *Definitions* in row one, and the information listed below in rows two through four. (Hint: to create the dash in the last two definitions, press Ctrl+Alt+- [minus on the numeric keypad].)

Database	**A collection of information organized for easy access and retrieval.**
Field	**One item of variable information—for example, a first name.**
Record	**All the information related to one set of fields—for example, all the data for one customer.**

3. Change the font size of all information to 12 points.

4. Adjust the cell widths to correspond with the cell contents.

5. Save the file to your Student Disk as **Terms**. Print and then close the file.

Exercise 2: Creating a Three-Column Table

To practice creating a table within a business letter, follow these steps:

1. Open a new document.

2. Assume that you are working with company letterhead, so set the top margin at two inches.

    Insert the current date at the top line of the document; then press ↵Enter six times.

3. Type the following text; then create a three-row by three-column table that itemizes each item purchased and provides a cell for the total of the items purchased. (Hint: After creating the initial table, select the third column and set a decimal tab in an appropriate location so that all dollar amounts entered in the column will align on the decimal point. Before entering an amount, be sure to press Ctrl+Tab↹ to move to the proper location in the cell.)

    Village Electronics
    1890 Sound Drive
    Duluth, GA 30136

    Enclosed please find your requested itemized list of purchases for last month. The enclosed list also includes the amount due at the end of the total row.

Item	Description	Price
A45	**Video camera batteries for Canon X25 model**	**$119.95**
C89	**CD (instructions for use of Canon X25 video camera)**	**$24.95**
Total		

4. Use a table formula to display the total amount of the purchases. (Don't forget to use an appropriate format for the value to be inserted.)

5. Format the entire table by choosing a format from the Table AutoFormat dialog box. Then make any necessary final formats.

6. Save the file to your Student Disk as **Invoice**. Print and then close the file.

Exercise 3: Inserting a Table into the Business Document

In this exercise, you create a job fair flyer that includes a table that lists the events of the job fair. Follow these steps:

1. Open a new document and change it to Landscape orientation.

2. Use a 36-point, regular, Arial font to enter the following title:

Job Fair — June 1

3. Center the title. Then place the insertion point at the end of the line, change the font to 20-point, regular, Arial. Press ⏎Enter twice, change the paragraph alignment to Left, and enter the following paragraph (press ⏎Enter twice after typing the paragraph):

Make your plans now to attend the Job Fair in the Smith Building on June 1, 8:00 a.m. to 3:00 p.m. See the table below for session information and pricing.

4. Change the font to 18-point, regular, Arial, and then create a table to include the following information. (Hint: To display the é character in the word *résumé*, press Ctrl+⟨·⟩ and then press ⟨e⟩.)

Session	Time	Topic	Room	Fee
Résumé	**8:00 a.m.-9:45 a.m.**	**Design and prepare camera-ready résumé**	**Suite C**	**125.00**
Interview	**10:00 a.m.-11:45 a.m.**	**Mock interviews with videotaping**	**Suite A**	**135.00**
Job Placement	**1:00 p.m.-3:00 p.m.**	**Review available jobs Match client to employers**	**Suite B**	**250.00**
Total				

5. Bold the contents of the first and last lines of the table; then manually change the thickness of the cell borders and add shading to appropriate rows in the table.

6. Use the appropriate formula to total the fees for all three sessions in the table.

7. Save the file to your Student Disk as **Job Fair**. Print and then close the file.

Exercise 4: Inserting a Table into the Fonts Document

In this exercise, you insert a table into a document that is similar to the Fonts document you created earlier. Follow these steps:

1. Open the Chap0801 file from your Student Disk; then immediately save the file back to your disk as **Fonts and Fonts Sizes 08**.

8

2. Move the insertion point to the end of the document and press ⏎Enter twice to create a blank row between the existing text and the table you are about to enter.

3. Create a table with six rows and two columns.

4. Using the default Times New Roman, Regular, 10-point font, add the following information to the table:

Font	Points
Times New Roman	12
Courier	14
Century Schoolbook	16
Arial	18
Courier New	20

5. Using a font that is not listed in your table, emphasize the heading row of the table through appropriate format commands.

6. Format the characters in rows 2–6, using the listed font and font size.

7. Adjust the cell widths to fit the largest entry in the column; then center the entire table across the page.

8. Save the revisions to your Fonts and Fonts Sizes 08 file. Print and then close the file.

Exercise 5: Inserting a Table into the Guideline Document

In this exercise, you insert a table into a document that is similar to the Employee Guidelines documents you created earlier. Follow these steps:

1. Open the Chap0802 file from your Student Disk and immediately save the file back to your disk as **Guidelines 08**.

2. Move the insertion point to the end of the document; then press ⏎Enter twice to create a blank line between the last line of text and the table you are about to enter.

3. Create a table with five rows and two columns.

4. Bold the headings *Name* and *Date*; then enter the following names and dates to create a personal day schedule for the employees:

Name	Date
Joseph King	August 11
Herman Munster	July 15
Calvin Hops	August 14
Katherine Lassie	July 7

5. Move the row that contains July 7 before the row that contains July 15.

6. Move the row that contains August 11 immediately above the row that contains August 14.

7. Attach a caption above the table that reads: **Table 1. Preliminary Summer Personal Day Requests.**

8. Save the revisions to your file. Print and then close your file.

Continuing Projects

Project 1: Practice in Using Word

In this exercise, you practice converting **existing tabbed text into a table.** Follow these steps:

1. Open the Chap0803 file from your **Student Disk; then** immediately save the file back to your disk as **Planning 08.**

2. Select the tabbed text at the end of **the document (on the** dates, fund-raisers, times, and fees) and convert the tabbed text into a table.

3. Reverse the order of columns 2 and 3.

4. Format the entire table by **choosing a format from the** Table AutoFormat dialog box. Complete any necessary final formatting. **(Hint: If you have trouble** shortening the width of the last (Fee) column, try dragging the **decimal tab a little to the** left.)

5. Center the table between the left **and right margins.**

6. Save the revisions to your file. Print **and then close the** file.

Project 2: Deli-Mart

Continue your work on the catalog for **the Deli-Mart by following** these steps:

1. Open the Chap0804 file from **your Student Disk; then** immediately save the file back to your disk as **Menu 08.**

2. Select the block of lines starting **with the line that includes the** headings *Menu Item*, *Number*, and *Description* through the line **starting with** *Special of the Day*. Convert this tabbed text into a three-column table.

3. Format the cells as needed to **make an attractive table.**

4. Save the revisions to the file. Print **and then close the** file.

Project 3: The Marketing Connection

After reviewing the newsletter, you decide **that a table describing each** product, as well as the fee, should be listed. Follow these steps:

1. Open the Chap0805 file from your **Student Disk and immediately** save the file as **Market 08**.

2. Place the insertion point on the **blank line immediately** above the *Sales* heading.

3. Press ⏎Enter once; then type the **following sentence:**

   Along with our newsletter, we also offer the services listed in Table 1 below.

4. Press ⏎Enter twice; then enter the following table:

Description	Fee
Brochure designs, selection of paper, and length of text	250.00
Radio, TV, and video preparation	750.00
Seminars with similar product marketing	500.00
Telemarketing (from the employee to the client)	350.00

5. Add a caption below the table identifying it as:

Table 1. Additional marketing services.

Then insert a blank line below the caption.

6. Format the table by choosing a format from the Table AutoFormat dialog box. Then make any necessary final format changes to the table.

7. Center the table and caption across the center of your page.

8. Save the revisions to your file. Print and then close the file.

CHAPTER 9

Merging Files

Merging involves drawing information from one file (such as a data source or database file) and combining it with a standard document to create a new, customized document. Merging is one of the most useful, yet underused, features in word processing. Word's mail merge feature enables you to use the merging procedure to quickly generate mass mailings, such as personalized form letters, along with envelopes and mailing labels. When mail merge is used correctly, it can save you a great deal of time and effort. The Mail Merge Helper in Word guides users through the process so that anyone who needs to merge documents can do so.

Nearly every organization has a mailing that needs to be sent to all its contacts, but most do not have the staff for such a task. By using the Word mail merge feature, however, you can create one form letter document and then customize it by merging into it the contact names and addresses from a data file. The result is a personalized letter for every contact. In addition, you can use the same list of names and addresses to generate envelopes or mailing labels for the letter.

Objectives

By the time you finish this chapter, you will have learned to

1. Understand the Basic Merge Procedure

2. Create a Main Document

3. Create a Data Source

4. Insert Merge Fields into the Main Document

5. Merge the Data Source into the Main Document

6. Merge to Create Mailing Labels or Envelopes

7. Use Advanced Merging Features

Objective 1: Understand the Basic Merge Procedure

Main document
A file containing the information you want to repeat from one copy of the document to another—for example, a letter.

Data source
The file containing the information that changes from one copy of the document to another—for example, names and addresses.

Database
A collection of information organized for easy access and retrieval.

Field
One item of variable information—for example, a first name.

Record
All the information related to one set of fields—for example, all the data for one customer.

Merge field
The name of a data source field that is inserted into a main document to indicate where the variable data should appear when the data source is merged with the main document.

To complete a merge, you must follow these four basic steps:

1. Create a *main document.*

The main document file contains the information that will be identical in each resulting merged document. In a form letter, for example, the main document contains the text of the letter, as well as the formatting. You can identify an existing document as the main document for a merge, or you can create a new main document.

2. Choose a *data source.*

The data source file contains the information that will vary from document to document, such as names and addresses. You can create a data source file, or you can use an existing file that is organized in columns and rows, such as a table or a *database.*

In a data source file, data must be organized in *fields* and *records.* A field is one piece of information, such as a first name or a ZIP code. A record is one set of related field entries, such as the name and address for one person.

3. Add *merge fields* to the main document.

To complete a main document, you insert *merge fields* as placeholders to indicate where the variable information should appear in the document. For example, a form letter would have merge fields for the recipient's name and address. The merge fields correspond to the fields in the data source, and they determine which pieces of information from the data source are inserted in the main document, and where.

4. Merge the data source into the main document.

After the main document and data source are complete, you conduct the merge. During the merge, Word replaces the merge fields in the main document with the actual information from the data source. The data from each record in the data source is used to create a new merged document. Therefore, if you have ten address records stored in your data source, the merge would create ten customized form letter documents.

The resulting letters, labels, or envelopes can be printed directly. They also can be edited and saved together as one long document.

> **Note**
>
> It is not always necessary to create one form letter for each record listed in the data source. In Objective 7 of this chapter, "Use Advanced Merging Features," you learn how to use filtering options to produce form letters using only the data source records that meet your predetermined criteria (such as people living in a particular ZIP code area).

Objective 2: Create a Main Document

The main document for a merge contains the information that is identical in each document and placeholders for the variable information (name, address, and so on) that will be inserted during the merge. You can use an existing document as a main document, or you can create a new document. A main document may include the same type of formatting as other documents—that is, you can use a variety of fonts, paragraph alignments, graphics, and so on.

When creating a form letter main document, you often include the date, the body of the letter, the closing, temporary placeholders for the merge fields, and a few spaces and punctuation marks inserted between the placeholders (for example, a comma between the city and state names). The main document for an envelope or mailing labels contains mostly placeholders, but it also may contain a return address, spaces, and punctuation.

In the following exercise, you open an existing file, save it under a new name, and then identify it as the main document.

Note

Creating a form letter from a blank document is similar to typing any other letter except that you may leave placeholders to indicate where merge fields will be inserted later.

Creating a Form Letter Main Document

To create a main document for a form letter, follow these steps:

❶ Start Word; then open the Chap0901 file from your Student Disk and immediately save it back to your disk as **Award letter**.

This is the document you will identify as the main document for the mail merge. The document has a two-inch top margin to allow for printing the letters on company letterhead. The placeholders in this letter are indicated by text within brackets ([]). You will replace these placeholders with the appropriate merge fields later in this chapter.

❷ Choose **T**ools, Mail Me**r**ge to display the Mail Merge Helper dialog box (see Figure 9.1).

The Mail Merge Helper provides access to the commands you need to complete a main document and a data source and then to conduct the merge.

❸ Choose **C**reate in the Main document area; then select Form **L**etters from the drop-down list that appears.

A dialog box prompts you to use the active document or create a new one (see Figure 9.2). If you did not have a document open, you would choose to create a new one. In this case, however, the document you want to use is already open in the active document window.

(continues)

9

Creating a Form Letter Main Document (continued)

Figure 9.1
Use the Mail Merge Helper to guide you through the steps of the merge.

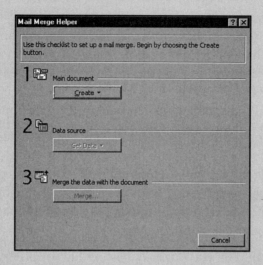

Figure 9.2
When you create a main document, you can use the document you opened before starting the merge.

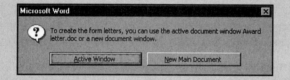

❹ Choose the **A**ctive Window button in the dialog box.

This action closes the message box and converts the Award letter document into a main document for merging.

The Mail Merge Helper dialog box remains open, but new information has been added. The Award letter document is now listed below the **C**reate button as the main document for the current merge. Your next step is to use the Mail Merge Helper dialog box to identify a data source. You do this in the next section.

Note

When you identify a Word document as a main document for use in a merge, Word codes it as a main document and assumes that it will always be used for merging. If you decide to use the document as a regular Word document in the future, you must tell Word that you no longer want to use the document as a main document. Simply open the Mail Merge Helper dialog box and select Restore to **N**ormal Word Document from the **C**reate drop-down list.

When you are creating your own main document, make sure to proofread the document a few times. A little extra effort spent at this point can save you from printing perhaps hundreds of copies of a document that contains errors.

Objective 3: Create a Data Source

After you create a main document, you specify a data source that you want to use for the merge. Remember, the data source is the file that contains the variable data that will change in each merged document. You can identify an existing table or database as the data source, or you can create a new data source. If the data source already exists (for example, if you have typed a mailing list into a Word table), you just open the existing file in the Mail Merge Helper. If you need to create a new data source file, Word helps you set up the fields and enter information in each record.

When you open an existing data source or create a new one, the data source file is attached to the main document file. Even when you exit and save your documents, the data source is still attached when you open the main document later. That way, you can repeat the merge without recreating the data source file.

Creating a New Data Source

If you don't have an existing table or database of information to use as a data source, you can create one using the Mail Merge Helper.

To create a new data source, you first define the fields you want to use, such as a field for the first name and a field for the last name; then you enter the actual data. The Mail Merge Helper comes with a list of commonly used fields from which you can choose, or you can define your own fields.

Defining Fields for the New Data Source

Before you enter information into a data source, you must name the fields you want to use, such as the various elements of an address and any other categories you want to include. The field names, up to 40 characters long, can include letters, numbers, or underscore characters (_) and must begin with a letter. They cannot include spaces. You can use capital letters to visually separate words in a field name, as in *FirstName*. To define the fields for your data source, follow these steps:

1 Determine which fields you want to include in the merged documents.

Taking a few minutes to plan now may save you hours later if you don't have to return to the data source and edit every record. In this case, if you look back at the main document form letter, you can see that to replace the temporary placeholders you need to include the following fields: Title (such as Mr., Ms., or Mrs.), FirstName, LastName, Address (such as 123 Main Street), City, State, PostalCode, and Product.

2 The Award letter document (your *main* document) and the Mail Merge Helper should still be open on-screen from the last exercise. If they are not open, choose **F**ile, **O**pen to open the Award letter document, and then choose **T**ools, Mail Me**r**ge to open the Mail Merge Helper.

(continues)

Defining Fields for the New Data Source (continued)

You use the Mail Merge Helper to create a data source. The main document must be open when you choose a data source so that Word can establish the necessary links between the two files.

❸ In the Mail Merge Helper dialog box, choose **G**et Data. The drop-down list appears (see Figure 9.3).

If a data source already exists, you would select it at this time. In this case, however, you need to create a new data source file.

Figure 9.3
Use the drop-down list to create a data source or to open an existing one.

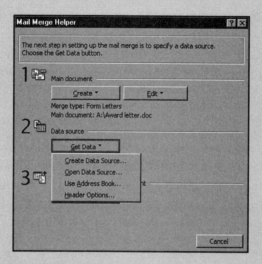

Header row
A row at the top of the data source file that contains the names of each field in a data source—for example, the header row for addresses may contain FirstName, LastName, City, State, and so on.

❹ From the drop-down list, choose **C**reate Data Source.

The Create Data Source dialog box is displayed (see Figure 9.4), showing an initial list of fields you can include in your data source. The fields are listed in the *header row* of the data source. Word assumes that you want to include all these fields in your header row. You must select the fields that you do *not* want to include, and you must add fields you want that are not on the list. You also may rearrange the order of the fields that you do want to include.

Figure 9.4
Use the Create Data Source dialog box to remove the merge fields you don't want to use in the data source file and to create new fields if necessary.

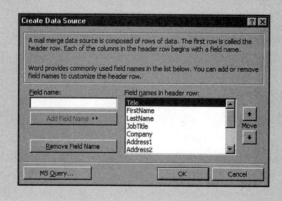

5 From the Field **n**ames in header row list box, select JobTitle (a field that you *don't* need in your data source) and choose the **R**emove Field Name button to remove the field from the list. Repeat this procedure to remove the Company, Address2, Country, HomePhone, and WorkPhone fields.

The only fields you need in the data source for this form letter are Title, FirstName, LastName, Address1, City, State, PostalCode, and Product (you create the Product field in step 6).

> **Note**
>
> In the preceding step, you removed the unneeded fields supplied by the Mail Merge Helper. You do not *have* to remove any of the generic field names supplied by the Mail Merge Helper. You may choose to keep the extra fields available (and just leave those field entries blank in each record). This enables you to return to the data source at a later time and easily add new information to each record.
>
> The disadvantage to including blank fields in your data source is the extra steps required to skip over the unneeded fields as you enter the data for each record.

6 Type **Product** in the **F**ield name box, and choose the **A**dd Field Name button. (This button becomes available as soon as you remove an existing field or type a character in the **A**dd Field Name box.)

The Product field is now added to the list. You can add as many fields as you want.

To change the order of fields in the Field **n**ames in header row list, select a field name and choose the up or down Move button on the right side of the dialog box.

You want the fields in the list in this order: Title, FirstName, LastName, Address1, City, State, PostalCode, and Product.

The order of fields in your data source doesn't matter for the form letter, but it is easier to enter data if the fields are in a logical order. If you copy information from a stack of business cards, for example, they may tend to show the company name first, and then first and last name, and so on.

7 Choose OK to display the Save As dialog box.

You save the Data Source file just as you would save any Word file.

8 Enter the name **Award recipients** in the File **n**ame box.

9 Choose **S**ave.

A dialog box then appears that indicates that you can edit either the data source or the main document (see Figure 9.5). You edit the data source to enter data or modify existing data. You edit the main document to insert the merge fields or modify the existing paragraphs. At this point, you want to enter the data for the data source (the Award recipients file).

9

(continues)

Defining Fields for the New Data Source (continued)

Figure 9.5

Word prompts you to edit the data source or the main document.

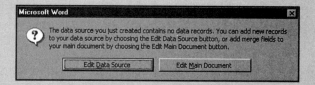

Form

A grid used to enter data into a database.

⑩ Choose the Edit **D**ata Source button from the dialog box.

⑪ The Data Form dialog box is displayed (see Figure 9.6). This dialog box represents a *form* that you can use to enter data into the data source. The Data Form dialog box lists all the fields you selected for your data source. Keep this dialog box open and continue to the next exercise.

Figure 9.6

Use the Data Form to enter the field data for each record in your data source.

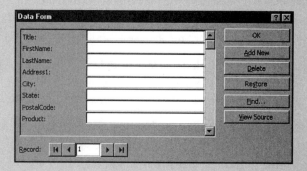

Your fields are set up, so all you have to do now is type the data. Each form represents one record. When you fill the record, a new blank form appears so that you can enter the data for the next record.

Entering Data in the Data Source

When you finish creating fields in the Create Data Source dialog box, Word prompts you to edit the data source. No data has been entered yet in the data source, so you must type it. You use the Data Form dialog box to enter the data. Follow these steps to enter the data in the Award recipients document.

❶ If the Data Form dialog box is not already open, open the Mail Merge Helper and choose Award recipients from the E**d**it drop-down list in the Data Source section.

To enter data in the Data Form dialog box, simply type the data in each field text box. Press Tab⇥ or ⏎Enter to move to the next field text box. If no data exists for a particular field, leave it blank and press Tab⇥ or ⏎Enter to continue to the next field.

❷ In the Title field, type **Mr.** and then press Tab⇥ or ⏎Enter.

The Title field data for the first record is entered, and the insertion point is moved to the next field. Continue entering data as follows:

FirstName: **Jack**
LastName: **Frost**
Address1: **10 Summer Lane**
City: **Marietta**
State: **GA**
PostalCode: **30066**
Product: **Furniture**

Figure 9.7 shows the Data Form dialog box with the data for the first record entered.

Figure 9.7
The data for the first record has been entered.

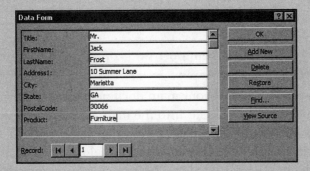

③ When you press ↵Enter after typing the data in the last field, a new blank form is displayed.

If you press Tab⇆ after typing data in the last field, you can move to the other fields and command buttons for the current record in the Data Form dialog box. You can edit the data typed in the fields, if necessary. When you are ready to move to a new, blank form to continue entering data, choose the **A**dd New button.

④ Repeat steps 2 and 3 until you have entered the two additional records listed below. (After typing the product entry for the last record, choose OK.)

Title: **Ms.**
FirstName: **Jennifer**
LastName: **Kayhill**
Address1: **890 Time Road**
City: **Orem**
State: **UT**
PostalCode: **84057**
Product: **Lighting**

Title: **Mrs.**
FirstName: **Alice**
LastName: **Seymour**
Address1: **243 South Drive**
City: **Chicago**
State: **IL**
PostalCode: **60604**
Product: **Carpet**

9

(continues)

Entering Data in the Data Source (continued)

⑤ When you have completed entering the three records, choose OK.

Word then displays the main document—in this case, the Awards letter document. Notice the Mail Merge toolbar located above the window work area.

If you have problems... The Mail Merge toolbar may be located in another screen location. Remember that you can move Word toolbars to meet your needs. If you want to reposition the toolbar, click on a gray line in the toolbar, drag the toolbar to the new location, and then release the mouse button.

---

⑥ Keep the main document open and continue with the next exercise.

After you have established your main document and the data source, you are ready to insert the merge fields into the main document. However, when working with data sources, you will often find it necessary to add, delete, or edit records. Before learning to insert the merge fields into your main document, complete the next exercise to learn how to edit your data source.

Editing a Data Source

You can edit a data source if you need to modify any records. To edit the Award recipient data source document, follow these steps:

① With the main document open, click the Edit Data Source button on the far right of the Mail Merge toolbar. The Data Form dialog box appears.

> **Note**
>
> Another way to open this dialog box is to choose **T**ools, Mail Merge and select the data source from the **E**dit drop-down list in the Mail Merge Helper.

② Choose the **A**dd New button to display a new, blank form; then add the following record:

Title: **Mr.**
FirstName: **Sean**
LastName: **O'Malley**
Address1: **457 Times Road**
City: **Sayersville**
State: **NJ**
PostalCode: **08871**
Product: **Bedding**

To go back and change a record you have already entered, type the record number in the **R**ecord box and press ⏎Enter.

If you don't know the record number, you can browse through the records one at a time. From left to right, the **R**ecord arrow buttons at the bottom left of the Data Form dialog box display the first, previous, next, and last records in the data source.

❸ Display the third record (the Alice Seymour record).

❹ Enter the name **Betty** in place of *Alice* in the FirstName box.

> **Tip**
>
> In steps 3 and 4 you edited an existing record in the Data Form dialog box. To delete a record from the Data Form dialog box, display the record; then choose the **D**elete button. Be careful, though; Word does not display a warning dialog box when you choose the **D**elete button. As soon as you choose the button, the record is deleted.

You have finished editing your records; at this point, the record information has not yet been saved in the Award recipient file. You will save the updated file in the next steps.

❺ In the Data Form dialog box, choose the View Source button to display the Award recipients file.

> **Tip**
>
> If the data source file is open, but the main document is displayed on your screen, you can display the data source file by choosing it from the **W**indow menu.

Although you enter data into the data source file using the Data Form dialog box, the data source file itself is formatted as a table. In the table, each field appears as a column, and each row represents one record. The first row in the table is the header row, which displays the field names. The other cells in the table contain the data you enter in the Data Form dialog box.

You can edit the data in this file just as you would edit data in a Word table. For example, if you want data to appear on two lines in one field, you can insert a paragraph mark within a field.

❻ Choose the Save button on the Standard toolbar to save the data source file under its current name.

> **Note**
>
> To open the Data Form dialog box again after editing the data source file, click the Data Form button on the Database toolbar, which appears automatically at the top of the data source file document window.

9

7 To display the main document, click the Mail Merge Main Document button on the Database toolbar. (Or, you can choose the Award letter file from the **W**indow menu.)

8 Let the Award letter main document display in your Word window for the next exercise.

You are now ready to insert merge fields into your main document.

Objective 4: Insert Merge Fields into the Main Document

When you create a main document, you typically use placeholders to identify the places in the document where you want to insert merge fields. When you create a data source, you provide the variable information to be inserted into your main document. You are now ready to replace the placeholders in the main document with merge fields that correspond to the fields in the data source.

When you merge a data source with the main document, Word replaces merge fields in the main document with the information in the corresponding field of the data source. The formatting you apply to the merge fields in the main document (such as bold or italics), as well as any other text typed in the main document, will appear in the final document.

Inserting Merge Fields in a Form Letter

After you have specified a data source, you can insert merge fields into the form letter main document. To insert merge fields, you make the main document active and use the buttons on the Mail Merge toolbar. Follow these steps:

1 From the preceding exercise, the Award letter main document should already be opened. If it is not, open the file now.

2 If it is not already active, choose the Show/Hide button to display the nonprinting characters in your main document window.

Whenever you need to edit a document, it is helpful to display the nonprinting characters.

3 Select the *[INSERT RECIPIENT'S Title, FirstName, and LastName MERGE FIELDS]* placeholder and delete it. Make sure that you do not delete the paragraph mark at the end of this line. (If you accidentally delete the paragraph mark, press ⏎Enter to reinsert the paragraph mark.)

In the next steps, you insert the Title, FirstName, and LastName merge fields on this line. (You will use spaces to separate the merge fields.)

4 Click the Insert Merge Field button on the Mail Merge toolbar (see Figure 9.8) and choose Title.

Figure 9.8

The Insert Merge Field button on the Mail Merge toolbar shows the merge fields from your data source.

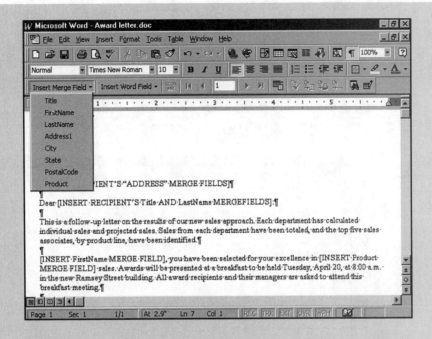

The Title merge field appears in the document. It is enclosed in chevrons (<<Title>>), indicating that it is a field, not actual data.

5 Press Spacebar, click the Insert Merge Field button, and choose FirstName.

The FirstName merge field is inserted in the document.

6 Press Spacebar, click the Insert Merge Field button, and choose LastName.

The LastName merge field is inserted in the document. You now have inserted all the merge fields necessary to complete the first line of the address on the form letter.

7 Move the insertion point to the beginning of the next line; select and then delete the entire [*INSERT RECIPIENT'S "ADDRESS" MERGE FIELDS*] placeholder. Again, be careful that you don't delete the paragraph mark at the end of the line.

8 Click the Insert Merge Field button again and choose Address1.

The Address1 merge field is inserted in the document.

9 Press ↵Enter. Then, on the new line, click the Insert Merge Field button again and choose City to insert the City merge field into the document.

10 Type a comma, press Spacebar once, and insert the State merge field. Then press Spacebar once and insert the PostalCode merge field.

This completes the address on the form letter.

11 Move the insertion point to the salutation line (the line beginning with *Dear*), remove the placeholder, being careful not to delete the colon, and then insert the Title and LastName merge fields. If you delete the colon accidentally, just type another in its place.

(continues)

Inserting Merge Fields in a Form Letter (continued)

Make sure that a space is displayed between *Dear* and the Title merge field, and another space is displayed between the Title and LastName merge fields.

12 Remove the placeholders and insert the appropriate merge fields in the second paragraph of the letter (see Figure 9.9).

Figure 9.9
The main document with all the merge fields inserted.

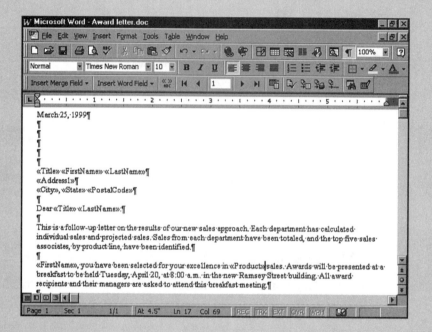

13 To see the form letter as it will appear with the data merged, click the View Merged Data button on the Mail Merge toolbar.

Word merges the data source with the main document and displays the results of the first record on your screen. You can see that the merge fields in the main document have been replaced with the corresponding data from the data source file. Use the First Record, Next Record, Previous Record, and Last Record arrow buttons on the Mail Merge toolbar to view the document containing data merged from the other records in the data source.

If you see mistakes in the form letter, such as spelling errors in the letter text, formatting problems, or missing spaces and punctuation between merge field data, you can edit the main document file. If you see mistakes in the merge field data, such as spelling errors in a name or address, you can edit the data source file.

14 Click the View Merged Data button again to view the main document with the inserted merge fields.

> **Note**
>
> To format a merge field but not the surrounding text, position the insertion point in the field and press Ctrl+⇧Shift+F9 to select the field before you apply the character formatting.
>
> If you want to remove a merge field you inserted, select the merge field you want to replace (press Ctrl+⇧Shift+F9); then press Del.

 15 When you have finished setting up the Award letter main document, save it by choosing the Save button on the Standard toolbar. Keep the main document open and move to the next exercise.

You ended the preceding exercise by previewing the merge. In the following exercise, you complete the merge.

Objective 5: Merge the Data Source into the Main Document

After you have created a main document, specified a data source, and prepared the main document by inserting merge fields, you are ready to merge the data source with the main document. Depending on your needs, you can merge directly to the printer, or you can merge to a new document so that you can save the merged documents for later editing and printing.

If you merge to a document, Word creates one long file with Next page section breaks between the merged documents for each record. You can then edit each document, adding individual notes or information, before printing.

Before performing the merge, you can have Word check the merge to identify potential problems. You can also sort the data source so that Word produces the merged documents in a particular order (for example, by ZIP code or alphabetically by last name). Several other options enable you to customize the merge.

Merging Form Letters

You can perform a merge and send the results to a printer or to a new document by using either the Mail Merge Helper or Mail Merge toolbar buttons. In either case, the main document must be active.

Merging from the Mail Merge Helper

9

To merge your form letters from the Mail Merge Helper, follow these steps:

1 Open the Award letter main document if it is not already open; then choose **T**ools, Mail Me**r**ge to open the Mail Merge Helper dialog box.

(continues)

Merging from the Mail Merge Helper (continued)

❷ Choose the **M**erge button under Merge the data with the document. The Merge dialog box appears (see Figure 9.10).

Figure 9.10
Use the Merge dialog box to specify options for the final merge.

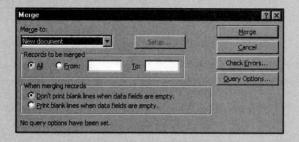

The Me**r**ge to drop-down list box (located in the top-left portion of the dialog box) provides the options to store the form letters in a new document, print them, or use the form letters in electronic mail.

❸ Accept the default option of New document in the Me**r**ge to drop-down list box.

Choosing the New document option instructs Word to store the merged documents in a new file with Next page section breaks between each letter when the merge is completed.

❹ In the Records to be merged section, choose **A**ll if it is not already selected.

This section provides the option to merge either all the records or just a certain range of records. To merge a specific range of records, enter the starting record number in the **F**rom text box and the ending record number in the **T**o box. To print documents containing the data from records 3, 4, 5, and 6, for example, enter **3** in the **F**rom text box and **6** in the **T**o text box.

You also can use this option to check the printer output by choosing and printing just a few merged documents.

❺ If it is not already selected, choose the **D**on't print blank lines when data fields are empty option in the When merging records section.

With this option selected, blank lines caused by an empty field in a record are not printed. For example, some addresses require two address fields (Address1 and Address2—possibly for a P.O. Box and a street address). Although the street addresses for most people in a typical data source file require only one address line, if some people require two address lines, you need to insert the two address merge fields in the main document. For the recipients needing only one address line, using the **D**on't print blank lines when data fields are empty option prohibits an extra blank line from being inserted in the recipient address portion of the letter.

❻ Choose the **M**erge button.

Word begins the merging process, creating a file from the new merged documents or printing them. If you create a new document, you must name and save it as you would any Word document. When you merge to a new document, Word assigns the default name Form LettersX (where X is 1, 2, 3, and so on for the number of times the main document and source file have been merged to create form letters during the current computer session). Alternatively, you can close the merge file without saving it.

Because it is relatively easy to create a merge if the main document and data source are saved, you may not want to take up disk space by saving your merged documents.

You have now completed the merge. You have a main document file, a data source file, and the customized form letters resulting from the merge. The next step is to create mailing labels or envelopes for the letters.

7 Look at the status bar to verify that you are viewing the first of four pages. Then use the vertical scroll bar to review the form letters in your merged document.

8 Close the merged document and the Award recipient data source files without saving any changes. Leave the main document open for the next exercise.

Merging with Toolbar Shortcuts

When the main document is active, the Mail Merge toolbar appears. You can click toolbar buttons to perform several of the merging tasks available in the Mail Merge Helper.

- Click the Mail Merge button on the Mail Merge toolbar to select options in the Merge dialog box.

- Click the Merge to New Document button on the Mail Merge toolbar to combine the results of the merge in a new document.

- Click the Merge to Printer button on the Mail Merge toolbar to print the results of the merge on the active printer.

Objective 6: Merge to Create Mailing Labels or Envelopes

To create mailing labels or envelopes for the form letters you created with a merge, you use the same basic steps used to create the form letter. You create the main document, choose a data source, set up the main document, and then conduct the merge.

When you create a main document for a mailing label or envelope merge, you identify a blank document as the main document, and Word automates most of the details. You simply choose the size and shape of the labels or envelopes and insert the merge fields in the correct positions.

9

In addition, when you merge to labels or envelopes, it is likely that the data source already exists. In the exercises for this objective, you use the existing data source file that was used when you created the form letters in the preceding exercise.

Merging Mailing Labels

When you set up a main document for a label merge, Word handles the difficult details, including calculating the number of labels that will fit on a page.

Creating the Mailing Labels Main Document

To create a new main document for mailing labels, follow these steps:

1 With the Award letter main document still displayed in your Word window from the preceding exercise, choose **T**ools, Mail Me**r**ge. The Mail Merge Helper dialog box appears so that you can create a mailing labels main document.

2 From the **C**reate drop-down list, select **M**ailing Labels. A dialog box asks whether you want to use the active document or create a new one.

3 Choose the **N**ew Main Document button.

This creates an empty main document for the mailing labels merge. The Mail Merge Helper is still open on the screen so that you can choose the data source (see Figure 9.11), which you do in the next section.

Figure 9.11
Use the Mail
Merge Helper to
create an empty
main document for
the mailing labels
merge.

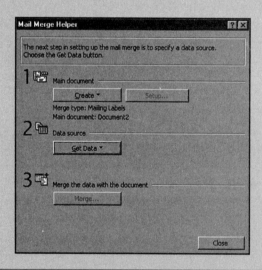

You are now ready to set up a data source for the mailing labels.

Opening an Existing Data Source

You can use the same data source for many different merges. In this exercise, you use the Award recipient data source document that you created for the form letter merge. Follow these steps to open the data source:

1 In the Mail Merge Helper dialog box (that should still be open on your screen from the preceding exercise), choose the **G**et Data button, and then choose the **O**pen Data Source option from the drop-down list.

The Open Data Source dialog box appears. This dialog box is similar to the Open dialog box you use to open any Word file.

2 Most likely, your student files are displayed in the Open Data Source dialog box. If so, choose the Award recipient document from the Look **i**n list; then choose **O**pen. (If necessary, work through the list of storage locations in the Look **i**n drop-down list box to move to the location holding your files; then choose the Award recipients file.)

Word associates the mailing labels main document with the Award recipient data source file and displays a message box prompting you to set up your main document.

3 Leave the message box on your screen as you continue to the next section.

Note

Conversion filter
A program that makes data entered in other applications compatible with Word.

You can use data created in other programs as a data source for a merge if the corresponding *conversion filter* was installed during the Word installation process. If all the Word converters were installed, you can open data created by many different applications, including previous versions of Word, WordPerfect, Microsoft Excel, Lotus 1-2-3, FoxPro, Access, dBASE, and Paradox.

You are now ready to set up the mailing labels you want to use for the merge.

Setting Up and Merging the Mailing Labels

To set up a mailing label main document, you must choose the type and size of the labels before you insert the merge fields. Follow these steps:

1 Choose the **S**et Up Main Document button from the message box still on-screen from the preceding exercise. The Label Options dialog box appears (see Figure 9.12). The default printer options correspond to the default printer used with your computer system. If necessary, you can choose other options.

Figure 9.12
Use the Label Options dialog box to choose from standard types of label sheets.

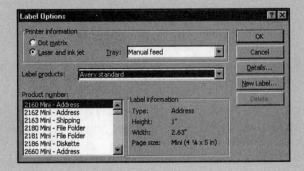

(continues)

Setting Up and Merging the Mailing Labels (continued)

The Label **p**roducts drop-down list enables you to select the general label type (or label manufacturer) you will use.

Most labels manufactured by U.S. producers are compatible with Avery products. A few other manufacturers appear when you select Other.

2 Accept the default choice of Avery standard. If the dialog box does not default to this choice, choose the Avery standard option.

From the Product n**u**mber list, select the labels you want to use in the merge.

If the product number of the labels you are using does not appear, you can select a product that has the same dimensions as the product you are using. To see the specific measurements of the selected product, choose the **D**etails button.

3 Choose the 5160-Address option from the Product n**u**mber list.

To learn about the type, height, width, and page size of the 5160 Address label option, review the information now displayed in the Label information frame of the dialog box.

4 Choose OK.

The Create Labels dialog box appears (see Figure 9.13). In the Create Labels dialog box, you insert the merge fields for your mailing labels main document.

Figure 9.13
You use the Create Labels dialog box to insert merge fields for the delivery address.

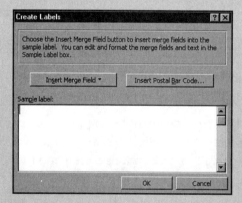

5 Click the Insert Merge Field button to display the list of merge fields available to you from the selected data source. Review the list and determine which merge fields, along with proper punctuation and character and line spacing, will be needed to create the mailing labels.

6 To complete the first, insert the Title merge field, press ⌷Spacebar⌷ once, insert the FirstName merge field, press ⌷Spacebar⌷ once, insert the LastName merge field, and press ⌷◄Enter⌷.

7 Enter the necessary remaining merge fields (along with the proper punctuation and spacing) to complete the mailing label information (see Figure 9.14); then choose OK.

Figure 9.14

The entries for the Create Labels dialog box.

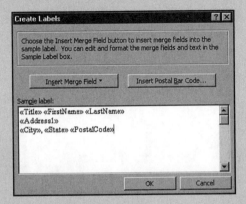

You are returned to the Mail Merge Helper dialog box. Meanwhile, Word has prepared a main document with the appropriate settings for the mailing labels.

8 Choose the **M**erge button in the Merge the data with the document section to display the Merge dialog box.

9 Make sure that the default options are selected in the Merge dialog box: the Me**r**ge to option is New document; the **A**ll option is selected in the Records to be merged section; and the **D**on't print blank lines when data fields are empty option is selected.

10 Choose the **M**erge button to complete the merge.

Word displays the merged mailing labels document on-screen (under the default name of Labels1), as shown in Figure 9.15. (You may need to adjust your zoom setting to about 75% to see the complete entries.) At this point, you can work in the document window to do any final editing necessary to prepare the mailing labels for printing.

Unlike repetitive form letters, some people prefer to save their merged mailing labels files. This is especially true for those who send frequent correspondence to the same group of people.

11 Save the merged document as **Mailing labels**; then close the document. Save the main document (the document with the mailing labels merge fields) as **Labels**; then close the Labels main document. Close the Award letter and any other open files.

(continues)

9

Setting Up and Merging the Mailing Labels (continued)

Figure 9.15
Word displays your merged label document and gives it the default name of Labels1.

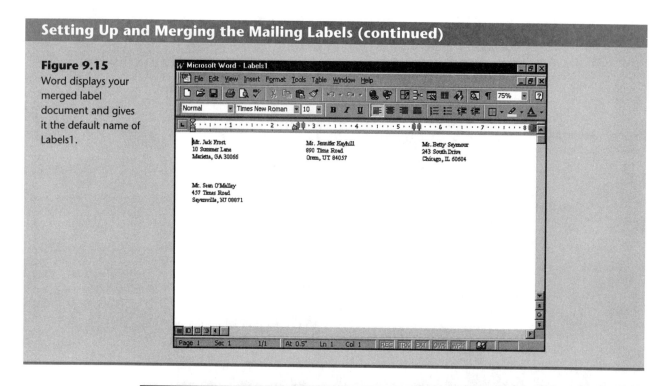

Note

You may have noticed that you were not instructed to print the labels in this exercise. If your printer does not have access to the specified labels during the printing process, there is a possibility that the printer will jam.

If you have access to the appropriate labels and have received an OK from your instructor or network administrator, try to print your Mailing labels file.

Merging Envelopes

You use the same basic steps to create merged envelopes as you did to create merged mailing labels. The major difference is that you set up the envelope main document to accommodate the size and type of envelopes that you are using.

The steps for merging envelopes and merging mailing labels are similar; therefore, no exercise for merging envelopes is included in the text.

One word of caution when working with envelopes: many printers have problems in the feeding of envelopes through the printer. Make sure that you select the appropriate type and size of envelopes during the envelope main document setup. Many printers will jam if the specified envelope is not present and properly aligned in the printer tray. Even when you are sure that the exact type and size of envelope have been correctly inserted in the main document and the printer, you may still want to stay by the printer during the envelope printing process.

Objective 7: Use Advanced Merging Features

Word offers powerful features for customizing merges to fit your needs. In this section, you learn how to check for errors, sort the data source, and filter the data source to print only certain records.

Checking the Merge for Errors

Before merging the data source with the main document, Word can check the merge for potential problems. Error-checking catches some common problems. If you change the name of a field in the data source after inserting merge fields in the main document, for example, the two names may not match. If your data source contains a record containing only blank fields, the check catches the error. You can check for errors in advance, without merging, or you can have Word run the check while it is creating the final merged documents.

After you have a completed data source file attached to your main document, you can check for errors by completing the following steps:

1. With the main document displayed in the Word window, choose the Check for Errors button on the Mail Merge toolbar to display the Checking and Reporting Errors dialog box (see Figure 9.16).

Figure 9.16
You can check for nonexistent fields or blank records before or during a merge.

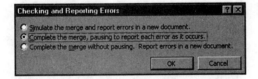

2. Select one of the error-checking options and choose OK.

The first option lets you simulate the merge to check each record and field for errors without actually performing the merge. Word lists the errors in a separate file. The second option lets you complete the merge, pausing each time an error is encountered. The third option enables you to complete the merge without pausing, which merges the documents without interruption and afterwards lists any errors in a new document window.

Before you merge the data source and the main document, you can sort the data source by field to produce documents in a particular order. To print form letters for a bulk mailing, for example, you may want to sort the data source by ZIP code. (The U.S. Postal Service requires that bulk mailings be broken into groups according to ZIP code.)

9

Sorting Data in a Data Source before Merging

The records in the data source have been entered as the names were received, but there are times when the records need to be in a sorted order. To sort the data source, follow these steps:

1 Open the Award letter main document from your Student Disk.

Because you earlier established this document as a main document, the Mail Merge toolbar is displayed in its document window. The Award recipients data source file is also still attached to the Award letter main document file.

2 Choose the Edit Data Source button on the Mail Merge toolbar. When the Data Form dialog box is displayed, choose the **V**iew Source button to display the Award recipients data source file in a table format (see Figure 9.17).

Figure 9.17
The Award Recipients data source table.

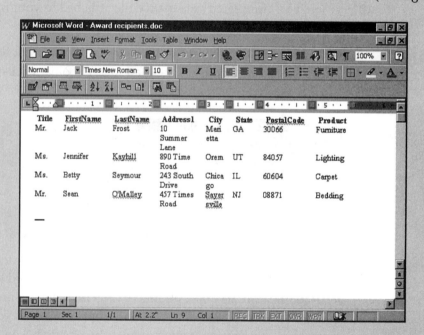

3 Click anywhere within the PostalCode heading (in row 1, the heading row) to anchor the insertion point in the PostalCode field name.

4 Choose the Sort Ascending button to use with the PostalCode field (the ZIP code) to sort the records from the smallest ZIP code number to the largest.

Notice that the Sean O'Malley record is now the first record, followed by Jack Frost, Betty Seymour, and Jennifer Kayhill.

Tip

If you sort the records in a data source and then add new records to the data source, you will need to repeat the sort procedure to integrate the newly added records into their proper positions.

5 Choose the Mail Merge Main Document button (or open the **W**indow menu and choose the Award letter file) to return to the Award letter main document window.

 6 Choose the Merge to New Document button on the Mail Merge toolbar to create the new merge.

7 Use the vertical scroll bar to scroll through the letters and see that they have been sorted (in ascending order) according to the recipient's ZIP code.

8 Close the merged document file without saving it. Then leave the Award letter and Award recipients files open for the next exercise.

Merging Only Certain Records

To limit which records Word includes in the merge, you can filter records to test for one or more conditions—or rules. Using these rules, you can merge to create only the documents you really need. Remember that any rule assumes that the data was entered consistently—for example, that all records use two-letter abbreviations for state names.

To merge only records with a New York address, you could include records where the State field is NY. You could merge only records with ZIP codes beginning with 8 by specifying that the PostalCode field be greater than or equal to 80000 *and* less than 90000.

Filtering Data to Merge Only Certain Records

If the data source contains a large number of records and you need only specific records, you can set up a filter to merge only selected records. Follow these steps:

1 Display the Award letter main document that should still be open from the preceding exercise.

 2 Choose the Mail Merge Helper button on the Mail Merge toolbar to display the Mail Merge Helper dialog box; then choose the **Q**uery Options button to display the Query Options dialog box (see Figure 9.18).

> **Tip**
>
> You also can display the Query Options dialog box by choosing the **Q**uery Options button in the Merge dialog box.

3 If necessary, select the **F**ilter Records tab so that your dialog box appears similar to the one in Figure 9.18.

(continues)

9

Filtering Data to Merge Only Certain Records (continued)

Figure 9.18
Use the filter options to merge only records that meet the conditions you set.

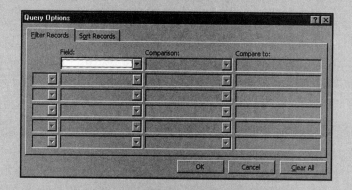

In this dialog box page, you choose the field you want to filter; then you enter the type of comparison (greater than, equal to, and so on) and the value to which you want to compare. The Field list box contains merge field names from the data source. The Comparison list box contains the operators you can use to test a field's contents. The Compare to box enables you to supply the value to check against the field. Together, the three boxes constitute a rule, such as State (the field name) Equal to (the comparison) UT (the value to compare).

❹ Set up a rule for using only those records of addresses in the state of Utah. Choose the field State, choose the comparison Equal to, and then type the value **UT** in the Compare to text box.

You can add another rule on the next line by selecting And or Or from the first box in the next row and filling in values for that row. For example, if you think you may have used complete state names in the data source file, you might want to select Or, the State field, the Equal to comparison, and then type the value **Utah** in the Compare to text box.

You can remove all existing rules on this page by choosing the **Clear All** button. If you are surprised at a small number of records that are displayed when you conduct a sort or filter on your records, make sure that all rules from previous filtering procedures have been cleared.

❺ You have defined your filter options; choose OK to close the Query Options dialog box, engage your filter, and return to the Mail Merge Helper dialog box.

Tip

In the preceding exercise, you completed a single-criterion sort—sorting the records in the data source by ascending ZIP codes. You can use the Sort Records page of the Query Options dialog box to use multiple criteria in your sort procedure—for example, creating a sort that arranges the records first by ZIP code, and then using the last name entries to create an alphabetized list of people within each ZIP code.

6 Choose the Merge button in the Mail Merge Helper dialog box.

7 After verifying that the New document option is selected in the Merge to section and that the **All** option is selected in the Records to be merged section (choose these options if necessary), choose the **Merge** button to complete the merge.

8 Review the results of your merge to see that only the Jennifer Kayhill form letter was produced in the merge.

This concludes the exercises for this part of the chapter.

9 Close all open documents without saving any changes made to the documents.

If you want to apply complicated combinations of filters, see the Word Help program, your instructor, or your technical support person for instructions about multiple rules. For simpler rules, remember that using AND *limits* the possible number of matching records, whereas OR *increases* the possible number of matching records. Consider the following examples:

> *LastName Less than H*

This selects records in which the last name begins with one of the letters from A through G.

> *LastName Greater than or Equal to J AND Title Equal to President*

This selects records in which the last name begins with one of the letters from J through Z, and the title is President. Notice that AND excludes people who have the appropriate last name but a different title. If you used OR in this example, you would include every record with the last name beginning with a letter from J–Z (no matter what title) as well as every record with the title President (no matter what last name).

Chapter Summary

In this chapter, you learned how to set up a merge in Word. You learned about fields and records and about the factors to consider when planning a merge file. You can see that using the merge feature can save time and increase productivity in an organization. In the next chapter, you learn how to further increase your productivity by using some of the Word features that automate your work.

If you have completed your work for this computer session, make sure that you properly exit all open programs. Then use the Windows Shut Down command to exit safely from Windows. To test your knowledge of the material covered in this chapter, answer the questions in the Checking Your Skills section immediately following this summary. Then complete the exercises in the Applying Your Skills section at the end of the chapter.

9

Checking Your Skills

True/False

For each of the following, circle *T* or *F* to indicate whether the statement is true or false.

T   F   **1.** The main document contains the information that is identical in each merged item.

T   F   **2.** To use a data source file in a merge, it first must be attached to the main document.

T   F   **3.** If your main and data source documents are saved, it is not always critical to save your merged document.

T   F   **4.** When you create a new data source, you define the fields you want to use and then enter the actual data.

T   F   **5.** The formatting you apply to the merge fields and any other text appears in the final document.

T   F   **6.** When you are filtering records in your data source, combining the second rule with an AND will reduce the number of records meeting the necessary conditions compared to combining the two rules with an OR.

T   F   **7.** Field names may be no longer than 30 characters and may include numbers and letters.

T   F   **8.** Word creates a table to hold the information in the data source file, using a column for each field defined.

T   F   **9.** When you merge a data source with a main document, Word replaces merge fields in the main document with information in the corresponding field of the data source.

T   F   **10.** In general, preparing a mailing labels main document is similar to preparing an envelope main document.

Multiple Choice

In the blank provided, write the letter of the correct answer for each of the following questions.

1. Which step is *not* related to the use of the Word Mail Merge Helper?

———

a. Create a main document.

b. Select a data source.

c. Add merge fields to the main document.

d. Merge the data and the document.

e. Select your printer.

2. A valid field name is ———.

a. Field Name

b. 2Address

c. NewName

d. Name Last

e. Sam Jones

3. To complete a merge, you need to replace the blanks or placeholder in the main document with _____.

 a. asterisks

 b. merge fields

 c. field names

 d. field sizes

 e. plus signs

4. A quick way to select a merge field in your main document is to place the insertion point in the merge field and then press _____.

 a. F9

 b. Ctrl + F9

 c. Shift + F9

 d. Alt + F9

 e. Shift + Ctrl + F9

5. When filtering records, the combination of the field name, comparison entry, and compare to value is called a _____.

 a. sort

 b. rule

 c. record

 d. character

 e. guideline

6. To insert merge fields, you make the main document active and use the buttons on the _____ toolbar.

 a. Standard

 b. Formatting

 c. Table

 d. Mail Merge

 e. Forms

7. In a data source, all the information related to one customer is typically considered to be one _____.

 a. field name

 b. merge field

 c. field

 d. record

 e. entry

8. Merge fields in the main document are enclosed in _____.

 a. chevrons (<< >>)

 b. quote marks (" ")

 c. asterisks (* *)

 d. brackets ([ ])

 e. braces ({ })

9. To combine the results of the merge in a new document from the Mail Merge toolbar, click the _____ button.

 a. Merge to New Document

 b. Merge to View

 c. Mail Merge

 d. Mail Merge to Printer

 e. Insert Merge File

10. Before you merge the data source with the main document, you may want to produce documents in a particular order, using the _____ Records feature.

 a. Search

 b. Find

 c. Sort

 d. Arrange

 e. Selecting

9

Fill in the Blank

In the blank provided, write the correct answer for each of the following questions.

1. The process of combining sets of information from one document with another document is known as _____.

2. To enter data in the Data Form dialog box, just type the data in each _____ text box.

3. Word replaces a(n)_____ field in the main document with information in the corresponding field of the data source.

4. If you merge to a document, Word creates one long document with _____ breaks between the documents for each record.

5. You can simulate the merge to check for _____ without actually completing the merge.

6. To create a new data source for use in the main document, you define the _____ of information in the data source, and then enter the data.

7. The _____ you apply to enhance the merge fields and any other text will appear in the final document.

8. The _____ toolbar appears when the main document is active.

9. To create a sort using two or more fields, use the _____ dialog box.

10. To limit which records Word includes in the merge, you can _____ records to test for one or more conditions.

Applying Your Skills

Review Exercises

Exercise 1: Creating a Main Document

To practice creating a main document for a merge, follow these steps:

1. Create the following main document for a "form memo" that is to be sent to all company employees to announce new choices in employee medical insurance. Put the placeholders, including the brackets, in the document for this exercise. In a later exercise, you will re-place the placeholders with merge fields.

Interoffice Memorandum

DATE   April 1

TO: [INSERT FIRST AND LAST NAME MERGE FIELDS]

FROM: Benefits

SUBJECT: New Choices in Medical Insurance

As of July 1, [INSERT INSURANCE MERGE FIELD] insurance (your current medical insurance) will no longer be offered through our company. Please stop by our office to pick up the necessary paperwork to change your insurance provider to one of the following: Blue Cross, MT Health Plan, or CompuCare. The Change in Medical Insurance forms must be submitted to our office by June 1.

Thank you.

2. Save the file as **Insurance Memo** to your Student Disk.

3. Leave the file open until you complete Review Exercise 5.

Exercise 2: Creating a Data Source

To practice creating a data source for a merge, follow these steps:

1. Use the following table to create a data source for the Insurance Memo document. (Address1 is the name of the field representing the employee's internal mailing address.)

LastName	FirstName	Insurance	Department	Address1
Sprechen	Vonni	ARCC	Records	205-W
Roberts	Don	ARCC	Education	123-S
Claudsen	Gilbert	MNSCU	Accounting	205-W
Hesski	Ken	Metro Partners	Marketing	205-W
Bonthos	Borgie	Champlin Health	Utilities	123-S

2. View the data source, checking for any errors, and then make any necessary corrections.

3. Save the file as **Employees** to your Student Disk.

4. Leave the file open until you complete Review Exercise 5.

9

Exercise 3: Sorting the Records in the Data Source

To practice sorting records in a data source, follow these steps:

1. Display the Employees data source you created in Review Exercise 2.

2. Sort the records in the Employees data source, by the LastName field, in ascending alphabetical order.

3. Save the changes to your file.

4. Keep the Employees data source file open for the next exercise.

Exercise 4: Merging

To practice creating a merge, follow these steps:

1. In the open Insurance Memo main document, replace the placeholders with the appropriate merge fields.

2. Create the "form memos" merge to a new document.

3. Review your merged documents for errors and make any necessary corrections.

4. Save the merge, to your Student Disk, in a new document called **Insurance Change Memo.**

5. Print the memos.

6. Close the Change Insurance Memo file.

Exercise 5: Creating Mailing Labels

To practice creating mailing labels, follow these steps:

1. Create a mailing label main document to be used with the Employees data source. Because this label is to be used for an internal employee mailing, just place the employee first and last names, department, and internal mailing address (the Address1 field) on the label. Use the Avery standard 5160 Address labels you used earlier in the chapter. Save the main document as **Labels**.

2. Perform the merge to a new document, check for errors, and then make any necessary corrections.

3. Save the merge document as **Employee Labels** to your Student Disk.

4. Close all the files used in the first five review exercises (do not save the Mailing Labels main document).

Continuing Projects

Project 1: Practice Using Word

In this project, you change an existing letter into a main document. Then, after creating a data source from the following records, you complete the necessary steps to create a merge and produce copies of the form letter.

1. Open the Chap0902 file from your Student Disk; then immediately save it as **Flyer** back to your Student Disk.

2. Make the Flyer document a main document for a merge. Leave the file open and move to the next step.

3. Use the following records to create a data source file named **Flyer Data** and attach it to the Flyer main document.

Title	First Name	Last Name	Address1	City	State	Postal Code
Ms.	Josie	Marie	1425 Town Street	Miconville	CT	14602
Ms.	Holly	Dusky	1463 W. Idaho	Miconville	CT	14601
Ms.	Nicole	Johnson	1212 Main Street	Miconville	CT	14601
Mr.	Matt	Stafford	134 East Avenue	Miconville	CT	14603
Ms.	Andrea	Larson	1123 Main Street	Miconville	CT	14604

4. In the Flyer main document, delete the inside address and the existing personal information in the salutation (the *Dear...* line) and insert the appropriate merge fields and punctuation.

5. Merge the main and data source documents to a new document. Check for errors and make any necessary corrections. Save the new document to your Student Disk as **Jolly Flyer**.

6. Print the Jolly Flyer document; then close all open files, saving all changes made to the open files.

Project 2: Filtering Your Data Source

Before completing a merge, practice filtering the records in a data source by following these steps:

1. Create a new (main document) form letter as shown in the following. Place the current date and merge field placeholders in the identified locations. Save the new main document as **Clean Rugs** on your Student Disk.

   [Insert the current date]

   [Insert the Title, FirstName, and LastName merge fields]

   [Insert the Address1 merge field]

   [Insert the City, State, and PostalCode merge fields]

   Dear [Insert the Title and LastName merge fields]:

9

> **The people living in your ZIP code area have been chosen to receive an extra 10% discount on our regular rug cleaning service. Our representative will be calling you within the next few days to set up your appointment.**
>
> **We are looking forward to seeing you.**
>
> **The Cleaner Carpets Corporation**

2. Attach the Flyer Data document as the data source for your Clean Rugs main document.

3. Use the appropriate filter options so that the form letter is sent to only the people living in the 14601 ZIP code area.

4. Merge the data source file with the main document to a new document, check for errors, and then make any necessary corrections.

5. Save the merged document as **Rug Letter** to your Student Disk. Then print the form letters. (Only two letters should be printed.)

6. Save and close all open files.

CHAPTER 10

Increasing Your Productivity

Word has several features that you can use to automate the repetitive aspects of your work. Using the automated features can help you maintain consistency in your entries, while also minimizing the amount of time required creating the entries. In Chapter 3, you learned about one of Word's automated features when you started using AutoCorrect to automatically correct frequent typing mistakes. The AutoCorrect feature affects individual characters in your document. This chapter focuses on the use of styles and templates, the AutoFormat feature, Wizards, AutoText, and macros—automated features that affect characters, paragraphs, or entire documents.

Objectives

By the time you finish this chapter, you will have learned to

1. Use Styles and Templates
2. Use AutoFormat
3. Use Wizards
4. Use AutoText
5. Use Macros

Objective 1: Use Styles and Templates

Style
A collection of settings that can quickly be applied to characters or paragraphs in your document.

The format you set for one part of your document (the font, line spacing, paragraph indentation, and so on) can be saved and then applied to other parts of the document if you use *styles*. The two types of styles available in Word are character styles and paragraph styles. By using character styles, you control the appearance of one or more characters. You control the appearance of complete paragraphs by using paragraph styles.

Using styles can make you more productive because they eliminate many of the repetitive tasks associated with formatting the content of a document. In most cases, a document consists of headings, subheadings, and paragraphs; each part commonly requires a different format. In a short document, formatting each part separately is not particularly difficult. In a longer document, however, formatting each part is time-consuming and tedious. In addition, when working with similar segments of the document split over numerous pages, users often forget exactly how the first segment was formatted when they format the second segment.

Although you do not have to use styles when creating documents, most Word users find that styles:

* Reduce the time and effort required to format the various parts of a document

* Ensure a consistent "look" when you format similar portions of a document

* Provide a convenient way to modify the look of all similar sections in a document—when you modify an existing style, all parts of the document using that style are automatically updated

Using Styles Stored in Templates

Template

A file in which Word can store a set of styles; specific character, paragraph, and page settings; text and graphics entries; macros; AutoText entries; field codes; custom menu commands and toolbar buttons; and shortcut keys.

Where are these "styles" saved, and how do you gain access to them? Styles are saved to a *template*. Every Word document you open or create is based on a template. Therefore, the styles currently available to you depend on the template on which your current document is based.

So far, all the documents you have created have been based on the *Normal* template. (Normal.dot is the name of this template file.) This is the default template that Word assigns to blank documents that are opened when you start Word.

If you created only one type of document, you would need only one set of styles, and only one template. However, you probably work with several types of documents: letters, memos, reports, and so on. Each type of document is formatted differently and requires different styles. Instead of grouping all possible styles into one huge template, Word provides a variety of templates designed to help you format standard documents, letters, memos, faxes, reports, and so on. When you open a new document, all the features of the selected template on which the document is based are available for your use.

You can open a new document, based on the Normal template, and then attach another template to your document. When you do this, Word updates the styles in the styles list and all other settings to correspond with the newly attached template. Attaching a new template does not change the content of existing document text. Alternatively, if you find that none of Word's templates meet your needs, you can create a new template or modify one of the built-in templates.

Note

As Word has evolved, some terms have taken on different meanings in different contexts. One of these terms is *Normal*, which is used in three contexts. As you have already learned, you can see a document in various views, one of which is Normal. When you choose the New button on the Standard toolbar, a new document, based on the *Normal* template is displayed. Finally, you will soon see that the Normal template contains several styles; one is named "Normal." When the word *Normal* appears, make sure that you understand whether it is referring to a view, a template, or a style.

Using Styles in the Normal Template

Character styles hold only character formatting and are applied to selected text or the word containing the insertion point. Character styles can include any option available from the Font dialog box. When you apply a paragraph style to a paragraph, Word formats all the text in the paragraph according to that style. These formats include the font and font size for characters; line alignment and line spacing within, before, and after paragraphs; tab settings; and indents. As you work through the exercises in this section, you learn that the default Normal template includes one character style and four paragraph styles.

You can select a style and then type the paragraphs that you want to display in that style; or you can type paragraphs, select them, and then apply a style to them.

Styles are most commonly applied to existing text through the Style box on the Formatting toolbar, the Style dialog box, or the keyboard shortcuts. Although applying styles through the keyboard shortcuts or Style box on the Formatting toolbar is a little faster and easier, using the Style dialog box provides more immediate information and options regarding the available styles.

Normal style
The paragraph style Word uses automatically unless you specify a different one.

Whenever the Formatting toolbar is displayed in your Word window, the Style box lists which style is applied to the paragraph that contains the insertion point. In Figure 10.1, notice that the style box at the far-left end of the Formatting toolbar contains the word Normal. Word uses *Normal style* as the default style; therefore, when you begin working with a document, you typically start working in Normal style. Further review of the Formatting toolbar tells you the font in the selected style is Times New Roman, the font size is 10 points, and the characters will be aligned against the left margin.

Figure 10.1
The Style box shows the style of the paragraph containing the insertion point.

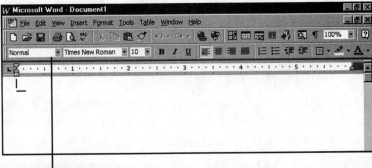

**The Style box indicates that
Normal style is currently in use.**

Figure 10.2 displays the Style dialog box. Notice the additional information available when you display the Style dialog box. Not only is there a detailed description of the style, Paragraph and Character preview sections are also included so that you can view the results of applying the style selected in the list box on the left side of the dialog box. Finally, among other features, the command buttons included in the dialog box provide access to apply, create, modify, or delete styles.

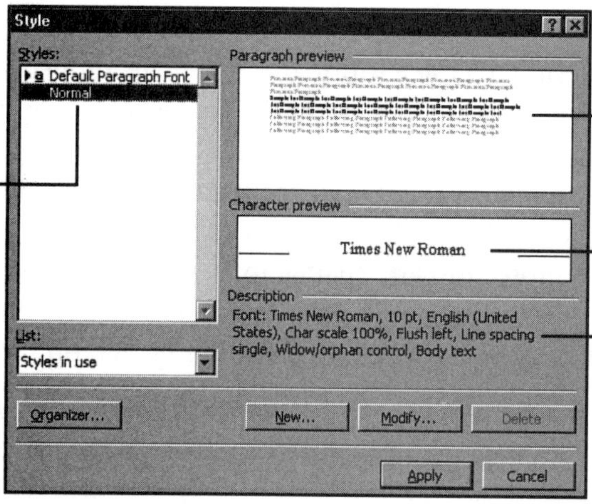

Figure 10.2

The Style dialog box.

List of styles available on the current template

Preview your paragraph formatting here.

Preview your character formatting here.

Read a description of the selected style here.

In the following exercise, you use both the Formatting toolbar and the Style dialog box to apply styles to various parts of a document. As with all predefined formatting in a software program, the formatting of the Microsoft Word Heading styles may or may not be appropriate for your needs. Use the default Word Heading styles for this exercise. Later in the chapter, you learn to modify existing styles. At that point, you may choose to modify some of Word's existing styles for your own personal work with Word.

Applying Styles in the Normal Template

To use styles in the Normal template, follow these steps:

1 Start Word and view the blank document (Document1) that opens when the Word window is first displayed.

Depending on how Word is set up on your system, some Word options may be activated that may cause a little confusion when you are first learning to work with styles. In the next steps, you make sure that these options are turned off. After you become familiar with the use of styles, you may choose to turn on these options again.

2 Choose **T**ools, **A**utoCorrect to open the AutoCorrect dialog box; then choose the AutoFormat As You Type tab to display the options on that page (see Figure 10.3).

3 If necessary, clear the check box in front of the Hea**d**ings option, located in the Apply as you type section, and the Define **s**tyles based on your formatting option, located in the Automatically as you type section. Then choose OK to close the dialog box.

4 Open the Chap1001 file from your Student Disk; then immediately save the file back to your disk as **College**. Then review the basic content of the document.

As you read the document, you'll notice that the entire document has been created in an Arial, Regular, 10-point font and that an ellipsis (...) follows the last character in the multiple-line paragraphs beneath each heading. For illustration purposes, the document has been shortened. The ellipses are used to represent the additional text that typically would be included if this were an actual document.

Figure 10.3
The AutoFormat As You Type page of the AutoCorrect dialog box contains numerous automatic formatting options.

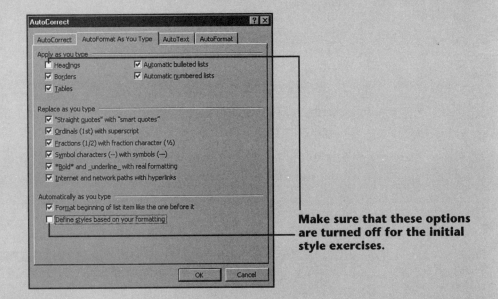

Make sure that these options are turned off for the initial style exercises.

⑤ Place the insertion point in the *Admission Information for River Valley College* line, the title line for the document. Then click the down arrow at the end of the Style drop-down list box to display a list of available styles (see Figure 10.4).

Because you will use a paragraph format for the entire title line (a one-line paragraph) it is not necessary to select all the characters in the line.

Figure 10.4
When the drop-down list is opened from the Styles box, the names of the styles are formatted similar to how they will apply to the document.

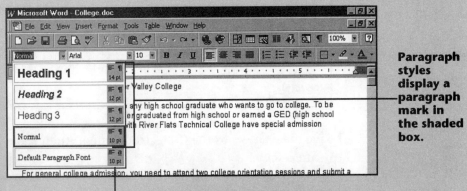

Paragraph styles display a paragraph mark in the shaded box.

Character styles display the underlined letter *a* in the shaded box.

⑥ Choose Heading 1 paragraph style from the list to close the list and display the first line in Heading 1 style.

Note that the Style box now displays Heading 1 style when the insertion point is in the first line of the document.

(continues)

Applying Styles in the Normal Template (continued)

7. Place the insertion point in the paragraph below the title line that begins with *River Valley College is open...*; then choose F**o**rmat, **S**tyle to display the Style dialog box.

8. Select Heading 1 paragraph style; then note the preview frames and read the Description section of the dialog box to learn the features included in Heading 1 style.

9. Select Normal paragraph style; then note the preview frames and read the Description section of the dialog box to learn what is included in Normal paragraph style.

10. Choose the **A**pply button to apply Normal paragraph style to the paragraph under the title of the document.

    After you complete this step, your document should look similar to the one in Figure 10.5.

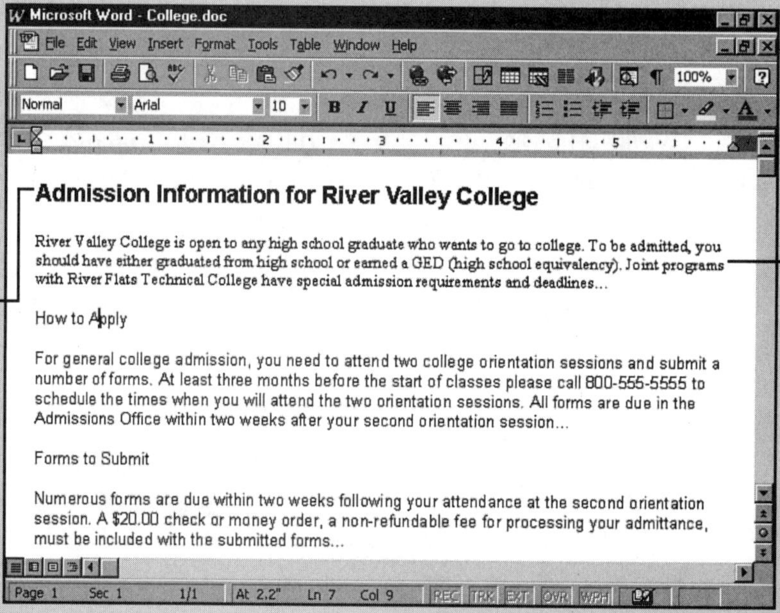
Microsoft Word - College.doc
File Edit View Insert Format Tools Table Window Help
100%
Normal
Arial
10
Admission Information for River Valley College
River Valley College is open to any high school graduate who wants to go to college. To be admitted, you should have either graduated from high school or earned a GED (high school equivalency). Joint programs with River Flats Technical College have special admission requirements and deadlines...
How to Apply
For general college admission, you need to attend two college orientation sessions and submit a number of forms. At least three months before the start of classes please call 800-555-5555 to schedule the times when you will attend the two orientation sessions. All forms are due in the Admissions Office within two weeks after your second orientation session...
Forms to Submit
Numerous forms are due within two weeks following your attendance at the second orientation session. A $20.00 check or money order, a non-refundable fee for processing your admittance, must be included with the submitted forms...
Page 1 Sec 1 1/1 At 2.2" Ln 7 Col 9 REC TRK EXT OVR WPH

Figure 10.5
Styles have been applied to the title and first text paragraph of the College document.

The Heading 1 style was applied here.

The Normal paragraph style was applied here.

11. Save the changes to the College document; then leave the file open for the next exercise.

Note

Word defines several heading styles, each having a special purpose. Some of the advanced automated features, like the Outline and Master Document features, use the occurrence of heading styles when automatically creating documents. Therefore, to prepare for future use of various Word tools, it is recommended that you format only headings (not paragraphs of text) with heading styles.

10

As an alternative to using the Formatting toolbar or Style dialog box to apply styles to paragraphs, you can use keyboard shortcuts for certain styles. First, place the insertion point within the text or paragraph to be formatted or select the specific text. Then apply the style that you want using the designated shortcut keys. Shortcut keys for the three heading styles in the Normal template are listed in the following table:

Shortcut Key	Paragraph Style
Alt+Ctrl+1	Heading 1
Alt+Ctrl+2	Heading 2
Alt+Ctrl+3	Headin g 3

Applying Styles with Keyboard Shortcuts

To practice all three ways to apply styles to portions of your document, follow these steps:

1 In the open College document, place the insertion point in the *How to Apply* heading.

This is a second-level heading. As you probably can guess, a second-level heading can be used to identify the start of a new section in your document; however, the format of a second-level heading is not as "dramatic" as the format of a first-level heading.

2 Format this heading in the Heading 2 style by pressing Alt+Ctrl+2. Then review the changes to the *How to Apply* heading.

3 Place the insertion point in the paragraph that begins with *For general college admission,...*; then open the Style drop-down list from the Style box on the Formatting toolbar and choose Normal paragraph style to change the font of the current paragraph to Times New Roman.

4 Place the *Forms to Submit* heading in the Heading 3 style by placing the insertion point within the line and pressing Alt+Ctrl+3.

5 Use the Style dialog box to place the paragraph beginning with *Numerous forms are due...* in Normal paragraph style. (Once the desired style is selected, choose the **A**pply button to apply the style to the current paragraph.)

When you complete this step, your document should look similar to the one in Figure 10.6.

(continues)

Figure 10.6
Most of the necessary styles have been applied to the parts of the College document.

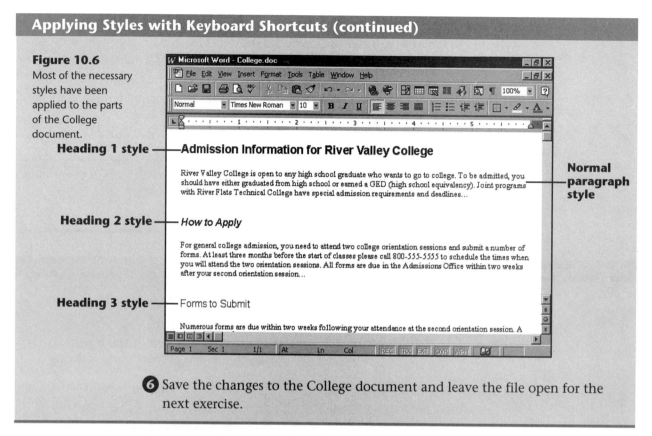

Heading 1 style — **Admission Information for River Valley College**

Normal paragraph style

River Valley College is open to any high school graduate who wants to go to college. To be admitted, you should have either graduated from high school or earned a GED (high school equivalency). Joint programs with River Flats Technical College have special admission requirements and deadlines...

Heading 2 style — *How to Apply*

For general college admission, you need to attend two college orientation sessions and submit a number of forms. At least three months before the start of classes please call 800-555-5555 to schedule the times when you will attend the two orientation sessions. All forms are due in the Admissions Office within two weeks after your second orientation session...

Heading 3 style — Forms to Submit

Numerous forms are due within two weeks following your attendance at the second orientation session. A

6 Save the changes to the College document and leave the file open for the next exercise.

Creating and Applying Your Own Styles

Using a style that you create is a two-step process. The first step is to create (or define) the style; the second step is to apply your style. You can create a style by example, or through the use of menu commands and dialog boxes. The easiest way is to create a style by example; just select the appropriate characters or paragraph, format the selection (the example text) with the desired attributes, and then name the selected example text in the Style box. You will use this technique in the following exercise.

Word will automatically add a new style that you create to the *document's* style list. If you want your new style to be available for other documents, however, you must complete the specific steps for saving the style to the current template, or create a new template that includes your new style.

Using Your Own Style

To create and apply your own styles, follow these steps:

1 In the open College document, select the fourth heading (*High School Transcript or GED Certificate*); then underline it.

2 With the underlined heading still selected, click in the Style box on the Formatting toolbar to highlight the name Normal.

3 Type **Heading U**.

> ### Note
>
> Although they are not always displayed in the Style box when the Normal template is in use, Word provides access to nine heading levels (Heading 1 – Heading 9). For this reason, do not use Heading 4 in step 3.
>
> To preview all the predefined styles that may be accessed from the Normal template, choose Format, Style to open the Style dialog box, click the down arrow at the end of the List drop-down list box, and choose All Styles.

The Heading U name replaces Normal in the Style box on the Formatting toolbar.

4 Press ⏎Enter to add the Heading U style to the document's style list. (You can verify the Heading U style has been added to the list of styles by clicking the drop-down arrow at the end of the Style box and locating the Heading U style on the style list.)

The Normal paragraph style remains unchanged. To verify this, complete the next step.

5 Format the paragraph below the *High School Transcript or GED Certificate* heading, the one beginning with *A transcript of high...*, in Normal paragraph style.

Now apply your new Heading U style to another heading in your document.

6 Place the insertion point in the *Forms to Submit* heading; then note the Heading 3 entry in the Style box on the Formatting toolbar.

7 Click the arrow at the end of the Style box, and then choose the Heading U style to apply your new style to the *Forms to Submit* heading.

Your document should now look similar to the one in Figure 10.7.

8 Save the changes to the document; then leave it open for the next exercise.

(continues)

Using Your Own Style (continued)

Figure 10.7
The College document with the new Heading U paragraph style applied to the last two headings.

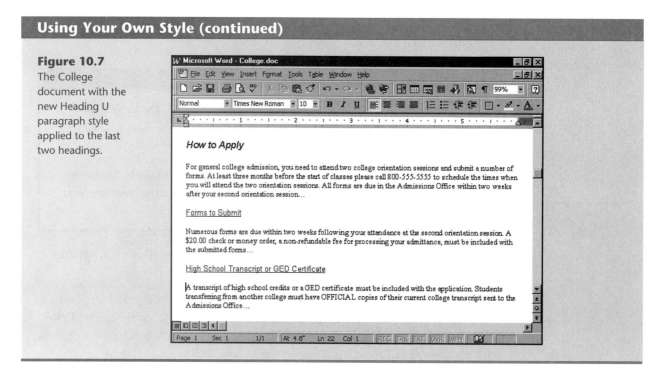

In the preceding exercise, you created a new style that was automatically attached to the document's style list. However, the style was not attached to the Normal template. When using Word, the Normal template is used so often that you want to be careful of any changes you make to this template. After you become more familiar with styles and templates, you may find yourself adding new styles to templates, or you may find that you need to modify an existing style.

In the next section, you learn to modify a style. The style you modify is the one you created in this section. This enables you to practice the procedure, without altering the settings in the Normal template.

Modifying a Style

To modify a style, you can open a new or existing document based on a template that contains that style, or you can open the template itself. In this section you work with an existing document that contains the style to be modified.

When you modify a style, Word automatically updates any text that has been formatted in that style.

Caution

Many of the styles in Word are based on the settings in Normal style. To tell if an existing style is based on Normal style (and then enhancements are made to establish the different style), start by displaying the Style dialog box. Then look in the Description section to see the listing of the style features. If the list starts with Normal +, the selected style is based on Normal style. It is important to remember that any change you make to Normal style will be reflected in all styles based on Normal style.

Modifying a Style

To practice modifying a style, follow these steps:

1 In the open College document, select the *Forms to Submit* heading, which is formatted in Heading U style.

2 Use the buttons on the Formatting toolbar to turn off the Underline feature, turn on the Bold feature, and then center the selected line.

> **Note**
>
> Along with using the toolbars, you can change any other component of character formatting by using the options in the Font dialog box.
>
> Similarly, you can change any other component of paragraph formatting by using the options in the Paragraph dialog box.

3 Click the down arrow at the end of the Style box on the Formatting toolbar; then choose Heading U style to display the Modify Style dialog box (see Figure 10.8).

Figure 10.8
The Modify Style dialog box is used to change the format of an existing style.

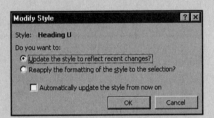

4 Make sure that the **U**pdate the style to reflect recent changes? option is selected; then choose OK to change the formatting of Heading U style.

> **Note**
>
> In the Modify Style dialog box, choosing the Reapply the formatting of the **s**tyle to the selection? limits the application of the new style to only the selected text.
>
> Choosing the Automatically up**d**ate the style from now on option instructs Word to redefine from now on a current style with a current selection's attributes without displaying the Modify Style dialog box.

5 Notice that, along with the *Forms to Submit* heading being changed, the *High School Transcript or GED Certificate* heading has been automatically updated to the new settings of Heading U style.

6 Save the changes to the College document; then leave it open for the next exercise.

In this section, you learned to modify a style. In the next section, you learn to delete a style.

Deleting a Style

After you create a number of personal styles, you may find that you no longer need a style. When this happens, you may want to delete the style. You can delete the styles that you create; however, you cannot delete Word's built-in styles. When you delete a style, all text formatted in the deleted style will become formatted in Normal style.

Deleting Personal Styles

To practice deleting a style that you created, follow these steps:

1. With the College document displayed in your Word window, choose Format, Style to display the Style dialog box.

2. Select Heading U style from the Styles list.

3. Choose the Delete button to display a message asking you to confirm the deletion of the style.

4. Choose Yes to confirm the deletion and close the message box.

5. Choose the Close button to close the Style dialog box. The two headings that were formatted in Heading U style are now displayed in the Normal style.

Now that you are familiar with some of the styles in the Normal template, you are ready to attach another template to your College document and explore the use of some of the other predefined styles.

Using the Style Gallery to Preview and Attach a Template to a Document

The Normal template is just one of the numerous predefined templates that come with Word. Although the Normal template is a general-purpose template, many of the other predefined templates have been created to help produce specific types of documents, such as memos, letters, reports, faxes, resumes, and Web pages.

Word templates are divided into three general layout categories: contemporary, elegant, and professional. For example, there are three Letter templates: a Contemporary Letter template, an Elegant Letter template, and a Professional Letter template. If your job consists of producing numerous documents that can be based on some of Word's predefined templates, you may choose all the templates from the same category (such as the Professional category) when you start to create a document. Basing your documents on templates from the same category can ensure a consistent look across all your documents.

In the following exercise, you use the Style Gallery dialog box to preview and attach a template to your College document. Remember that when you attach a template, you update the existing similarly named styles to the styles of the newly attached template. After attaching a template, you view the results of having the updated styles applied to the components in your document.

Previewing and Attaching a Template

To practice displaying all available styles, and previewing and attaching a template to your current document, follow these steps:

1 In the open College document, format the *Forms to Submit* heading in the Heading 3 style.

In the next steps, you will expand the list of available styles and then use a predefined style to format the last heading in the College document.

2 Place the insertion point in the *High School Transcript or GED Certification* heading; then choose F**o**rmat, **S**tyle to display the Style dialog box.

3 If necessary, click the down arrow at the end of the **L**ist drop-down list box and choose the All Styles options to display all the styles currently available to you in the Styles list box.

4 Scroll through the list to find, and then select, the Heading 4 style.

5 Choose the **A**pply button to close the Style dialog box and display the fourth heading in Heading 4 style.

6 Choose F**o**rmat, Style **G**allery to display the Style Gallery dialog box (see Figure 10.9).

Figure 10.9
The Style Gallery dialog box.

Select a template here.

Select the document option to preview your document.

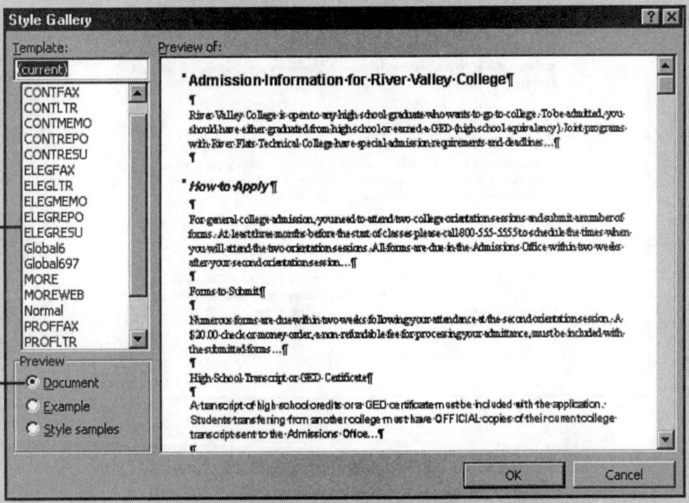

7 Make sure that the **D**ocument option is selected in the Preview portion of the dialog box; then select the Contemporary Report (in Figure 10.9, it's listed as CONTREPO) option in the **T**emplate list box. (Depending on the installation of your system, the template names may appear differently in your list. For example, your system may list the Contemporary Report option as *Contemporary Rep*.)

After a few seconds, the **P**review of section displays how your College document will appear if you attach the Contemporary Report template to the document.

(continues)

Previewing and Attaching a Template (continued)

8 Select the Elegant Report option (in Figure 10.9, it's listed as ELEGREPO) in the **T**emplate list box, wait a few seconds, and then view how the College document will appear if you attach the Elegant Report template to the document.

9 Select the Professional Report option (it may be listed as PROFREPO) in the **T**emplate list, wait a few seconds, and then view how the College document will appear if you attach the Professional Report template to the file.

10 Choose OK to attach the Professional Report template to the College document and close the Style Gallery dialog box.

11 Move the insertion point to the top of the document; then choose **V**iew, **F**ull Screen to display your College document in Full Screen view.

Your College document should now look similar to the one in Figure 10.10.

Figure 10.10
Full screen view.

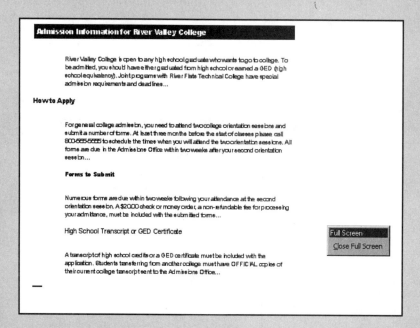

12 Choose the **C**lose Full Screen command in the Full Screen box (or press Esc) to return to the Normal view of your document.

13 Place the insertion point in different document locations and note that the name of each style (listed in the Style box in the Formatting toolbar) has not changed. However, the formatting of the styles has changed once you attached another template to the College document.

14 Save the changes to the College document; then close the file. Leave the Word window open for the next exercise.

In the preceding exercise, you saw that if you apply styles to the various components of the document, the look of your document could quickly change when you attach another template to the document.

Sometimes, when you assign styles or attach a template, you may need to complete additional formatting to your document. For example, the heading styles in the Professional Report template include spacing after the headings. The original College document included a blank line between each section heading and the paragraph following the heading. Currently, there is too much space separating the headings and the following paragraphs. Because the College document is just a practice document, there is no need to correct the spacing at this time. However, it is important to review your document when you use some of the automated formatting tools provided in Word.

In the next exercise, you let Word automatically format your entire document through the AutoFormat feature.

Objective 2: Use AutoFormat   3/26/99

If you need to format a document in a hurry, using AutoFormat may enhance the quality of your work. The AutoFormat feature enables Word to automatically format your document (by applying various styles to the components in your document) while you focus on the content of the document. Remember that because AutoFormat is automatic, the feature does not always make the formatting choices that you might make yourself.

Applying Formatting to Your Document

To apply automatic formatting to a document, follow these steps:

1 Open the Chap1002 file from your Student Disk; then save it back to the disk as **College list**.

As you can see, this document is a list of things that need to be done in preparation for attending River Valley College.

The College list document is based on the Normal template, and all paragraphs are in Normal style. The following are some of the layout features of the document.

- A blank line is placed below the first heading (*Forms I need to collect or complete:*), but there is no blank line below the second heading.

- Each item in the two list sections starts with a hyphen (-).

- The (r) following the word Microsoft, at the end of the document, represents the Registered symbol.

2 Choose Format, AutoFormat.

Word displays the AutoFormat dialog box (see Figure 10.11).

3 Make sure that the **A**utoFormat now option is selected and the General Document option is displayed in the drop-down list box; then choose OK to let Word automatically format your List document.

(continues)

Applying Formatting to Your Document (continued)

Your document should now look similar to the one in Figure 10.12.

Figure 10.11
The AutoFormat dialog box.

Figure 10.12
The results of letting AutoFormat format your document for you.

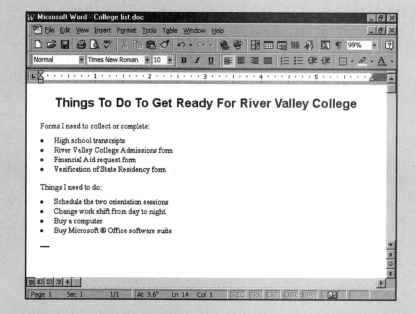

In this example, the results of using the AutoFormat feature are acceptable. However, this is not always the case. If you are ever dissatisfied with the results of using the AutoFormat feature, you can manually format any area of the document, or choose the Undo button to return your document to its previous appearance.

Note

To gain control over each change proposed by AutoFormat, choose the Auto-Format and **r**eview each change option when you first display the AutoFormat dialog box.

❹ Save the changes to the College list document; then close the file.

At this point, space prohibits a more detailed discussion of the AutoFormat feature. However, before concluding your work with AutoFormat, check out at least one topic of the AutoFormat information in the Word Help program.

10

5 If you have the Office Assistant activated, display it, enter **AutoFormat** in the search text box, and choose **S**earch.

Or, if the Office Assistant is not active, choose **H**elp, **C**ontents and Index; change to the Index page of the Help dialog box (if necessary); enter **AutoFormat** in the text box; and then choose the **D**isplay button.

6 When the list of AutoFormat topics appears, display the Let Word format my documents and WordMail messages topic and then review the topic's information.

If you want, choose any of the jump buttons in the Help information to view related information on AutoFormat.

7 When you have finished reviewing the Help AutoFormat information, close the Help program and return to your Word window. Leave Word running for the next exercise.

You just completed an exercise that formatted an entire document in one pass, by using the AutoFormat feature. Word also includes an AutoFormat As You Type feature that does many of the same things as AutoFormat; however, as the name implies, it completes the formatting as you type. The AutoFormat As You Type options include the formatting of headings, bulleted and numbered lists, borders, numbers, symbols, and more. To view the list of options, choose **T**ools, **A**utoCorrect; then choose the AutoFormat As You Type tab to view the options.

When the various options of the AutoFormat As You Type feature are activated, they work in the same way as when you make corrections using AutoCorrect. After a particular entry has been made and then the (Spacebar), (↵Enter), close parenthesis ()), and so on, has been entered, the appropriate option from the AutoFormat As You Type feature is activated.

Word includes numerous automated features to help you quickly produce effective documents. You have now used the AutoCorrect and AutoFormat features; later in this chapter, you learn to use the AutoText and the AutoComplete features. To learn more about other automated features, review the information included in the Word Help program.

Objective 3: Use Wizards

Wizards
Automated templates that lead you step-by-step through the process of creating a document.

Wizards are extensions of templates. They are useful for creating specific kinds of documents, such as agendas, fax cover sheets, newsletters, résumés, and so on. Wizards can save you a great deal of time if you don't mind accepting the built-in formats that Word provides.

Using the Memo Wizard

To practice using the Memo Wizard, follow these steps:

1 In the open Word window, choose **F**ile, **N**ew to display the New dialog box, choose the Memos tab to display the Memos page, and then click once on the Memo.wiz icon (see Figure 10.13). (As was the case in a previous exercise, your installation of Word may display the names under the icons in a different manner. For example, in this step you may see the term *Memo Wizard.wiz*, instead of *Memo.wiz* on your screen.)

Figure 10.13
The Memos page of the New dialog box.

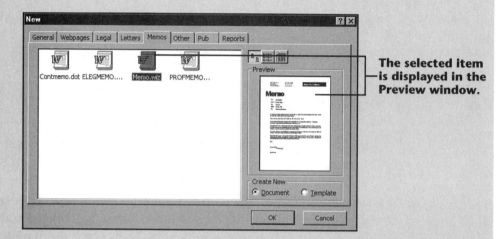

The selected item is displayed in the Preview window.

2 Make sure that the **D**ocument option is selected in the Create New section of the dialog box; then choose OK to start the Memo Wizard.

Within a few seconds, the first page of the Memo Wizard is displayed (see Figure 10.14).

Figure 10.14
The first page of the Memo Wizard.

Steps to complete in the Memo Wizard

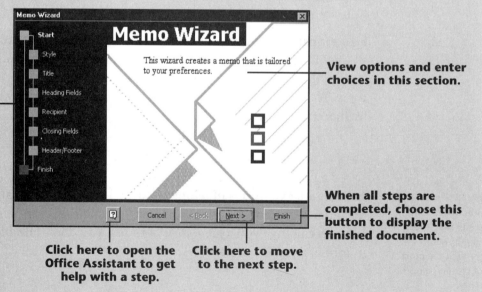

View options and enter choices in this section.

When all steps are completed, choose this button to display the finished document.

Click here to open the Office Assistant to get help with a step.

Click here to move to the next step.

3 Review the initial information in the first Memo Wizard window; then choose the **N**ext button to move to the next step in creating your memo.

As you continue to choose the **N**ext button, you can monitor your location in the total process by noting the highlighted box in the outline on the left side of the Memo Wizard box.

❹ Choose the **C**ontemporary style option; then choose the **N**ext button to move to the next step.

> ### Tip
>
> While working in the Wizard boxes, choosing the **B**ack button lets you return to a previous page to change a selected option.

❺ If the Yes. Use this text option is already selected and Interoffice Memo is displayed in the text box, choose the **N**ext button. (If necessary, change the current entries so that Interoffice Memo will be used for the memo title; then choose the **N**ext button.)

❻ Make sure that today's date has been placed in the **D**ate text box; then place your name in the **F**rom text box and **River Valley College Admission** in the **S**ubject text box. Leave the **P**riority check box blank.

Your Wizard page should look similar to the one in Figure 10.15.

Figure 10.15
Make sure that the date is current, your name is listed in the From box, and River Valley College Admission is placed in the Subject box of the Memo Wizard page.

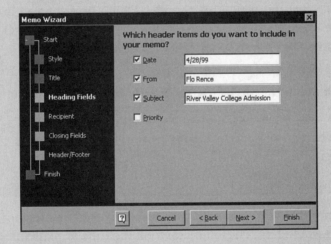

> ### Note
>
> By default, the Memo Wizard uses the mm/dd/yy format for the date entry. If you want to change the format, select and delete the current date entry; then enter the date in the desired format.

❼ Choose **N**ext to move to the next page.

(continues)

Using the Memo Wizard (continued)

You enter the recipient's name on this page and the names of the people receiving copies (**C**c) of the memo. If you are using the Address Book feature, you can choose the **A**ddress Book button to open the Address Book and select the recipient. However, for this exercise, you'll just enter a name directly in the **T**o box.

8 Enter the name **Donald Snuke** in the **T**o box, (if necessary) clear the check box in front of the **C**c option and make sure that N**o** is selected for the Do you want a separate page for your distribution list? option. Then choose **N**ext.

9 For this example, leave all the closing items boxes blank; then choose the **N**ext button to move to the Header/Footer page of the Wizard.

10 In the Header options, select only the **T**opic option. In the Footer options, select only the **P**age Number option. Then choose the **N**ext button.

11 At the Memo Wizard Finish screen, read the displayed information; then choose the **F**inish button to instruct Word to use the information you have provided to create the basic memo document.

After the memo is displayed on your screen, the Office Assistant (if active) asks whether there is anything else you want to do with the basic form of the memo. At this point, you can choose an option or close the Office Assistant (by choosing Cancel) and complete your memo.

For this exercise, you do not need to add body text to the memo. Your work with the Memo Wizard is completed. Scan through the document to see the results of your work.

12 Save the document as **College memo** to your Student Disk; then, if you want, print the document. Close the file, but leave the Word window open for the next exercise.

The memo that you created in the preceding exercise may not have the layout that you would have chosen if you took the time to plan and design it yourself. If you will create a number of memos as part of your daily work, you probably will want to create your own memo template. However, for now, when you need to create a quick memo, the Memo Wizard can be quite helpful.

Remember that after a Wizard has created a document, you still can enter the document and edit or format any portion of the file.

Objective 4: Use AutoText

AutoText
A stored portion of text or graphics, of any size, that can be quickly inserted into any document.

The Word *AutoText* feature enables you to save text, graphics, logos, or symbols you use regularly in the documents you create. When you want to use an item that you saved as an AutoText entry, you don't have to type it or select it again; you only have to type a shortcut to insert that AutoText entry. For example, if you use a standard closing for all your letters, you can store the entire selection in an AutoText entry named *cl*. (This selection can include your digitized signature, if you have the items needed to insert your signature into your Word document.) Then, whenever you need to end a letter, you simple type **cl** and press F3 to instruct Word to insert the stored information into the letter.

In addition to making your own AutoText entries, Word has more than 40 predefined AutoText entries, including letter salutation, header, footer, reference line, and mailing instruction entries.

Creating an AutoText Entry

When you create an AutoText entry, you assign it a short name to indicate the contents of the entry. Whenever you want to use the AutoText entry, you can type the short name and press F3. The name you assign should be long enough to identify the entry, but short enough to enable you to type it quickly.

To create an AutoText entry, follow these steps:

1 Display a blank document in your Word window.

2 Type the following information regarding a River Valley College policy:

The college will use the requested information to create an academic record for the applicant and make appropriate admissions decisions. Social Security number and birth date are voluntary items used for proper identification of records.

3 Select the paragraph you just entered.

> ### Tip
>
> Remember that all the formatting for a paragraph is stored in the paragraph mark at the end of the paragraph. To capture the formatting used in the AutoText entry, make sure to include the paragraph mark. If you are capturing text entered in Normal style, selecting the paragraph mark is optional.

4 Choose **I**nsert, **A**utoText, **N**ew to display the Create AutoText dialog box (see Figure 10.16).

Figure 10.16
Use the Create AutoText dialog box to name an AutoText entry.

Based on the first characters in the AutoText selection, a name will be suggested in the **P**lease name your AutoText entry text box. You can either accept the suggested name or replace it with the name of your choice. It is assumed that you will change the suggested name; that is why the name is highlighted. All you need to do is start typing the new name, and the old one will be erased.

(continues)

Creating an AutoText Entry (continued)

Tip

You can also display the Create AutoText dialog box by pressing Alt+F3.

❺ Enter the name **ap** into the text box; then choose OK to save the entry, close the box, and return to your Word document.

❻ Press Ctrl+End to place the insertion point at the end of the document and deselect the text; then press ↵Enter twice to create a blank line between the preceding paragraph and the one you are about to enter.

In the following steps, you create another AutoText entry. This time you'll save it through the AutoText page of the AutoCorrect dialog box, which gives you greater control over the saving of the entry.

❼ Type the following paragraph to be placed on all forms related to students applying for admission to River Valley College:

> **River Valley College does not tolerate discrimination based on race, color, national origin, sex, sexual orientation, religion, age, or disability in employment or in the provision of our services.**

❽ Select the new paragraph; then choose **Insert**, **AutoText**, AutoText to display the AutoText page of the AutoCorrect dialog box (see Figure 10.17).

Figure 10.17
The AutoText page of the AutoCorrect dialog box provides for the most control over the AutoText entries.

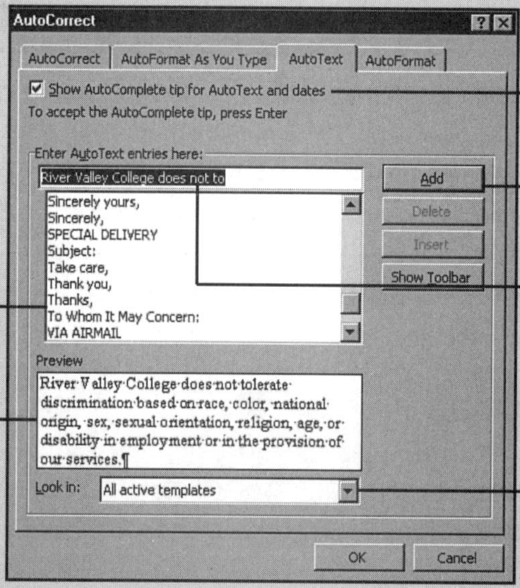

List of available AutoText entries

Preview your AutoText entry here.

Make sure this option is checked to use AutoComplete.

Click here to add the current AutoText entry to the template(s) displayed in the Look in box.

Enter the name for the AutoText entry here.

Click here to display a list of available templates to which the current AutoText entry may be attached.

By default, Word saves the AutoText entry in the Normal.dot template. (Also by default, the All active templates option is displayed in the **L**ook in box of the dialog box. With this option displayed, the AutoText entry is saved in all templates attached to the current document. If only the Normal.dot template is in use, this option saves the entry to just the Normal.dot template.) To limit the AutoText entry to documents based on a particular template, display that template in the **L**ook in drop-down list box.

9 Enter the name **discpol** (an abbreviation for *discrimination policy*) in the Enter AutoText entries here text box.

10 Choose **A**dd to save the AutoText entry, close the AutoText dialog box, and return to the Word window.

11 Close the document displaying the two AutoText entries you created, without saving the document changes. Then leave the Word window open for the next exercise.

After you have created your AutoText entries, it's easy to enter them into your documents.

Inserting AutoText Entries

To practice inserting AutoText entries, follow these steps:

1 Open the College document you created earlier in this chapter; then place the insertion point on the blank line following the paragraph beginning with *For general college admission,...* that is located under the *How to Apply* section of the document.

2 Press `⏎Enter` once.

3 Type **ap** and then immediately press `F3` (if you insert a space after ap you will not be able to insert the AutoText entry with this technique).

The ap AutoText entry should now be inserted in the College document. The newly inserted paragraph should be formatted in the same style as other similar paragraphs.

If you are not sure of the name of an AutoText entry, you can use the AutoText dialog box to find, and then insert, the entry.

4 Position the insertion point at the end of the College document; then press `⏎Enter` once.

5 Choose **I**nsert, **A**utoText, AutoText to display the AutoText page of the AutoCorrect dialog box; then scroll through the entries in the list box, in the center of the dialog box, until you see the discpol entry.

6 Click once on the discpol entry in the list box to select it; then preview the entry in the Preview box to make sure that it is the one you previously entered.

7 Choose the **I**nsert button to close the AutoCorrect dialog box and insert the discpol AutoText entry at the insertion point.

8 Leave the College document open for the next exercise.

Another way to insert AutoText entries is by using a new Word feature called AutoComplete. This features enables Word to automatically complete the following items:

- The current date
- A day of the week
- A month
- Your name (if it was used when you first installed your system and application software)
- AutoText entries

The first step in using the AutoComplete feature is to make sure that the **S**how AutoComplete tip for AutoText and dates check box is marked in the AutoText page of the AutoCorrect dialog box. Then, when you type the first few letters of one of the preceding items, a tip box, containing the entire entry or the beginning of the AutoText entry, is displayed by the insertion point. To accept the tip and have the item automatically completed, press ⏎Enter or F3. To reject the tip, keep typing.

Using AutoComplete to Insert AutoText Entries

To practice inserting entries by using AutoComplete, follow these steps:

1 In the open College document, place the insertion point on the blank line at the bottom of the document and press ⏎Enter once.

2 Start typing the AutoText entry discpol and stop typing as soon as you see the AutoComplete tip box by the insertion point (see Figure 10.18).

Figure 10.18
Typing the first few letters of an AutoText entry displays the AutoComplete tip box.

AutoComplete tip box

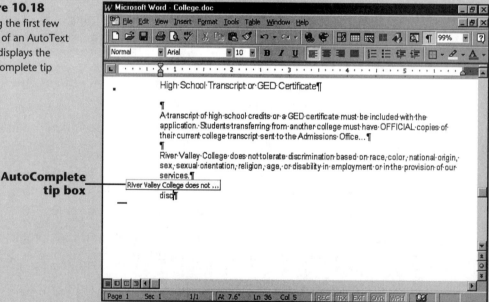

3 Press ⏎Enter to accept the tip and insert the AutoText entry at the insertion point. Note that the first letters of the name of the AutoText entry that you typed were automatically erased when the paragraph was inserted.

4 Save the changes to the College document; then leave it open for the next exercise.

If you realize that an AutoText entry contains an error, or needs to be updated, you can quickly change the contents of an entry.

10

Editing an AutoText Entry

To edit an AutoText entry, follow these steps:

1 In the open College document, place the insertion point at the beginning of the second paragraph under the *How to Apply* section; this is the ap AutoText entry paragraph beginning with *The college will use*....

2 Delete the first word *The* and the lowercase *c* in *college*. Then rewrite the beginning of the paragraph so that it starts with *River Valley College will use*....

3 Select the entire paragraph (to prepare to enter the revised paragraph as an AutoText entry). To stay consistent with the original ap entry, make sure to include the paragraph mark at the end of the last sentence in your selection.

4 Choose Insert, **A**utoText, AutoText to display the AutoText page of the AutoCorrect dialog box; then locate and select the ap entry in the list box.

5 Choose the **A**dd button to display a dialog box asking whether you want to redefine the AutoText entry.

6 Choose **Y**es to redefine the entry, close the dialog box, and return to the college document. The AutoText entry is still selected.

7 Place the insertion point on the blank line below the selection; then press ⏎Enter once.

8 Type **ap** and press F3 to insert the edited ap AutoText entry. Then verify that the entry has been updated.

9 Save your changes; then leave the College document open for the next exercise.

To keep your AutoText list from becoming cluttered, you can easily remove entries that you no longer use.

Deleting an Entry from the AutoText List

To practice deleting entries from the AutoText list, follow these steps:

1 In the open College document, choose Insert, **A**utoText, AutoText to display the AutoText page of the AutoCorrect dialog box; then select the ap entry in the list box.

2 Choose the **D**elete button in the AutoText page to remove the entry from the list.

3 Choose OK to close the AutoCorrect dialog box.

(continues)

Deleting an Entry from the AutoText List (continued)

④ Place the insertion point at the end of the College document, press ⏎Enter once, type **ap,** and press F3 to *try* to insert an AutoText entry.

⑤ When the AutoText entry is not inserted, read the note in the status bar at the bottom of the window stating that the characters you just typed are not a valid AutoText name.

If the AutoText entry is inserted, repeat the first three steps again to delete the entry.

⑥ Remove the discpol AutoText entry by using the same procedure you used to remove the ap AutoText entry.

⑦ Save the College document; then close it. Leave the Word window open for the next exercise.

The AutoText feature is most frequently used to automate the insertion of text into the document. Macros can insert text too. In addition, macros can control formatting and other document features. In the next section, you learn to work with simple macros.

Objective 5: Use Macros

Macros
A group of actions that you record and play back to accomplish specific tasks.

Macros are used to perform repetitive tasks—such as changing formatting—by grouping a number of formatting and editing commands into one command (the macro). When the macro is activated—by using the keyboard, toolbar, or menu command—an entire series of dialog box options, toolbar button choices, and menu commands may be completed.

You can create your own macros or use one of the many Word built-in macros. This section focuses on creating and running your own macros. After you learn to run your own macros, you also know how to run Word's built-in macros.

Most of the built-in Word macros are located within the Macros folder, which is normally found inside the Word or Microsoft Office folder. If you want to run the built-in macros, start by seeing your instructor or network administrator to learn the exact location of the Word macros and how to set up Word to access the macros. Then, use the procedures for running macros that you learn about in this section.

Record Macros

Word records the macro as a series of Word commands in the Visual Basic for Applications programming language. Although you can write the macro using this programming language, most Word users choose to *record* their macros with the help of the macro recorder. All you have to do is start the Word macro recorder, perform the actions that you want to record, and then stop the recorder. By default, Word stores macros in the Normal template so that they are available for use with every Word document. However, if you choose, you can place a macro on another template and remove it from the Normal template.

Recording a Macro

To record your own macro, follow these steps:

1 Open a new document in your Word window.

2 Choose **T**ools, **M**acro, **R**ecord New Macro to start the macro recording process by displaying the Record Macro dialog box (see Figure 10.19).

Figure 10.19
Use the Record Macro dialog box to name your macro and start the recording process.

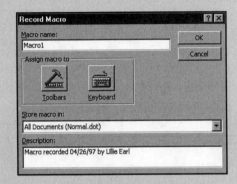

3 In the Macro name text box, type **CentArialB16ShSc** as the name for your macro.

Note

You can accept the suggested name, Macro1, but it is better to use a descriptive name. You cannot include spaces in the name, but you can use uppercase letters to indicate the beginning of each word (for example, InsertDate).

4 Select the current entry in the Description box; then erase the entry by typing: **This macro centers selected text and places it in an Arial, Bold, 16-point font with Shadow and Small caps effects.**

It is not necessary to include a description of the purpose of the macro, although when you create a large number of macros, descriptions can help you quickly remember the purpose of each macro.

This is normally the desired place to create a shortcut key command, or place a button on a toolbar, for the macro you are about to create. (You use the buttons inside the Assign macro to section of the dialog box to start the procedure.) However, we'll skip this procedure now to concentrate on creating the macro. In a later exercise, you learn an alternative way to create a shortcut for running your macro.

5 Choose OK.

The Macro Record toolbar appears, REC is displayed in the status bar, and a small cassette icon is attached to the mouse pointer until you turn off the recorder (see Figure 10.20).

(continues)

Recording a Macro (continued)

Figure 10.20

While recording a macro, you can click the Stop Recording or Pause Recording buttons in the Macro Record toolbar.

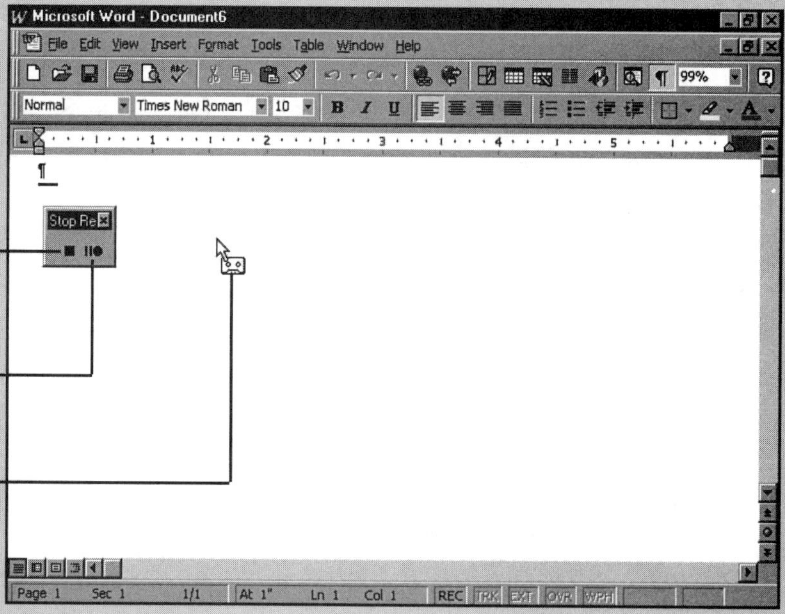

Stop Recording button

Pause Recording button

Macro Record pointer

 6 Click the Center button on the Formatting toolbar.

> ### Note
>
> Mouse actions in menus, dialog boxes, and toolbars are recorded in Word macros; however, mouse movements in the window work area are not recorded.

7 Choose F**o**rmat, **F**ont to display the Font dialog box.

8 Choose Arial, Bold, and 16 in the top row of option boxes; then choose the Shado**w** and S**m**all caps options in the Effects section.

9 Choose OK to close the dialog box and return to your document.

 10 Click the Stop Recording button on the Macro Record toolbar to indicate that you have completed your recording.

Word temporarily stores the macro in the Normal template, the Macro Record toolbar is closed, REC is dimmed in the status bar, and the small cassette icon is removed from the mouse pointer.

11 Close the document without saving the changes, but leave the Word window open and continue to the next exercise.

If you need to end your computing session at this time, when you exit Word, you will be prompted to save changes to the Normal template—in this case the change is your new macro—so that the changes can be used in future Word documents. When you see this prompt, click the **Yes** button if you want to save your new macro.

10

Tip

You also can double-click REC in the status bar at the bottom of the window to begin recording a macro.

Now that you know how to create a macro, you need to make sure that you can run one. Word provides you with a variety of ways to access macros so that you can work as efficiently as possible. If you do not use macros often, running them from the Macros dialog box may be sufficient for your needs. Running a macro from the dialog box requires no customizing after the macro has been recorded.

Running a Macro

In the preceding exercise, you created a macro named CentArialB16ShSc. To run your new macro from the Macros dialog box, follow these steps:

1 Open a new Word document; then type the following text (make sure to press ↵Enter after each line you type):

River Valley College
100 River Road
St. Paul, MN 55113

2 Select the name and address of the college.

3 Choose **T**ools, **M**acro, **M**acros from the menu (or press Alt+F8) to display the Macros dialog box (see Figure 10.21).

Figure 10.21
The Macros dialog box.

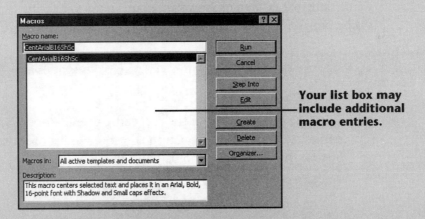

Your list box may include additional macro entries.

4 If you do not see the CentArialB16ShSc macro name in the **M**acro name list box, choose All active templates and documents from the **M**acros in drop-down list.

Word displays a list of all macros available to you from the active templates.

5 Select the CentArialb16ShSc macro from the **M**acro name list.

6 Choose the **R**un button.

7 Deselect your text and view the result.

(continues)

The college name and address should be centered and appear in the Arial, Bold, 16-point font with the Shadow and Small caps effects.

8 Keep this document open for the next exercise.

The Macros dialog box enables you to complete many macro-related functions. You can choose command buttons to run, edit, and delete macros. You can use the Macros dialog box to access the Visual Basic Editor for those who want to create or edit macros in the Visual Basic for Applications programming language. Finally, you can use the Macros dialog box to access the Word Organizer, a dialog box that enables you to copy, rename, and remove macros from templates.

If you use a macro frequently, you may get frustrated with the time it takes to constantly open the Macros dialog box. As an alternative to running macros through the Macros dialog box, you can assign the macro to a shortcut key combination, a toolbar button, or even a new menu command. This text shows you how to assign a shortcut key combination to the macro. Please refer to the Word Help program to learn how to create a macro toolbar button or menu command.

In the Record Macro dialog box, you can specify a macro name, a description, and alternative ways of running the macro before you actually record it. To assign a shortcut-key combination, click the **K**eyboard icon in the Assign macro to section and then enter the shortcut key combination in the following dialog box.

Most likely, you did not assign a shortcut key when you created the CentArialB16ShSC macro; however, you can do so now by using the Customize dialog box.

Specifying a Shortcut Key for a Macro

To assign a key combination to your new macro, follow these steps:

1 With the document from the preceding exercise open, select the college name and address lines, open the drop-down list of styles from the Style box on the Formatting toolbar, and then choose Normal style.

The text should now be displayed in Times New Roman, Regular, 10-point, and be left-aligned.

2 Choose **T**ools, **C**ustomize to display the Customize dialog box (see Figure 10.22).

3 Choose the **K**eyboard button to display the Customize Keyboard dialog box (see Figure 10.23).

4 Make sure that the Sa**v**e changes in drop-down list box displays the Normal.dot template.

5 Scroll through the **C**ategories list until you see the Macros category; then select Macros.

The Macros list displays a list of available macros.

Figure 10.22
Use the Customize dialog box to customize the entries on the toolbar and the menus and access the Customize Keyboard dialog box.

Click here to display the Customize Keyboard dialog box.

Figure 10.23
Use the Customize Keyboard dialog box to create shortcut keys for your macros.

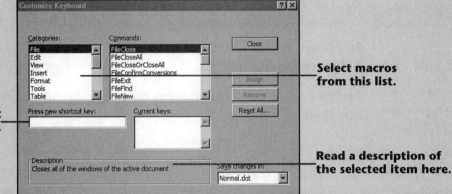

Enter new shortcut key here.

Select macros from this list.

Read a description of the selected item here.

❻ In the Macros list box, select the CentArialB16ShSc entry.

You are now ready to assign a shortcut key to your macro.

❼ Click in the Press **n**ew shortcut key text box to place the insertion point in the box; then press Alt+C to assign that key combination to the macro.

If no other items have been assigned to the Alt+C combination, Word displays the phrase Currently assigned to: [unassigned] below the Press **n**ew shortcut key text box.

If you have problems...   If the dialog box indicates that another item is already using the Alt+C shortcut key, keep trying other combinations until you find one that is available. You may want to avoid potential key combinations consisting of Ctrl and a letter because this combination is already used for numerous Word commands.

---

❽ Click **A**ssign to assign the keystrokes that you entered as the new shortcut keys for the macro.

❾ Click Close to close the Customize Keyboard dialog box; then click Close to close the Customize dialog box and return to the Word document.

(continues)

Specifying a Shortcut Key for a Macro (continued)

⑩ If necessary, select the college name and address. Then test your new shortcut key combination for the CentArialB16ShSc macro by pressing `Alt`+`C`.

⑪ Deselect your text and view your results. The college name and address should now be centered and displayed in the Arial, Bold, 16-point font with the Shadow and Small caps effects.

⑫ Leave the file open for the next exercise.

Use the following steps to remove a shortcut-key combination from a macro.

1. Open the Customize Keyboard dialog box.

2. Choose Macros in the **C**ategories list, select the macro in the Macros list, and select the key combination in the **C**urrent keys list box.

3. Choose the **R**emove button; then close the Customize Keyboard and Customize dialog boxes.

When you do this, you are removing only the shortcut key, not deleting the macro itself.

When you no longer need a macro, you can delete it. You learn how to delete a macro in the following exercise.

Deleting a Macro

To delete a macro, follow these steps:

❶ With the document open from the preceding exercise, choose **T**ools, **M**acro, **M**acros to display the Macros dialog box.

❷ If necessary, choose All active templates and documents from the **M**acros in drop-down list.

> **Note**
>
> If the macro does not appear in the list, you first must open the template in which the macro is stored.

❸ Select the CentArialB16ShSc macro from the **M**acro name list.

❹ Choose the **D**elete button.

❺ Choose **Y**es when you are prompted to delete the macro.

❻ Click the Close button to return to your document.

❼ In your open Word document, select the college name and address; then choose Normal paragraph style from the Style box in the Formatting toolbar to return the selected text to the default font and alignment.

❽ Press `Alt`+`C` (or the shortcut keys you assigned to the CentArialB16ShSc macro) to see if your macro runs on the selected text. (No macro should run at this time.)

9 Choose **T**ools, **M**acro, **M**acros to display the Macros dialog box.

10 If necessary, choose All active templates and documents from the Ma**c**ros in drop-down list; then scroll through the list to see whether you can find the CentArialB16ShSc macro.

The CentArialB16ShSc macro should no longer be listed.

11 Choose Cancel to close the Macros dialog box.

12 Close your document without saving the changes.

This concludes your work with macros. In this section, you learned to record, run, and delete a macro, and you learned to assign a shortcut key to your macro. You can edit existing macros using the Visual Basic for Applications programming language. However, when working with simple macros, you may find it easier to delete the incorrect macro, and then record a new one that consists of the proper steps.

Chapter Summary

In this chapter, you worked with styles, templates, the AutoFormat feature, wizards, AutoText, and simple macros to automate your work and save you time. You learned to apply styles to different parts of your document; then you watched as your entire document was reformatted by attaching a different template to it, or by using the AutoFormat command. You also learned that AutoText entries store text or pictures, whereas macros can store instructions for executing Word commands.

In the final chapter of this text, you will build on all the information you have learned so far as you start to work with the desktop publishing features that are part of Word.

If you have completed your work for this computer session, make sure that you properly exit all open programs; then use the Windows Sh**u**t Down command to safely exit Windows. To test your knowledge of the material covered in this chapter, answer the questions in the Checking Your Skills section immediately following this summary. Then complete the exercises in the Applying Your Skills section at the end of the chapter.

Checking Your Skills

True/False

For each of the following, circle *T* or *F* to indicate whether the statement is true or false.

T   F   **1.** The use of character styles lets you quickly add numerous character formats to selected text with just a few clicks of the mouse button.

T   F   **2.** Paragraph styles can include tab settings, line spacing, and character formatting.

T   F   **3.** Styles can be saved on templates.

T   F   **4.** An AutoText entry may contain text, graphics, and even a digitized signature.

T   F   **5.** The only way to create a macro is to start the recorder and record the desired actions.

T   F   **6.** When you key the first few letters of an AutoText entry, the AutoComplete feature displays a small text box with part or all of the AutoText entry it "thinks" you are about to type.

T   F   **7.** When you create or modify a style, you can specify a style for the paragraph that follows it.

T   F   **8.** The AutoFormat and AutoFormat As You Type features are identical.

T   F   **9.** A wizard is an automated program that leads you through the process of creating part of a document or the entire document.

T   F   **10.** You can create macros, but you cannot delete them until you restart Word.

Multiple Choice

In the blank provided, write the letter of the correct answer for each of the following questions.

1. When you apply a style to a paragraph, Word applies the style to all the _____.

    a. text in the paragraph

    b. text in the section

    c. characters in each line of the page

    d. text on the page

    e. text in the document

2. Which of the following is not an area where Word includes a predefined AutoText entry? _____

    a. footnotes

    b. reference lines

    c. mailing instructions

    d. salutations

    e. subject line

3. One way to display an AutoText entry is to type the short name and press _____.

    a. F2

    b. F3

    c. Ctrl + A

    d. F4

    e. Alt + C

4. Which of the following is not one of the general layout categories for the Word templates? _____

    a. Contemporary

    b. Elegant

    c. Professional

    d. Standard

10

5. Which of the following steps is *not* used in recording a Word macro? _____

  a. Start the macro recorder.

  b. Perform the actions.

  c. Open the Customize dialog box.

  d. Stop the recorder.

6. To see a list of available templates and a preview of how your current document will appear when a selected template is attached to the document, open the _____ dialog box.

  a. Style Gallery

  b. Style

  c. Templates

  d. Character Style

  e. Paragraph Style

7. To move back one screen in a wizard, choose the _____ button.

  a. **H**elp

  b. **R**everse

  c. **C**ancel

  d. **B**ack

  e. There is no button to back up one screen.

8. Wizards are helpful in creating specific kinds of documents—such as agendas, fax cover sheets, and newsletters—and are an extension of _____.

  a. styles

  b. formats

  c. templates

  d. customization

  e. frames

9. When you create a new style, Word automatically adds it to the list of styles on the _____ template.

  a. Normal

  b. Document

  c. Universal

  d. Character style

  e. Wizard

10. Unless you specify differently, Word will use the _____ style for the paragraph style in your documents.

  a. Universal

  b. Times New Roman

  c. Regular

  d. Automatic

  e. Normal

Fill in the Blank

In the blank provided, write the correct answer for each of the following questions.

1. A _____ for a document provides the basic framework on which you create a document.

2. You can use _____ to save words, phrases, or graphics that you use regularly.

3. A _____ can contain text or graphics, but it does not have to. It could just contain formatting commands for selected text.

4. _____ text or graphics are saved in a template and appears in every document that is based on that template.

5. By default, the _____ template automatically loads when you open a file without attaching a different template.

6. Many characteristics of the current style can be found by viewing the _____ toolbar.

7. When you create a(n) _____ entry, you assign it a short name so that you can later type the name; then immediately press F3 to display the entire entry.

8. When you see an AutoComplete entry displayed on your screen, press _____ to insert the rest of the entry.

9. When you want Word to format your entire document in one pass, choose the _____ command.

10. If you don't want Word to automatically change the lists you create to bulleted or numbered lists, turn off the corresponding options in the _____ page of the AutoCorrect dialog box.

Applying Your Skills

Review Exercises

Exercise 1: Applying Styles

In this exercise, you practice applying styles to the headings in a report. All the headings are temporarily right-aligned to make them easy to find. When you finish the exercise, there should be no right-aligned headings.

1. Open the Chap1003 file from your Student Disk; then save the file as **Headings** back to your Student Disk.

2. Select the *MEMORY AND STORAGE* title and place it in Heading 1 style.

3. Place the *Memory* heading and the *Storage* heading in Heading 2 style.

4. Place the *Common Secondary Storage Media* heading in Heading 3 style.

5. Save the revisions to your file; then print it.

6. Leave the Headings file open for Exercise 2.

Exercise 2: Attaching a Template to an Existing Document

In this exercise, you attach a template to an open document.

1. If the Headings file is not still open from Exercise 1, open it now; then save it as **Headings Elegant Report** back to your Student Disk.

2. Attach the Elegant Report Template to the Headings document.

3. Save the revisions to the Headings Elegant Report file.

4. Print the revised file and be prepared to discuss the differences between the two Headings documents.

5. Close the file.

Exercise 3: Create and Apply a New Style

In this exercise, you create and apply a paragraph style to an entire document. Then you modify the style and apply the modified paragraph style to the entire document.

1. Open the Chap1004 file from your Student Disk and immediately save the file as **Business 10** back to your Student Disk.

2. Create a new paragraph style, named Busletter, which includes the following characteristics:

    a. One-inch left and right indents

    b. Line spacing set to 1.5 lines

    c. 12 points inserted after a paragraph

    d. the Arial, Italic, 12-point font

3. Apply the Busletter style to the entire document.

4. Preview the letter. Then make the following modifications to the Busletter style:

    a. Change the left and right indents to .3 inches.

    b. Insert 6 points after a paragraph.

    c. Change the font size to 11 points.

5. Save the changes to the Busletter style, and then make sure that the entire document has been reformatted to the revised style.

6. Save the revisions to the file; then print it and close the file.

Exercise 4: Working with AutoFormat

In this exercise, you use styles to format a document; then you use the AutoFormat command to format your document and compare the differences. In the initial file, the headings are right-aligned for easy identification. When you finish, no headings should be right-aligned.

1. Open the Chap1005 file from your Student Disk; then immediately save it as **Planning 10** back to the disk.

2. Create you own Heading A style and apply it to the title *Schedule of Events*.

3. Create your own Heading B style and apply it to the February 28, March 6, and April 8 date headings, plus the *Upcoming Summer Events* section heading.

4. Print your formatted document.

5. Use the AutoFormat feature to format the entire document. When prompted, accept all of Word's suggested changes.

6. Print the current document and compare the results of the AutoFormat to the manual formatting you applied in steps 2 and 3. Be prepared to discuss the differences between the two printouts.

7. Save the final revisions to the file; then close the file.

Exercise 5: Using the Letter Wizard

1. Choose **F**ile, **N**ew to display the New dialog box.

2. Choose the Letters tab.

3. Select the Letter Wizard icon and read the description of the function of this wizard.

4. Create a one-paragraph letter to your instructor, describing the two most important things you learned in this chapter.

5. Save the file as **Letter** to your Student Disk, print, and then close the file.

Continuing Projects

Project 1: Practice Using Word

Practice creating macros in Word by completing the following steps:

1. Open the Chap1006 file from your Student Disk and immediately save the file as **Guidelines 10** back to your disk.

2. Write a macro to center the title and place it in an Arial, Bold, 15-point font.

3. Write a macro to apply automatic numbering to the five guidelines and format the text in an Arial, Regular, 11-point font.

4. Format the document, using the two macros.

5. Save the revisions, print, and then close the file.

Project 2: Deli-Mart

In this exercise, you practice applying styles and creating an AutoText entry.

1. Open the Chap1007 file from your Student Disk and immediately save the file as **Menu 10** back to your disk.

2. Apply Heading 3 style to each menu item name. (If necessary, readjust the tabs to separate the item name from the item number.)

3. Create an AutoText entry for the title of the document and place the AutoText entry at the bottom of the document.

4. Save the revisions to the file, print, and then close the file.

Project 3: The Marketing Connection

Continue working with the newsletter by creating a style for the section headings and then creating a macro to apply the heading style to each heading.

1. Open the Chap1008 file from your Student Disk and immediately save the file as **Market 10** back to your disk.

2. Format the title of the newsletter in an appropriate style.

3. Create a new style for the section headings.

4. Create a macro that will apply the new style to a selected section heading.

5. Use the macro to apply your new style to each section heading.

6. Save the revisions to your file, print, and then close the file.

CHAPTER 11

Introduction to Desktop Publishing

Desktop publishing
The use of a computer system and software to combine text and graphics in advanced layout formats to produce a visually attractive document.

In this chapter, you learn about a number of Word features that can help turn ordinary-looking text into an eye-pleasing document. As you learn to add columns, special effects, and pictures to a document, you learn about features that bridge word processing and *desktop publishing*. After you complete this chapter, you are ready to use the Word Help program, or other resources, to learn more about Word's desktop publishing features.

Objectives

By the time you have finished this chapter, you will have learned to

1. Create Columns
2. Use AutoShapes
3. Create WordArt Entries
4. Apply Borders and Shading to Paragraphs and Pages
5. Insert Drop Caps
6. Insert and Manipulate Pictures

Objective 1: Create Columns

Side-by-side columns
Short blocks of text (or paragraphs) displayed next to one another, as in a table.

Newspaper columns
Text that flows from the bottom of one column to the top of the next.

Some documents look best and are easiest to read when they are divided into columns. Sometimes, you can actually place more information onto fewer pages when you format the document into columns. In Word, you can divide pages of your documents into *side-by-side columns*, similar in concept to a table. Or you can divide your text into *newspaper columns*, in which your text fills the first column and then starts at the top of the next column, just as it does in newspapers and magazines. In this chapter, you learn to use the newspaper column format.

When you create a new document, Word applies the single-column format by default. If you want to format a document in two or more columns, you can specify the column format before you start typing the text, or you can complete the text and then divide the document into columns.

One way to activate the Columns command is to choose the Columns button on the Standard toolbar. When using this technique, the width of each new column is identical. You can use the move column marker on the ruler to adjust the width of columns, following the same procedures you used when using the ruler to adjust the width of the cells in a table. For greater control over the column formatting, including setting the number of columns, the width of each column, and the space between columns, use the Columns dialog box.

When you apply the Columns command, the entire document is placed in the specified number of columns, unless the document has been divided into sections. If a document is divided into sections, only the current section is affected by the Columns command. Remember that if you want to have different column formats within the same document, you must divide your document into sections.

Inserting Section Breaks and Column Breaks

In Chapter 6, you learned to work with **N**ext page section breaks as you divided documents into a number of sections to control the information displayed in page headers and footers. In those instances, each section started at the top of a new page.

A Con**t**inuous section break is used when you need the text following the break to continue on the same page as the text before the break. For example, suppose that you want to create a page in which the text is in two columns; however, you need a single-column heading stretching above both columns of text. To do this, use a Con**t**inuous section break to break the page into two sections; the top section will be formatted in a single column for the heading, and the bottom section formatted into two columns for the text.

You can apply continuous section breaks from the Break dialog box (displayed by choosing **I**nsert, **B**reak) or from the Columns dialog box.

If you are displaying the nonprinting characters and you insert a section break on a blank line, a nonprinting, dotted, double line is displayed across the document window. The double line includes the words *Section Break* and the type of section break (**N**ext page, Con**t**inuous, **E**ven page, **O**dd page) inserted.

If you insert a section break after the period at the end of a paragraph, only part of the nonprinting double line is displayed.

Word stores all section formatting in the section break. If you delete a section break, the preceding text assumes the formatting of the following section.

When using columns, you can end one column and begin another by inserting a column break at the desired location. The Break dialog box is used to insert column breaks (and section breaks). Alternatively, pressing `⇧Shift`+`Ctrl`+`↵Enter` also inserts a column break. When the nonprinting characters are displayed, column breaks are represented by a single dotted line displaying the words *Column Break* in the center of the line.

To delete a column or section break, position the insertion point in the single or double dotted line and press ⒟ⓔⓛ. Alternatively, you can position the insertion point immediately after the break and press ⟨←Backspace⟩.

Formatting an Existing Document into Columns

To format an entire document into two columns and practice breaking the columns at different points, follow these steps:

1 Start Word, open the Chap1101 file from your Student Disk, and immediately save the file back to your disk as **Column Report**. Then choose the Show/Hide ¶ button to display the document's nonprinting characters.

2 Choose the Columns button in the Standard toolbar, to display a pop-up, four-column grid below the button (see Figure 11.1).

Figure 11.1
The column grid is displayed when you click the Columns button.

3 Move the pointer to the grid's second column (from the left) to highlight the first two columns; then click in the second column to issue the command to format the document into two equal-width columns.

> ### Tip
>
> As you move the pointer across the columns in the grid, the lower section of the grid lists the number of columns selected.
>
> To divide the page into five or six columns, rest the pointer on the fourth column, press the mouse button, and drag the mouse to the right until the fifth and six columns in the grid are displayed.

Word divides the document into two columns and places it in Page Layout view (see Figure 11.2).

> ### Note
>
> Although a document may be divided into two or more columns, Normal view will display only one continuous column aligned against the left margin.

(continues)

Formatting an Existing Document into Columns (continued)

Figure 11.2
The document is divided into two equal-width columns. The horizontal ruler shows the positions of the columns and the space between the columns.

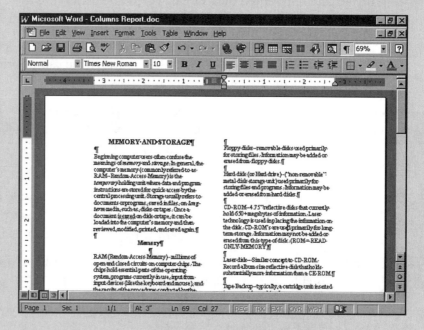

❹ Scroll through the document to briefly note the information included in the document.

Note that the *Common Secondary Storage Media* heading is at the bottom of the first column, but the corresponding text is at the top of the second column. (If the section heading was placed at the top of your second column, modify the following steps on inserting a column break as desired.)

You can end a column at the place of your choice by entering a Column break command.

❺ Place the insertion point immediately in front of the *Common Secondary Storage Media* heading; then choose **I**nsert, **B**reak to display the Break dialog box.

❻ Select the **C**olumn break option in the Insert section and choose OK to close the dialog box and move the text following the column break to the top of the second column.

❼ Scroll through the document to review your changes; then scroll to the bottom of the page to view the end of the first column and the nonprinting Column Break dotted line.

To delete a column or section break, place the insertion point on the break line and press (Del).

❽ Delete the column break you just entered to return the columns to their previous content.

When using the Columns button or Columns menu command to create columns, Word fills the first column with text and then continues the text into the next column. When there are more than two columns, this pattern continues in subsequent columns. If not enough text exists to fill a page, this process results in columns of unequal length.

To instruct Word to try to balance the amount of lines in each column, insert a Continuous break at the end of the last column.

9 Place the insertion point at the end of the document, open the Break dialog box, select the Continuous section break option, and then choose OK to close the dialog box and return to the document.

The two columns in the document should now be close to equal in length.

10 Choose the Print Preview button to display your document. Note that the two columns are almost equal in length; then close the Print Preview window.

11 Save the changes to your document and keep it open for the next exercise.

In the exercise you just finished, you use the Columns button on the Standard toolbar and the Break dialog box to control the number and content of your columns. In the next exercise, you use the Columns dialog box to control your columns.

Using the Columns Dialog Box

To practice using the Columns dialog box to control the formatting of the columns in your document, follow these steps:

1 In the open Columns Report document, place the insertion point immediately in front of the first character in the first paragraph, the paragraph beginning with *Beginning computer users...*.

2 Open the Break dialog box and insert a Continuous section break immediately in front of the first paragraph.

Make sure that the nonprinting characters are displayed so that you can easily see the section break location. Don't be concerned when it looks as if the section break has jumped to the top of column 2.

> **Note**
>
> Remember, if you have changed back to Normal view, you will not see the columns as they will be printed.

Note that the left side of the status bar now indicates that the insertion point is in section 2 of the document.

3 Move the insertion point up into the first section of the document.

4 Choose Format, Columns to display the Columns dialog box (see Figure 11.3).

(continues)

Using the Columns Dialog Box (continued)

Figure 11.3

Use the Columns dialog box to set the number of columns, column width, and spacing; place a line between columns; and insert new sections into a document.

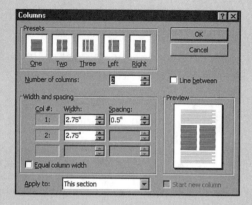

⑤ Make sure that the This section option is displayed in the **A**pply to box in the lower-left part of the dialog box. Then change the number of columns in the first section to one by selecting the **O**ne Presets option in the Columns dialog box and choosing OK.

Tip

You can also change the number of columns in a section by placing the insertion point in the section, choosing the Columns button, and then dragging across the number of desired columns.

For ease in reading, you should use no more than three columns when the page is displayed in portrait mode, and no more than five columns in landscape mode.

Your document should now look similar to the one in Figure 11.4.

Figure 11.4

Section one of the document is formatted to one column; therefore, the title is centered over the two columns of text.

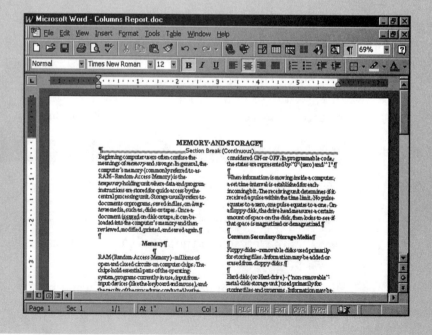

The Columns dialog box also makes it easy to change the width of columns.

6 Place the insertion point in section two of the document; then choose Format, Columns to open the Columns dialog box.

7 If necessary, deselect the Equal column width option in the Width and spacing section.

8 Change the value in the column one Width box to 3.5 inches by clicking the up spinner arrow at the end of the box.

Note that as you click the column one Width increase (or up) spinner arrow, the value in the Spacing box remains the same; but as the column one value increases, the column two Width value decreases in an equal amount.

> **Note**
>
> You can also change column width by dragging the column markers in the ruler.

9 Select the Line between option to activate it.

10 Make sure that the This section option is displayed in the Apply to box in the lower-left part of the dialog box. Then choose OK.

The column widths have changed, and a line appears between the columns (see Figure 11.5).

Figure 11.5
Document columns may be in equal or unequal widths.

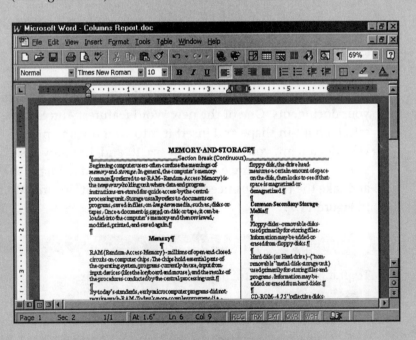

11 Save the changes to your document; then close it. Leave the Word window open for the next exercise.

Many newsletters are placed in column format. In the next exercises, you create a newsletter.

The text in Figures 11.6 and 11.7 is almost identical; however, the use of columns, pictures, and special effects makes the document in Figure 11.7 more visually appealing. The remaining exercises in this chapter lead you through the steps needed to change the text document in Figure 11.6 into the newsletter in Figure 11.7. Along the way, you learn to use some of Word's special effects tools, and you learn to insert pictures into your document.

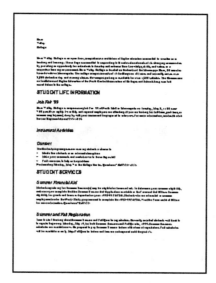

Figure 11.6
A text document.

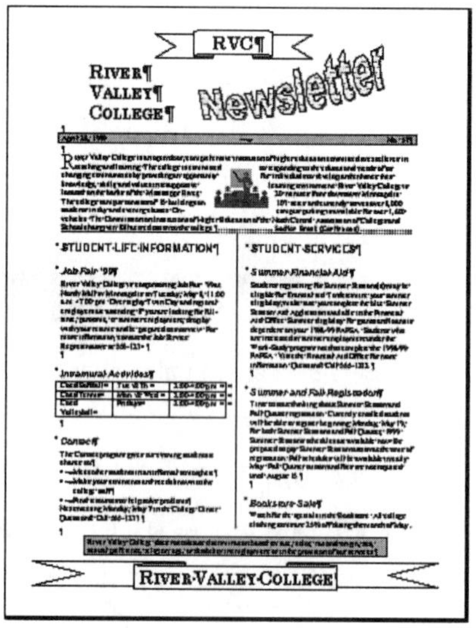

Figure 11.7
The document from Figure 11.6 formatted with special effects, a picture, and columns.

Objective 2: Use AutoShapes

Word has a number of features that help you insert eye-catching effects into your documents. One of the new Word features, AutoShapes, enables you to select a built-in shape and insert it into your document. Once the shape is in your document, you can move it; size it; and, in many cases, add text to the shape. In the following exercise, you open the document shown in Figure 11.6 and take the first steps needed to transform that document into the one you see in Figure 11.7.

Inserting and Editing an AutoShapes Image

To practice using AutoShapes, follow these steps:

❶ In the open Word window, open the Chap1102 file from your Student Disk. If the document is not already displayed in Normal view, choose the Normal View button, the first of four buttons in the lower-left part of the window. Save the file, as **N57**, back to the disk.

In this example, you create a newsletter for River Valley College. The name N57 is given to the document because it is assumed that the person creating the newsletters for the college saves all the newsletters in the same Newsletters folder. This would be the 57th newsletter in the series.

If the nonprinting characters are not already displayed, choose the Show/Hide ¶ button to display those characters now.

② Choose **I**nsert, **P**icture, **A**utoShapes, to display the AutoShapes toolbar.

 ③ Choose the Stars and Banners button to display a menu of related shapes (see Figure 11.8).

By default, when the AutoShapes toolbar is displayed, the Drawing toolbar is displayed along the bottom of the Word window.

Stars and Banners button

Figure 11.8
The menu of stars and banner images that can be inserted into your current document.

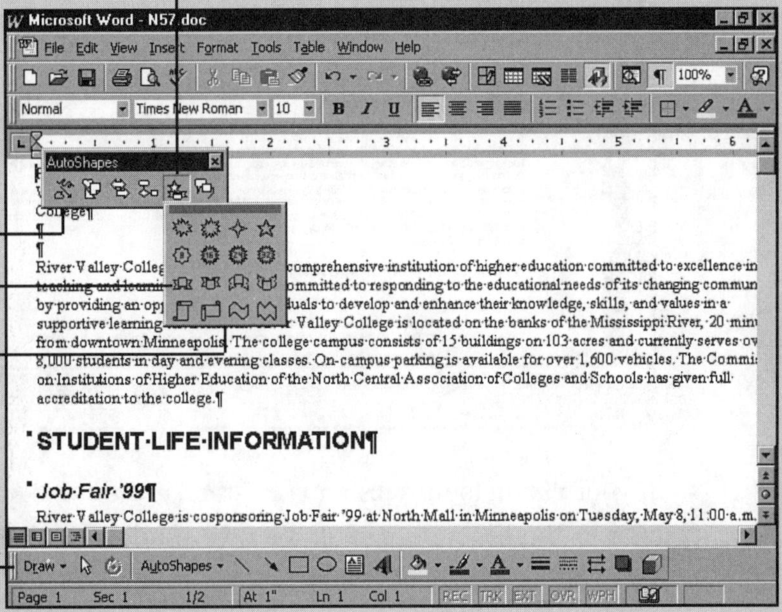

AutoShapes toolbar
Up Ribbon button
Stars and Banners menu

Drawing toolbar

④ Rest the pointer on the first image in the third row to see the ScreenTip identifying the Up Ribbon image button; then click the mouse button.

When you click the Up Ribbon button, Word automatically changes to Page Layout view. However, the image is not immediately displayed on your document.

⑤ Read the message on the status bar instructing you to click and drag to create the initial Up Ribbon image.

⑥ Use the vertical and horizontal rulers as guides to place the pointer about one-half inch down from the top edge of the page and a half-inch in from the left edge of the page. With the pointer in place, use the mouse to drag a three-inch-wide by one-half-inch-high rectangle; then release the mouse button.

(continues)

Inserting and Editing an AutoShapes Image (continued)

If you have problems...	If the rulers are not displayed in your window, choose **V**iew, **R**uler to display the vertical and horizontal rulers.

The Up Ribbon image is now "sized" according to the rectangle you created. The image remains selected as shown by the eight small boxes (these are sizing handles) encompassing the AutoShapes image. Your window should look similar to the one in Figure 11.9.

Figure 11.9
After selecting the AutoShapes image, create it by clicking and dragging the mouse.

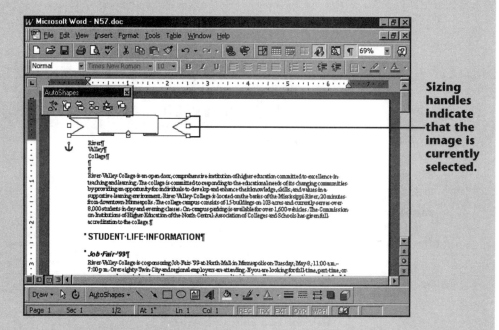

Sizing handles indicate that the image is currently selected.

If your ribbon looks substantially different from the one in Figure 11.9, use the sizing handles to modify the shape of the ribbon. Dragging a corner handle simultaneously changes the height and width of the ribbon, while maintaining the same height and width proportions. Dragging one of the middle sizing handles changes either the height or width of the ribbon, while keeping the other dimension constant.

7 Close the AutoShapes toolbar by clicking the Close button on its title bar.

8 Move the ribbon to the top center of the document by placing the pointer inside the image (when the pointer rests on the image, it changes to a four-headed arrow) and then dragging the image until it is centered across the page.

The document uses one-inch left and right margins. Therefore, when moving the ribbon, use the 3.25-inch mark on the horizontal ruler as your centering guide. Try to keep the top edge of the ribbon one-half inch below the top edge of the page. Repeat the move procedure as often as needed. (When you insert an object like an AutoShapes image into a document, Word initially "floats" the image over your text.)

9 Right-click inside the image to display the context-sensitive shortcut menu; then choose the Add Text command to place the insertion point within the ribbon and surround the ribbon with a frame of slash marks. (Refer to Figure 11.10 to view the frame around the ribbon.)

> ### Note
>
> If a Text Box toolbar is displayed when you choose the Add Text command, just close the toolbar. This toolbar provides access to additional tools, such as changing the direction of the text. Although you do not need it for this exercise, you may want to learn more about this toolbar after you are more familiar with the features covered in this chapter.

10 Change the font to a Century Schoolbook, Bold, 22-point font; then enter **RVC**.

> ### Note
>
> If the Century Schoolbook font is not available, choose another font.
>
> If you cannot see the complete letters, or if there is too much space above or below the letters, adjust the ribbon size until it resembles the one in Figure 11.10. Don't worry about trying to make a "perfect match." However, if the ribbon is too big, it may overlap some of the elements you will add in the next few exercises.

11 Choose the Center button on the Formatting toolbar to center the text within the ribbon (see Figure 11.10).

Figure 11.10
The completed top ribbon in the N57 document.

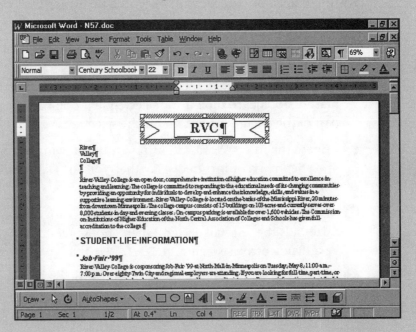

(continues)

11

Inserting and Editing an AutoShapes Image (continued)

⓬ Click within the document to deselect the ribbon and view your results. Then save the N57 document and leave it open for the next exercise.

When working with special effects and graphics, you'll find that your document can change very quickly. Therefore, it is recommended that you save your document every few minutes—compared to about every 10 minutes—when working with only text.

Objective 3: Create WordArt Entries

WordArt enables you to apply special effects to ordinary text, such as curving and rotating text; expanding and condensing letter spacing; or adding colors, borders, and shadows to text. When you work in WordArt, the selected text is treated as an *object*—the generic name for a segment of text, a graphic, table, sound byte, video clip, or any other item that can be inserted into a document.

WordArt graphics are based on text. This means that you can access any font installed on your computer and use most of the character-formatting tools when you create your WordArt entry.

Using WordArt

The following steps lead you through the process of changing the font of some existing text and then using WordArt to create a word displayed with special effects.

❶ In the open N57 document, select the first three lines of text (*River Valley College*); open the Font dialog box; change the font to a Century Schoolbook, Bold, 22-point font; and activate the **Sm**all caps effect. Choose OK to close the dialog box and format the selected text.

❷ Keep the text selected; then choose the Increase Indent button on the Formatting toolbar to indent the selected text one-half inch. Click in the top part of the document to turn off the selection.

❸ Choose the Insert WordArt button in the Drawing toolbar; or choose **In**sert, **P**icture, **W**ordArt to display the WordArt Gallery dialog box (see Figure 11.11).

❹ Click the fifth box in the fourth row to select that design (a black rectangle surrounds the selected design); then choose OK to display the Edit WordArt Text dialog box (see Figure 11.12).

❺ Replace the selected entry in the **T**ext box by typing **Newsletter**, accept the default font and font size options, and then choose OK to insert the WordArt object into your document and display the WordArt toolbar.

Figure 11.11
The WordArt Gallery provides 30 formatting options for your WordArt object.

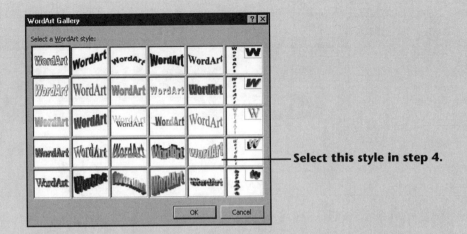

Select this style in step 4.

Figure 11.12
The Edit WordArt Text dialog box.

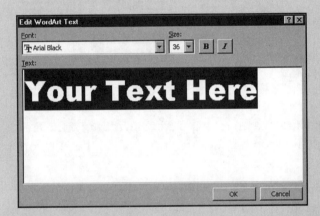

> **Note**
>
> Although the WordArt object appears in color, if you have a black-and-white printer, the printed image will consist of black letters with a gray shadow.

Don't be concerned where the WordArt object is initially placed in your document. You move a WordArt object in the same way you moved the ribbon at the top of your document.

6 Drag the WordArt object into the blank space to the right of the *River Valley College* text. Position the *N* in *Newsletter* about an inch to the right of the college name. The center of the *N* in *Newsletter* should be at the same height as the *Valley* line of the college name (see Figure 11.13).

7 Locate the three sizing handles on the right side of the WordArt object; then drag the middle sizing handle about one-half inch to the right to stretch the object into a little wider shape.

8 Choose the Free Rotate button on the WordArt toolbar.

(continues)

Using WordArt (continued)

Figure 11.13
The WordArt object is located in the title area of the newsletter.

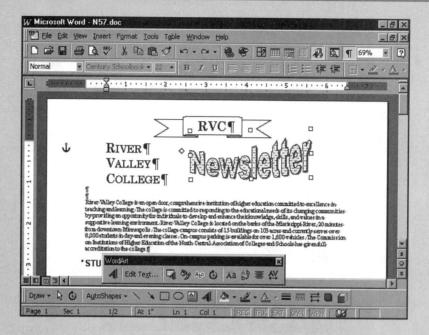

The pointer changes to include the image on the Free Rotate button, and round rotation handles are displayed on the four corners of the WordArt object.

❾ Rest the pointer on the upper-right rotation handle of the selected WordArt object; then drag the handle up about one-half inch. Release the mouse button and review your changes.

The letters in the right side of the object should now clearly be higher than the letters in the left side of the object (see Figure 11.14).

Figure 11.14
The WordArt object has been stretched, moved, and rotated.

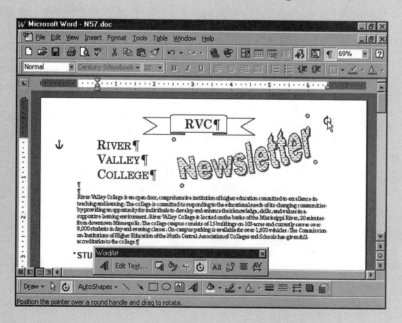

🔟 Click inside the text area of the document to deselect the WordArt object and close the WordArt toolbar.

⓫ Right-click anywhere on the Drawing toolbar to display a pop-up list of toolbars; then deselect the Drawing toolbar to remove it from your window.

⓬ Save the N57 document; then leave it open for the next exercise.

11

Now that you know how to create, move, size, and rotate a WordArt object, you are ready to experiment with some of the other tools on the WordArt and Drawing toolbars. At this point, space prohibits a further explanation of those tools; however, feel free to experiment with these tools on your own.

Objective 4: Apply Borders and Shading to Paragraphs and Pages

A more subtle way to apply emphasis to text is with borders. A border consists of lines placed around a paragraph—above, below, at either side, or by any combination of these positions. Borders can be drawn in various line styles, thickness, and colors, and can include a *shadow*. A shadow adds a three-dimensional look to the border.

Borders may be applied to selected paragraphs through the Borders toolbar or the Borders and Shading dialog box. The Borders and Shading dialog box also enables you to place a border around an entire page.

You can also add emphasis to text by shading it. Traditionally, most shading has been in a gray color because of the abundant use of black-and-white laser printers in business offices. With the advent of low-cost color laser printers, many offices will be using color to emphasize key parts of their correspondence. The shading exercises in this text call for gray shading; however, you would use similar techniques to shade in different colors to add emphasis to your documents.

Applying Borders and Shading to Selected Text

To practice applying borders to selected text, follow these steps:

❶ In the open N57 document, place the insertion point in front of the paragraph mark two lines below the *River Valley College* name you formatted in the preceding exercise.

❷ Insert today's date at the beginning of the line.

❸ Set a Right Tab just inside the right margin, press Tab⇥, and type **No. 57**; then press ⏎Enter once.

(continues)

Applying Borders and Shading to Selected Text (continued)

4 Select the current line containing the date and No. 57; then click the down arrow to the right of the Borders button on the Formatting toolbar to display the Borders toolbar (see Figure 11.15).

Figure 11.15
When first displayed, the Borders toolbar is initially attached to the Formatting toolbar.

5 Rest the pointer on the various buttons to see the corresponding Screen-Tips; then click the Outside Border button to place a border on all four sides of the selected paragraph.

6 Deselect the date line to view the border around the one-line paragraph. Then select the paragraph again and choose Format, Borders and Shading to display the Borders and Shading dialog box.

> ### Note
> If you don't select a paragraph, Word applies the border or shading formatting to the paragraph that contains the insertion point.

7 Choose the **S**hading tab to display the Shading options. Then click the second box, in the second row, of the grid in the Fill section, to set the shading at Gray-20% (see Figure 11.16).

Figure 11.16
The Shading page of the Borders and Shading dialog box.

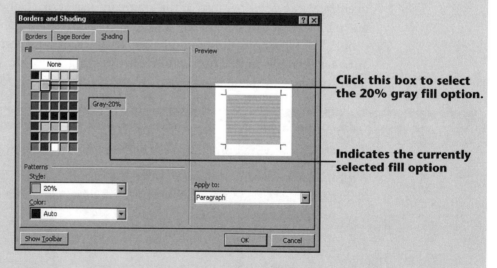

Click this box to select the 20% gray fill option.

Indicates the currently selected fill option

8 Choose OK to close the dialog box and shade the selected paragraph at a 20% gray setting. Click outside the selection to view your results.

To remove shading from selected paragraphs, choose None in the Fill section of the Shading page of the Borders and Shading dialog box and then choose OK.

> ### Tip
>
> Before you spend too much time shading paragraphs throughout a document, shade a typical paragraph, print it, and examine the results. If you use anything more than a light shading, text within the shaded paragraph may become difficult to read. The effect is even more pronounced when you make photocopies of shaded paragraphs.

9 Open the Borders and Shading dialog box again; then select the **P**age Border tab to display the Page border options (see Figure 11.17).

Figure 11.17
The Page Border page of the Borders and Shading dialog box.

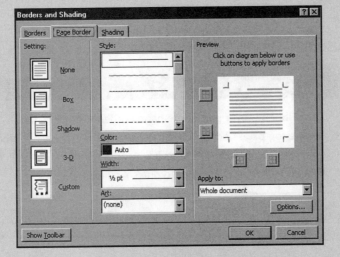

10 Choose the Bo**x** option in the Setting frame. Then make sure that a single solid line is selected in the St**y**le section, the ½-point option is selected in the **W**idth section, and Whole document is displayed in the App**l**y to drop-down list box.

11 Choose OK to place a single-line, ½-point border around the pages (currently, the document consists of two pages) of the N57 document.

At this point, you may need to "fine-tune" the placement of the objects at the top of the document.

12 Make any adjustments necessary to the ribbon or the WordArt object at the top of the document to make it look similar (it need not look exactly like) the top of the document in Figure 11.18.

(continues)

Applying Borders and Shading to Selected Text (continued)

Figure 11.18
The completed top of the newsletter.

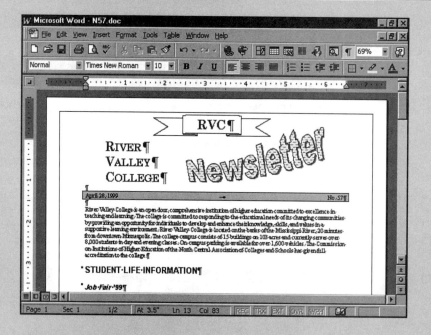

Note

If the ribbon is over part of the page border, move the ribbon down until you can see the top page border. If the top page border appears in broken lines, display your document in the Print Preview window; then return to Page Layout view. This should return the top border to one solid line.

⓭ Save the N57 document; then leave it open for the next exercise.

Objective 5: Insert Drop Caps

A *drop cap* is typically displayed as a larger-than-normal first letter of a paragraph. Word provides the option of dropping the capitalized first letter of the paragraph into the paragraph itself, or displaying the oversized letter in the margin to the left of the paragraph.

Inserting a Drop Cap

To insert a drop cap into a paragraph, follow these steps:

❶ In the open N57 document, place the insertion point anywhere inside the first paragraph, the one beginning with *River Valley College is an open door....*

❷ Choose F**o**rmat, **D**rop Cap to display the Drop Cap dialog box (see Figure 11.19).

Figure 11.19
The Drop Cap dialog box.

❸ Select the **D**ropped option box and enter the number **2** in the **L**ines to drop box.

The default size of the drop cap is three lines; however, for this document, a two-line drop cap is sufficient.

❹ Choose OK to close the dialog box and format the first letter of the paragraph to be two lines tall. Click outside the selected letter to deselect the first letter of the paragraph; then view your results (see Figure 11.20).

Figure 11.20
A drop cap has been inserted into the first paragraph.

The drop cap

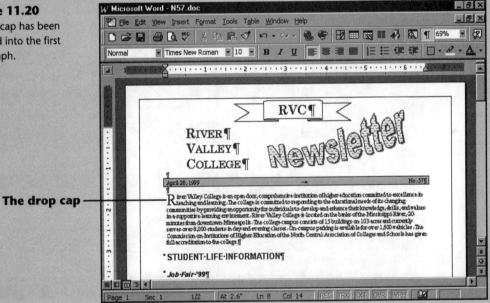

❺ Save the changes to the N57 document; then leave it open for the next exercise.

Objective 6: Insert and Manipulate Pictures

Word uses the term *pictures* to represent the various graphic images (clip art, digitized photos, scanned images, charts, and so on) that can be inserted into a document. After the image is in the document, you can move and size the image; wrap text around it; and, if desired, place it behind or in front of existing text.

Graphic files are stored in many different formats. Word, by itself, can work with many different graphic formats. If the graphic you want to use cannot be read by Word, you can usually install a "filter" file that enables Word to read the corresponding graphic file. The names of graphic files typically include file extensions such as .BMP, .WMF, .EMF, .JPG, .PCX, .PIC, and .TIF.

In the following exercises, you learn to insert a picture (a clip art file) into your document, move and size the picture, and then wrap text around the picture.

Inserting and Manipulating a Picture in a Document

To insert a picture into a document, follow these steps:

1 In the open N57 document, place the insertion point in the middle of the first line of the paragraph with the drop cap; then choose **Insert**, **Picture**, **Clip Art** to display the Microsoft Clip Gallery 3.0 dialog box.

2 If necessary, choose the **Clip Art** tab and then select the Academic category from the category list box on the left side of the dialog box (see Figure 11.21).

Selected category is highlighted

Figure 11.21
The Clip Art page of the Microsoft Clip Gallery 3.0 dialog box.

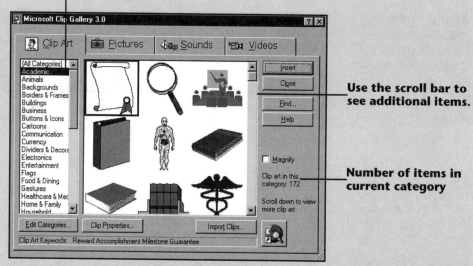

Use the scroll bar to see additional items.

Number of items in current category

Note

The computer system that was used to create the illustration in Figure 11.21 contains a complete installation of Microsoft Word. Depending on your system, your Clip Art page may contain a different number of clip art categories and illustrations available in the Academic category.

3 Select the third picture on the first row. (Included in this picture is a person in front of a group of people seated around a table.)

If this image is not available to you, pick another one.

4 Choose **Insert** to close the dialog box and place the image above the current paragraph.

Notice that the clip art picture is selected and that it has the same type of sizing handles you have already used when you worked with the AutoShapes ribbon and the WordArt object.

5 Drag the upper-right sizing handle diagonally down to the left to reduce the width of the picture to about one inch while maintaining the current height-to-width proportions.

6 Place the pointer in the center of the picture (the pointer changes to a four-headed arrow), press the mouse button, drag the picture to the center of the paragraph, and then release the mouse button.

To determine the location of the vertical center of the paragraph, try to display about the same number of lines above and below the picture. To determine the location of the horizontal center, use the AutoShapes ribbon and 3.25-inch mark on the horizontal ruler as guides.

As you can see, you move a picture the same way you moved a WordArt object. When you complete the move procedure, the paragraph text is split (see Figure 11.22).

Figure 11.22
When a picture is first placed within a paragraph, the lines of the paragraph move either above or below the picture.

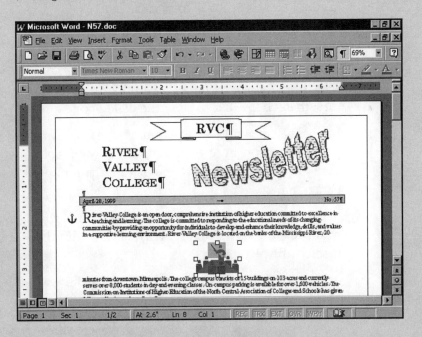

7 Save the document; then leave it open for the next exercise.

In the preceding exercise, you made your best guess regarding the sizing and placement of the picture in your document. If you want to be exact, you can use the pages of the Format Picture dialog box when working with your picture. In the next exercise, you use the Format Picture dialog box to instruct Word on how to wrap text around the picture in the document.

Wrapping Text Around a Picture

To wrap paragraph text around a picture, follow these steps:

1 In the open N57 document, right-click the picture of the people to display the shortcut menu; then choose the Format Picture command to display the Format Picture dialog box.

2 Choose the Wrapping tab to display the wrapping options (see Figure 11.23).

Figure 11.23
The Wrapping page of the Format Picture dialog box.

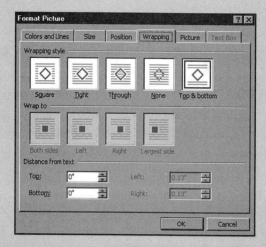

By default, the Top & bottom Wrapping style option is selected; you choose another option in the next step.

3 Select the Tight Wrapping style option to place text on all sides of the picture; then choose OK to close the dialog box.

When the paragraph is displayed, you may be surprised to find that your picture is no longer in the center of the paragraph. There is a good chance that you will have to move the picture again to place it in the center of the paragraph.

4 Make any final adjustments to the picture and the paragraph text that is wrapped around the picture. Then click within the text in the paragraph to deselect the picture.

At this point, your document should look similar to the one in Figure 11.24.

Note

It usually requires a few moving and sizing procedures before you are satisfied with the appearance of a picture in your document. Then, when you wrap text around the picture, you may decide that you need to make a few more modifications to the picture or the text.

For the purposes of this exercise, try to keep the drop cap paragraph to nine lines of text when the paragraph includes the clip art picture. This will leave enough room in the document for the information you will add in the next exercises.

Figure 11.24

The paragraph text is wrapped around the picture.

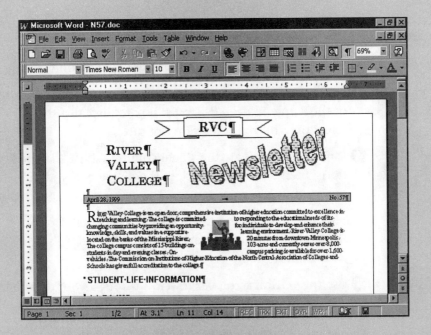

The final work to be completed in the first paragraph is to attach a horizontal line under the last line of the paragraph. This line is actually a bottom border. When you attach it to the paragraph, it will stretch between the left and right margins.

5 Make sure that the insertion point is within the drop cap paragraph; then click the arrow to the immediate right of the Borders button on the Formatting toolbar to display a menu of border choices.

6 Choose the Bottom Border button to place a horizontal line across the page immediately below the last line of the current paragraph.

If you have problems... If a single, thin, black line is not displayed below the paragraph, another line style may be chosen. If this happens, choose the Undo button to remove the bottom border line. Then open the **B**orders page of the Borders and Shading dialog box and select the options to use single, ½-point, black line style border.

7 Save the changes to your file; then leave it open for the next exercise.

Complete the Newsletter

In the final chapter exercises you use some of the formatting tools you worked with in the earlier exercises. You also learn a new way to move quickly to specific points in your document, as you learn to use Online Layout view and Word's Document Map.

Using Columns in the Newsletter

To format part of your N57 document in columns, follow these steps:

1 In the open N57 document, place the insertion point in front of the *S* in the *STUDENT LIFE INFORMATION* heading.

2 Choose F**o**rmat, **C**olumns to display the Columns dialog box.

3 Select the T**w**o option in the Presets section; then click the arrow at the end of the **A**pply to drop-down list box to display a short list of choices and select the This point forward option.

4 If necessary, activate the **E**qual column width and the Line **b**etween options; then choose OK to close the dialog box and return to your document.

This step inserts a continuous section break in front of the *STUDENT LIFE INFORMATION* heading and formats the second section into two equal-width columns.

5 Use the vertical scroll bar to scroll through your document—you should now be viewing a one-page document. Then choose the Online Layout View button (located in the group of buttons attached to the left end of the horizontal scrollbar) to display the document in Online Layout view (see Figure 11.25).

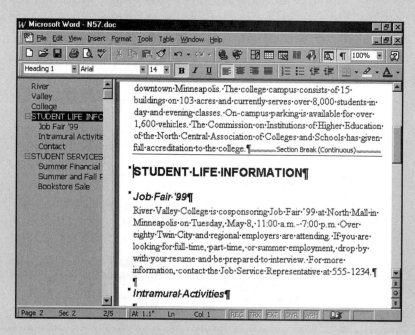

Figure 11.25
The Document Map is located in the left pane; the document (with rewrapped text for ease in reading) is displayed in the right pane.

In this view, the screen is split vertically into two panes. The Document Map is located in the left pane. Your document (with revised word wrapping in place to make the content easy to read) is in the right pane.

Note

You can display the Document Map in any view by clicking the Document Map button on the Standard toolbar. However, only Online Layout view "rewraps" your text to make it easy to read. Remember that your document will not print in the same way it appears in Online Layout view.

The Document Map entries consist of the section headings that were formatted with a heading style. For example, note that the *STUDENT LIFE INFORMATION* heading is formatted in Heading 1 style.

Clicking on a Document Map entry moves the insertion point directly to the corresponding document location.

Tip

If the Document Map pane is too narrow to display an entire entry, rest the pointer on the partial entry to see a pop-up text box displaying the entire name of the entry.

You can adjust the width of the panes by moving the vertical bar separating the two panes. To do this, rest the pointer on the vertical bar until it changes to the Resize pointer (a pointer consisting of two short vertical lines displayed between a left and a right arrow); then drag the pointer (and vertical bar) to the desired location.

The Intramural Activities portion of the STUDENT LIFE INFORMATION section is currently blank. Complete the next steps to quickly move to that section and insert a table of activities.

6 Click the *Intramural Activities* entry in the Document Map to move the insertion point to that heading.

7 Choose **V**iew, **P**age Layout to change to Page Layout view.

8 Place the insertion point in front of the paragraph mark on the blank line below the *Intramural Activities* heading.

9 Choose the Insert Table button from the Standard toolbar; then drag across the grid to create a 3 × 3 table and release the mouse button.

Notice that the cells are automatically adjusted to fit within the available column width.

10 Enter the following text in the corresponding cells of the table:

Coed Softball	**Tue. & Th.**	**2:00-4:00 p.m.**
Coed Tennis	**Mon. & Wed.**	**2:00-4:00 p.m.**
Coed Volleyball	**Fridays**	**2:00-4:00 p.m.**

(continues)

Using Columns in the Newsletter (continued)

11 Choose the Document Map button to display the Document Map in **P**age Layout view.

A telephone number is incomplete in another portion of the document. Correct this mistake by completing the next two steps.

12 In the Document Map, select the *Summer Financial Aid* heading to move the insertion point to the beginning of that section.

Don't worry if the text is too small to work with in the right pane of the window.

13 Choose the Document Map button again—this time to close the Document Map.

14 Move to the end of the *Summer Financial Aid* section and complete the telephone number by adding **1232**.

15 Scroll through your document to view the changes; then save your revisions and leave the document open for the next exercise.

In the final exercise, you enter a new paragraph; then place a border around it and shade it. You also insert a second ribbon into the document. The last two items provide some "visual weight" to the bottom of the document so that the newsletter appears "visually balanced."

Visually Balancing the Newsletter

To enter items to visually balance the top and bottom of the newsletter, follow these steps:

1 In the open N57 document, place the insertion point at the end of the last paragraph, the one ending with ...*the month of May.*

2 Choose F**o**rmat, **C**olumns, to display the Columns dialog box.

Use the Columns dialog box to enter a continuous section break to format the bottom of the newsletter in one column.

3 Select **O**ne in the Presets section, select the This point forward option in the **A**pply to section, and then choose OK to close the dialog box.

The bottom of the newsletter should now be in the one-column format. You can verify this by looking to see that the horizontal ruler does not display any column markers. Because you inserted the continuous break at the end of a line, you may not be able to see very much, if any, of the nonprinting double-line indicating the existence of a section break.

4 Move the insertion point to the end of the document; then type the following text in the third section of the document (if desired, adjust the Zoom setting to help you view the text you are entering):

River Valley College does not tolerate discrimination based on race, color, national origin, sex, sexual orientation, religion, age, or disability in employment or in the provision of our services.

5 Select the paragraph, place a single-line black border around the paragraph, and then use a 20% gray setting to shade the paragraph.

6 Keep the paragraph selected, open the **I**ndents and Spacing page of the Paragraph dialog box, set the left and right indents to .5 inches, and then choose OK.

7 Deselect the paragraph, save the revisions to the document, and then keep the file open for the next steps.

8 Choose **I**nsert, **P**icture, **A**utoShapes to display the AutoShapes toolbar.

9 Choose the Stars and Banners button to display the corresponding menu of shapes; then choose the Down Ribbon button.

10 Use the page borders and the bottom border of the last paragraph as guides for you to drag a rectangle that fills most of the available space below the last paragraph and between the page borders (see Figure 11.26).

Figure 11.26
The Down Ribbon fills most of the available space between the page borders and the bottom border of the last paragraph.

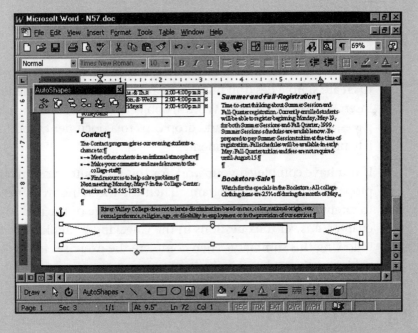

11 Right-click in the middle of the Down Ribbon graphic; then choose the Add text command.

12 Change the font to a Century Schoolbook, Bold, 22-point font, with the Small caps effect; type **River Valley College**; then center the text, using the Center button on the Formatting toolbar.

(continues)

11

Visually Balancing the Newsletter (continued)

If you have problems... If the last word disappears as you type it, the text space in the ribbon is not quite large enough to display all the letters in the text. Stretch the ribbon a little closer toward the page borders until the entire college name is displayed on the ribbon.

⓭ Review your entire document and complete any necessary final edits. Then close the AutoShapes and Drawing toolbars.

⓮ Save the document, print it, and then close it.

If you have trouble displaying all the page borders in your printouts, you may choose to remove the page borders or experiment with some of the page border settings. In either case, start by displaying the **P**age Border page of the Borders and Shading dialog box. Then, to remove the page border, choose **N**one in the Setting section and choose OK. To experiment with the settings in the Border and Shading dialog box, choose F**o**rmat, **B**orders and Shading, choose the **P**age Border page, and then choose the **O**ptions button to display the current settings. Change these settings as needed.

Chapter Summary

In this chapter, you were introduced to a few of the Word tools that can be used to create simple desktop publishing documents. You learned to use columns, insert AutoShapes, create WordArt objects, place borders around paragraphs and pages, shade paragraphs, add drop caps to a document, and insert and manipulate pictures in your document.

If you have completed your work for this computer session, make sure that you properly exit all open programs. Then use the Windows Sh**u**t Down command to safely exit Windows. To test your knowledge of the material covered in this chapter, answer the questions in the Checking Your Skills section immediately following this summary. Then complete the exercises in the Applying Your Skills section at the end of the chapter.

Checking Your Skills

True/False

For each of the following, circle *T* or *F* to indicate whether the statement is true or false.

T   F   **1.** Although you can insert an AutoShape item into your document, you cannot size it.

T   F   **2.** A graphic file typically includes an extension such as .WMF, .BMP, .PCX, .PIC, or .TIF.

T   F   **3.** WordArt enables you to place words into shapes, rotate text to any angle, and use other eye-catching features.

T   F   **4.** The Borders toolbar button enables you to apply borders to the current or selected paragraph, but not shading.

T   F   **5.** You cannot divide a page displayed in portrait mode into more than three columns.

T   F   **6.** To divide the top part of a page into three columns, and the bottom part of the page into two columns, a section break must be created between the top and bottom parts of the page.

T   F   **7.** To add text to an AutoShape entry, right-click the entry, choose **A**dd text, and enter the desired text.

T   F   **8.** To apply shading to a selected paragraph, you must use the Paragraph dialog box.

T   F   **9.** The Document Map can help you move the insertion point to a specific heading in your document.

T   F   **10.** Although you can insert clip art pictures into a Word document, you cannot insert a digitized photograph.

Multiple Choice

In the blank provided, write the letter of the correct answer for each of the following questions.

1. To change the layout of text from one column (that stretches between the left and right margins) to two columns, and start the two columns on a new page, choose _____ from the Break dialog box.

    a. **P**age break

    b. **C**olumn break

    c. **N**ext page

    d. **C**ontinuous

    e. **E**ven column

2. If you display a two-column document in **N**ormal view, you see _____.

    a. both columns

    b. both columns and a line dividing the columns

    c. only one column

    d. only one column enclosed in a box with the number 2 representing the two-column format

    e. only one column with the text stretching between the left and right page margins

3. Which of the following Word views automatically displays the Document Map by default? _____

    a. Normal

    b. Online Layout

    c. Page Layout

    d. Outline

    e. Print Preview

4. After you display the AutoShapes toolbar and choose a specific image, the next thing you need to do is _____.

    a. Close the Document Map

    b. Click and drag to size the AutoShape image

    c. Close the AutoShapes toolbar

    d. Close the Drawing toolbar

    e. Display the Document Map

5. You can apply a border to a selected paragraph by using the Borders button on the _____.

    a. Standard toolbar

    b. Formatting toolbar

    c. Paragraph dialog box

    d. Line dialog box

    e. AutoShapes toolbar

6. When you use Word's automated command to make the first letter of a paragraph significantly larger than the other letters, you are using the _____ command.

    a. Drop Cap

    b. Large Cap

    c. Special Font

    d. Special Letter

    e. Box Cap

7. To display 3-D text and use special features like text rotation, use the _____ tool.

    a. SpecialText

    b. TextArt

    c. OfficeArt

    d. LetterArt

    e. WordArt

8. When using columns in portrait page mode, it is recommended that you use no more than _____ columns across your page.

    a. three

    b. four

    c. five

    d. six

    e. seven

9. The two dialog boxes that enable you to insert continuous section breaks are the _____ dialog boxes.

    a. Paragraph and Columns

    b. Paragraph and Break

    c. Sections and Breaks

    d. Paragraph and Section

    e. Columns and Break

10. To determine an initial shape for your WordArt object, choose an entry from the _____ dialog box.

    a. Style Gallery

    b. Clip Gallery

    c. WordArt Gallery

    d. Stars and Banner Menu

    e. WordStyle menu

Fill in the Blank

In the blank provided, write the correct answer for each of the following questions.

1. To place a border around your entire page, display the **P**age Border page of the Borders and Shading dialog box; then choose the _____ Setting option.

2. A(n) _____ is the general name used to refer to pictures, AutoShapes images, and other items you can place in your document.

3. When you insert an AutoShapes image into your document, Word initially _____ it over your text.

4. All the formatting for a section is held in the _____.

5. The _____ of a component in your document determines whether the component is listed in the Document Map.

6. The _____ Word view automatically displays the Document Map in the left pane and "rewraps" the text in the right pane for easy reading.

7. To create close to equal column lengths, use the _____ column break at the end of the section containing the columns.

8. When you place the pointer on a graphic or WordArt object to prepare to move the item, the pointer changes to a(n) _____ arrow.

9. To place a line border immediately below the current paragraph, choose the _____ Border button.

10. Only the _____ character of a paragraph can be made into a drop cap for the paragraph.

Applying Your Skills

Review Exercises

Exercise 1: Creating Columns

Practice creating columns in an existing document by following these steps:

1. Open the Chap1103 file from your Student Disk and immediately save the file as **Content 11** back to your disk.

2. For this document, change the page orientation to landscape; however, do not change the margins or the font settings.

3. Create a Continuous section break immediately in front of the *Chapter 1 Objectives* heading.

4. Place all of section 2 in three equal-width columns and display a line between the columns.

5. Adjust the column breaks so that:

    a. the *Chapter 1 Objectives* heading is at the top of the first column;

    b. the *Chapter 5 Objectives* heading is at the top of the second column; and

    c. the *Chapter 9 Objectives* heading is at the top of the third column.

6. Save the revisions to your file; then print and close the file.

Exercise 2: Creating a Letterhead with Fonts and Borders

Practice creating a letterhead by following these steps:

1. Open the Chap1104 file from your Student Disk and immediately save the file as **Business 11** back to your disk.

2. Place the insertion point at the top of the document; then press ⏎Enter twice to create some room at the top. Then move the insertion point to the top of the document.

3. Create a letterhead for the Jolly Fine Furniture Company, using the company name and address (123 Main Street; Allentown, PA 16057), an appropriate set of fonts, and a multiple-line bottom border.

4. Make any necessary final adjustments to the letter, save the revisions to your file, print, and close the file.

Exercise 3: Creating Similar Length Columns

Practice using clip art pictures and creating equal-width columns by following these steps:

1. Open the Chap1105 file from your Student Disk and immediately save the file as **College List 11** back to your disk.

2. Place an appropriate clip art picture under the last item in the *Forms I need to collect or complete* section. Size the picture into a two-inch square; then center the picture under the text.

3. Place an appropriate clip art picture under the last item in the *Things I need to do* section. Size the picture into a two-inch square; then center the picture under the text.

4. Use the Columns dialog box to create a continuous section break immediately in front of the *Forms I need to complete* heading. (Hint: Use the appropriate option in the **A**pply to section of the Columns dialog box.) Then, format the second section into two columns.

5. Place the insertion point at the end of the second section; then use the Break dialog box to activate the option to make the columns approximately equal in length.

6. If necessary, move the clip art pictures to appropriate locations within your document.

7. Save the revisions to your file, print, and then close the file.

Exercise 4: Inserting AutoShapes and Borders

Practice inserting AutoShapes into your document and using borders and shading by following these steps:

1. Open the Chap1106 file from your Student Disk and immediately save the file as **Guide-lines 11** back to your disk.

2. Set the top margin to two inches.

3. Place an AutoShapes image in the upper-left corner of the document. Enter the text **Jolly Fine Furniture Company** inside the shape. Use the font of your choice.

4. Place a second AutoShapes image in the upper-right corner of the document. Enter the text **Worker Vacation or Personal-Day Guidelines** inside the shape. Use the font of your choice.

5. Make any necessary adjustments to the two AutoShapes images so that the page appears "visually balanced."

6. Place a single-line border around the second guideline.

7. Place a double-line border around the fourth guideline and shade the guideline, using the 20% gray shading setting.

8. Place a single-line border around the entire page.

9. Save your revisions to the file, print, and then close the file.

Exercise 5: Using AutoShapes and Wrapping Text Around a Picture

Practice using AutoShapes and wrapping text around pictures by following these steps:

1. Open the Chap1107 file from your Student Disk and immediately save the file as **Report 11** back to your disk.

2. Place an AutoShapes ribbon at the top of the page; then enter the title **Memory and Storage** in the text area of the ribbon.

3. If it is available, insert the picture of the hand holding a 3.5-inch disk into your document. This picture is located about halfway down through the rows of images available on the **P**ictures page of the Microsoft Clip Gallery dialog box. If this picture is not available, insert an appropriate clip art image.

4. Size the image to fit in the first paragraph under the title of the report.

5. Wrap the text around the image, using the **Sq**uare Wrapping style.

6. Save the revisions to your file, print, and then close the file.

Continuing Projects

Project 1: Practice Using Word

If your system has a complete installation of Word, you should have access to the Word Newsletter wizard (*newslttr.wiz*) on the Pub tab of the New dialog box. Choose **F**ile, **N**ew to display the New dialog box. If you have access to the Word Newsletter wizard, create a brief newsletter about yourself, a friend, your family, your job, or your school. When you have completed all the steps in the wizard, feel free to do any final formatting to the document. Save the document as **My Newsletter** to your Student Disk. Print and then close the document.

Project 2: Deli-Mart

Complete your work on the Deli-Mart menu by following these steps:

1. Open the Chap1108 file from your Student Disk; then save the file as **Menu 11** back to your disk.

2. Place a pair of AutoShapes images (such as an up ribbon and a down ribbon) at the top and bottom of the page.

3. Use WordArt to place the title **Deli-Mart International Delicatessen** in an eye-pleasing form below the AutoShapes image at the top of the page.

4. Enter a section break immediately in front of the name of the first menu item, and place the section containing the menu items into two equal-width, equal-length columns.

5. Place an appropriate clip art image in the lower-left part of the page. Place a copy of the WordArt title in the lower-right part of the page. You may need to size the copy of the WordArt object to make it fit on the right side of the page. (Hint: you may prefer to create a third, single-column section to do this.)

6. Open the Zoom drop-down list, choose Whole Page, and examine the page layout. Complete any necessary steps to produce a "visually balanced" document.

7. Save the revisions to the file, print, and then close the file.

Project 3: The Marketing Connection

Complete your work on the newsletter for the Marketing Connection by following these steps.

1. Open the Chap1109 file from your Student Disk; then save the file as **Market 11** back to your disk.

2. Place a small AutoShapes image in the upper-right corner of the page.

3. Using the phrase **The Marketing Connection** for the title, use WordArt to create for the newsletter an attractive title that is centered between the left and right page margins.

4. Place the rest of the content of the document into two equal-width columns.

5. Use the Document Map to locate the *Public Relations Group* heading; then place an appropriate clip art picture in the first paragraph under the heading. Make sure that the picture is appropriately sized to fit inside the paragraph; then use the **T**ight Wrapping style to wrap the paragraph text around the picture.

6. Use the Document Map to locate the *Travel* heading; then place an appropriate clip art picture in the paragraph under the heading. Make sure that the picture is appropriately sized to fit inside the paragraph; then use the **T**ight Wrapping style to wrap the paragraph text around the picture.

7. Place a single-line page border around the entire document. (Make sure to keep the document to one page.)

8. Enter the appropriate command so that the two columns are approximately equal in length.

9. Save the revisions to your file, print, and then close the file.

11

Appendix A

Working with Windows 95

Graphical user interface (GUI) A computer application that uses pictures, graphics, menus, and commands to help users communicate with their computers.

Microsoft Windows 95 is a powerful operating environment that enables you to access the power of DOS without memorizing DOS commands and syntax. Windows uses a *graphical user interface* (GUI) so that you can easily see on-screen the tools you need to complete specific file and program management tasks.

This appendix, an overview of the Windows 95 environment, is designed to help you learn the basics of Windows.

Objectives

By the time you finish this appendix, you will have learned to

- Start Windows 95
- Use a Mouse
- Identify the Elements of a Window
- Understand the Start menu
- Exit the Windows 95 Program

Objective 1: Start Windows 95

The first thing you need to know about Windows is how to start the software, and in this lesson, you learn just that. Before you can start Windows, however, it must be installed on your computer. If you need to install Windows, refer to your Windows manual or ask your instructor for assistance.

In most cases, Windows starts automatically when you turn on your computer. If your system is set up differently, you must start Windows from the DOS prompt (such as C:\>). Try starting the Windows program now.

Starting Windows

Desktop
The background of the Windows screen, on which windows, icons, and dialog boxes are displayed.

1. Turn on your computer and monitor.

   Most computers display technical information about the computer and the operating software installed, and then Windows 95 starts automatically. If Windows 95 starts, you can skip step 2. Otherwise, you will see the DOS prompt (C:\>) in the upper-left corner of the screen.

2. At the DOS prompt C:\>, type **win** and then press Enter.

   When you start the Windows program, a Microsoft Windows 95 banner displays for a few seconds; then the *desktop* appears (see Figure A.1).

Figure A.1
The Windows 95 desktop appears a few seconds after a Windows 95 banner.

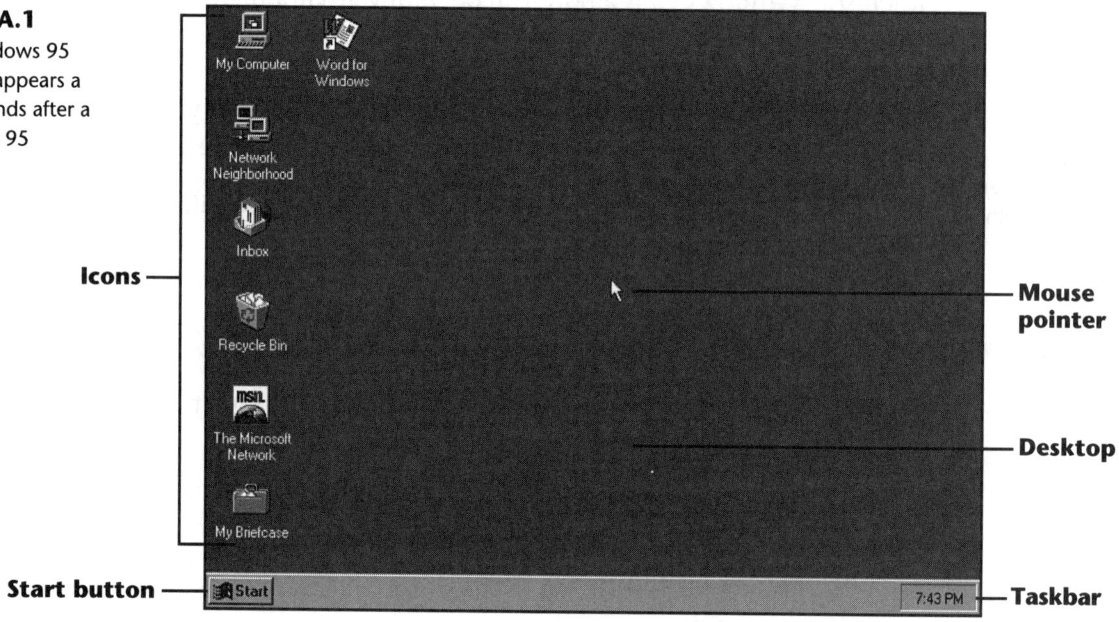

Icon
A picture that represents an application, file, or system resource.

Program *icons* that were created during installation (My Computer, Recycle Bin, Network Neighborhood) are displayed on the desktop. Other icons may also appear, depending on how your system is set up. *Shortcuts* to frequently used objects (such as documents, printers, and network drives) can be placed on the desktop. The *taskbar* appears along the bottom edge of the desktop. The *Start button* appears at the left end of the taskbar.

Objective 2: Use a Mouse in Windows

Shortcut
Gives you quick access to frequently used objects so you don't have to look through menus each time.

Windows is designed to be used with a *mouse*, so it's important that you learn how to use a mouse correctly. With a little practice, using a mouse is as easy as pointing to something with your finger. You can use the mouse to select icons, to make selections from *pull-down menus* and *dialog boxes*, and to select objects that you want to move or resize.

A

On the Windows desktop, you can use a mouse to:

- Open windows
- Close windows
- Open menus
- Choose menu commands
- Rearrange on-screen items, such as icons and windows

The position of the mouse is indicated on-screen by a *mouse pointer*. Usually, the mouse pointer is an arrow, but it sometimes changes shape depending on the current action.

On-screen the mouse pointer moves according to the movements of the mouse on your desk or on a *mouse pad*. To move the mouse pointer, simply move the mouse.

There are four basic mouse actions:

- *Click*   To point to an item, and then press and quickly release the left mouse button. You click to select an item, such as an option on a menu. To cancel a selection, click an empty area of the desktop. Unless otherwise specified, you use the left mouse button for all mouse actions.

- *Double-click*   To point to an item, and then press and release the left mouse button twice, as quickly as possible. You double-click to open or close windows and to start applications from icons.

- *Right-click*   To point to an item, and then press and release the right mouse button. This opens a Context menu, which gives you a shortcut to frequently used commands. To cancel a Context menu, click the left mouse button outside the menu.

- *Drag*   To point to an item, and then press and hold down the left mouse button as you move the pointer to another location, and then release the mouse button. You drag to resize windows, move icons, and scroll.

If you have problems...   If you try to double-click but nothing happens, you may not be clicking fast enough. Try again.

Objective 3: Understand the Start Menu

The Start button on the taskbar gives you access to your applications, settings, recently opened documents, the Find utility, the Run command, the Help system, and the Shut Down command. Clicking the Start button opens the Start menu. Choosing the Programs option at the top of the Start menu displays the Programs menu, which lists the *program folders* on your system. Program folders are listed first, followed by shortcuts (see Figure A.2).

Taskbar
Contains the Start button, buttons for each open window, and the current time.

Start button
A click on the Start button opens the Start menu.

Mouse
A pointing device used to make choices, select data, and otherwise communicate with the computer.

Pull-down menus
Menus that cascade downward into the screen whenever you select a command from the menu bar.

Dialog box
A window that opens on-screen to provide information about the current action or to ask the user to provide additional information.

Mouse pointer
A symbol that appears on-screen to indicate the current location of the mouse.

Mouse pad
A pad that provides a uniform surface for a mouse to slide on.

Program folder
Represented by an icon of a file folder with an application window in front of it, program folders contain shortcut icons and other program folders.

Figure A.2
Click the Start
button to open the
Start menu. All your
programs are
grouped together in
the Programs
menu.

Programs folder ——

Programs menu ——

Shortcut ——

Start menu ——

Start button ——

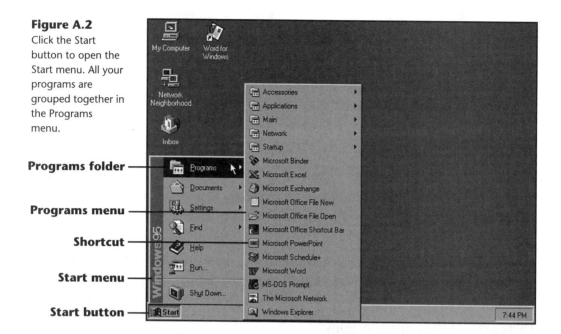

When the Start menu is open, moving the mouse pointer moves a selection bar through the menu options. When the selection bar highlights a menu command with a right-facing triangle, a submenu opens. Click the shortcut icon to start an application. If a menu command is followed by an ellipsis, clicking that command opens a dialog box.

Objective 4: Identify the Elements of a Window

In the Windows program, everything opens in a window. Applications open in windows, documents open in windows, and dialog boxes open in windows. For example, double-clicking the My Computer icon opens the My Computer application into a window. Because window elements stay the same for all Windows applications, this section uses the My Computer window for illustration.

The Title Bar
Across the top of each window is its title bar. A title bar contains the name of the open window as well as three buttons to manipulate windows. The Minimize button is for reducing windows to a button on the taskbar. The Maximize button is for expanding windows to fill the desktop. The Close button is for closing the window.

The Menu Bar
The menu bar gives you access to the application's menus. Menus enable you to select options that perform functions or carry out commands (see Figure A.3). The File menu in My Computer, for example, enables you to open, save, and print files.

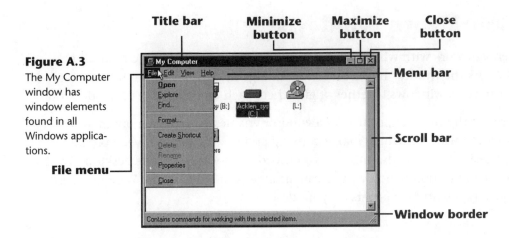

Figure A.3
The My Computer window has window elements found in all Windows applications.

File menu

Some menu options require you to enter additional information. When you select one of these options, a dialog box opens (see Figure A.4). You either type the additional information, select from a list of options, or select a button. Most dialog boxes have a Cancel button, which closes the dialog box without saving the changes; an OK button, which closes the dialog box and saves the changes; and a Help button, which opens a Help window.

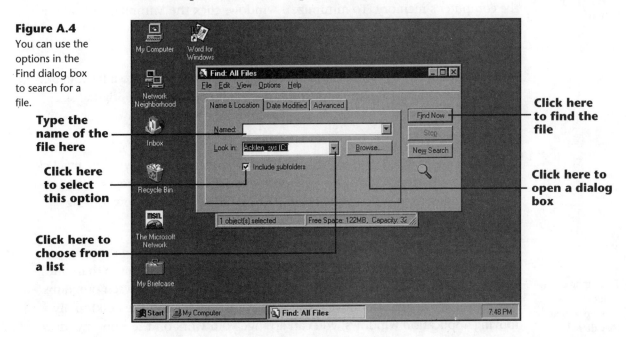

Figure A.4
You can use the options in the Find dialog box to search for a file.

Type the name of the file here

Click here to select this option

Click here to choose from a list

Click here to find the file

Click here to open a dialog box

Scroll Bars

Scroll bars appear when you have more information in a window than is currently displayed on-screen. A horizontal scroll bar appears along the bottom of a window and a vertical scroll bar appears along the right side of a window.

The Window Border

The window border identifies the edge of the window. In most windows, it can be used to change the size of a window. The window corner is used to resize a window on two sides at the same time.

Objective 5: Work with Windows

When you work with windows, you need to know how to arrange them. You can shrink the window into a button or enlarge the window to fill the desktop. You can stack windows together or give them each an equal slice of the desktop.

Changing the size and position of a window enables you to see more than one application window, which makes copying and pasting data between programs much easier. You can also move a window to any location on the desktop. By moving application windows, you can arrange your work on the Windows desktop just as you arrange papers on your desk.

Maximizing a Window

Maximize
To increase the size of a window so that it fills the entire screen.

You can *maximize* a window so it fills the desktop. Maximizing a window gives you more space to work in. To maximize a window, click the Maximize button on the title bar.

Minimizing a Window

Minimize
To reduce a window to a button.

When you *minimize* a window, it shrinks the window to a button on the taskbar. Even though you can't see the window anymore, the application stays loaded in the computer's memory. To minimize a window, click the Minimize button on the title bar.

Restoring a Window

When a window is maximized, the Maximize button changes into a Restore button. Clicking the Restore button restores the window back to the original size and position before the window was maximized.

Closing a Window

When you are finished working in a window, you can close the window by clicking the Close button. Closing an application window exits the program, removing it from memory. When you click the Close button, the window (on the desktop) and the window button (on the taskbar) disappear.

Arranging Windows

Tile
To arrange open windows on the desktop so that they do not overlap.

Cascade
To arrange open windows on the desktop so that they overlap, with only the title bar of each window (behind the top window) displayed.

Changing the size and position of a window enables you to see more than one application window, which makes copying and pasting data between programs much easier. You can also move a window to any location on the desktop. By moving application windows, you can arrange your work on the Windows desktop just as you arrange papers on your desk.

Use one of the following options to arrange windows:

- Right-click the taskbar; then choose Tile Horizontally.
- Right-click the taskbar; then choose Tile Vertically. See Figure A.5 for an example.
- Right-click the taskbar; then choose Cascade. See Figure A.6 for an example.
- Click and drag the window's title bar to move to the window around on the desktop.

• Click and drag a window border (or corner) to increase or decrease the size of the window.

Figure A.5
The windows are tiled vertically across the desktop.

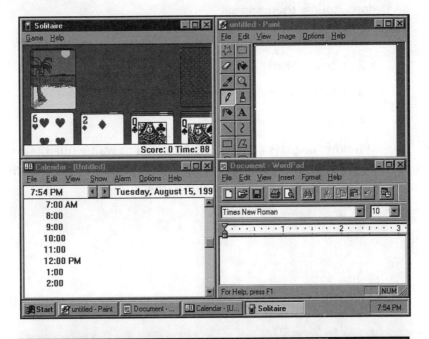

Figure A.6
The windows are cascaded on the desktop.

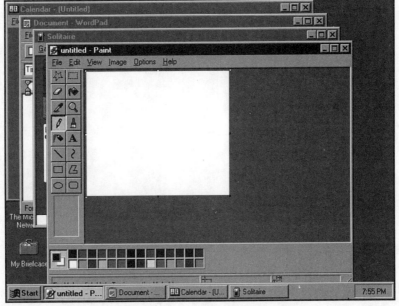

Objective 6: Exit the Windows Program

In Windows 95, you use the Shut Down command to exit the Windows program. You should always use this command, which closes all open applications and files, before you turn off the computer. If you haven't saved your work in an application when you choose this command, you'll be prompted to save your changes before Windows shuts down.

Exiting Windows

You should always exit Windows before turning off your computer. To exit Windows, follow these steps:

1. Click the Start button on the taskbar.

2. Choose Sh**u**t Down.

3. Choose **S**hut down the computer.

4. Choose **Y**es.

Windows displays a message asking you to wait while the computer is shutting down. When this process is complete, a message appears telling you that you can safely turn off your computer now.

Glossary

Active window   The window containing the document on which you are currently working.

Antonyms   Words that mean the opposite (or nearly the opposite) of other words. The thesaurus suggests antonyms for some.

AutoText   A stored portion of text or graphics, of any size, that can be quickly inserted into any document.

Cell   The intersection of a row and a column in a table.

Characters   Letters, numbers, punctuation marks, and symbols that appear in a document.

Clipboard   A temporary storage area for selected text, graphics, sound clips, and video clips.

Column   A vertical line of cells. Word identifies columns alphabetically from left to right. (Also see newspaper columns.)

Conversion filter   A program that makes data entered in other applications compatible with Word.

Data source   The file containing the information that changes from one copy of the document to another—for example, names and addresses.

Default   The original settings for a program when it is first installed on a computer system. Most default settings can be changed to reflect your preferences.

Desktop publishing   The use of a computer system and software to combine text and graphics in advanced layout formats to produce a visually attractive document.

Dictionary   An alphabetical list of words frequently used in documents. Word's main dictionary may not contain all the words used in your document, so Word also enables you to create custom dictionaries.

Document   A file that contains the work created by a program.

Endnotes   Reference text or comments that appear at the end of a document, or end of a section.

Field   One item of variable information—for example, a first name.

Font   A set of characters that have the same appearance (a distinctive typeface). In most cases, the typeface is available in a variety of sizes and styles.

Footers   Text that appears at the bottom of each page.

Footnotes   Reference text that appears at the bottom of the page containing the corresponding reference mark.

Formulas   Expressions that perform mathematical operations on data in cells in a table.

Gridlines   Printing or nonprinting lines indicating the cell borders in a table.

Gutter   An extra margin at the inside edge of facing pages to allow space for binding.

Hard page break   A break that you insert into a document to force Word to begin a new page.

Headers   Text that appears at the top of each page.

Header row   A row at the top of the data source file that contains the names of each field in a data source—for example, the header row for addresses may contain FirstName, LastName, City, State, and so on.

Insertion point   The flashing vertical bar in the work area of the document.

Insert mode   A mode in which characters you type move existing characters to the right and down.

Macros   A group of actions that you record and play back to accomplish specific tasks.

Main document   A file used when merging documents containing the information you want to repeat from one copy of the document to another—for example, a letter.

Merge field   The name of a data source field that is inserted into a main document to indicate where the variable data should appear when the data source is merged with the main document.

Newspaper columns   Text that flows from the bottom of one column to the top of the next.

Nonprinting characters   Keys, such as ⏎Enter and Tab↹, that do not display or print a character.

Normal style   The paragraph style Word uses automatically unless you specify a different one.

Orientation   The placement of text and graphics on the page. Your document can usually be printed in vertical or horizontal orientation.

Overtype mode   A mode in which the characters you type replace existing characters.

Pagination   The way in which Word separates your document into pages.

Panes   Portions of a window.

Point   A unit used to measure the size of typographic characters. One point is approximately 1/72 inch.

Readability statistics   Data analyzing how difficult a document is to read. The data includes word, character, paragraph, and sentence counts; a calculation of the average number of sentences per paragraph, words per sentence, and characters per word; and the reading level.

Record   All the information related to one set of fields—for example, all the data for one customer.

Right-click   To click the right mouse button.

Row   In a table, a horizontal line of cells. Word numbers rows consecutively from top to bottom.

Scalable font   A font that can be enlarged or reduced to any size within a wide range without visual distortion.

Select   To highlight a specific part of a document. The highlighted portion will be affected by the next program action.

Selection bar   An unmarked region between the first character in each line and the left border in the window work area. The selection bar is used to select text with the mouse.

Shortcut menu   A context-sensitive menu that appears after you right-click the mouse.

Side-by-side columns   Short blocks of text (or paragraphs) displayed next to one another, as in a table.

Soft page break   A page break that Word inserts after calculating that the page cannot display the next character or graphic.

Style   A collection of settings that can quickly be applied to characters or paragraphs in your document.

Synonyms   Words that have the same (or nearly the same) meanings as other words. The thesaurus suggests synonyms.

Table   A method of organizing and displaying data in a collection of rows and columns.

Template   A file in which Word can store a set of styles; specific character, paragraph, and page settings; text and graphics entries; macros; AutoText entries; field codes; custom menu commands and toolbar buttons; and shortcut keys.

TrueType fonts   A type of font, included in Windows, Word, and many other software packages, where the same font-generating program used to create the font on the screen is used to create the font at the printer.

Wild-card characters   Characters that you can use to represent one or more other characters.

Word wrap   A Word feature that automatically moves a complete word to the beginning of a new line whenever text overflows the right margin.

Index